THAT DISN—— ——AGIC!

The magic of Bambi, battling deep in the heart of the forest for the doe who has won his heart—

—of Captain Nemo, voyaging through the deeps of the sea into the farthest reaches of adventure

—of Mary Poppins, soaring high in the sky over London

—of Davy Crockett, braving the dangers of the untamed American frontier

—of Peter Pan, ruling his youthful band in Never-Never-Land

Each of us has a favorite spot in the wide and wonderful world that Walt Disney created—and you will find it here, in the book that puts it all together to celebrate the unique vision and style of one of the supreme masters of the movie art.

The
DISNEY FILMS

Abridged and Updated

Leonard Maltin

POPULAR LIBRARY ■ NEW YORK

THE DISNEY FILMS

Published by Popular Library, a unit of CBS Publications,
the Consumer Publishing Division of CBS Inc., by arrange-
ment with Crown Publishers, Inc.

ISBN: 0-445-04276-1

Printed in the United States of America

10   9   8   7   6   5   4   3   2   1

Dedicated

to the memory of

WALT DISNEY

AUTHOR'S NOTE

THIS PAPERBACK EDITION OF THE DISNEY FILMS HAS been updated, to incorporate new information and corrections which have come to light since 1973, when the book first appeared.

In this abridged version, the emphasis is on Disney's career in general, and the animated films in particular; discussion of live-action films is limited to those features that played a significant part in the history of the Disney studio. A complete list of the live-action films appears in the back of the book.

One final note: throughout this book reference is made to the dates when Disney features were reissued. In 1975, Disney's distribution company, Buena Vista, broke policy by booking special summer "festivals" into many theaters, showing major Disney films that otherwise would have waited seven years for an airing. The studio has also permitted 16mm non-theatrical distribution of many titles previously held under wraps. These special exceptions are not specifically noted in the release data included in this book.

CONTENTS

PREFACE

ONCE UPON A TIME THERE WAS A WRITER WHO WANTED to do a list of Walt Disney's films. He assembled such a list and published it in his own magazine, *Film Fan Monthly*. He dreamed of expanding the list into a book-length study of the Disney films. One day he did. And he lived harriedly ever after.

I am that writer, and I am now a nervous wreck. What started out as a fairly simple project blossomed into a formidable job of deciding what to include and what to put aside in preparing a book that wouldn't go on for seven volumes. It would take a full seven volumes to do complete justice to the films of Walt Disney, because he did so much in so many fields: early silent cartoons, talking cartoons, live-action short subjects, over eighty feature films, hundreds of television shows, scores of public-service, sponsored, and wartime films, and what can only be described as miscellany. The point is, even Disney miscellany is worth watching and discussing.

Something had to give. Therefore, the bulk of this book concerns Disney's feature films. I have screened every one of them, sought out background material, and interviewed participants to try to put each one in its proper perspective. The brief chapters on the shorts and the television shows are meant as summaries, and the indexes as basic lists. Each topic could, and should, fill a book by itself, and, unfortunately, much of the necessary information is not currently accessible (for example, there were no credits on the cartoon shorts until the early 1940s).

In cataloging the feature films I decided to write my own critique for each one, rather than simply reprinting old reviews and letting it go at that. For one thing reviews of Disney films fall into several extreme categories: laudatory to the point of blindness (in the early days), harshly critical of good films because they weren't great (middle period), and apathetic (late period, with exceptions).

What is more, many contemporary reviews have little meaning today, for viewed *out* of context the films take on qualities that everyone seemed to ignore at the time of release. *Fantasia* and *The Three Caballeros*, both severely criticized in their day, have emerged as two of Disney's most astoundingly imaginative works in the 1970s; it seems incredible that anyone could disparage such overwhelming creativity. Perhaps it is because those films came at a time when hundreds of good films were being made, and now, when any films, not to mention good ones, are sparse, and television has blurred our sense of values, they stand out like oases in a desert of mediocrity.

In any event I have tried to strike a balance by reporting my own views as well as those of others, and noting the public response via box-office returns.

One note on spelling of names: there is simply no consistency to the spelling of the names of Disney's staff over the years. Every effort has been made to check the accuracy of such tricky names. For the sake of sanity and uniformity, where a staffer has used various forms of his name (Bob, Bobby, Robert) over the years, his full name has been used every time.

Obviously, this book could not have been done without the cooperation of the Walt Disney organization. I am deeply indebted, more than I can say, to Vincent Jefferds, Tom Jones, and Arlene Ludwig of Walt Disney Productions; David R. Smith, head of the Disney Archives; Chris Behrens and her entire staff in the 16mm Division, as well as Bill Birch, formerly of the 16mm Division. Their kindness and generosity went far beyond

9

the call of duty. I have also drawn upon an interview with Ward Kimball recorded several years ago for *Film Fan Monthly,* before this book was ever planned; I belatedly thank him for his candor and keen insights.

I was fortunate in being able to discuss individual films with the men who directed them, specifically Ken Annakin, Charles Barton, Byron Haskin, Francis D. Lyon, H. C. Potter, and Harold Schuster, as well as assistant director William Beaudine, Jr., and Robert Florey, who directed numerous Disney television shows. For their patience and kindness, I am truly grateful.

As always, the staffs of the research library at Lincoln Center in New York, the Motion Picture Section of the Library of Congress, and the Teaneck Public Library have been unfailingly helpful.

For providing material, answering questions, helping with research, and putting up with my phone calls, I thank Alan Barbour, Gordon Berkow, Panayotis Carayannis, John Cocchi, William K. Everson, Joel Jacobson, Miles Kreuger, Al Marill, Doug McClelland, Don Miller, Drew Simels, Lou Valentino, Jerry Vermilye, and John Willis. Very special thanks are due to Mike Barrier, editor of *Funnyworld,* whose knowledge of animation and skill in expressing his thoughts embarrass me; and Al Kilgore, the staunchest Disneyphile I know, for reading the manuscript and making valuable suggestions.

Also, I have to thank my family and friends, for lending moral support and keeping me company in my lonely projection room this past year. Special awards of merit are due Dennis Fine, Rosalie Palladino, Dennis Reer, Drew Simels, and sometimes Louis Black, for sitting through the endless parade of films.

Finally, I really would like to thank every individual who ever worked with Walt Disney, for making these films in the first place. They have made a great many people happy, and there is no finer achievement in life. I hope I have done them justice in this book.

LEONARD MALTIN

1 · Introduction

EVEN WALT DISNEY COULD NEVER EXPLAIN THE phenomenal worldwide acclaim that greeted him and his cartoon creations in the 1930s, and which continued until his death in 1966. The answer, it seemed, was self-evident: he made good films, both animated and live action, that appealed to the young and young-at-heart around the world.

But why Walt Disney? There were cartoons being made before he arrived in Hollywood, and good cartoons being produced all during his reign as the King of Animation. Others made good family pictures with wide appeal.

So why, and how, did Walt Disney get to the top of the heap and stay there? Most of the answers are to be found in the man himself. He was born in Chicago in 1901; his father, Elias Disney, moved his family with him as he traveled throughout the Midwest seeking success at some kind of work—first with a construction company, then a farm, later a newspaper delivery service. One of five children, Walt was raised in an atmosphere of hard work and tight purse strings. When his father bought the newspaper route, Walt (then nine) and his older brother Roy had to get up every morning at three thirty in order to begin the delivery. Late in life, Disney recalled: "The papers had to be stuck behind the storm doors. You couldn't just toss them on the porch. And in the winters there'd be as much as three feet of snow. I was a little guy and I'd be up to my nose in snow. I still have nightmares about it."

11

For relief from the drudgery of such work, Walt usually had to amuse himself. Drawing caught his fancy at an early age, since he was not athletically inclined. A gift he received of a pad of paper and some pencils set him to work, and as years went by he became more serious about drawing, and he enrolled in a class at the Kansas City Art Institute when he was fourteen.

From his earliest years he was closely attached to his brother Roy, eight years his senior, and when Roy decided to join the navy in 1918, Walt thought it would be a good idea too. Being only sixteen, he enlisted in the Red Cross Ambulance Corps, and served as a driver in France during the last year of World War I. When he returned to America in 1919, he went to Kansas City to seek employment as an artist, and got his first job with a commercial art studio. It didn't last long, but it was there that Disney met Ub Iwerks, another young artist who, when Disney was let go, went with him to form their own commercial art company.

Disney abandoned the firm to take a job with the Kansas City Film Ad Company, which made animated commercials for various concerns and showed them in local theatres. Before long, Iwerks was working there too, and the two men worked together at night making their own animated cartoons. They sold them to the Newman Theater, and named them Newman Laugh-O-Grams. They were successful enough that Disney was able to leave the Kansas City Film Ad Company and start an animation firm of his own, which he called Laugh-O-Gram.

Looking at one of these Kansas City-made cartoons today, *Puss 'n Boots*, one sees an undeniably primitive, but bright, imaginative, and funny little film—full of inventive touches, and some ambitious animated effects. (How much easier it would have been to have a motionless crowd than to animate movement as Disney did in a bullfight scene.) Though it would be foolish to read too much into one early cartoon, *Puss 'n Boots does* show that Disney was striving for quality, certainly a luxury in a business as small as his was at this time.

12

Disney poses with his staff in Hollywood in the 1920s: Rollin (Ham) Hamilton, Roy Disney, Hugh Harman, Walt, "Alice" of the *Alice in Cartoonland* series, Rudolf Ising, Ub Iwerks, and Walker Harman. Hugh Harman and Ising later had their own cartoon studio, as did Iwerks. *Courtesy British Film Institute*

A scene from Disney's early *Puss 'n Boots*. Note the full range of gray tones, something of a luxury for most silent-film cartoonists. *Courtesy Adam Reilly/Cinemaesthetics*

13

Indeed, Disney continually got himself into financial crises, never being able to make any profit from his films. Though the amounts involved were small, and he was already cutting corners, it is safe to conjecture that one reason for this was that Disney wanted a good product above all else. To come up with the results he wanted, he would impulsively spend more time on it than he should have, then later suffer the consequences. The consequences, in this case, meant leaving Kansas City, something of a failure—at least, monetarily. Disney decided to go to Los Angeles, hoping to find any sort of work. When none was waiting for him in Movieland, he decided to set up shop himself, again.

Just as he was about to go into the same kind of Laugh-O-Gram production he had done in Kansas City, word came from the East that a company that had taken one of his films—a combination cartoon and live-action reel called *Alice's Wonderland*—had sold an independent producer on the idea of making an *Alice* series. The distributor, M. J. Winkler, offered $1,500 per reel, and when Walt, joined as production partner by his brother Roy, turned out the first film for $750, the mood was nothing short of triumphant.

Like most loners who start in business for themselves, Walt wanted to do everything himself; it seemed the only way to get real satisfaction in every department of filmmaking. But before long it became evident that he simply could not handle the various chores alone, and he sent to Kansas City for his friend and ex-partner Ub Iwerks to join him. Walt insisted on putting each film's profits back into their filmmaking enterprise to improve the quality of the shorts, but even so, they did not set the world on fire. The addition of Iwerks has been credited with revitalizing the series when it looked as if it might be discontinued.

The *Alice* films were made on a makeshift basis, with little thought given to fresh ideas beyond those employing the gimmick of combining the actions of a live girl with cartoon backgrounds and props. The stories and gags were tantamount to those seen in cheap one- and two-reel comedies made during the silent era, with movement, more than anything else, being the principal ingredient.

In 1927 Disney's distributor encouraged him to drop *Alice* and start a new series. The result was Oswald the Rabbit, a character that gave Disney and his staff more latitude in concocting amusing adventures than they had enjoyed with Alice. Charles Mintz and his brother-in-law George Winkler were releasing the *Oswald* cartoons through Universal, and when Disney went to New York late that year to ask for a raise (he was getting $2,250 per short), they refused, told him that they wanted to cut back the amount, threatened to hire away his staff, and reminded him that they had copyrighted Oswald in *their* name. Disney refused to go along with them, and was forced to sever his relations with the company. (The *Oswald* series was subsequently taken over by Walter Lantz and Universal.)

On the train returning to California, the story goes, the inspiration came to Disney to initiate a new cartoon series starring a mouse. The character was first named Mortimer, but then rechristened Mickey. He was drawn in a simple manner, in the style of animal characterization then popular. Having made enough money to feel somewhat more secure than before, Walt and Roy decided to make their first films, and *then* seek distribution. Thus, in early 1928, Disney produced the first Mickey Mouse cartoon, *Plane Crazy,* quickly followed by a second, *Gallopin' Gaucho.* Both of these were, of course, silent.

But just at this time *The Jazz Singer* was sweeping the country, unveiled by another struggling family of producers, the Warner Brothers. Its astounding success not only made the brothers Warner instant movie magnates, but it dealt the first deathblow to silent pictures. Most Hollywood showmen could not deny the impact of the talkie sequences in *The Jazz Singer,* but at the same time they expressed conservative views of sound's future. Indeed, it took two full years for silent films to cease production in Hollywood, by which time it

15

was clear that talkies were here to stay.

Walt Disney was in the right place at the right time. And he had the nerve to try out the new medium when other more established filmmakers were holding back. After all, not only did he have nothing to lose (except money), he had much to gain from the idea. Disney, and his chief aids, Ub Iwerks and Wilfred Jackson, decided to experiment with sound on their third Mickey Mouse cartoon, *Steamboat Willie*. They calculated that if film ran at ninety feet a minute (twenty-four frames a second), they could animate their silent cartoon to a musical beat by planning it out in advance. Their simple tunes could be played at two beats a second, so markings were made on the film every twelve frames, both as a guide to the animator, and, later, as an indicator for the orchestra, which would synchronize the musical track.

In September 1928 Walt took his completed film, and a written score, to New York. He had definite ideas about how the sound track should be made, and they did not coincide with those of RCA or Western Electric, which owned the sound-recording patents. Disney then allied himself with P. A. ("Pat") Powers, whose bootleg Cinephone Process was responsible for recording the first sound cartoon. After a calamitous initial recording session, with a twenty-piece band led by Carl Edwourds, a second session was held (at great expense) with only fifteen pieces, and everyone more willing to listen to Walt's original conception of how to do the track. Disney did the high-pitched voice of Mickey Mouse (the story goes that while auditioning actors, he tried to show one what he wanted, and it came out so well he decided to do it himself), and after no little aggravation, the finished product was ready.

Not long after completing *Steamboat Willie*, Disney embarked on another, entirely different kind of cartoon. The origin of the idea is not clear; veteran musical director Carl Stalling, then working for Disney, has said that he initiated the idea, which Walt liked immediately. Wilfred Jackson, then an animator and the harmonica

16

player who originally worked out the score of *Steam-boat Willie* with Disney, has recalled that Disney, in an effort to soft-pedal Stalling's desire to have music take precedence over action in the Mickey Mouse cartoons, promised him that they would do another series where action would be matched to music, instead of the other way around.

However the idea originated, Disney liked it, and before long he had produced the first "Silly Symphony," *The Skeleton Dance,* a cartoon with skeletons coming alive and dancing to music (always erroneously referred to as Saint-Saëns's "Dance Macabre"), written by Stalling, including a fragment of Edvard Grieg's "The March of the Dwarfs."

In both cases Disney had trouble getting distribution for his shorts, but in both cases the success of his films was gauged—as it has been ever since—by audiences. Individual producers and distributors who screened the shorts were not always impressed, but when the cartoons were shown in theatres, the reaction was always favorable, and usually overwhelmingly so.

Looking at the early Disney cartoons today, the word "primitive" instantly comes to mind. To understand the cartoons' success, one must try to put oneself back to 1928. There is no way to overstate the tumultuous effect of talking pictures. Indeed, in many cases, all previous criteria for judging films—both by critics as well as moviegoers—were completely forgotten. Sound became the principal factor in a film's evaluation, and if it talked, it hardly mattered if it moved, made sense, or did anything else. One need only look at two of 1929's biggest hits today—*The Cock-Eyed World* and *In Old Arizona,* both absolutely deadly—to see just how much critical taste suffered during this period.

This is not to disparage Disney's early animated efforts, but merely to place them in proper perspective. Though *Steamboat Willie* was pleasant enough, it is safe to say that had it come two years earlier, Disney never would have achieved the phenomenal success he did.

Here are samplings of the reviews *Willie* received,

17

which were heavily publicized by Disney's distributor, Pat Powers, at the time: *The New York Times* wrote: "It is an ingenious piece of work with a good deal of fun. It growls, whines, squeaks and makes various other sounds that add to its mirthful quality." *Variety* said: ". . . a high order of cartoon ingenuity cleverly combined with sound effects. The union brought forth laughs galore." *Film Daily* noted: "This is what *Steamboat Willie* has: First, a clever and amusing treatment; secondly, music and sound effects added via the Cinephone method. The result is a real tidbit of diversion."

Steamboat Willie's influence was still felt three years later when the fledgling Warner Brothers cartoon department made a short called *Smile, Darn Ya, Smile,* starring a character named Foxy. Both Foxy and the short itself owed so much to *Willie* and Mickey Mouse as to be almost absolute plagiarism.

A corollary question must now be asked: Were those audiences laughing at Mickey, or at the sound effects and gags? The answer is clear. Mickey Mouse was not unlike many comedians of the silent-film era, who gained considerable, but transient, fame. Men like Billy Bevan and Snub Pollard made innumerable silent comedies, most of them quite funny, but the humor always arose from situations and sight gags—never from their characterizations. As long as the material was funny, *they* were considered funny. But when the material ran dry, as it did for Pollard in the late twenties, they stopped getting laughs.

Mickey Mouse, like his mentor, was in the right place at the right time. And when people left the theatres after seeing *Steamboat Willie* or one of the other cartoons that soon followed it, they were thinking of Mickey, not of Disney, or the gags, or anything else. He stayed in their minds most of all, and before long, he became a star . . . more by default than anything else.

It wasn't long before Mickey was surrounded by costars—Minnie, his every-faithful girl friend, and Pegleg Pete, the villain, appeared with him in his first cartoon. Pluto, his dog, Horace Horsecollar, and Clarabelle Cow entered the scene not long thereafter. And, invariably, one's attention was focused on them, not the Mouse (Pluto even outranked Mickey as a cartoon star by the 1940s). Yet Mickey was the star, and that he remained through the late 1930s.

In 1935 L. H. Robbins, in the *New York Times Magazine,* wrote, quite accurately: "Mickey Mouse is the best known and most popular international figure of his day." He continued:

What is the secret of his appeal? How has an imaginary creature only 6 years old, going on 7, captured the interest of almost every tribe on this terrestrial ball? Why is it that university presidents praise him, the League of Nations recommends him, Who's Who and the Encyclopaedia Britannica give him paragraphs, learned academies hang medals on him, art galleries turn from Picasso and Epstein to hold exhibitions of his monkey-shines, and the King of England won't go to the movies unless Mickey is on the bill?

. . . World-weary philosophers find in Mickey's antics "a release from the tyranny of things." He declares a nine-minute moratorium on the debt we owe to the iron facts of life. He suspends the rules of common sense and correct deportment and all the other carping, conventional laws, including the law of gravity, that hold us down and circumscribe and cramp our style.

These observers tell us there is in human nature a streak of rebellion, a yearning to cut loose, to be free to overlap the moon if we like, even at the cost of a headache and an unpleasant taste in the cold gray dawn of the morning after. This craving of ours, Mickey, with his absurdities, his defiance of reason and his accomplishment of the impossible, gratifies for us vicariously.

Some years later, on Mickey's twenty-fifth birthday,

Walt Disney with his special "Oscar" of 1932, and the mouse that won it for him. *Courtesy British Film Institute*

Walt Disney told the same magazine: "This is tough, trying to explain Mickey. It's been done by experts and the best any of us have been able to come up with is the fact that Mickey is so simple and uncomplicated, so easy to understand, that you can't help liking him."

The likability factor was all-important in Mickey's metamorphosis in the 1930s. At the outset, Mickey, like most other cartoon characters, was often rather crude. Would-be attackers of Walt Disney point with glee to scenes such as the famous one in *Steamboat Willie* where Mickey, in improvising various muscial instruments, "plays" a cow's udder. Again, one cannot use 1970s standards to criticize a 1928 cartoon. Animated cartoons, which had existed since the first decade of the century, were still in their embryonic stage in the late 1920s. Disney was still feeling his way, like most of his colleagues. The humor of the early Mickey Mouse cartoons was not *his* humor, but the humor of the day; and though it is easy to criticize Disney for the cow's udder gag, one must also remember that it drew one of the short's biggest laughs in the leading theatres of this country.

Once Mickey became a star—an almost overnight process—Disney and his staff had to be more conscious of what they did with the Mouse. He still had to get laughs, but, after all, there are some things a star just doesn't do. Surely this thought dictated much of what went into the Mickey Mouse cartoons of the early 1930s; it was certainly responsible for delegating many of the gags to subsidiary characters.

Evidence of the regard people had for Mickey can be found in an erudite article by playwright William Kozlenko that appeared in *The New Theatre* magazine, in which, at one point, he compared the Disney creations to Max Fleischer's Popeye.

Popeye evinces no niceties of character. He is a tough, though apparently kind-hearted, pug. The salient features of his personality are illiteracy, stupidity, gruffness, and a pair of powerful muscles.

21

(How versatile and refined, by comparison, is such a subject as Mickey Mouse, who can play the piano, ride a horse, conduct a band, fly an airplane, build a house, and do other constructive things with equal proficiency.)

As Mickey became more likable, he became more popular. It is staggering to try to conceive of the impact he had around the world; before long he was the merchandising king of America, and it has been said, probably accurately, that the Disney studio couldn't have survived just making cartoons, that it was the supplementary income from the literally hundreds of licenses for everything from bookends to thermometers that kept the studio afloat.

Though Mickey remained a superstar in the eyes of the world, he became more of a problem to the Disney staff. Some years later, Disney explained: "Mickey's our problem child. He's so much of an institution that we're limited in what we can do with him. If we have Mickey kicking someone in the pants we get a million letters from mothers telling us we're giving their kids wrong ideas. [This was especially embarrassing because Mickey Mouse merchandising was being used to get kids to eat, wash, etc.] Mickey must always be sweet, always lovable. What can you do with such a leading man?"

The answer was in Mickey's supporting cast. Pluto rapidly became a major cartoon star in his own right; he was not only allowed to have a temper, but somehow, with his canine personality, the fits of anger seemed to suit him well, and frustration became a major trait in his appearances. But in 1934 the Disney people hit upon another character who not only was everything that Mickey wasn't, but who quickly surpassed him in popularity: Donald Duck.

Legend has it that Disney heard a fellow named Clarence Nash on a local radio show, doing his act, which was highlighted by his impression of a duck reciting "Mary Had a Little Lamb." Nash was hired to repeat the recitation for a Mickey Mouse cartoon, *The Orphans' Benefit,* at which a gangly sort of white duck tries to get through this speech despite the razzing of the youngsters in the audience. His peculiar voice, and inimitable way of expressing vociferous anger and frustration, caught on immediately, and the Disney people knew they had something special on their hands. (Donald's actual debut was in a cartoon called *The Wise Little Hen.*)

Donald reappeared the following year in what this writer considers to be the best Disney cartoon short—*The Band Concert.* In it, Mickey is conducting a Sunday afternoon concert in a park bandstand; the band is trying to play the *William Tell* Overture, but among other hazards, they are continually interrupted by Donald Duck, who's trying to sell ice cream to the spectators. When Donald hears the music, he produces (apparently out of his sleeve) a fife and begins to play "Turkey in the Straw" in exact counterpoint to the band's portion of *William Tell.* Before long, the whole band catches on with him and is playing "Turkey in the Straw," until maestro Mickey quiets them down and breaks Donald's flute in half. But the resourceful duck apparently has an endless supply of instruments, and he continues to confound Mickey throughout the piece. Further problems arise when a tornado approaches the town. The residents in the park scurry for shelter, but Mickey and his musicians are too wrapped up in the opening bars of "The Storm" section of the overture to notice. As the tornado hits them full force, they go into the appropriate part of the piece, their music matching the circumstances exactly as they are swept up into the air, along with the band shell and sundry other objects from the town.

Like the music, *The Band Concert* is perfectly orchestrated, a prime example of setting action to music, a formula later capitalized on by Walter Lantz in his many "cartunes," by Warner Brothers in such shorts as *Rhapsody in Rivets,* MGM in *Cat Concerto,* and, of course, Disney himself in *Fantasia* and the later

23

musical omnibus features.

Surprisingly enough, *Concert*, the first Mouse cartoon to be made in Technicolor, also gave Mickey one of his best "roles." He was never seen to better advantage than as the fiery conductor, whose brass-button uniform, several sizes too large, proved a major obstacle to his conducting efforts. As a vehicle for Mickey, the film was ideal, but once again it was Donald who stole the show. From that film on, he was a regular character in the Disney organization. The very next film, *Mickey's Service Station*, costarred the Mouse with both Donald and another character who was gaining in popularity, Goofy. Originally named Dippy Dawg, Goofy was a dumb but amiable fellow whose innocent ignorance and delightful voice (that of Disney staffer Pinto Colvig) made him another favorite character around the world.

During this time, the *Silly Symphonies* were also going full steam ahead, having made their conclusive mark in 1932 when Disney exployed Technicolor for the first time for his short *Flowers and Trees*. From that time on, he made the series exclusively in color, waiting three years before giving Mickey a chance to do likewise. The *Silly Symphonies* dominated the cartoon category at the Academy Awards for many years, beginning with *Flowers and Trees* and continuing until 1940.

Though most of the *Symphonies* were quite enjoyable, color was as important to their success as sound was to *Steamboat Willie*'s. Disney's Christmas cartoons, *Santa's Workshop* (1932) and *The Night Before Christmas* (1933), were true holiday treats because the rich, vivid colors were so vital to the toyland theme. (In addition, color keeps them fresh, even today. Times have changed quite a bit since 1932, but the magic of *Santa's Workshop* remains intact after forty years—largely due to the brilliant colors.)

Film historian Lewis Jacobs has written:

Disney was the first to realize that color in motion pictures need not bear any resemblance to color in real life, that objects on the screen could be endowed

24

with any pigmentation dictated by the imagination. Furthermore, he recognized that color on the screen need not be static, but could move, and that such mobility, affecting the emotions, produced new visual experiences. . . . When Pluto, lost and frozen blue in the Alps, was found by a St. Bernard who forced whiskey down Pluto's throat, a luminous warm color slowly seeped back into his body as he thawed out; when the wolf tried to blow down the house of the three pigs, he literally blew himself blue in the face; when the north wind swept through an autumn forest, the entire color scheme changed from golden red to icy blue . . .

Disney was equally meticulous about the technical aspects of color. Director H. C. Potter recalls:

He discovered that with Technicolor film, no matter what color you photographed, a certain blue would come out a little bit deeper, or a little bit lighter. Invariably there would be an alteration in the color value. His technical people finally worked out a whole palette that his artists used religiously. They would take the original color, and a chart on the wall would show how much change there was from what the artist had conceived into what the Technicolor would print. It ran six, seven feet high, and three or four columns. I always thought it was an example of how meticulous Walt was in trying to get something right.

The most famous *Silly Symphony* of all was *The Three Little Pigs,* made in 1933. Disney had always known the importance of music to his cartoons, but here the impact of a song really made itself known. Frank Churchill composed a bright little song that went along with the classic story of the three pigs and their enemy, the wolf; several members of the staff contributed words, and the result, "Who's Afraid of the Big Bad Wolf?" not only had much to do with the film's success, but became one of the most popular songs of the 1930s, a symbol, many

25

said, of the American people's spirit during the darkest days of the Depression.

The Three Little Pigs was but one of many *Silly Symphony* cartoons that derived from longtime favorite fairy tales and Mother Goose stories, which lent themselves especially well to Disney treatment. Others included *Spider and the Fly, The Ugly Duckling, Old King Cole, Pied Piper, The Grasshopper and the Ant, The Tortoise and the Hare,* and *Who Killed Cock Robin?* The latter is well remembered for its use of a Mae West voice and personality for the character of Jenny Wren.

Most cartoon entrepreneurs used caricatures of movie stars in their films, but few of them with the scope of Disney. His first such attempt was in 1933 with *Mickey's Gala Premiere,* at which the premiere of a Mickey Mouse cartoon is attended by a bevy of movie celebrities, all delightfully caricatured: John, Ethel, and Lionel Barrymore, Wallace Beery, Marie Dressler, Laurel and Hardy, Joe E. Brown, Greta Garbo, Charlie Chaplin, Harold Lloyd, Wheeler and Woolsey, and numerous others. (P.S. It all turns out to be a dream.) Disney had similar success with *Mickey's Polo Team* in 1936 and *Mother Goose Goes Hollywood* in 1938, in which Katharine Hepburn was featured as Little Bo-Peep.

If Disney was free to ''borrow'' stars from other movie studios, he was equally generous with his own resources. He permitted Columbia's *Screen Snapshots* and Pathé's *Pathé Parade* to film sequences showing his studio at work, and when Hal Roach wrote him for permission to use the characters of the Three Little Pigs in his Laurel and Hardy feature, *Babes in Toyland,* Disney wrote a warm letter back not only granting permission, but offering his services in securing the women who did the pigs' voices, getting music clearance, and helping in any way possible. Thus, though Disney was not socially affiliated with most of his confreres in Hollywood, he earned their utmost respect and admiration, not only as a businessman, but as a gentleman.

Some of Disney's employees did not always hold him

in such high regard, but this was not the usual employer-employee type of situation. Disney, as we have seen, would have loved nothing better than to do everything himself. It soon became obvious to him that he couldn't, and he began assembling a staff. At this time Disney's work was his life's blood—like most men burning with creative energy, he had no use for relaxation—and it meant everything to him. When others joined in his enterprise, he implicitly expected them to feel the same way. Most of them *were* dedicated men, but dedication does not always take the place of money, good working hours and conditions, and public recognition. It took a bitter strike, in 1941, to settle most of these points of contention.

Despite the bitterness that sometimes came to the fore, Disney did engender remarkable loyalty from his associates, most of whom stayed with him for decades, and some of whom are now running his studio. Some of these men did not stay because they loved Walt as a human being; most of them realized that they were working in a unique enterprise, one of the few places in Hollywood where the creative spark did mean more than the bankbook. Disney became more and more aware of money matters, but it was his brother Roy who became the business head of the studio, who had to oversee financial problems; to Walt, nothing, but nothing, was more important than the quality of his product. Fortunately in Roy he had not only a confidant with business sense, but someone who shared his enthusiasm and was willing to take risks that many more prudent advisers would have rejected.

Thus, it was not for monetary reasons that Disney first started thinking about an animated feature film. To be sure, the Disney studio was not as prosperous as it deserved to be in the 1930s. In 1934 the studio revealed that *The Three Little Pigs* had cost $60,000 to make, and had grossed only $64,000, an outstanding income for any short subject, but for the fact that it had cost so much to produce. Therefore, one must not discount the fact that Disney stood to make considerably more money from an

One mark of Hollywood success: a formal portrait with his wife by Clarence Sinclair Bull. *Movie Star News*

animated feature than he would from shorts; but it can be said with some assurance that it was not his principal motivation.

Throughout his career Disney always sought new worlds to conquer. By the mid-1930s he was the idol of millions around the world and the darling of America's intelligentsia. (It was only later, when he became more ambitious, that the critics first reared their heads.) He thought of the tremendous challenge of making a full-length animated feature. And he thought about the prestige.

Definite ideas took shape as early as 1934, as Disney started augmenting his staff, encouraging his animators to take art lessons, and signing on apprentices to learn the ropes at the studio. Meanwhile, some members of the Disney staff, principally Bill Garity, were developing a machine that was to revolutionize Disney animation, the multiplane camera.

It would not be quite accurate to say that Disney had gone as far as he could in technique by the mid to late 1930s. But there *had* been great advances, and certainly the animation style of the studio had progressed immeasurably since 1928. But a cartoon was still, after all, just a cartoon. Disney longed to top himself by doing something more than just an ordinary cartoon. One answer was length: doing a feature film. Another answer was artistic quality: hence the art lessons and additional staff. But the third answer, techical advancement, was provided by the multiplane camera.

This device made it possible, for the first time, to use camera movements which live-action films had been doing for years as a matter of course, but which the one-dimensional animated cartoon format had never been able to accomplish. The camera could now move backward and forward, filming the drawings as if they were live objects, and not having to worry about size distortion. Since this camera was capable of shooting through many separate layers of drawings, spaced according to perspective, there was a greater feeling of depth, and foregrounds and backgrounds could be made more elaborate. Best of all, the animators could now do special effects—a "blur" effect for underwater, the vague glow around a fire that could never be drawn on a conventional cell, etc.—by implementing these things on separate panels in the multiplane system.

In short, the multiplane camera enabled the Disney staff to make their cartoons look more realistic, a goal that has been criticized by many who find a nonartistry in merely duplicating live action in animated form. What these critics miss is the fact that Disney never favored *realism* in his cartoons at all; rather, it was an *idealization* of real life, which was made possible by this technical advance. Indeed, even Disney's live-action films seldom sought a realistic feeling.

Disney's animated features strove for the effect of a fantasy world set against realistic backgrounds: just true enough to be believable, just fanciful enough to be make-believe. One sees this formula in most of the classic films, most notably in *Pinocchio* and *Dumbo*.

The multiplane camera was not perfected soon enough to be used throughout *Snow White*, so the entire film, as impressive as it is, does not have the majestic scope of, say, *Pinocchio*, although the multiplane was responsible for several sequences—the witch sailing her boat through the swamp and bringing it ashore, for example—none of them, except the wishing-well scene, being particularly ostentatious.

Meanwhile, the Disney staff was experimenting, and finding out just how much they could do with the camera. Publicity for *Donald's Lucky Day*, a 1939 short, enthused: "Walt Disney is putting his magical multiplane camera to increasing good use, as is seen in *Donald's Lucky Day*. A waterfront at night forms most of the locale for Donald's newest funfest, which means that the backgrounds are not only unbelievably beautiful, but that they look almost real because of the illusion of depth brought to the screen by this new camera process."

This was not the first time that a cartoonmaker had tried this technique; in the mid-1930s Max Fleischer touted a so-called 3-D process utilizing tabletop photography (slightly blurred foregrounds and backgrounds), with sharply defined characters as the center of attention. Though not exactly 3-D, the effect was quite striking, especially in color, as in *Popeye Meets Ali Baba and the Forty Thieves*.

For an even greater sense of realistic movement, the Disney staff decided to film live-action versions of their feature films, so the animators could study body movement in the various situations the plot presented. Marjorie Bell (Belcher), the wife of animator Art Babbitt, was recruited to pose as Snow White, and later as the Blue Fairy in *Pinocchio*. (She later became well known as Marge Champion.) In addition, a new department was established at the studio to provide scale models of every character, and, in some cases, every object (such as the toy clocks in Geppetto's workshop) in the cartoons. For Monstro, the whale, in *Pinocchio*, the staff even rigged up a rib cage and lungs in the scale model that could be pumped to simulate breathing action!

Furthermore, countless tests were shot of every scene before final animation was approved. Reporter Paul Harrison wrote in 1939:

I have just seen some *Pinocchio* sequences, photographed in black and white from the original drawings, and several color tests. Both provide new evidence of the meticulous caution used in making such a feature.

From the animators' pencil sketches the complete picture is shot—along with dialogue and sound effects—so that Disney and his editors can criticize it. When they have refined it as far as possible in that medium, the sketches are cleaned up so that the figures can be traced on the celluloid sheets, or "cells."

Throughout the picture key scenes are completely painted with minute variations, then photographed and projected as color tests. For example, I saw seven slightly different treatments of the scene in

The multiplane camera that did so much to broaden the horizons of the Disney cartoons. *Courtesy British Film Institute*

Two of Disney's gagmen, Joe Grant and Dick Huemer, at work on *Dumbo.* Notice the detailed model of Dumbo in front of them; the studio made intricate models of every character who appeared in the feature films for the writers and animators to study. *Movie Star News*

which the woodcarver finishes painting the face of Pinocchio and then picks him up and walks away.

One test would be in rather bright colors, another paler; one would use dark shadows behind the figures, another light shadows, a third no shadows. Such tests have been made on hundreds of scenes. The labor involved is staggering even to think about.

It was most staggering to animators and directors working for other cartoon studios in Hollywood. They were often allowed to be more individually creative, and they certainly had a more freewheeling sense of humor and daring, but virtually every figure in this golden age of animation has admitted that he, at one time or another, longed to have the resources to turn out something as good-looking as Disney's cartoons. Even disenchanted ex-employees do not hesitate to admit what invaluable experience it was to work for Disney during this period.

As the animated features started coming out, entertaining millions and racking up impressive box-office figures, Disney became more of a target for certain highbrow critics. After all, there wasn't much one could say about a man making cartoon shorts, but once Disney showed more ambition, it was easier to throw stones. Even Walt himself found something lacking in calling a work such as *Snow White* a "cartoon."

It was mainly on artistic grounds that Disney was criticized. Famed caricaturist Al Hirschfeld wrote of *Snow White:*

. . . the characters Snow White, Prince Charming, and the Queen are badly drawn attempts at realism: they imitate pantographically the actions of their counterparts in factual photography. The illusion created by a well-directed pen line is an art not to be confused with the gingerbread realities of a Snow White. Disney's treatment of these characters belongs in the oopsy-woopsy school of art practiced mostly by etchers who portray dogs with cute sayings. Snow

33

White with her full complement of fingers and fingernails, eyelashes, one-dimensional head, bare arms without solidity and uninventive neck is an anatomic automaton. These awkward symbols do not articulate, and the lovely voice with which she is endowed only heightens the effect of a ventriloquist's dummy. The staccato movements of Snow White and her cardboard lover, both wired for sound, are distinctly bad influences in this new art form. To imitate an animated photograph except as satire is in poor taste.

Thomas Burton, writing about *Pinocchio* in *Saturday Review,* said:

His [Disney's] is the art of soft-focus caricature, of picturing animals and men as lovable and amusing people. His art is all good-natured curves. Disney has discarded the straight line as bad for animation and the pure joy he sees in life. Both his technical limitations and his background have kept him from being another 'Rowlandson, Daumier, Leech, Gavarini, or Hogarth. He cannot, like them, be casually cruel or see with their cold artistic lassitude.

This gives him all his talents to be put into surface entertainment. There is no place for social bite, grand manner, art theory in his work. Walt Disney in *Pinocchio* lets nothing confuse his story. He sees it and tells it with a charm, a wit, a beautiful sense of pace and mounting. . . . It will keep you living in a wonderful world of form and color and excitement.

What many critics could not understand was that Disney had no desire to inject "social bite, grand manner, art theory" in his work. Like the man who says "I don't know anything about art, but I know what I like," Disney knew exactly what he liked, and as has been pointed out so many times, his audiences were Walt Disney multiplied many times over. His taste matched his audience's perfectly.

Throughout his career, when sniped at by critical attacks, Disney's answer was as logical as it was natural. He pointed to his films' overwhelming success around the world. And what better criterion for a man whose avowed purpose in making these films was to entertain people?

"This above all: to thine own self be true." Disney was true to himself every step of his career. When dissatisfied with *Pinocchio,* he completely scrapped five months of finished product. Why? It didn't look right to him. This kind of judgment was always based on integrity—personal integrity—and a dedication to the one goal Disney held above all others: entertainment.

It was wrong for critics to chide Disney for not living up to his potential, for it was his potential as *they* saw it. Disney was satisfied with his films because they lived up to his own visions of them, and when released to theatres, his judgment was echoed by countless millions who delighted in what he gave them.

Disney strove for something special with *Fantasia,* a *succès d'estime* if not a box-office smash (until recently), and then in the 1940s went into new areas of endeavor. He tackled live action, initially in *The Reluctant Dragon,* and to a greater extent as the decade wore on. Some of his staunchest supporters berated him for deserting the realm of animation, but Disney defended himself, saying:

> I'll keep on making pictures all-cartoon, mixed with human actors, or with an all-live cast. It's the story that appeals to me and the manner of treatment is dictated from that. Yes, I've heard some people say I ought to stick to features like *Snow White* or *Pinocchio,* and it's true that the cartoon is my first love. I'll always go back to it. But I'm still experimenting and I've got to keep a busy schedule to make enough money to finance the big all-cartoon feature folks seem to expect of me.

During the war he went into a whole new sphere of

filmmaking: the instructional film. In 1941 he produced a film called *Four Methods of Flush Riveting* for the Lockheed Aircraft Company; it was the beginning of four years of wartime morale, training, and instructional films, and the cornerstone of a new career for Disney in the nontheatrical film field.

Shortly after the Lockheed project, John Grierson, then head of the National Film Board of Canada, commissioned Disney to make four shorts promoting the Canadian War Savings plan and an army training film called *Stop That Tank*. The United States government ordered the first of many films when it assigned Disney the task of making a theatrical short explaining the wartime tax situation to Americans. (The resulting film, *The New Spirit*, starred Donald Duck, and was warmly received by everyone but the Senate, which raised questions about the wisdom of paying large sums of money for such movies during wartime. One must remember that the government's involvement with filmmaking as a means of communication was virtually nonexistent until World War II.)

Before long the Disney studio was busier than ever, churning out scores of films serving every conceivable purpose for members of the Armed Forces, Americans at home, and people of other countries as well. The Museum of Modern Art has saved a number of these films in its permanent collection, calling Disney's army-navy training films "[deserving of] study as among the most mature examples of the instructional film." Other notable wartime endeavors include *Out of the Frying Pan into the Firing Line* (1943), an Office of War Information short distributed to American theatres, with Minnie Mouse showing why it was important for housewives to save fat, and *Water, Friend or Enemy* (1943), one of a series of health films designed to be shown in South America and sponsored by the Coordinator of Inter-American Affairs. The museum's notes declare: "Here the lesson about the right and wrong place for a well, about the necessity of boiling water, is clarity itself."

Disney possessed an uncanny ability in the making of such films. He managed, with live action and animation, to take literally any subject (and his wartime shorts certainly ran the gamut) and make it interesting, while peerlessly getting across the point of the film. Some observers have labeled these films "nonhumorous" and made a distinction between them and Disney's theatrical product. This is not entirely true. These films were made with a keen awareness of the audience that would be watching them. Some of the training films are not only of a quality well up to contemporary animated films being shown in theatres, but contain an abundance of humor that appeals directly to the servicemen it was created for. There is even so-called barracks humor in many of the films.

In a 1944 speech Disney called the animated film "the most flexible, versatile, and stimulating of all teaching facilities." Indeed, schoolchildren (and a great many adults, too), who have been exposed to such Disney films as *Our Friend the Atom, Donald in Mathmagic Land*, and the informative *People and Places* series, sigh with annoyance that all their instruction cannot be as lively and intriguing as that of Disney.

Disney also, of course, got into commercial films in a big way after the war, and lent his touch to films for everyone from U.S. Steel to Kleenex. Many companies whose "sponsored films" either don't get shown, or are projected to lethargic audiences, have discovered the advantage of having Walt Disney prepare movies for them.

The war disrupted many of Disney's plans, but it kept his studio busy and also kept a money flow coming through the gates. Disney produced one propaganda film for theatrical release, *Victory Through Air Power*, and two pet projects, combination live-action and cartoon salutes to the beauty of South America, *Saludos Amigos* and *The Three Caballeros*.

With the war over he was able to return to full production and revive some plans that had been dormant for the duration. A unique feature of the Disney studio throughout its history has been the length of time some ideas persisted in the studio before coming to fruition. The idea for *Peter Pan* existed as early as 1935. (It wasn't finished until 1952.) The rights to T. H. White's book *The Sword in the Stone* were bought in 1939 and the animated feature released twenty-four years later!

Often, projects were begun, then shelved temporarily; this was true of *Bambi,* which was planned to follow *Snow White,* and *Sleeping Beauty,* which first took shape in 1950. It was put aside in the middle of the decade when the studio concentrated its efforts on its TV shows and the new Disneyland park, only to be revived in 1956, when production began at full pace for a 1959 release.

Another discovery that Disney made in the 1940s was the value of his film backlog. Reissues are as old as the film industry itself, but Disney was uniquely equipped to take advantage of the system, since his films were basically timeless, unhampered by social change that rendered many other Hollywood films commercially impotent after several years. With the passage of time, reissues have proved to be the backbone of the Disney company, an asset whose monetary value is infinite. Disney discovered this relatively early in his career, and to date no one (except MGM with *Gone With the Wind*) has had greater success with reissues. In 1948 in an unprecedented move, Radio City Music Hall booked the 1933 cartoon *The Three Little Pigs* for a very successful engagement, followed by two hundred other theatres across the country.

Disney also continued to make new one-reel cartoons over the years, a source of wonder to many in the industry who gave up on short subjects in the late 1940s. Ward Kimball, veteran Disney animator and director, has explained why Disney continued to produce short cartoons well into the 1950s:

That was done as a buffer for animators. Schedules can't always be timed to accommodate your full working crew full time on features. Try as hard as we may, we can never seem to make one feature start

38

right in step with the one we've just finished. There is always a period of animation doldrums while we are preparing the next feature. Back when we used the shorts as a filler, they would provide temporary work for animators between features. When we discontinued the shorts program, TV shows then provided this buffer.

In 1961 Disney told columnist Art Buchwald: "I saw the handwriting on the wall about ten years ago. I'll make an occasional short now to go with one of my features, just to keep the theatre owners from booking some horrible short subject with my own picture, but it costs $100,000 to make a seven-minute cartoon, and you can't get your money back."

Even so, the Disney cartoons continued to be amusing, ingenious, and full of verve right to the last (in 1957), after which Disney's only cartoon shorts were featurette-type "specials." In 1953 the studio briefly succumbed to the then-popular 3-D craze, with a Donald Duck/Chip 'n' Dale cartoon called *Working for Peanuts*. The press book stated: "The gags with 3-D are plentiful as the chipmunks catch peanuts from the audience and Donald almost sticks a foot in the aisle as he searches for the playful chips." Just to be sure, the studio made the film available in regular versions for theatres that weren't interested in handing out the special glasses.

The quality of the cartoons remained exceedingly high in the 1950s, although the animation staff did follow the trend of foregoing very detailed backgrounds for more impressionistic views of trees, buildings, and such. They did not go along with the swing to "limited animation," led by the much praised UPA studio, although the Disney people found it useful for deliberate comic effect in their Academy Award-winning *Toot, Whistle, Plunk, and Boom*, a lighthearted history of music, which was also the studio's first cartoon in CinemaScope. Adding further to the experimental nature of the short, the sound was conceived for stereophonic effects (used again in another short, *Grand Canyonscope*). The car-

39

Disney accepts his Oscar for *Water Birds*, a nature short, in 1953 from Jane Wyman and Ray Milland. *UPI photo*

toon was enthusiastically received, and the Disney staff took special pride in being acclaimed for a short where limited animation was used in such a creative rather than economical way.

Disney's greatest and most surprising success in the late 1940s and early 1950s, however, was not with cartoons, short or long, or even with live-action features, but with a series of nature films! For years Disney publicity stories have claimed that this idea came about by chance, that Disney was vacationing in Alaska and happened to meet camera-store owners Alfred and Elma Milotte, who impressed him with their amateur wildlife movies. The truth is that Disney hatched the idea himself and then went looking for someone to actually make the first film. Emery F. Tobin, publisher of *The Alaska Sportsman* magazine, recommended the Milottes, who happened to be in Los Angeles at the time showing their wildlife films on tour. Disney contracted for footage on

Alaskan seals, and the result was edited down to a half-hour color short called *Seal Island*.

Everyone thought Disney was crazy when he tried to promote it; no one would play it. But Disney had it shown in one California theatre in order to qualify for the Academy Awards, and, much to everyone's surprise, it won an Oscar for Best Short Subject Documentary of the year. Not only did the theatre owners come running, but the film was a tremendous financial success. It was the beginning of Disney's *True-Life Adventure* series, which collected many awards, much praise, a lot of money, and led to another series, *People and Places,* and a string of feature films that continue to be made to this day.

The shorts also raised considerable controversy, and even Richard Schickel, one of Disney's harshest critics, had to admit:

> The nature films indeed present one of the most difficult problems of critical evaluation in the entire Disney history. On the one hand, no one can doubt that Disney's photographers did bring back the pearls and that they were displayed in a variety and profusion previously unknown on the theatre screens of the world. . . . In their sheer technical virtuosity, in their ability to put on the screen rarities and oddities from the natural world, the Disney films were so far above their competition as to deserve a category all to themselves. In them he satisfied the simplest, most basic demand of film making: he gave us a chance to see things we might not otherwise have ever seen. And yet he falsified this material in precisely the ways his critics suggested.

For all the wonder and delight and awesomeness of the films, one cannot help but bristle at some of the hoke Disney injected into them. Some of the ideas were good: a flight of birds set to Liszt's Second Hungarian Rhapsody provided a charming sequence that only served to emphasize the beauty of their ascent. But gimmicking

41

up the film so that two rocky mountain sheep butted each other to the "Anvil Chorus," or clowning up a fight to the death of two natural enemies, did not sit quite so easily.

This might have been somewhat easier to take, too, had not the Disney people assumed such a pretentious attitude toward the films. In a promotional booklet, writer-director James Algar stated:

> Factual honesty in essence as well as in detail is the distinguishing hallmark of the *True-Life Adventure* films. The theme of a Disney factual is usually elemental—often it is the fight for survival. The tempo of the telling must be leisurely. The tone must be respectful—no ridicule. No condescension, particularly when dealing with the wisdom of the ages and the tales of the master story-teller.

Factual honesty? No ridicule? No condescension? It was a bit hard to swallow.

Still, as Schickel pointed out, the scales were balanced to a large degree by the positive aspects of these films—and they were many, especially in the feature films *The Living Desert, The Vanishing Prairie, The African Lion,* etc. Here one must forgive Disney's misdirected showmanship; one *cannot* lambaste the man for making the films available in the first place, and though some people claim that the road to hell is paved with good intentions, Disney's route only led him slightly astray.

It is also worth noting that apparently the Disney staff took note of the films' criticism, for after the initial feature films in the series, such "gimmicky" treatment was generally abandoned in favor of a more sober approach. In the long run there is more good to say about the series than bad, and it remains a notable, if tarnished, achievement in Disney's career.

The 1950s were a decade of evolution for Walt Disney. He continued to make animated features that came out every year or two, but the period between them grew longer as the decade progressed. By the 1960s it had stretched to four years. Theatrically, the 1950s saw the change from an emphasis on animation to live action. Disney initially set up live-action filming in England with his memorable *Treasure Island,* followed during the next few years by three period swashbucklers.

His first ambitious undertaking on home ground was *20,000 Leagues Under the Sea.* It was filmed in CinemaScope and color, with a prestigious cast (James Mason, Kirk Douglas, Paul Lukas, Peter Lorre) and impressive production values, directed, oddly enough, by Richard Fleischer, the son of Disney's onetime competitor Max Fleischer. It was also the first film, except for the nature feature *The Living Desert,* to be released by Disney's own distribution company, Buena Vista. The film was a tremendous box-office success, but instead of following it up with a string of other life features, Disney turned his attention to a new medium—television.

In 1950 Disney turned down an offer of $1 million—for the television rights to his 350 cartoon shorts. "The television people want to buy my films," he explained, "but I'm not selling. Why should I? They're still good for movie theatres. And, because they're timeless, they always will be." Disney did agree to mount a one-hour television special for Christmas viewing several years in a row. "But I insisted on one thing, and sponsors agreed with me. No commercials. All we do is tell you the name of the sponsor . . . and that's that."

But by 1954 Disney changed his tune slightly. He still wasn't going to sell out to any network or sponsor. He decided to produce his own *Disneyland* TV series, a weekly hour show that he would host; the series would be comprised of some material from the backlog, used sparingly, a lot of hours filmed especially for the show (most of this live action), and considerable coverage of his new amusement park, Disneyland.

Because Disney hated to cut corners, the cost of producing his hour-long films for TV most often exceeded the amount he earned on them. Asked about this procedure, Disney explained: "Television makes lots of friends. It's just good policy. When four million people see your television show, they carry away with them an image of what we're doing."

Of course, viewers carried away more than just an image. Many of the hour programs were really glorified advertisements for new Disney theatrical features or upcoming reissues. When during the show's first season Disney presented an hour called "Operation Undersea," about the difficulties of making *20,000 Leagues Under the Sea*, industry pundits labeled it "The Long, Long Trailer," but the show won an Emmy Award as the Best Individual Program of the Year.

And although Disney's critics are quick to point out how he exploited the TV show to his own advantage in myriad ways, it should also be remembered that he couldn't have done any of it if the material he presented wasn't entertaining. Disney's plugs for feature films were often more enjoyable than hour-long installments of other series. And the original material shot for the series was bright, handsomely turned out programming, one of the most consistently good series on the air.

Disney decided to host the show himself; all reports of him being taciturn and/or shy were dispelled as he presented the various programs week after week with a natural and completely winning style that reminded one of a benign relative. Indeed, he was the best possible choice for a host, and in his twelve-year stint in that position he cemented forever the public image of Walt Disney that no amount of critical writing can eradicate from Americans' minds.

Disney soon learned that TV was also a useful proving ground for actors, writers, directors, and ideas in general. Often he would plan a segment for the TV show and it would turn out so well that he would release it as a feature instead—something that could never have been accomplished had Disney been using the same economical shooting methods as other TV producers.

But the biggest outgrowth of the TV series in the 1950s was a fellow named Davy Crockett. Disney produced a three-part program on the famous United States folk hero, and before he knew what was happening, the whole country was Davy Crockett-crazy. Disney reaped a fortune from merchandising rights as every red-blooded American boy (this writer included) donned coonskin caps and other Crockett regalia. The three TV hours were edited into a feature film, which then warranted a sequel. The shows also made a star of Fess Parker, who appeared in such other Disney films as *The Great Locomotive Chase* and *Westward Ho the Wagons*.

Disney's hold on the small fry of the 1950s was completed with the emergence of *The Mickey Mouse Club*, which debuted on October 3, 1955. A daily filmed half-hour TV show that aired on ABC at five o'clock, the *Club* featured a group of likable youngsters known as the Mouseketeers, led by singer-actor Jimmy Dodd, who entertained, presented various travel and educational segments, appeared in serialized stories ("The Hardy Boys," "Spin and Marty," "Corky and White Shadow"), and showed old Disney cartoons with Mickey, Donald, Goofy, and the other favorite characters.

The show was phenomenally successful; 260 hours and 130 half hours were filmed, and the series enjoyed a healthy run on the network, and later on local stations when additional material was filmed to bring the shows up to date. We needn't go into a comparison of the quality of this program to most of today's commercial kiddie fare.

The name of Disney's hour-long program was changed to *Walt Disney Presents*, as he continued to come up with quality material week after week. Eventually, several series within the series sprang up, including *Texas John Slaughter,* starring Tom Tryon, *The Swamp Fox, Elfego Baca, Moochie,* and *Zorro,* the latter proving so popular and so flexible that it was developed as a half-hour series starring Guy Williams, Henry Calvin, and Gene Sheldon, which ran on ABC and subsequently in endless reruns in syndication.

When Disney severed his relations with ABC and moved to NBC in the fall of 1961, the name of the show was changed once more, to *Walt Disney's Wonderful World of Color,* an indication that the show was to be aired in color, and a prestigious tie-in for NBC and RCA, the program's sponsor. In announcing the move Disney stated that all previously established characters would be abandoned and that the NBC program would present all new ideas. The most prominent of these was a new cartoon figure, Professor Ludwig von Drake, an erudite but absent-minded duck whose delightful voice was provided by Paul Frees. The program, aired at seven thirty every Sunday night, has remained at the top of the rating charts every year, a considerable feat in the fickle television world, and it looks to be a permanent fixture in the future. (When Disney died, the name of the show was changed to *The Wonderful World of Disney.*)

The late 1950s saw the beginning of Disney's real plunge headfirst into live-action feature film production, which continues unabated to this day. The standard formulas (action-adventure, animal films, lightweight comedy) have served the studio well, and with features and TV programs in constant production, the studio has established various favorites over the years who have found themselves in the enviable position of being steadily employed by Disney. It can truly be said that Disney was responsible for making Fred MacMurray a star of the first magnitude once more, and his studio has developed its own stars as well, most notably Hayley Mills. Directors Robert Stevenson, James Neilson, and Norman Tokar have been responsible for the majority of the company's live-action product.

The great success of such fanciful comedies as *The Shaggy Dog* and *The Absent Minded Professor* led the studio to concentrate more and more on innocuous family comedies, predicating a feeling in some circles that the Disney magic was wearing thin. Then came *Mary Poppins.* The big-budgeted (nearly $5 million) live-action/animation musical grossed an estimated $40 million, and let it be known to all doubters that there

46

was still only one Walt Disney and he was alive and well in Burbank.

Poppins was followed by another host of amiable comedies and a few adventure films, none of them outstanding, all of them adhering to certain patterns that had been set up over the years (clean-cut hero, wholesomely good-looking heroine, plenty of slapstick in the comedies, etc.).

If these films weren't up to what one likes to consider "the Disney standard," it is probably because Walt himself wasn't involved with them to the extent he was in times gone by—or even in the case of a major production like *Mary Poppins*. Disney always had to have new worlds to conquer, and having set up his moviemaking machine at the Burbank studio, the excitement of it started to diminish. Certainly Disney took much more pride and interest in the development of his Audioanimatronics (automatically controlled robots, such as the famous one of Abraham Lincoln built for the New York World's Fair and later installed in Disneyland) than he did in *The Monkey's Uncle*. In Audioanimatronics he found something new and challenging—a way to recreate a likeness of Lincoln delivering a speech as if he were alive!

He took special pride in Disneyland and had great plans for his Florida complex, Walt Disney World. All this meant more to him than films or television toward the end of his life. For after all it would have been difficult for Disney to top himself filmwise at this stage of the game. There were few mountains left to climb in the field of animation. There wasn't even the satisfaction of turning out a Mickey Mouse cartoon in a few weeks anymore. In some ways sheer size defeated Walt Disney; there could no longer be the simplicity and innocence of a *Dumbo* (or even the brevity—*Dumbo* was sixty-four minutes, *Mary Poppins* 139!). It took a fresh and beguiling subject—A. A. Milne's classic *Winnie the Pooh*—to bring out the very best in Disney and his staff once more. *Winnie the Pooh and the Honey Tree* and its sequel, *Winnie the Pooh and the Blustery Day*, were un-

In 1961 Disney introduced a new character, Ludwig von Drake (officially Donald Duck's uncle), on his NBC television show.
NBC photo; © 1961 Walt Disney Productions

doubtedly the most charming cartoons, both visually and otherwise, that the Disney studio had created in years. It is worth noting that both films were less than a half hour in length.

One thing never changed at the studio, and that was the professionalism that Walt had instilled in every member of his staff. Even Disney's color quality was better than most other studios, simply because the studio insisted on the very best results from Technicolor labs. (Technicolor was glad to comply, since Disney was largely responsible for putting the company on the map in the 1930s.) The special effects in Disney's live-action films far surpassed rival companies', with matte and process-screen work that puts many a Hollywood epic to shame. Disney was even able to use animation to create undetected effects in his films—the long shot of the mansion in *Blackbeard's Ghost*, scenes of fish swimming by Captain Nemo's observation window in *20,000 Leagues Under the Sea*, etc.

Roy Disney said that "it was Walt's wish that when the time came he would have built an organization with the creative talent to carry on as he established and directed it through the years." This came to pass on December 15, 1966, when Walt Disney died of acute circulatory collapse after surgery for the removal of a lung tumor one month earlier.

The world mourned the loss of its greatest fantasist, the one man who entertained more people in more ways than any other person of our era.

There were many who felt that the studio would never last without him, but Roy Disney's words were more than just an empty statement. Disney actually had built up his studio to the point where it could run quite smoothly without him. Men who were animators in the 1930s were now in charge of various facets of production, along with other writers, directors, and technicians who were so rewarded for their longtime loyalty to the Disney company.

So it is that Walt Disney Productions has continued to prosper, both with reissues of its classic films and a steady flow of new product, both animated and live action.

But if something seems to be missing at times, it is not imagined, for even in his final years Walt Disney was no figurehead at the studio. Recalling the making of *Snow White and the Seven Dwarfs* on the occasion of its fifth reissue in 1967, UB Iwerks commented: "It would probably cost $20 million to make in today's market. But there's more to it than that. I don't think we could find the necessary talent or the enthusiasm it took in those days.

"Walt provided the enthusiasm," he concluded, "and our staff was young. Most of us were in our late twenties or early thirties. I think Walt was only thirty-five or thirty-six when he made *Snow White.*"

No, Walt Disney was not a figurehead, as some have called him, nor an exploiter. He was a showman, an entertainer by proxy, a storyteller. One must forgive the cliché that he "brought joy to millions," because he really did. His films continue to entertain millions today and undoubtedly will do so for many years to come.

And that, above all, is the living testament to the talent—genius, if you will, of Walt Disney.

2 · The Feature Films

SNOW WHITE AND THE SEVEN DWARFS

RELEASED BY RKO RADIO PICTURES; WORLD PREMIERE, December 21, 1937, released February 4, 1938. Multiplane Technicolor. Adapted from *Grimm's Fairy Tales*. Supervising director: David Hand. Sequence directors: Perce Pearce, Larry Morey, William Cottrell, Wilfred Jackson, Ben Sharpsteen. Supervising animators: Hamilton Luske, Vladimir Tytla, Fred Moore, Norman Ferguson. Story adaptation: Ted Sears, Otto Englander, Earl Hurd, Dorothy Ann Blank, Richard Creedon, Dick Richard, Merrill De Maris, Webb Smith. Art directors: Charles Philippi, Hugh Hennesy, Terrell Stapp, McLaren Stewart, Harold Miles, Tom Codrick, Gustaf Tenggren, Kenneth Anderson, Kendall O'Connor, Hazel Sewell. Character designers: Albert Hurter, Joe Grant. Animators: Frank Thomas, Dick Lundy, Arthur Babbitt, Eric Larson, Milton Kahl, Robert Stokes, James Algar, Al Eugster, Cy Young, Joshua Meador, Ugo D'Orsi, George Rowley, Les Clark, Fred Spencer, Bill Roberts, Bernard Garbutt, Grim Natwick, Jack Campbell, Marvin Woodward, James Culhane, Stan Quackenbush, Ward Kimball, Wolfgang Reitherman, Robert Martsch. Backgrounds: Samuel Armstrong, Mique Nelson, Merle Cox, Claude

Coats, Phil Dike, Ray Lockrem, Maurice Noble. Music arrangers: Frank Churchill, Paul J. Smith, Leigh Harline. Running time: 83 minutes.

Songs by Frank Churchill, Larry Morey, Paul J. Smith, and Leigh Harline: "I'm Wishing," "One Song," "With a Smile and a Song," "Whistle While You Work," "Heigh Ho," "Bluddle-Uddle-Um-Dum," "The Dwarfs' Yodel Song," "Some Day My Prince Will Come."

Voices: Adriana Caselotti (Snow White), Harry Stockwell (The Prince), Lucille LaVerne (The Queen), Scotty Mattraw (Bashful), Roy Atwell (Doc), Pinto Colvig (Grumpy), Otis Harlan (Happy), Pinto Colvig (Sleepy), Billy Gilbert (Sneezy), Moroni Olsen (The Magic Mirror), Stuart Buchanan (Humbert, The Queen's Huntsman), Marion Darlington (bird sounds and warbling), The Fraunfelder Family (yodeling).

How does one begin to talk about *Snow White*—the first full-length animated feature, the turning point in Walt Disney's career, a milestone in film history, and, as more and more people realize with each passing year, a great film?

Perhaps the way to start is with what exists on film—beginning, as most of Disney's subsequent animated features were to do, on a close-up of a storybook with "Some Day My Prince Will Come" being played on the sound track at a brisk tempo. The storybook opens and establishes in its first few pages the background of our story: the beautiful Snow White, orphaned at birth, growing up forced to do menial work in the Queen's household.

It is with a long shot of the Queen's castle that the action begins, as the majestic lady, proud and vain, approaches her Magic Mirror to ask, as she always does: "Who is the fairest of them all?" Today the Mirror replies that it is one within her very home . . . Snow White.

The Wicked Queen orders Snow White killed, and her heart returned in this box. © *Walt Disney Productions; courtesy Al Kilgore*

At this point the picture dissolves to our first scene of Snow White, doing her work with the garden birds fluttering happily about her. She does long for one thing (having long since accepted her tedious work), and as she goes to the well to fill her wash pail, she sings ''I'm Wishing,'' an echo duplicating her voice as she tells in song of her yearning for the man she loves to find her and take her away. As she finishes the song, a handsome prince who has heard her approaches, singing the last line of the song, much to Snow White's surprise. Although she is embarrassed and runs away, it is clear that here is the very man she has been wishing for.

Meanwhile, the Queen has sent for her huntsman, ordering him to take Snow White to the forest that afternoon and slay her. He must bring back her heart in order to prove that the deed has been done. That day the unsuspecting Snow White goes with the man into the forest, and while picking wild flowers, turns to see him raising his gleaming hunting knife. But he cannot go through with it. He begs her forgiveness, and tells her to run—flee—escape from the power of the evil Queen.

She takes off into the forest, frightened not only by what has just happened, but by the specters her mind imagines around her. Finally she falls to the ground in tears, but then some of the haunting eyes that have peered at her from the brush emerge; they are merely the animals of the forest, as frightened of Snow White as she has been of them.

As they gingerly approach, however, she realizes her mistake, and brightens, making friends with the animals. Trying to forget her nightmarish experience, she sings "With a Smile and a Song," and the animals lead her out of the deep forest toward a house in the clearing. Finding the quaint little cottage caked with dust and its belongings in wild disarray, she decides to clean it up with the help of her animal friends, singing "Whistle While You Work."

Meanwhile, some distance away, the Seven Dwarfs are introduced in song as they "dig dig dig" in their mine. With the end of the workday approaching, they pack up their tools and head for home, singing "Heigh Ho" as they march back to their cottage.

Snow White, having finished her chores, explores the second floor of the house, and falls asleep draped over several of the curiously tiny beds in the room. When the animals hear the Dwarfs approaching the house, they scurry off in all directions, leaving Snow White alone.

When the Dwarfs arrive at the cottage, they find it has undergone an amazing transformation. It's spotlessly clean, with everything in its place. They decide that whoever is responsible must be upstairs, and they elect a patsy to go up and have a look around. This

Snow White flees through the forest, letting her imagination run away with her. © *Walt Disney Productions; courtesy Al Kilgore*

Six of the dwarfs try to get the seventh, Grumpy, to wash his hands and face before dinner. © *Walt Disney Productions*

simpleminded Dwarf creeps into their bedroom, but with a vivid imagination, and with the shadows cast by his lantern, envisions the figure covered by a bedsheet to be a scary ghost!

When they all finally tiptoe into the room, Snow White wakes up and surprises them by identifying each one by name (having read the unusual names on each bedpost): Doc (the "leader"), Happy, Sleepy, Sneezy, Bashful, Grumpy, and Dopey. When she tells of her plight—and offers to cook and keep house for them if they will let her stay—they happily agree, except for Grumpy, who doesn't want any part of her or her problems.

She baffles them by insisting that they wash before sitting down to dinner, but before long she has won them over completely and the house sparkles as it never had before. When the Dwarfs go off to work the next morning, they beg Snow White to be careful while they're gone (even Grumpy showing interest in her well-being), and she kisses them good-bye, Dopey playfully coming back for seconds and thirds.

The night before, however, the Queen has discovered the trick played on her by the Huntsman, by asking the Magic Mirror who is the fairest and being told that Snow White is still alive. Determined to get rid of her for good, she hatches a diabolical scheme; she will disguise herself as an ugly old woman and offer Snow White a poisoned apple. She stalks down to her dungeon laboratory that night, where she mixes the ingredients for her transformation: a scream, to turn her hair white, etc. She drinks the potion, and detail by detail turns into a cackling old crone. Then she prepares the deadly apple, and during the foggy night sails her boat through the swamp to reach Snow White by morning.

After the Dwarfs have gone, the Queen appears and offers Snow White the luscious red apple to use in baking a pie, exhorting her to taste it. She does, and falls to the ground in a dead faint, which, according to the Queen's curse, cannot be broken except by love's first kiss.

The animals see what has happened, and rush to get the Dwarfs, who race back to catch the Queen. Amidst thunder and lightning, they chase her up rocky terrain, causing her to back out onto a ledge that gives way. Screaming, she falls to her death, two hungry vultures circling down after her.

The Dwarfs are crushed by Snow White's death; even Grumpy dissolves into tears at the sight of her. A subtitle explains that she was "so beautiful, even in death, that the Dwarfs did not have the heart to bury her." Instead, they create a bier where she lies in state for all the forest animals, as well as the Dwarfs, to pay their respects.

But another comes to see Snow White; it is the Prince who approaches, and as a farewell gesture he kisses her. Miraculously, she awakens, and grief turns into joy as the Dwarfs and animals cheer for Snow White and the Prince who has finally come to take her off where they will live happily ever after.

The story of *Snow White and the Seven Dwarfs* is, of course, an old and fairly simple one. But here, for the first of many times, the Disney staff faced the challenge of taking a simple tale and stretching it out to the length of a feature film, achieving the proper balance between the plot motivation of the central character(s) and the comedy relief supplied, in this case, by the Dwarfs.

Just as Disney learned that his hero Mickey Mouse was downright dull in comparison with such colorful sidekicks as Pluto and Donald Duck, he quickly discovered that the heroes and heroines of fairy-tale stories were frequently the least interesting aspects of those tales. Yet one couldn't eliminate them or relegate them to supporting roles; the answer was to have their actions intertwined with those of the comedy characters so subtly that it would never seem as it did, for example, in the archetypal Broadway musical comedies of the 1920s and 1930s that two separate and distinct elements were at work.

One way of achieving this goal was seeing that the action never stayed with one character or setting too long.

Practically every key scene in the film is interrupted by crosscutting to simultaneous action elsewhere. (The Dwarfs are introduced in the middle of Snow White's housecleaning sequence; the Queen's transformation takes place amid scenes of the after-dinner party at the Dwarfs' cottage.)

Mike Barrier has said it best: "The story is never just an excuse for the Dwarfs' comedy; instead, most of what they do has direct bearing on the plot. We care more about what happens to Snow White because the Dwarfs—far more vivid personalities than she—care so much for her, and much of the comedy arises from their concern."

Disney also realized that operetta-style villainy would never work in these films, so instead he went out for totally evil characterizations and sequences that were firmly rooted in horror elements. Snow White's peril is made distressingly real by the character and actions of the Queen. (For example, leaving her dungeon laboratory, down a winding staircase past prison cells, she spots the skeletal figure of what was once a man lying on the ground, his bony hand reaching through the bars for a pitcher of water that is *just* beyond his reach. She says mockingly: "Thirsty? Have a drink!" and kicks the cup and the skeleton into a dozen directions as she laughs wickedly. An ugly yellow and black spider scurries out of the overturned cup. This is just one of many truly terrifying vignettes throughout the film.)

With these factors—the sweetness of Snow White, the wickedness of the Queen, and the humor of the Dwarfs—firmly established, the film moves at a firm, steady pace, never seeming rushed or contracted (as some of the cartoon features did), or prolonged with dull stretches. The sequences lead one into another with perfect precision and harmony, seeming to flow as if this were the way the story had always been told.

Much of this fluidity, of course, was the result of judicial editing, a vital part of the four-year period spent making this film. Whole sequences were animated and fit into the film, and then taken out because they hindered the progress of the story.

The film originally showed Snow White's mother dying in childbirth; this was cut from the film at the very last minute. Indeed, stills from this sequence were printed in *Look* magazine's preview of the film, and the sequence itself was part of all the authorized book versions, comic strips, comic books, and related material that came out in advance of the film. (This, incidentally, was a practice Disney followed for years, having syndicated comic versions of his films appear before they were to be released to theatres, so that by the time youngsters went to see the film, they were fully versed in the background and plot of the film—an educated audience, as it were.)

Ward Kimball recalls:

I animated on *Snow White and the Seven Dwarfs*, and that was one of the early tragedies of my life. I was made a full-fledged animator, and they decided that Kimball would do a good job on the eating sequence, after Snow White makes the Dwarfs wash up. I would do the soup sequence, because I did funny stuff. I animated the whole sequence, and it got big laughs in the sweat box (Walt's projection room), but when Walt started seeing the whole picture, he thought that was one of the places that we ought to get on with the story, go right from making them wash to the next sequence. So as much as he hated to do it—he even called me up on the phone and apologized—he had to take it out of the picture. So then I went on a bed-building sequence; they had a big, ornate bed that the Dwarfs were building as a present to Snow White. This also was taken out after I'd animated it, because it didn't help the story along.

The animated pencil test of the "soup sequence" was later shown on one of Disney's 1956 TV hours, "The Plausible Impossible."

But these personal setbacks were, as Kimball well realized, made for the good of the picture, and, indeed, when the last cut was made, Disney had a film with not one wasted minute, and a story that held the audience's attention from the first frame to the last.

There was not a detail of the film that had not been discussed, picked apart, tried, rejected, tried again, and perhaps again and again and again.

Thirty years later, Wolfgang Reitherman recalled:

> I remember when I first came here as an animator and did the mirror sequence in *Snow White,* the atmosphere in the studio was alive with creativity, a marriage of many minds and talents. It was great to work under those conditions. We fabricated whole characters from thin air. We made life happen in cartoon form. There were no movie actors to fall back on to make the cartoon figures click. From our imagination we created frame by frame spontaneity.

The design of the human characters bothered Disney the most. Although, as in all later features, live models were used for the animators to achieve realism (Marjorie Belcher, the wife of animator Art Babbitt, posed for Snow White, and Louis Hightower for the Prince), it was for the drawing of the central human characters that Disney was most severely criticized.

Archer Winsten, in criticizing the film for the *New York Post,* wrote:

> I am completely at a loss to understand how anyone can fail to sense the difference in the quality of draftsmanship between the animals, and the dwarfs on the one hand and Snow White, Prince Charming, the Huntsman, and the Wicked Queen. Now to place it on an artistic plane, one can say that the former come to life completely whereas the latter remain drawings, not very pleasing ones, that move.

The Disney staff was more acutely aware of this problem than many may have guessed. They deliberately brought Prince Charming into the picture
60

for only two brief scenes (at the beginning and the end), because they felt he looked unbearably stiff. (Today, ironically enough, with the soft, cuddly style of drawing on the outs and more realistic drawing popular, the Prince looks better than any of the other human characters in the film.)

The design of the Dwarfs provided a challenge of a different kind. Here the idea was to create seven distinct personalities who would be readily identifiable visually, not by their voices or actions. Once the characters' names were set, the artists went to work on their conceptions of the Dwarfs. These were revised and revised again before meeting with general approval. In general, the orders on these revisions was to make them look "more cute." Along these lines, someone came up with the idea of having Dopey's clothes and hat be far oversized, giving him a floppy, carefree look. The final version of the character was patterned after character comedian Eddie Collins.

According to one contemporary account:

Posture was also an important factor in defining the dwarfs' personalities. Doc always stands well back on his heels, his hands pressed behind whenever possible, which adds to his pompousness. Bashful's back is slightly arched and his stomach is out. Frequently he stands on one foot and twists the other around his ankle. . . . Grumpy has a slight hunch to his shoulders and a swagger to his walk which makes him look pugilistic.

Matching the voices to these characters was another important step. Disney auditioned dozens of young girls for the role of Snow White, staying in his office while their voices were piped through, so he wouldn't be affected by their appearance. Reportedly, he turned down Deanna Durbin for the job, saying she sounded too mature. He finally decided on a young girl named Adriana Caselotti, whose highpitched voice still sounds disconcerting to this writer whenever he sees the film, although, it must be admitted, this discomfiture disappears after the first few scenes.

For the Dwarfs, various actors and veteran studio jack-of-all-trades Pinto Colvig (who was also the voice of Goofy) were pressed into service. In a few special cases distinctive voices were sought. Vaudeville comic Roy Atwell, famous for his spoonerisms (substituting the first syllables of consecutive words), was hired to play Doc, and he used his amusing malaprops as part of the character. When comedian Billy Gilbert read in *Variety* that one of the Dwarfs was to be called Sneezy, he telephoned Disney, who agreed to an impromptu audition. In Walt's office, Gilbert went into his famous sneezing routine; Disney smiled and said "You're my man."

Lucille LaVerne, a skilled actress most famous for her old hag characterizations in such films as *Orphans of the Storm* and *A Tale of Two Cities*, was the ideal choice for both the voice and model of the Queen-turned-Witch.

Of course, there was no voice problem when it came to Dopey, who was cast as a mute. At first, it was reported that he was going to be a chatterbox, but then someone came up with the marvelous idea of enhancing his endearing witlessness by having him remain silent (also provoking the comment that he was patterned after Harpo Marx). In the film his condition is explained by one of the Dwarfs, who, asked by Snow White if he can talk, replies: "He don't know—he never tried!"

Music played a more important role in the making of *Snow White* than in virtually any other Disney film, excepting, of course, *Fantasia*, for the songs in *Snow White* were designed from the very beginning to become integral parts of the story. (Reportedly, some twenty-five tunes were written before Disney settled on the eight used in the film.) What is more, however, the *entire film* was planned out to a musical beat. Some examples are obvious, such as the prolonged sequence that begins with Snow White and the animals in the forest, and ends with them going into the song "Whistle

While You Work'' in the Dwarfs' cottage. Between those two points, all movements, and all of Snow White's dialogue, are done in rhythm. The introduction of the Dwarfs in the mine, picking away in time to the "dig dig dig" verse they sing, is just a rhythmical lead-in to the marching theme of "Heigh Ho," which they sing as they walk back home.

Naturally, the most prominent and important aspect of *Snow White* was the visuals, and it was here that Disney did his most impressive work. The film is filled to overflowing with beautiful images, both spectacular and throwaway. Those in the former category owed much to the new multiplane camera, which, although it wasn't ready when animation began on *Snow White,* still was used in quite a few scenes.

In Snow White's run through the forest, there are many dark, winding, ominous trees in the foreground as well as in the background. As she scurries through, her mind visualizes various distortions: driftwood in the stream becomes alligators, hollows in the trees become elongated eyes staring at her, etc. What is important here is that Snow White is not running on a straight path, parallel to our eye view, but on a wildly twisting path that takes her back and forth at varying distances from the camera, with material passing in front of her as well as behind her. The feeling of *depth* is astounding.

The Queen's transformation scene is justifiably famous, a marvel of *directing* and *editing* as well as animation. After mixing the brew in her harshly candlelit laboratory, with her pet raven observing on the sidelines, she pulls the cup close to her, and we see her reflection on the side of the glass. She swallows it down, and starts to gag on the drink, as the entire room begins to spin around her! One by one in the maze we see the characteristics of the Witch overtake her—the scream turning her hair a ragged white, her hands growing into masses of wrinkles and bones, her voice changing into a cackle. When done, she has her back to us, and turns around in her black-hooded cape, keeping her face covered in best Dr. Jekyll fashion, until the camera moves in and she unveils her ugly countenance for the first time.

Much of the horror in this scene is conveyed not by the Witch, but by the reactions of her pet raven, who is truly frightened when the Queen completes her metamorphosis.

Cartoonist Al Kilgore feels that "the witch's trip from her castle to the forest, on her way to the Dwarfs' cottage, in the fog-shrouded dawn is the most underrated scene in the entire film. It is the most subtle use of multiplane, color, and realistic animation."

Color is used with great care throughout the film. It was decided that to employ the bright, vivid colors of the one-reel cartoons throughout a feature would be a mistake. Instead, muted colors are used in most sequences (as in the forest, where there are no really rich greens) so that key color sequences would stand out all the more. A prominent example is the stunning silhouette of the Dwarfs marching home over a log, set against a dazzling sunset.

More than anything else, people were impressed with *Snow White*'s realistic touches in 1937; they are just as striking today. Few cartoons, before or since, depicted rain so vividly—not just having a torrent of drops superimposed over a setting, but actually showing the drops splashing on the ground! Seldom had there been such a concentration on shadows, from realistic ones such as that of the Huntsman as he towers over Snow White in the forest, to deliberately exaggerated ones cast by the Dwarfs' lanterns as they tiptoe into the darkened room where Snow White is asleep.

Few people will ever forget the menacing gleam of the Huntsman's knife just before he raises it to kill Snow White. And having the face in the mirror blur as wisps of smoke rise around it . . . well, it was just too much.

Other little things stand out in memory: Dopey's marvelous expressions, tongue protruding from the side of his mouth when he shows determination, eyes rolling in carefree abandon as he snaps his fingers and dances with Snow White . . . the haunting establishing shot of the Castle at twilight, seen from the forest below through a brace of branches as the Queen is about to make her potion . . . and the famous scene of Snow White's face reflected in the well when she sings "I'm Wishing."

There is also something more than mere animation in the final sequences of the film. The animals rushing to get the Dwarfs, the Griffithlike intercutting between the Dwarfs riding bareback and the Witch trying to escape, as lightning and thunder help set the mood, and then the absolute deadly silence after the Witch's fall over the cliff, with the Dwarfs timidly peering over the edge as two vultures silently swoop down into the mist to claim their prey.

Without seeing it, it's difficult to envision the emotional impact of *Snow White and the Seven Dwarfs*. There is terror (and that is the correct word) in the horrific scenes of the Queen/Witch, and there is heart-rending sorrow in the apparent death of Snow White, with the Dwarfs' unspeakable sadness. (Mike Barrier has commented on Grumpy's reaction in particular: "He's obviously crushed almost beyond endurance, his eyes wide with horror and disbelief. Grumpy's relationship with Snow White is handled very well; his attitude toward her changes subtly, so that his grief is more affecting.")

But most of all the film exudes a feeling of joy, a radiant glow of happiness that is so persuasive that, at the end of the film, you're ready to believe that somewhere in this world there must be happy endings such as this—they've just *got* to be real.

There is no way to overstate the effect of *Snow White and the Seven Dwarfs* on the film industry, the moviegoing public, and the world in general.

Howard Barnes of the *New York Herald Tribune* wrote:

After seeing *Snow White and the Seven Dwarfs* for the third time, I am more certain than ever that it belongs with the few great masterpieces of the screen. It is one of those rare works of inspired artistry that weaves an irresistible spell around the beholder. Walt Disney has created worlds of sheer enchantment before with his animated cartoons, but never has he taken us so completely within their magic bounds. *Snow White and the Seven Dwarfs* is more than a completely satisfying entertainment, more than a perfect moving picture, in the full sense of that term. It offers one a memorable and deeply enriching experience.

His comments were echoed by critics around the world, but more importantly by the public. It ran for an unprecedented five weeks at New York's Radio City Music Hall, an amazing thirty-one weeks in Paris, and set new attendance records around the world.

It was dubbed into ten languages, with such titles as *Blanche Neige et les Sept Nains* (France) and *Schneewittchen und die Sieben Dwerge* (Germany). It was under a partial ban in several countries, such as England, where censors ruled that children under sixteen would not be allowed to see the film unless accompanied by adults, for fear of the tots having nightmares after seeing the film's horror sequences. Most of the other restrictions in countries ranging from South Africa to the Netherlands were lifted in response to public outcry (having been presold on the film by the same merchandising boom that took root in this country). At one point there was talk of Lily Pons recording the voice of Snow White for the French-language print, but apparently nothing came of it.

In Hollywood rival movie studios gave serious consideration to full-length animated features, which a year before they wouldn't have touched. Paramount insisted that Max Fleischer, who supplied them with *Popeye* and *Betty Boop* cartoons, produce a cartoon feature; the result was *Gulliver's Travels*, which was released for Christmas 1939. Universal announced that its resident cartoon producer, Walter Lantz, would make a feature called *Aladdin and His Wonderful Lamp,* on a budget of $750,000. (*Snow White,* which had originally been budgeted at $250,000, wound up costing $1,480,000.) Lantz even signed up Disney's music staffer Frank Churchill, but this feature never came to fruition.

Warner Brothers' cartoon department had no thoughts of doing a feature, but they did make one atypically "serious" short, *Tom Thumb in Trouble* (1940, directed by Chuck Jones), which was clearly patterned after the Disney style, and even had an original song. Several years later they came up with a more typical reel called *Coal Black and the Sebben Dwarfs,* which for obvious reasons is not widely shown today.

In 1938 it was estimated that *Snow White* had earned $4.2 million in the United States and Canada alone, with its subsequent reissues in 1943, 1952, 1958, and 1967, it earned a domestic gross of $15,950,000 and an estimated worldwide gross of nearly $30 million.

As for Walt Disney, *Snow White* was little more than an experiment. "We've worked hard and spent a lot of money, and by this time we're all a little tired of it," he told reporter Paul Harrison just before the film's release. "I've seen so much of *Snow White* that I am conscious only of the places where it could be improved. You see, we've learned such a lot since we started this thing! I wish I could yank it back and do it all over again."

So for Walt Disney *Snow White and the Seven Dwarfs* was not a crowning achievement, as so many critics were to say. For him, it was only the beginning.

PINOCCHIO

Released by RKO Radio Pictures; world premiere, February 7, 1940, released February 23, 1940. Technicolor. Based on the story by Collodi (Carlo Lorenzini). Supervising directors: Ben Sharpsteen, Hamilton Luske. Sequence directors: Bill Roberts, Norman

Ferguson, Jack Kinney, Wilfred Jackson, T. Hee. Animation directors: Fred Moore, Franklin Thomas, Milton Kahl, Vladimir Tytla, Ward Kimball, Arthur Babbitt, Eric Larson, Wolfgang Reitherman. Story adaptation: Ted Sears, Otto Englander, Webb Smith, William Cottrell, Joseph Sabo, Erdman Penner, Aurelius Battaglia. Music and lyrics: Leigh Harline, Ned Washington, Paul J. Smith. Art directors: Charles Philippi, Hugh Hennesy, Kenneth Anderson, Dick Kelsey, A. Kendall O'Connor, Terrell Stapp, Thor Putnam, John Hubley, McLaren Stewart, Al Zinnen. Character designers: Albert Hurter, Joe Grant, John P. Miller, Campbell Grant, Martin Provensen, John Walbridge. Animators: Jack Campbell, Berny Wolf, Don Towsley, Oliver M. Johnston, Jr., Don Lusk, John Lounsbery, Norman Tate, John Bradbury, Lynn Karp, Charles Nichols, Art Palmer, Joshua Meador, Don Tobin, Robert Martsch, George Rowley, John McManus, Don Patterson, Preston Blair, Les Clark, Marvin Woodward, Hugh Fraser, John Elliotte. Backgrounds: Claude Coats, Merle Cox, Ed Starr, Ray Huffine. Running time: 88 minutes.

Songs: "When You Wish Upon a Star," "Little Woodenhead," "Hi Diddle Dee Dee (An Actor's Life for Me)," "I've Got No Strings," "Give a Little Whistle."

Voices: Dickie Jones (Pinocchio), Christian Rub (Geppetto), Cliff Edwards (Jiminy Cricket), Evelyn Venable (The Blue Fairy), Walter Catlett (J. Worthington Foulfellow), Frankie Darro (Lampwick), Charles Judels (Stromboli and The Coachman), Don Brodie (Barker).

Pinocchio is one of Disney's most visually innovative films and. also his "meatiest" animated feature. If parents worried about their young ones having bad dreams after watching *Snow White*, they would have done well to spare them the trauma of seeing *Pinocchio*, which has some of the most terrifying scenes of any of

Disney's films—although, oddly enough, much of the terror, and some of the nuances of the allegory, are too subtle for very young minds to understand.

Although *Pinocchio* has a definite direction, the story is very episodic. Indeed, five months' worth of animation was scrapped at one point during production in order to start from scratch.

But the film does not seem to ramble, and its sequences tie together quite naturally. The emotional high points are cleverly spaced throughout the film so that one will not dissipate the impact of the other.

Jiminy Cricket sings "When You Wish Upon a Star" over the main titles; we see him finish the song as he rests on a shelf above a storybook entitled *Pinocchio*. He says hello to the audience and, referring to the song's message (that when you wish upon a star your dream will come true), says, "I bet some of you don't believe that." He tells us that he didn't believe it either until a startling experience changed his mind. He opens the storybook and starts to narrate the tale of Pinocchio.

One night, the only lighted window in town was that of the wood-carver, Geppetto. "So," says Jiminy, "I hopped over," and the camera literally hops into town, toward the shop, where Jiminy creeps in and makes himself at home.

Geppetto comes in and finishes painting the smile on his latest marionette, that of a little boy he names Pinocchio. Before he goes to sleep, Geppetto looks up and sees the Wishing Star; he wishes that somehow Pinocchio could be a real live boy. As he sleeps, the Blue Fairy descends from the sky into his shop and transforms Pinocchio into a living being—albeit still a wooden one. She tells him that if he can prove himself brave, unselfish, and able to tell right from wrong, he will become a real live boy. When Jiminy unwittingly reveals himself, she decides to appoint him Pinocchio's conscience. He asks if he'll get a gold badge for doing so, and she tells him he might.

At this point Geppetto wakes up and, with his cat Figaro and goldfish Cleo, celebrates Pinocchio's miracu-

Geppetto puts the finishing touches on his wooden doll as Figaro, the cat, and Cleo, the goldfish, look on admiringly.
© *Walt Disney Productions*

Jiminy and Pinocchio (partially converted into a jackass) wonder how to save Geppetto. © *Walt Disney Productions*

lous transformation. The next morning he sends Pinocchio off to school, but on his way he encounters a sly fox named J. Worthington Foulfellow ("Just call me Honest John") and his feline sidekick Gideon. When they realize what Pinocchio really is, they sense a way to make a small fortune. The Fox dissuades Pinocchio from going to school by telling him the wonders of the stage, singing "An Actor's Life for Me," and succeeding in getting Pinocchio stagestruck. Jiminy's admonitions go unheeded.

That night Jiminy goes to see Pinocchio's premiere as part of Stromboli's puppet show. He comes out and sings "I've Got No Strings," and does a dance with a group of other marionettes. Although he is unsure of himself, his fumbling only makes him more popular with the audience. From this Jiminy concludes that perhaps that *is* the life for Pinocchio.

He goes to bid his wooden friend good-bye aboard his wagon in the troupe's caravan, only to discover that Pinocchio is locked in a cage! Stromboli is a wicked slave driver who has threatened to chop Pinocchio into firewood if he does not obey. Jiminy tries to undo the lock on the cage, but to no avail. Just then who should appear but the Blue Fairy, who asks Pinocchio how he got into this predicament. He invents a tall tale about the situation, and as he spins the yarn, his nose grows longer and longer—even sprouting branches! The Fairy explains that "a lie grows and grows until it's as plain as the nose on your face." He promises never to do it again, and she decides to give him (and Jiminy) a second chance. She unlocks the cage, enabling them to escape and start anew.

But it isn't long before they run into Foulfellow and Gideon once more. This time, the Fox convinces Pinocchio to join a band of young boys who are headed for Pleasure Island. Jiminy goes along to keep an eye on his ward. Little do they dream that the Fox has been hired by an unscrupulous rascal who sends them to the island "never to return . . . as boys." When they arrive, he exhorts them to have fun, live it up as much as they want, as they are bound "to make jackasses" out of themselves.

Late that night all is dark and deserted on the island, except in the pool hall (shaped like an eight ball), where Pinocchio and his newfound friend, Lampwick, are playing pool, smoking cigars, and drinking beer. Jiminy tries to talk Pinocchio out of such behavior, but he refuses to listen, so Jiminy stalks out. Lampwick makes fun of Jiminy's warnings.

"You'd think something was going to happen," he says mockingly, at which instant he sprouts donkey's ears! While Pinocchio is gawking at him, he grows a tail. When Pinocchio also grows long ears, Lampwick laughs, but the sound is that of a donkey's hee-haw. Realizing what is happening, he grows frantic, looks in the mirror, and tries to stop it, but can't. In another instant Lampwick has become a donkey!

Meanwhile, Jiminy has seen what is happening on the other side of the island—boys-turned-asses are being shipped overseas by the mercenary scoundrel who brought them there. He hurries back to grab Pinocchio just in time to stop him from the same fate. They run to the edge of the island and jump off a high cliff into the ocean below. They swim to shore and return to Geppetto's workshop, only to find it deserted. A dove brings them a message from the Blue Fairy explaining that Geppetto went to sea and was swallowed by Monstro, the Whale, but he is still alive inside Monstro's giant stomach.

Pinocchio announces that he must save his father . . . and Jiminy reluctantly goes along. They dive into the water, weighted down, and ask the fish about Monstro's whereabouts, causing them to scatter in all directions. When they do find the Whale, it's just as Monstro is about to have lunch; when he opens his gigantic mouth, Pinocchio is caught in the avalanche of water and fish that go inside. Once there, however, he is fished up by Geppetto, who is still aboard his little, wrecked boat with Figaro and Cleo.

There is a happy reunion, but then Geppetto tells the

boy that it is hopeless. Pinocchio disagrees and says that if they light a fire, Monstro will sneeze, and they can get out on the raft Geppetto has built. They manage to do so, but once outside, they see that Monstro is angry about the trick they've played, and is coming after them. There is a frantic chase, with Pinocchio and Geppetto paddling for their lives; they try to reach a rocky cove where Monstro cannot follow, but they are forced to abandon their raft when the Whale's tail lashes down on it.

Floating in the water, Geppetto tells Pinocchio to save himself, but the boy will hear none of it. He drags Geppetto toward the cove and freedom. But when the wood-carver wakes up onshore, joined by Jiminy, he sees Pinocchio's body lying along the water's edge—dead.

Back in Geppetto's workshop, there is great sorrow as Pinocchio lies on the bed, his friends grieving his noble death. But then the Blue Fairy's voice is heard, echoing her promise that if Pinocchio were to prove himself worthy, he would become a real live boy—and he does. It is, indeed, a miracle, and joy becomes elation. During the celebration Jiminy says, "This is where I came in," and steps outside. He looks up, sees the Blue Fairy's twinkling star, and thanks her for all she's done. Just then a shiny gold medal appears on his chest, reading "Official Conscience/18 Kt." Jiminy loves it and uses it to twinkle back at the star. As the camera moves in toward the star, we hear Jiminy and chorus reprise "When You Wish Upon a Star."

Pinocchio is a film of amazing detail and brilliant conception. Sheer technical virtuosity would mean nothing, if it were not employed so beautifully. Like all of Disney's best work, it has tremendous emotional impact as well, although as a whole the film is characterized by action, excitement, and terror more than humor.

Indeed, one can see where the Disney staff was hard pressed to maintain a humorous element throughout the film. Pinocchio himself is not a funny character,

Cecil B. De Mille poses with Pinocchio and Jiminy Cricket in this publicity still for the *Lux Radio Theatre*, which broadcast the story on Christmas Day, 1939. *CBS photo; courtesy David Chierichetti*

although he is more interesting and appealing than many other Disney "heroes." Jiminy could hardly be called comedy relief, since he serves such an important function in the film, but he *is* one of the characters who provides humorous sidelights on otherwise straightforward scenes. (When Pinocchio is swallowed by

Monstro, Jiminy is left outside; he bangs on the Whale's locked teeth, shouting, "C'mon, Blubbermouth, open up!" In fact, most of Jiminy's humor is in the form of contemporary wisecracks.)

Geppetto's absentmindedness is good for several laughs and serves to relieve tension in a number of scenes. At the end of the film, when Pinocchio comes to life, he asks, "Father, what's wrong?" "Lie down, son," says Geppetto, "you're dead." Which, of course, is followed by a double take, as in the scene where Geppetto fishes Pinocchio out of Monstro's mouth and thinks he's a fish.

Similarly, Figaro offsets much of the sentimentality in the film with his puckish sense of humor. For instance, while Geppetto is wondering why Pinocchio hasn't come home from school, Figaro's only thought is eating the celebration dinner that's been prepared. While Geppetto is wishing at night for a real boy of his own, Figaro is tossing and turning in frustration, unable to get to sleep.

Foulfellow's cohort Gideon is one of the few purely comic characters in the film, offsetting his partner's treachery with constant bungling.

The elements of terror are much more vivid and widespread in the film. While traveling with Stromboli, Pinocchio has his first taste of the seamy side of life. "When you grow too old," says the puppeteer, "you will make good firewood," as he tosses his hatchet into the remnants of another ragged marionette, now a pile of splinters and sawdust, a meekly smiling face the only reminder of its former "life."

The Pleasure Island segment of the film builds masterfully to its exciting climax. At the outset the neon lights, rides, and general atmosphere of the place have a decidedly creepy tone. (With one throwaway gag: the pool hall is in the shape of an eight ball, with a cue standing alongside, a neat takeoff on the Trylon and Perisphere of the 1939 New York World's Fair.) But the first shock comes when we see the slave driver carting off the donkeys for shipment. He whips one donkey who hasn't yet

75

lost his ability to talk, kicking him against the wall with others like him. Then we see his hulking shadow over them as he whips the whole group once more.

Back in the pool room, the transformation of Lampwick starts almost as a joke, with his ears. But the direction of the scene and the music create a growing sense of fear and fright. He begs for Pinocchio to help him, and we see Pinocchio's reaction over Lampwick's shoulder as his hands turn into hoofs. As he becomes more frantic, the music grows louder and more discordant. Finally, with the metamorphosis almost complete, he screams "Mama!!" his cry turning into a long, loud bray as we see the finishing touches of his shadow on the wall. William K. Everson has called this scene "surely one of the screen's supreme moments of horror," and that it is, as downright terrifying as any fright sequences devised by others for live-action movies.

The Monstro sequence is the film's other highlight, a matchless exercise in *excitement,* made all the more fascinating because of the very concept of being inside a whale, much less being chased by one. The shot of Monstro's mouth opening, as seen from the *inside,* as a cascade of water, fish, and Pinocchio pour in is unforgettable. The chase is beautifully staged, draining audience emotion as Pinocchio and Geppetto do their best to outdistance the seagoing monster. The tension reaches its apex when Monstro tries to plow into them, misses, but in turning around lashes his tail behind him. Geppetto looks up and a broad shadow starts to cover the raft. We look up with him and get a first-person view of the tail about to crash down. "JUMP!" shouts the wood-carver, as the tail strikes the raft and smashes it into a thousand pieces.

The underwater scenes with Pinocchio and Jiminy are much more easygoing and a lot of fun. As they drop to the ocean floor, Pinocchio says, "Gee, what a big place," his words gurgling from the sound track. (How this effect was accomplished was a source of great wonderment at the time of the film's release—proof that the full potentials of sound had hardly been scratched in the dozen-odd years since its development.)

There are other delightful, lighthearted scenes: Geppetto's workshop coming alive with his dozens of music boxes, each an intricate contraption with a myriad of moving parts (and for each of which, incidentally, a model was built for animators to work from); Pinocchio's stage debut, singing "I've Got No Strings" as backdrops and wooden costars are changed all around him; Foulfellow and Gideon marching along with Pinocchio through the city streets as they sing "An Actor's Life for Me" (this scene "shot" from the city rooftops); and the sidelight glimpses of Figaro and Cleo, who became very popular Disney characters, Figaro appearing in a number of subsequent short cartoons.

In addition to well-executed action sequences and delightful characterizations, *Pinocchio* has some fantastic detail work made possible by the multiplane camera, most notably a breathtaking shot of the village on the morning after Pinocchio's coming to life. The shot shows the church bell tower in the foreground, and the city below, stretching off as far as the eye can see, toward the distant hills. This is not a painting, but an amazingly lifelike panorama, each house having depth and dimension of its own. Reportedly, some twelve separate planes were employed in the filming of this one shot, which pans down into the town and Geppetto's workshop for the next scene.

When Jiminy first comes into Geppetto's house, he warms up by the fireplace; the flames not only look real, but there is actual heat distortion above them! Shadows on both characters and objects in this opening segment are also quite lifelike, and on the other end of the spectrum we get an amusing view of Pinocchio, as Cleo the fish sees him blurred and elongated through her fishbowl.

When Jiminy attempts to stop Pinocchio from going with Honest John and Gideon, he chases after them, and we see the villains from Jiminy's point of view. When he jumps up, the camera cuts to a bird's-eye view with Jiminy landing atop Honest John's hat. The use of perspective and cutting are most impressive here.

One of the film's most amazing pieces of animation, from a technical standpoint, occurs when Pinocchio is trapped in a cage inside Stromboli's wagon. The wagon is moving, and Pinocchio is inside the swinging cage, while lightning flashes outside cause changes in color and shadows!

Once again the sound track is as important to the film's success as the picture on the screen. Disney chose twelve-year-old child actor Dickie Jones for his lead character because he had "a typical nice boy's voice." The role of Jiminy Cricket gave a new lease on life to Cliff Edwards, who had scored a hit in the 1920s as "Ukulele Ike," and added his ebullience to many films of the 1930s. Unlike most other characters originating in Disney features, Jiminy became a staple of Disney films, appearing in one other feature (*Fun & Fancy Free*), numerous shorts (most notably the *I'm No Fool* series), and on the *Mickey Mouse Club* television show. Edwards later did the voice for one of the Black Crows in *Dumbo* as well.

Christian Rub *was* Geppetto, having essayed essentially the same characterization in most of his other films; indeed, he served not only as the voice, but as the model for the character. Evelyn Venable's pure, sweet voice was ideal for the Blue Fairy, an ethereally lovely blonde, blue-eyed woman. (Walt insisted that "although she must give the appearance of loveliness, she can't look like a glamour girl." Marjorie Belcher, who had posed for Snow White, was the model for the Fairy.) Walter Catlett, like Christian Rub, was used to playing characters much like the one he voiced in *Pinocchio*, J. Worthington Foulfellow, and Frankie Darro, the voice of Lampwick, was fairly well established as one of the screen's leading tough kids. Charles Judels's voice as Stromboli was readily recognizable from the whinnying sound of frustration that was the comic actor's trademark.

Miss Venable recalls that she recorded all her lines separately, and they were later intercut with those of the

78

other characters. "I recorded it line by line, each line several times with different inflections, emphasizing different words each time (I kept the pacing about the same each time, though). Then they chose whichever recording captured the dramatic feeling they wanted."

The musical score was one of the finest Paul J. Smith ever wrote for Disney, not only supplementing the action but playing a major role in creating the desired moods. Smith explained to Rose Heylbut of the *Etude Music Magazine* how he prepared the score for the animated film:

The songs are the first basis of the complete score. We like to use them as leitmotifs, to suggest both characters and situations throughout the picture. Take, for instance, the little theme with the hoppity-hop rhythm that symbolizes Jiminy Cricket. It is stated as the Cricket's tune, and appears as the inner voice of a more important theme, or merely as a rhythmic suggestion, in every scene in which Jiminy is about to assume the center of the stage. The star song is sung but twice in the picture, but it appears (in free variation, parallel chords, and so on) in every sequence where Jiminy and the Fairy combine their powers in working out Pinocchio's destiny. The development of these variations of the theme requires the most detailed care. The spectator must be aware of the theme and of its slightly altered form, but neither theme nor variation may at any time rise to the point of occupying his conscious attention.

In *Pinocchio*, Disney reached not only the height of his powers, but the apex of what many of his (later) critics considered to be the *realm* of the animated cartoon. The wonder, the brilliance of *Pinocchio*, is in depicting the wondrous fantasy of the story—a boy turning into a donkey, a man living on a boat inside the stomach of a whale—things that could not be shown with equal effectiveness by a live-action movie. It was when Disney tried to make his films more and more lifelike that the criticism mounted.

But most critics had only complimentary things to say about *Pinocchio*. Archer Winsten, who had criticized Disney's first feature film, wrote: "The faults that were in *Snow White and the Seven Dwarfs* no longer exist. In writing of *Pinocchio*, you are limited only by your own power of expressing enthusiasm. To put it in the simplest possible terms, this film is fantastically delightful, absolutely perfect, and a work of pure, unadulterated genius."

There were some complaints that Disney had changed the original story and altered its characterizations, but none so strong as that of Paolo Lorenzini, nephew of the fable's author, who asked the Italian Ministry of Popular Culture to sue Walt Disney for libel in portraying Pinocchio "so he easily could be mistaken for an American," when, indeed, he was Italian. Apparently nothing came of the protest.

The film cost an estimated $2.5 million. It was dubbed into seven languages at a reported additional cost of $65,000. Unfortunately, at the time of *Pinocchio*'s release, the European market was cut off, due to the war, and Disney lost one of his major sources of revenue for the film. This problem continued through the mid-1940s, and was partially responsible for Disney's involvement with South America at that time. Nevertheless, the film was successful in the United States, both critically and at the box office, and has since performed admirably in reissue, amassing some $13 million in United States and Canada grosses alone.

With *Pinocchio*, Disney found that his originally stated goal of turning out two feature-length animated films a year was a mere pipe dream, in spite of a staff of approximately eleven hundred, and a new studio facility in Burbank. But in spite of the time factor involved in producing animated features, Disney set to work on a number of projects at once, buying and negotiating for several properties at the same time and seeing to it that his studio would be busier than ever. He then tackled the most ambitious film of his career.

FANTASIA

Released by rko radio pictures; world premiere, November 13, 1940, no general release date. Technicolor, Fantasound. With Leopold Stokowski and the Philadelphia Orchestra. Narrative introductions by Deems Taylor. Production supervisor: Ben Sharpsteen. Story direction: Joe Grant, Dick Huemer. Musical director: Edward H. Plumb. Musical film editor: Stephen Csillag. Recording: William E. Garity, C. O. Slyfield, J. N. A. Hawkins. Running time: 120 minutes.

"Toccata and Fugue in D Minor" by Johann Sebastian Bach. Director: Samuel Armstrong. Story development: Lee Blair, Elmer Plummer, Phil Dike. Art director: Robert Cormack. Animators: Cy Young, Art Palmer, Daniel MacManus, George Rowley, Edwin Aardal, Joshua Meador, Cornett Wood. Background paintings: Joe Stanley, John Hench, Nino Carbe.

"The Nutcracker Suite" by Peter Ilich Tchaikovsky. Director: Samuel Armstrong. Story development: Sylvia Moberly-Holland, Norman Wright, Albert Heath, Bianca Majolie, Graham Heid. Character designers: John Walbridge, Elmer Plummer, Ethel Kulsar. Art directors: Robert Cormack, Al Zinnen, Curtiss D. Perkins, Arthur Byram, Bruce Bushman. Animators: Arthur Babbitt, Les Clark, Don Lusk, Cy Young, Robert Stokes. Background paintings: John Hench, Ethel Kulsar, Nino Carbe.

"The Sorcerer's Apprentice" by Paul Dukas. Director: James Algar. Story development: Perce Pearce, Carl Fallberg. Art directors: Tom Codrick, Charles Philippi, Zack Schwartz. Animation supervision: Fred Moore, Vladimir Tytla. Animators: Les Clark, Riley Thompson, Marvin Woodward, Preston Blair, Edward Love, Ugo D'Orsi, George Rowley, Cornett Wood. Background paintings: Claude Coats, Stan Spohn, Albert Dempster, Eric Hansen.

Poetry in motion, from the ''Dance of the Hours'' sequence.
© *Walt Disney Productions*

Chinese mushrooms strike a pose from ''The Nutcracker Suite.''
© *Walt Disney Productions*

"The Rite of Spring" by Igor Stravinsky. Directors: Bill Roberts, Paul Satterfield. Story development and research: William Martin, Leo Thiele, Robert Sterner, John Fraser McLeish. Art directors: McLaren Stewart, Dick Kelsey, John Hubley. Animation supervision: Wolfgang Reitherman, Joshua Meador. Animators: Philip Duncan, John McManus, Paul Busch, Art Palmer, Don Tobin, Edwin Aardal, Paul B. Kossoff. Background paintings: Ed Starr, Brice Mack, Edward Levitt. Special camera effects: Gail Papineau, Leonard Pickley.

"Pastoral Symphony" by Ludwig van Beethoven. Directors: Hamilton Luske, Jim Handley, Ford Beebe. Story development: Otto Englander, Webb Smith, Erdman Penner, Joseph Sabo, Bill Peet, George Stallings. Character designer: James Bodrero, John P. Miller, Lorna S. Soderstrom. Art directors: Hugh Hennesy, Kenneth Anderson, J. Gordon Legg, Herbert Ryman, Yale Gracey, Lance Nolley. Animation supervision: Fred Moore, Ward Kimball, Eric Larson, Arthur Babbitt, Oliver M. Johnston, Jr., Don Towsley. Animators: Berny Wolf, Jack Campbell, John Bradbury, James Moore, Milt Neil, Bill Justice, John Elliotte, Walt Kelly, Don Lusk, Lynn Karp, Murray McLennan, Robert W. Youngquist, Harry Hamsel. Background paintings: Claude Coats, Ray Huffine, W. Richard Anthony, Arthur Riley, Gerald Nevius, Roy Forkum.

"Dance of the Hours" by Amilcare Ponchielli. Directors: T. Hee, Norman Ferguson. Character designers: Martin Provensen, James Bodrero, Duke Russell, Earl Hurd. Art directors: Kendall O'Connor, Harold Doughty, Ernest Nordli. Animation supervision: Norman Ferguson. Animators: John Lounsbery, Howard Swift, Preston Blair, Hugh Fraser, Harvey Toombs, Norman Tate, Hicks Lokey, Art Elliott, Grant Simmons, Ray Patterson, Franklin Grundeen. Background paintings: Albert Dempster, Charles Conner.

"Night on Bald Mountain" by Modest Mussorgsky, and "Ave Maria" by Franz Schubert. Director: Wilfred

Jackson. Story development: Campbell Grant, Arthur Heinemann, Phil Dike. Art directors: Kay Nielsen, Terrell Stapp, Charles Payzant, Thor Putnam. Animation supervision: Vladimir Tytla. Animators: John McManus, William N. Shull, Robert W. Carlson, Jr., Lester Novros, Don Patterson. Background paintings: Merle Cox, Ray Lockrem, Robert Storms, W. Richard Anthony. Special animation effects: Joshua Meador, Miles E. Pike, John F. Reed, Daniel MacManus. Special camera effects: Gail Papineau, Leonard Pickley. Special lyrics for "Ave Maria" by Rachel Field; "Ave Maria" chorus directed by Charles Henderson; Juliette Novis, soloist.

Fantasia was Disney's most ambitious undertaking and in all respects his most controversial endeavor. Not much of a money-maker in its initial release, it has, in the past few years, become a phenomenal favorite of the younger generation, who have no concern with Disney's tampering with the musical pieces, and no deep thoughts about possible sacrilege in pictorializing these compositions. They are simply bowled over by the film's imagination.

The idea grew out of plans to make a Mickey Mouse short of "The Sorcerer's Apprentice" in 1938. Reportedly, Disney met the great conductor Leopold Stokowski at a party around this time (Stokowski had been working in several Hollywood features in the late 1930s), and mentioned the idea. Stokowski was enthusiastic and agreed to conduct the score for the cartoon, which he did in Los Angeles with a group of local musicians.

But Stokowski, always an innovator, prodded Disney about expanding his idea and doing a whole series of visualizations of musical themes. Disney was intrigued, and embarked on a series of discussions with the conductor and members of his staff. Disney also brought in Deems Taylor, the popular musicologist whose reputation for making music meaningful to American audiences (notably on New York Philharmonic radio broadcasts) made him a logical candidate for inclusion in this project.

The result, even the film's critics (and they were many) had to admit, was completely different from anything that had ever been done before.

The opening title card appears on a silent screen; as it fades, a curtain opens to reveal a blue cyclorama, as silhouetted musicians, talking among themselves, walk onto the orchestral platform. As they sit down and begin to tune up, colored lights emanate from each of the instruments playing.

Then Deems Taylor walks onto the podium to introduce the film. Although wearing white tie and tails, he puts his hand in his pocket when he begins to speak (a rather too-obvious attempt to show that this is not going to be a highbrow occasion). He tells us that there are three kinds of music: music that tells a story, music that paints a picture, and "absolute music," or music for music's sake. The first piece of music, the "Toccata and Fugue in D Minor," fits into this latter category, so the Disney artists have illustrated it in abstract fashion.

The silhouette of Leopold Stokowski walks to the podium. As the first strains of the piece are played, bright yellow light is cast upon his face from below, indicating the sound coming from the orchestra slightly below him.

The first images we see are colored silhouettes of the various musicians, some superimposed on each other. Then Stokowski's face dissolves into a vision of clouds. We see a partial picture of bows playing on floating strings, and then a series of impressions of waves, concentric circles, beams of light, and other patterns in time with the music on the sound track. The beams of light finally consolidate into a huge orange sun, as at sunrise, and as the final strains of the composition are heard, Stokowski's figure is superimposed over the brilliant orange sky. During the final notes the camera moves in to end the piece on a tight shot of the conductor.

We return to Deems Taylor, who introduces the next piece on the program, "The Nutcracker Suite." A close-up of Stokowski fades into a screenful of fireflies, which evolve into luminescent ballerinas, who perform "The Dance of the Sugar Plum Fairies." The dew droplets these creatures spread throughout the forest wake up other little fairies who cascade around the forest for a most ethereal celebration of nature.

The second section of the suite, "Chinese Dance," is performed by mushrooms, who assume an Oriental appearance with their crowns becoming hats for their wide, round heads.

"The Dance of the Reed Flutes" is enacted by petals cascading in the breeze and mingling with the lily pads floating on the water. This segues into an underwater setting for "Arabian Dance," highlighting a group of fish with magnificent, flowing tails. A flurry of bubbles, which introduced the scene, also provides the transition aboveground for the next sequence, the "Russian Dance," energetically performed by thistles, whose long, lean shape resembles that of a cossack, and orchids, whose petals are made to appear like peasant dresses.

This dance ends with the flower-dancers in close-up, filling the screen. As they form a still life, the picture dissolves into a vision of the forest. Butterflies fly through and bring with them the colors of autumn, causing the leaves to drop from their branches and create the setting for the final segment of the composition, "The Waltz of the Flowers." The swirling leaves form a ballet troupe, followed by milkweeds, all of whom are laid to rest by the Frost Fairies who come and spread the setting of yet another season. Snowflakes complete the change, and end the ballet with a lovely snowy pattern.

The next segment is "The Sorcerer's Apprentice," which opens with the mystical Sorcerer practicing his craft, conjuring up smoky spirits that create the misty form of a butterfly above him. But it's late, and he is ready to go to sleep. He leaves behind his tall, conelike hat, which glows as an indication of the powers it holds within. His hardworking apprentice (none other than Mickey Mouse), who is tired out from carrying buckets of water back and forth to do his cleaning chores, spies the hat and can't resist trying it out himself. He points his now powerful hands at a broom leaning against the wall, lures it to an upright position, and makes it grow arms and hands that take the bucket for him and do the bulk of his work while he just sits back.

His laziness overcomes him, however, and as the broom's shadow passes over him, going back and forth for water, he falls asleep and dreams of reaching greater heights—controlling cascades of stars in the sky with the flick of a wrist and even having oceans perform as he commands. But he suddenly awakens to find himself waist-deep in water, and an ocean already created before his very eyes by the persistent broom, which walks right over Mickey when he tries to stop it. Frantically, he grabs an ax and (shown in shadow on the wall) splits the broom into dozens of pieces. Then, in unison, each splinter rises up and becomes a broom, complete with arms, hands, and a bucket! They stubbornly march toward the well, pouring the water again and again. Mickey's attempts to bail out the room are doomed to failure. He floats along on his master's book of magic, looking for an antidote to the problem, and is suddenly caught in the swirl of a whirlpool.

By now the brooms are totally submerged, but continue to march underwater, and go through the motions of pouring still more water. Just then, at the head of the stairs, the Sorcerer himself appears, surveys the situation, and, with a majestic sweep of his hands, causes the water to disappear. He summons Mickey forward to reclaim his belongings. His eyes are glowing candles, his expression absolutely piercing. There is perhaps just the faintest hint of amusement. Mickey coyly smiles at him, hands him the broom, and starts to walk away. The Sorcerer takes the broom and whacks Mickey in the rear, sending him out of the room as the music whirls to a close.

The next shot is of Stokowski, again in silhouette on his podium. Suddenly, the silhouette of Mickey Mouse, still wearing his costume, runs up to the platform and tugs on the conductor's coat. He just wants to congratulate Mr. Stokowski for his work. "Thank you, Mickey," says the conductor, "and congratulations to you, too." Mickey runs off excitedly, and Stokowski waves after him.

Stravinsky's once revolutionary composition "Rite of Spring" becomes a depiction of the creation of the world, beginning with a cosmos in space and evolving through the universe until a planet is created (first as a sphere that flies right into the camera's eye). Then we first see clouds, hills, volcanoes—giant eruptions that send mountains jutting out of the surface, and lava that carves out patterns in the earth.

Microscopic particles are shown. They form and split and gradually metamorphose into undersea life—first as floating particles, then as fish. From the beginning the earliest living creatures have natural enemies, as these fish discover. Above water, on land, are other beings—dinosaurs, roaming the earth and learning the fight of survival. Pterodactyls fly above land, but one who comes too close to water level is snatched by a sea creature, which pulls the prehistoric bird underneath.

There are enemies on land as well, and the tyrannosaurus rex, stalking his domain, confronts and does battle with a stegosaurus, as Nature provides a dramatic setting with rain, thunder, and lightning.

Time passes, and the sun grows brighter, drying everything it touches. The animals migrate, in hope of finding some relief from the blazing heat. One by one they drop to the ground, others managing to carry on into the misty horizon. Soon only skeletons remain.

An eclipse of the sun brings the dawn of a new era. The planet trembles and the land crumbles under the pressure of tremors. Mountains spring up from the ground, other chunks of rock fall off and create caverns and valleys. Finally a new element is added as the ocean roars its presence on the planet. As the eclipse reaches its apex, the planet lies still. Earth has been created.

It is now intermission, and for relief the musician on string bass starts plucking out a jazz tempo. Other musicians join in for a brief, informal jam session. Then

Deems Taylor introduces one of the major, unsung stars of this concert: the sound track. Timid at first, it finally comes on camera and shows us how it reproduces various sounds from the orchestra (harp, violin, flute, trumpet, bassoon), concluding with a jazzy solo from the drummer and a final chime from the triangle, which creates, amusingly enough, a triangular shape on the track.

Next on the program is Beethoven's "Pastoral Symphony," interpreted with freedom by the Disney people as a paean to the characters of Greek mythology. By a beautiful countryside, unicorns, centaurs, and nymphs cavort in a gay celebration of life. Female centaurs bathe in the stream, and then spruce up with the help of some enthusiastic cupids, in anticipation of a call by their male friends, who go off with them for an idyllic afternoon. When one female centaur and a male counterpart are left stranded, the cupids go to work and strike up a match between them.

A feast is planned, and wine is pressed for the occasion. Cherubic Bacchus is soon happily soused, blissfully riding about on his unicorn, enjoying the party with the others.

But soon clouds cast a grim shadow over the festivities, and a storm brews. It's Zeus, happily tossing bolts of lightning to earth as they are handed to him by Vulcan, who fashions them on his anvil in the clouds. A bolt strikes the wine vat, creating a river of wine, a not unhappy turn of events for Bacchus below. But soon enough Zeus grows tired and goes to sleep, rolling the clouds over him like a blanket. They roll away, and Iris, goddess of the rainbow, signals that all is calm once more. The creatures below come out to admire the sun—symbolized by Apollo, riding a fiery chariot in the sky.

Then, as sunset approaches, Morpheus flies over the land bringing a cloak of darkness. It is time for sleep, and below all is quiet. While above, the crescent moon reveals the goddess Diana, who shoots her arrow into the air and creates the stars that shine down on our peaceful springtime setting.

Now we turn to ballet and "The Dance of the Hours." This charming set piece is beautifully executed by an ostrich, backed by a chorus of her peers, a hippopotamus who emerges from a lily pool in the midst of the Great Hall where all this takes place, a group of elephants who surround the sleeping Hippo, and a male chorus of crocodiles who playfully duet with the lead Hippo and her cronies. For the finale there is a mad chase, with the leering crocodiles leaping after the hippos (the principal figures having done a pas de deux), which climaxes in a grand finale featuring all the hippos, elephants, ostriches, and crocodiles who have appeared in the piece. The camera dollies back through the Great Hall's procession of columns to its entrance, where the iron doors slam shut and crumble off their hinges.

For the finale of the program there is a medley of "Night on Bald Mountain" and "Ave Maria," which, as Taylor explains, provides a picture of the struggle between the profane and the sacred. As night falls, near Bald Mountain, spirits rise in the local graveyard and travel, amid a flurry of devil bats, to the mountain for a celebration of Evil—a ritualistic bow to Tchernobog, the Black God. The flames become dancers, then animals, then lizards, at the whim of the fire monster. The Black God revels in this passionate exhibition; the ghostly figures swirl before the camera as in a whirlpool, with the smoke, flames, and fiery flashes covering the mountainside throughout the night.

Then, with morning approaching, church bells are rung. The Black Monster recoils in horror; with each tolling of the bell he is driven farther back until he hovers on the ground vanquished. As the sky lightens, the specters return to their graves. Monks carrying torches stand out in the morning mist, as they proceed over a bridge and into the forest on their mission. We travel through the dark forest into a beautiful pasture, its canvas painted by the first rays of daylight. The sunlit trees, the clear sky, the clouds create a heavenly vision on earth, as the strains of "Ave Maria" bless God's
90

Mickey Mouse, as the Sorcerer's Apprentice, teaches the brooms to do his work. © *Walt Disney Productions*

Walt Disney goes over the storyboards for *Fantasia* with Deems Taylor and Leopold Stokowski. *UPI photo*

presence. The camera travels upward as the hymn comes to a close, remaining fixed on the brilliant rays of the sun.

Fantasia is a tribute to the brilliance of Walt Disney's staff of artists and animators. Throughout the 1930s he had urged them to improve their work, sent them to art classes, insisted on greater and still greater quality. Toward what end? Many feared it was moving toward a goal of total realism in animation, which they felt would be disastrous.

Fantasia answered their questions and showed them what the skill of these artists, combined with the imagination of the Disney people, and the progress being made by studio technicians, could accomplish. For here was a whole new concept in animation—not only in appearance, but in content. Here was an opportunity to showcase visual fantasy that would never present itself again.

As much as some of the pictorial ideas bothered music critics, none of the sequences seems to have disturbed Leopold Stokowski, who was in on every phase of preparation for the film. He realized the potential impact of the film, not for his regular followers, or a handful of music aficionados, but for a much wider audience than would ever be seen in a concert hall or listen to a radio concert. He knew that here was a way to create a new medium of presenting this music, not to reduce it to the lowest common denominator, but to enhance the music's inherent qualities with the addition of visuals, and thus intrigue a segment of the public that had kept a closed mind with regard to classical music.

Thus, it was not "sacrilege," as some critics said, to portray the "Rite of Spring" as the creation of the world, or the "Pastoral Symphony" as a mythical celebration.

As Pare Lorentz commented in *McCall's:*

I advise you to disregard the howls from the music critics; *Fantasia* is a Disney and not a classical conception of a concert, and even though the music is broader and more powerful than any you've ever heard from the screen, it is the imagery, and not the scores you will follow during the show. Thus, you can dismiss the complaints of the little hierarchy of music men who try to make music a sacrosanct, mysterious, and obscure art. Disney has brought it out of the temple, put it in carpet slippers, and an old sweater, and made it work to surround, and support, and synchronize a brilliantly-drawn series of animated color sketches.

Stokowski, said music critic Virgil Thomson at the time, was the only symphonic conductor who "has given himself the trouble to find out something about musical reproduction techniques and to adapt these to the problems of orchestral execution. Alone among the famous musicians who have worked in the films, he has forced the spending of money and serious thought by film producers and engineers."

Thus, it was undoubtedly he who convinced Disney that *Fantasia* warranted something more than the usual sound system. Disney agreed and had his staff, led by chief engineer Bill Garity, look into the concept of a broader recording and playback method for the film. The result was dubbed "Fantasound," and it predated many of the stereophonic "innovations" of the 1950s and 1960s.

The film's score was recorded over a two-month period in 1938 at the Philadelphia Academy of Music. Nine "sound cameras" were at work, one recording the entire orchestra and each of the other eight focusing on one specific section. There were thirty-three microphones in all. Some 420,000 feet of film were used during the marathon recording sessions, of which 18,000 ended up in the final print.

The impact did not come from the method of recording alone, of course. The effect of Fantasound was determined by the playback system, and the first working model was built by RCA at a cost of $100,000.

Each additional unit cost $30,000.

Of the process Sam Robin wrote in the *New York Times Magazine:*

> When the waters hurl Mickey Mouse down a flight of stairs in Dukas' "The Sorcerer's Apprentice," the music pours out of one corner of the theatre and floods the auditorium . . . [but it] has not been used to play little jokes on the music of the composers represented on the program. It has been used to obtain greater depth and roundness for the works themselves . . .

Great care was taken in producing the ballet sequences of the film as well. Members of the Ballet Russe, notably Roman Jasinsky, Tatiana Riabouchinska, and Irina Baranova, modeled for the elephants, hippos, and ostriches (respectively) in the "Dance of the Hours" sequence. They wholeheartedly approved of the ballet spoof and agreed to pose for the animal caricatures. Indeed, the sequence was one of the least criticized in the entire film, except, ironically, by Pare Lorentz, who praised the feature but noted:

> I feel Disney should have had an old-fashioned low comedy selection in his second section, and I presume he felt that was what he was doing in "The Dance of the Hours," but either the high company of the Messrs. Taylor and Stokowski subdued him, or he felt low comedy out of place in such an austere presentation; whatever his reason, "The Dance of the Hours" isn't as earthy and violent as a number in this place in the concert should have been.

Dance critic Walter Terry wrote that "in *Fantasia* Walt Disney has assembled the richest qualities of his choreography: humans, animals, and flowers dance in ballets which poke fun at dancing and in ballets which exalt it. . . . Dance lovers will find much of *Fantasia* rewarding in its choreographic scope, stimulating in its brilliant use of a great art . . . bringing great dance and
94

simple dance to everyone."

Music critics were less enthusiastic, for nearly every work used in the film had been "adapted" in one way or another to meet animation demands or time restrictions. Stravinsky was reportedly very upset that his "Rite of Spring" had been altered, although the Disney studio has always reported that the composer, after seeing the film, was moved to comment, "Ah yes, I suppose that is just what I meant."

Each critic had different thoughts on various sequences in the film. One of the most frequently criticized was the "Pastoral Symphony," which was one piece of music that had been created with a specific image in mind, and which Disney had matched to an entirely different pictorialization. Furthermore, in the opinion of such critics as John Rosenfield, "Stokowski's conducting of the 'Pastoral' . . . was so distorted as to be objectionable."

Dorothy Thompson, in the *New York Herald Tribune*, wrote:

I left the theater in a condition bordering on nervous breakdown. I felt as though I had been subjected to an attentat, to an assault, but I had no desire to throw myself in adoration before the two masters who were responsible for the brutalization of sensibility in this remarkable nightmare. . . . Since the chief characteristic of this decade of the twentieth century is the collapse of the civilized world, the impetus to the collapse everywhere given by the very persons and groups most certain to be destroyed with it, the *Fantasia* is a social symptom worth this column's recording.

What Miss Thompson and many other critics objected to was not just the specifics of *Fantasia*, but the idea. Disney was attacked on the grounds that the music was not meant to be visualized, and that in doing so he had removed one of music's basic qualities, letting the listener create his own concept of its meaning.

But many other critics, even those with reservations about the film's success, praised Disney for his boldness in undertaking such an experiment in the first place. *Look* magazine called it a "masterpiece" and proclaimed: "Disney revolutionizes movies again . . ." Bosley Crowther in the *Times* deemed it "simply terrific," and Howard Barnes in the *Tribune,* while voicing some qualms about the film's format, still called it "a courageous and distinguished production."

Disney had special plans for *Fantasia*'s release. He wanted to treat it as a concert, instead of a film (there was even talk, for a time, of opening it in concert halls instead of conventional theatres). Because of the expense of installing Fantasound equipment, he planned to have the film playing in a limited number of theatres at any one time, each one having exclusivity in its location. Gradually, the film would move around to other theatres, perpetually playing as a reserved-seat attraction, and perhaps never going into neighborhood theatres at all. He even visualized filming new numbers and inserting them into the print at various times, making *Fantasia* a permanent fixture in movie theatres around the country.

(Debussy's "Clair de Lune" had been part of the film as late as July 1939, when it was still being referred to as "Concert Feature." *Fantasia,* a working title, was kept when no one could think of a better name for the film. When it opened in New York, the souvenir program announced that "from time to time the order and selection of compositions on this program may be changed." They never were.)

From the start there was trouble with Fantasound. Preparing the Broadway Theater in New York (formerly the Colony, where, ironically, *Steamboat Willie* had premiered) with the special sound equipment, a labor dispute arose between the International Alliance of Theatrical Stage Employees and the International Brotherhood of Electrical Workers, as to who had jurisdiction over installation of the new machinery.

Fortunately, a compromise was reached, and both unions set to work on twenty-four-hour shifts to get the theatre ready in time for the November 13 opening.

Then, with twelve Fantasound units ready, the government stepped in and declared that national defense priorities would prevent RCA and Disney from completing any further sets for the time being. Plans to open *Fantasia* in seventy-six theatres across the country were scotched.

Although Disney was willing to wait, his backers weren't. These were financially precarious times for Disney, who had spent the profits he made from *Snow White* on future films like this, and a large new studio in Burbank. To make matters worse, a labor strike was in the offing.

Disney was forced to submit to pressure and put *Fantasia* into general release, with a standard sound track. For this release the film was cut to eighty-eight minutes (most of the cuts involving Deems Taylor and orchestral interludes).

The film did not do well, despite Disney's proclamation that "it isn't highbrow to like good music." Apparently, the public that had flocked to see *Snow White* and *Pinocchio* was simply put off by the hightoned aura of *Fantasia*. The film, which cost $2¼ million, was many years in recouping its investment. Another attempt to reach the masses in 1946 was heralded by the catch line, *"Fantasia* will amaze-ya," a source of subsequent embarrassment for all involved.

The proposed additions to the film never were made. Among the properties in the talking stage were Weber's "Invitation to the Waltz," featuring Peter Pegasus from the "Pastoral Symphony" segment, "Humoresque," featuring the mushrooms from the "Nutcracker Suite," a reinsertion of "Clair de Lune," Sibelius's "Swan of Tuonela," Wagner's "Ride of the Valkyries," and "Peter and the Wolf," which *did* find its way into a later feature.

Among the boosters of *Fantasia,* there was comment that Disney should turn his hand to an illustrated film of popular music, an idea he did pick up after the war.

Fantasia was reissued in 1944, 1946, 1953, 1956, 1963, and 1969 (since which time it has remained in release). In the 1950s, to beef up business, it was decided to show the animated portions of the film in SuperScope, a wide-screen process that sent the film's devotees running from the theatres in horror. (It should be noted that Disney had originally wanted to do the film in a wide-screen format, but this idea never came to fruition.) Portions of the feature were shown on the Disney TV hour, and the "Rite of Spring" sequence was distributed on 16mm to schools as a geology film.

Walt Disney did not live to see his film be taken up by the younger generation of the 1970s, who adore the film (and who have caused no little embarrassment for the Disney image by using it as an adjunct to pot smoking). No doubt he would be pleased to see that these kids, some thirty years after the film was made, have finally given it the praise it so richly deserves, as one of the most dazzlingly imaginative films, both in concept and in execution, ever made.

Disney himself, when the film was first released, was quoted as saying, "*Fantasia* is timeless. It may run ten, twenty, thirty years. *Fantasia* is an idea in itself. I can never build another *Fantasia*. I can improve. I can elaborate. That's all."

THE RELUCTANT DRAGON

RELEASED BY RKO RADIO PICTURES ON JUNE 20, 1941. Technicolor. Live-action director: Alfred L. Werker. Cartoon directors: Hamilton Luske, Jim Handley, Ford Beebe, Erwin Verity, Jasper Blystone. Screenplay: Ted Sears, Al Perkins, Larry Clemmons, Bill Cottrell. Live-action cameramen: Bert Glennon, Winton Hoch. Art director: Gordon Wiles. Technicolor color director: Natalie Kalmus. Cartoon art directors: Ken Anderson, 98

Hugh Hennesy, Charles Philippi. Special effects: Ub Iwerks, Joshua Meador. Animators: Ward Kimball, Fred Moore, Milt Neil, Wolfgang Reitherman, Bud Swift, Walt Kelly, Jack Campbell, Claude Smith, Harvey Toombs. Film editors: Paul Weatherwax, Earl Rettig. Running time: 72 minutes.

Songs: "Oh Fleecy Cloud," "To an Upside Down Cake," "Radish So Red," " 'Tis Evening," by Frank Churchill and Larry Morey. "I'm a Reluctant Dragon" by Charles Wolcott and Larry Morey.

With Robert Benchley (himself), Frances Gifford (studio artist), Nana Bryant (Mrs. Benchley), Buddy Pepper (studio guide), Florence Gill and Clarence Nash (themselves), Truman Woodworth, Hamilton McFadden, Maurice Murphy, Jeff Corey, Henry Hall (studio cop), Frank Faylen (orchestra leader), Lester Dorr (Slim), Gerald Mohr (guard), Alan Ladd and John Dehner (animators), and members of the staff, including Walt Disney, Ward Kimball, and Norman Ferguson. With the voices of Barnett Parker (The Dragon), Claud Allister (Sir Giles), Billy Lee (The Boy), The Rhythmaires, Clarence Nash (Donald Duck), Pinto Colvig (Goofy), Gerald Mohr (*Baby Weems* narrator).

The Reluctant Dragon served two purposes for Walt Disney. The first was to capitalize on his worldwide popularity and do what many people had asked him to do—show how cartoons are made. The other purpose was to produce some working capital for future projects by making a relatively inexpensive feature (it was budgeted at $600,000) that would bring in a substantial return.

The film was only a partial success in meeting both goals.

It was decided to use Robert Benchley to provide the admittedly thin thread that held the picture together. The film opens at the Benchley home, where Mrs. B. (Nana Bryant) urges Benchley to take a charming

Robert Benchley is his usual bumbling self when he joins Walt Disney in a screening room during a scene from *The Reluctant Dragon.* © *Walt Disney Productions*

children's book she has just read, *The Reluctant Dragon,* to Walt Disney and suggest that he film it. Benchley doesn't like the idea, and has to be pushed into going to the Disney studio. His wife drops him off at the studio gate.

A distressingly eager young boy arrives to give Benchley a tour of the studio and bring him directly to Walt. But Benchley has other ideas, and repeatedly sneaks away from his tour guide, inadvertently getting a better look at studio life than he would have otherwise. He stumbles into a story conference, where a group of animators (one portrayed by Alan Ladd) asks for his reaction to a prospective project now in the storyboard stage called *Baby Weems.*

He walks into a recording session and meets a young girl (Frances Gifford) doing special voice effects; she explains how the sound track for a cartoon is created, with an orchestra following special timing, and sound-effects

100

men coming up with the appropriate noises. Then she takes him into a room where the cartoons are shot (as he walks into the room the film switches from black and white to color, and Benchley, noticing the change in his clothing, remarks upon the transformation).

He meets an animator (Ward Kimball) who shows him his latest work, a Goofy cartoon called *How to Ride a Horse;* a cameraman, who is photographing a Donald Duck cartoon (*MacDonald's Farm*), during which process Donald himself explains to Benchley how his movements are made; the paint department, a studio art class, the model department, and yet another recording session where he witnesses a historic duet between Clarence Nash and Florence Gill as Donald Duck and Clara Cluck.

Finally, he can avoid it no longer, and the energetic tour guide gets Benchley into a projection room where he meets Walt Disney and some of his staff, about to watch their latest product, an animated version of *The Reluctant Dragon*.

Driving home from the studio that day, Mrs. Benchley starts nagging her husband about his procrastination, and finally Benchley displays one of the tricks he's learned at the studio, squawking back at his wife à la Donald Duck.

The Reluctant Dragon is an extremely pleasant film, but little more. In its attempt to tell a mass audience how cartoons are made, it whitewashes much of the technique and omits most of the detail. It gives the erroneous impression that the sound track is matched to the cartoon, instead of vice versa. It uses actors in the roles of animators, musicians, cameramen, and never lets us in on the real creative process that produces Disney's cartoons. It's certainly a far cry from the cinema-verité technique that has more recently been used to show filmmakers at work!

There is little of Benchley's humor in the film; he too is relegated to the position of actor, and though he is an engaging one, it is a far cry from the humorist who

The remarkable Baby Weems is presented with a college diploma
in a scene from *The Reluctant Dragon*.

achieved such popularity in his series of how-to short subjects.

The film *does,* however, have its moments. Best of all is the *Baby Weems* sequence, which is a classic that deserves wider exposure. It is shown as a series of still frames, as one would see them on a storyboard, with occasional animation within each frame—a unique method for Disney.

The delightful story deals with a baby born to two happy young parents. When he is two days old, the baby opens his mouth and begins to talk! Not just baby talk, but fantastically intelligent conversation. What is more, the youngster is a genius.

Overnight Baby Weems becomes a celebrity. Albert Einstein and George Bernard Shaw come to learn from him. Newspapers feature him on the front page. He endorses various products. He composes symphonies on his toy piano. His poor parents can't even get to see him; they must be content to watch him in the newsreels and hear him on the radio.

One evening Baby Weems is set to broadcast to the world his theory on "How to Find Happiness." Everyone is listening; his parents rock their little radio in Baby Weems's cradle. Suddenly, the baby takes ill. His fever rises, and the world holds its breath. (A giant thermometer is erected on the Eiffel Tower to keep track.)

He recovers and goes before a multitude of microphones to speak. When he opens his mouth, however, only "goo-goo" and gurgling sounds come out.

The fickle public denounce him as an impostor; he is dropped like a cold potato and forgotten by everyone. Everyone, that is, except his parents, who are happy to have him back for themselves, and happier still that he is just a normal, happy baby.

Baby Weems is a charming cartoon that seems as fresh, both in its style and content, as the day it was made. Though seemingly it is an innocuous tale, its satiric thrust is quite sharp, and there are some marvelous throwaway gags throughout the sequence, poking fun at the world's penchant for exploitation and

104

Disney artists and writers prepared this elaborate storyboard to help director Alfred Werker visualize the live-action sequences in *The Reluctant Dragon.* Even camera instructions are included. *From the private collection of Alfred L. Werker*

commercialization.

The Goofy short, *How to Ride a Horse,* is a typically fast-paced, funny entry from the Goofy sports series of the 1940s. But the final segment, *The Reluctant Dragon,* is something of a letdown. It is reminiscent of *Ferdinand the Bull* in depicting a supposedly ferocious animal who in reality is rather peaceful; its spoofing of the veddy-British stereotypes (both in the Dragon and in the Knight who comes to slay him) was done with much greater success some years later in *The Wind in the Willows.*

The live-action portion of the film is quite well made, having been directed by veteran 20th Century–Fox contractee Alfred Werker. He recalls:

The Reluctant Dragon was the first live-action film that the studio made. They had a soundproof building which had been used to record the orchestra for *Fantasia*. This we converted into a small sound stage. I brought a young art director from Fox to do the sets, and we were in business. We rented lighting equipment, etc., and there were no difficulties in setting up the facilities.

Technicolor sent a color consultant, and as Walt had worked a lot in color cartoons, the color was beautiful. It was, of course, Walt's idea to go from black and white to color when Benchley entered the color department. Walt was deeply involved in the production of the film, but never intruded. As I remember, we had a six weeks' shooting schedule.

An interesting aspect of the project was how the script was prepared. The entire story was drawn in a series of sketches which were placed on what they called a story board, and when we had a story conference, the story board took the place of a script. Although I followed the sketches in general, Walt gave me a completely free hand in making the picture.

One of these storyboards is reproduced here for the first time. This technique was so successful that Disney used it from that point on for his live-action films. It enabled him to visualize a live scene with almost as much thoroughness as he could an animated sequence—a great boon in preparing to shoot a film.

Werker calls Disney "one of the nicest people I ever worked with, and the studio [was] the happiest one I ever saw. Walt had a delightful sense of humor and a fine understanding of what people wanted to see."

And, in this case, Disney was correct in assuming that people wanted to get a look at his studio. The trouble was that most moviegoers were unprepared for such an unspectacular, casual kind of film. Having enjoyed the richness of his previous features (*Snow White, Pinocchio, Fantasia*), they thought they were being somehow cheated with this film.

Oddly enough, looking at the film today, it seems almost lavish. The color is stunning, and the sets have a bright yet natural look about them. The cast is appealing and fairly believable.

But critics in particular complained that customers should not be expected to pay good money to see an "advertisement" for Walt Disney studios. Most of the reviewers singled out such sequences as *Baby Weems*, but thought on the whole that the film was a cheater and a disappointment in coming from quality-oriented Disney.

Ironically enough, this same complaint has been lodged against the Disney TV show, which often devotes segments to promotions of Disney, the studio, Disneyland, and forthcoming films. But in this instance, the public not only doesn't object, but can't get enough of it. The difference is probably that television is free.

The Reluctant Dragon was never reissued, although parts of it have been reused and shown on TV. A twenty-minute excerpt called *Behind the Scenes of Walt Disney Studio* was distributed on 16mm.

The film does not really deserve such obscurity. It is an interesting footnote to Disney's career, and, if only for *Baby Weems*, should be more widely shown.

DUMBO

RELEASED BY RKO RADIO PICTURES ON OCTOBER 23, 1941. Technicolor. From a story by Helen Aberson and Harold Pearl. Supervising director: Ben Sharpsteen. Screen story: Joe Grant, Dick Huemer. Story director: Otto Englander. Sequence directors: Norman Ferguson, Wilfred Jackson, Bill Roberts, Jack Kinney, Sam Armstrong. Animation directors: Vladimir Tytla, Fred Moore, Ward Kimball, John Lounsbery, Arthur Babbitt, Wolfgang Reitherman. Story development: Bill Peet, Aurelius Battaglia, Joe Rinaldi, George Stallings, Webb

Smith. Character designers: John P. Miller, Martin Provensen, John Walbridge, James Bodrero, Maurice Noble, Elmer Plummer. Art directors: Herb Ryman, A. Kendall O'Connor, Terrell Stapp, Donald Da Gradi, Al Zinnen, Ernest Nordli, Dick Kelsey, Charles Payzant. Animators: Hugh Fraser, Howard Swift, Harvey Toombs, Don Towsley, Milt Neil, Les Clark, Hicks Lokey, Claude Smith, Berny Wolf, Ray Patterson, Jack Campbell, Grant Simmons, Walt Kelly, Joshua Meador, Don Patterson, Bill Shull, Cy Young, Art Palmer. Backgrounds: Claude Coats, Albert Dempster, John Hench, Gerald Neivus, Ray Lochrem, Joe Stahley. Music: Oliver Wallace, Frank Churchill. Lyrics: Ned Washington. Orchestrations: Edward H. Plumb. Running time: 64 minutes.

Songs: "Look Out for Mr. Stork," "Baby Mine," "All Aboard," "Pink Elephants on Parade," "When I See an Elephant Fly," "Casey Junior," "Song of the Roustabouts."

Voices: Edward Brophy (Timothy Mouse), Herman Bing (ringmaster), Verna Felton (elephant), Sterling Holloway (stork), Cliff Edwards (Jim Crow).

Dumbo is one of the shortest animated features Disney ever made. It is one of the least pretentious. It is also one of the finest.

Ward Kimball, who has worked on virtually every animated feature at the studio, says:

Sure, we've done things that have had a lot more finish, frosting, and tricky footwork, but basically, I think the Disney cartoon reached its zenith with *Dumbo*. To me, it is the one feature cartoon that has a foolproof plot. Every story element meshes into place, held together with the great fantasy of a flying elephant. The first time I heard Walt outline the plot I knew that the picture had great simplicity and cartoon heart.

Dumbo was also one of the cheapest films we ever made. It came in for around $950,000 which was damn reasonable, even for 1940, when our cartoon features like *Bambi* climbed into the $2 million or $3 million bracket. The reason we brought it in for a low price was that it was done quickly and with a minimum amount of mistakes. The story was clear and air-tight to everyone involved in the project. We didn't do a lot of stuff over due to story-point goofs. There were no sequences started and then shelved, like in *Pinocchio*. Walt was sure of what he wanted and this confidence was shared by the entire crew. *Dumbo*, from the opening drawing, went straight through to the finish with very few things changed or altered.

The story *is* quite simple. The stork pays a visit to the circus, blessing most of the animals with new arrivals, including Mrs. Jumbo, the elephant. The other elephants come to admire the youngster, who suddenly sneezes, and as he does his ears enlarge to huge proportions. The other female elephants express horror, sarcasm, and disdain, saying he ought to be called Dumbo instead of Jumbo.

When some of the other circus people mistreat Dumbo, Mrs. Jumbo gets frantic and causes a commotion. The ringmaster orders her locked up as a "mad elephant." Left alone and brokenhearted, Dumbo finds an unlikely friend and champion in a saucy little mouse named Timothy. They become inseparable pals.

Dumbo is made part of the clown act, a great humiliation for him, but a great success for the clowns. During their celebration they accidentally knock a bottle of champagne into a bucket of water. When Dumbo gets the hiccoughs, he drinks from the bucket, and gets very, very drunk. After a nightmarish hallucination, he and Timothy awaken the next morning perched high in a tree!

Some local crows can't get over the sight, but in trying to figure it out Timothy discovers that Dumbo *flew* up into the tree. With the help of the crows, he gets Dumbo

Mrs. Jumbo loves her little Dumbo, even if none of the other elephants do. © 1940 Walt Disney Productions

It's "Pink Elephants on Parade" all right. © 1940 Walt Disney Productions

to fly again. That night at the circus, during the clown act, he surprises everyone by exhibiting his newfound talent. Overnight he becomes a sensation, the star of the circus. Now, when the circus travels, Mrs. Jumbo has her own streamlined car on the circus train, with Dumbo flying alongside.

Because the story was so simple, the Disney staff had plenty of elbow room to come up with ingenious ideas to add sparkle to the narrative. The result is a film over-flowing with delightful touches and memorable sequences.

For instance, Dumbo doesn't speak, and his mother never speaks directly to him, except in the song "Baby of Mine." The story is told *visually*, and as delightful as the sound track is, especially with Timothy's dialogue, one could turn it off and still follow every scene.

There are innumerable details that contribute to the whole. When the circus arrives at its new destination, and the arrival is heralded with a circus parade, the animals, still tired at this early morning hour, are shown yawning, just barely awake. When the circus train tries to climb a steep hill, the locomotive (Casey Jones, Jr.) chugs "I think I can, I think I can . . ." all the way up the hill; just making it over the crest, it chugs "I thought I could, I thought I could," as it goes downhill.

When Mrs. Jumbo sings a lullaby, "Baby of Mine," to her young one, we see similar scenes of mothers and offspring throughout the circus, including Mrs. Hippopotamus and her baby, resting underwater, and sending bubbles to the surface as they snore away.

The fantasy of a flying elephant and talking animals is played against a realistic background. There are some beautiful shots in the film, including the impressive master shot of the circus winter headquarters as the train pulls in to take them away. When they arrive, it's nighttime and rain is falling; men jump off the cars and start to pitch the tent, with the elephants' help. (The men are kept in shadow, since this is basically an animal film and the humans are only incidental. Later, when the

111

clowns celebrate their success, we see them in silhouette from outside their tent; when one of them voices a hesitation to making Dumbo leap from a high platform in their act, another says, "Ahh, elephants ain't got no feelings.")

One critic said that *Dumbo* had "more camera angles than *Citizen Kane*," and, indeed, its highlight sequences are brilliantly conceived. When Dumbo makes his initial appearance as part of the elephant act, he stumbles over his own ears and causes a "wall" of elephants to tumble. There is tremendous intercutting as the toppling pachyderms systematically wreck the entire circus, knocking over poles, hitting one another, propelling further destruction, and climaxing with the entire tent collapsing. Now all is quiet, as the camera moves in from a long shot to show Dumbo's trunk emerging from under a flap in the tent, waving the little flag he was to use in the act. As he does, the banner falls off the wooden flagpole for a quiet finale to a raucous scene.

There is no way to overpraise the "Pink Elephants" scene. It is one of the best things ever done at the Disney studio, and, to use a much overworked but appropriate phrase, years ahead of its time. It begins when Dumbo takes a trunkful of the spiked water, gulps it down, and starts to feel woozy. He hiccoughs champagne bubbles. Timothy tests out the "water" and likes it so much he falls in to get the most of it. Then he starts challenging Dumbo to blow various kinds of bubbles through his trunk; one of these turns into the shape of a pink elephant.

That elephant blows another elephant out of *his* trunk, and soon there are four elephants using their trunks as trumpets to herald the song "Pink Elephants on Parade." This begins the surreal fantasy of design, space, color, light, and gags, all to the tune of this minor-key march. For example, two elephants are marching along, one big one stepping on the small one in front of him, causing the little one to inflate as he does. Finally the little one kicks the big one in the rear, causing the big one to split into three giant elephants. Then the little one inflates, takes a pair of gold cymbals and crashes them on the three elephants, who are squished into a dozen or more tiny ones, who march out of the picture and start climbing up the side of the frame, over a close-up of Dumbo's face, as he watches the march with dreamy-eyed amusement.

For a finish, the elephants start to "melt," as the predominantly black background lightens and turns into the morning sky, with the elephants evolving into clouds. The sequence ends as the camera pans over to one prominent tree on the horizon, whose leaf formations give the vaguely rounded impression of being elephants. Fade-out.

The characterizations in *Dumbo* are, of course, a major part of the film's success. The idea of having a mouse as Dumbo's pal is marvelous; in the film Dumbo follows Timothy around, holding his tiny tail in his trunk. Ed Brophy is ideal as the voice of Timothy, who takes pleasure in scaring off the other "catty" elephants who have been picking on Dumbo, and then prodding his pal to have more confidence in himself.

Sterling Holloway, who has probably done voices for more Disney cartoons than anyone else, is charming as the one stork who arrives late at the circus, having lost his map of Florida. When he finally delivers Dumbo to Mrs. J. on the circus train, he takes out a pitch pipe and dutifully sings "Happy Birthday" to the baby elephant.

The other voices are all first-rate, with Cliff Edwards as the Black Crow who sings the jaunty song "When I See an Elephant Fly," full of delightful puns ("I've seen a peanut stand, I've seen a rubber band . . .").

There has been considerable controversy over the Black Crow sequence in recent years, most of it unjustified. The crows are undeniably black, but they are black *characters,* not black *stereotypes.* There is no denigrating dialogue, or Uncle Tomism in the scene, and if offense is to be taken in hearing the blacks call each other "brother," then the viewer is merely being sensitive to accuracy.

There is another interesting aspect to the crow se-

Disney artists Norman Ferguson and John Lounsbery work on the design for Timothy the Mouse, as Timothy's voice and inspiration, character actor Ed Brophy, looks on. *Movie Star News*

quence, as Ward Kimball tells it. "I was in charge of the crows, [and] I wanted to try something different; I wanted to make each crow a separate character. One example was the little crow with the big horn-rimmed glasses. When he rolled his eyes, the eyes went out beyond the head mass, they rolled around inside the big glasses."

The last sequence in the picture, a montage showing Dumbo's success, has many of the "little" throwaway gags that popped up so much in Disney cartoons. A series of headlines show the worldwide attention given Dumbo—he sets atmospheric records, his ears are insured for a million dollars, and, lastly, his manager, Timothy Mouse, signs a Hollywood contract for the famed elephant.

Dumbo was not only cheaper than other Disney feature cartoons, but only a year and a half in production, from inception, when Walt read the galleys of a story by Helen Aberson and Harold Pearl, to story construction and design (which took six months), and completion (another year).

The critics welcomed it as a breath of fresh air, *Newsweek* commenting that *Fantasia* wasn't the "real" Disney, and *The Reluctant Dragon* was a "disappointment."

Cecilia Ager summed everything up in her review of the film in *PM*:

> *Dumbo* is the nicest, kindest Disney yet. It has the most heart, taste, beauty, compassion, skill, restraint. It marks a return to Disney first principles, the animal kingdom—that happy land where Disney workers turn into artists; where their imagination, playfulness, ingenuity, daring flourish freest; where, in short, they're home.
>
> *Dumbo*'s the most enchanting and endearing of their output, maybe because it's the least pretentious of their works, the least self-conscious. It tries only to be a wonderful example of a form they themselves created—the fable expressing universal human truths in animal guise.

Indeed, the viewer feels a warmth and empathy for Dumbo and his friends that is rare in *any* kind of film. And perhaps it is this, more than anything else, that makes *Dumbo* such a special film.

BAMBI

RELEASED BY RKO RADIO PICTURES ON AUGUST 13, 1942; world premiere, Radio City Music Hall, August 13, 1942. Technicolor. Based on the book by Felix Salten. Supervising director: David Hand. Story director: Perce Pearce. Story adapter: Larry Morey. Story development: George Stallings, Melvin Shaw, Carl Fallberg, Chuck Couch, Ralph Wright. Sequence directors: James Algar, Bill Roberts, Norman Wright, Sam Armstrong, Paul Satterfield, Graham Heid. Art directors: Tom Codrick, Robert Cormack, Al Zinnen, McLaren Stewart, Lloyd Harting, David Hilberman, John Hubley, Dick Kelsey. Supervising animators: Franklin Thomas, Milt Kahl, Eric Larson, Oliver M. Johnston, Jr. Animators: Fraser Davis, Bill Justice, Bernard Garbutt, Don Lusk, Retta Scott, Kenneth O'Brien, Louis Schmitt, John Bradbury, Joshua Meador, Phil Duncan, George Rowley, Art Palmer, Art Elliott. Backgrounds: Merle Cox, Tyrus Wong, Art Riley, Robert McIntosh, Travis Johnson, W. Richard Anthony, Stan Spohn, Ray Huffine, Ed Levitt, Joe Stahley. Music: Frank Churchill, Edward H. Plumb. Orchestrations: Charles Wolcott, Paul J. Smith. Conductor: Alexander Steinert. Choral arrangements: Charles Henderson. Running time: 69 minutes.

Songs: "Love Is a Song," "Let's Sing a Gay Little Spring Song," "Little April Shower," "Twitterpated," "The Thumper Song," "Looking for Romance (I Bring You a Song)."

Note: Although no voice credits were issued, it is known that Peter Behn did the voice of Thumper.

Bambi is the gentlest of Disney's animated features, a delicate rendering of Felix Salten's classic story. It stands unique among the Disney cartoons in its style and atmosphere, and indeed, it would be quite some time before the studio would again go to such lengths to

116

achieve the realistic detail found in this film.

Its theme and format, however, became the basis for many of Disney's later True-Life features, and *Perri* in particular owes much to *Bambi* for its basic framework.

The opening music, "Love Is a Song," and script titles set the initial mood for *Bambi*. The film opens on a slow pan through the dim forest, somewhat hazy in outline. A flying owl is the first sign of life in this idyllic setting, as dawn slowly breaks. The owl has been up all night and is about to go to sleep, when one by one the other animals awaken and come to tell him the exciting news: the Prince has been born. He goes with them to see the Little Prince, a newborn fawn, open his eyes for the first time. His father stands majestically on a cliff overlooking the forest.

Mother starts to teach the young one such things as walking, but much of his education is taken over by a young rabbit friend named Thumper; they are soon joined by a third friend, a skunk named Flower. Bit by bit Bambi learns about life, picking up words from Thumper, learning about the forest, being exposed to lightning and thunder for the first time during an April shower.

The next day Mother takes him for the first time to the meadow, which she tells him is a wonderful place. But before they can go out in the field, he must wait. Mother explains that "out there, we're unprotected." She goes out first to see if it is safe, then she calls for Bambi, and they romp together throughout the meadow. He also meets another deer for the first time—a female dear named Faline, who teases him and engages in a chase around the meadow.

Bambi thus strays away from his mother and encounters many of the older deer, who stand silently as the Great Prince of the Forest walks by—a noble animal indeed, who stops to look at Bambi before continuing on. His mother later explains who he is, telling Bambi: "He is very brave, and very wise." Then suddenly there is noise. The Great Prince leads the others in scurrying for shelter. Bambi is lost and confused; his mother

Thumper gives Bambi a hand as he falters on the ice.
© *Walt Disney Productions*

calls for him but he cannot hear her. The Great Prince comes by and urges him to run, eventually leading him back to Mother. After much commotion, with all the deer back in the forest, there is quiet once more, and Mother says simply: "Man was in the forest."

Time passes and autumn arrives, followed quickly by winter and Bambi's first snowfall. Thumper coaxes him out onto the ice, where Bambi discovers that he isn't very graceful as a skater. Winter is very long, and Bambi soon gets bored. Then one day Mother calls him to show him the first patch of new grass growing out from the melting snow. They are in the meadow now, and suddenly Mother senses something wrong. She tells

Bambi first meets Flower, the skunk, in this scene.
© *Walt Disney Productions, courtesy of Al Kilgore*

Bambi to move, to run as fast as he can and don't look back. The two of them scurry for the forest, and, as Bambi presses on, there is a shot, and soon he is running alone. He gets back home, but doesn't see his mother. He goes back to look for her as it starts to snow again, and he finds the Great Prince waiting for him. He tells Bambi: "Your mother can't be with you any more."

Soon it is spring again and much has changed. Bambi, Thumper, and Flower are now grown, Bambi having grown antlers. Their old friend the owl tells them about love, but they scoff at the idea; as they walk along, however, each one meets an attractive female and is drawn away from the group. Bambi gets his turn as well, when he meets Faline once more. She kisses him, and he is soon on Cloud Nine, in a dream sequence of Bambi and Faline romping through a forest of clouds.

He is brought back to reality by the presence of another deer who is vying for Faline's attention. Bambi is forced to do battle against his will with the other deer. Locking horns, ramming each other, they move into the darkness of the forest; Bambi wins the fight, only to discover that yet another peril is present: man. The animals hide as the sound of man gets closer and closer. One quail can't stand the suspense and tries to fly away, only to be shot down.

Panic grows, and the Great Prince tells Bambi to run, but Bambi's only thought is of Faline. He runs to find her, and discovers her being trailed by a pack of vicious hunting dogs who have her trapped on a ledge several feet up in the air. He takes on the whole pack and urges her to run. She escapes, and he follows behind, leaping over a precipice to safety, but being shot in midair. He lands wounded on the edge of the forest.

Meanwhile, the humans' campfire spreads, and sets the entire forest ablaze. Fire is everywhere, and the Great Prince comes to find Bambi to tell him to flee. The weakened Bambi follows instructions, and, with the Prince's help, runs from the quickly attacking flames in and out of paths and through streams, finally over a waterfall to safety along the river's shore with most of the other animals, including his waiting Faline. They are together once more, safe from both man and the fire.

The cycle now becomes complete; it's spring again, the owl is trying to sleep, and the children wake him to tell him that a young Prince has been born. Indeed, it is Flower's child (named Bambi) who spreads the news. Faline has given birth to twins, and, as they are admired by the forest animals, high on a cliff overlooking the forest is Bambi, now a majestic prince himself. The camera pulls back into the forest, and the film ends as it began.

Bambi is a beautiful film, and the extraordinary effort that went into making it shows in the finished product. The project was initiated in 1937 when Disney read Felix Salten's book and decided it would be a good project for the studio. He discovered that the rights had already been bought by director Sidney Franklin, and negotiated with him to acquire the story. Franklin capitulated, and served as a sort of artistic consultant on the project. A title card on the film reads: "To Sidney A. Franklin, sincere appreciation for his inspiring collaboration."

When Disney announced that he was going to make *Bambi*, the Maine Development Commission sent two live fawns to serve as models for Bambi and Faline. The artists were able to follow the young fawns' growth over the years they worked on the film, and soon augmented their little zoo to include other animals appearing in the film.

Maurice ("Jake") Day was sent to Maine to take hundreds of photographs in the forests there. He had specific instructions to get shots of trees after snowstorms, light coming into the forest at various times during the day, spider webs covered with dew, etc. It is precisely this kind of detail that makes *Bambi* so striking, most notably during the "April Shower" sequence, with drops landing on various plants and trees in the forest and lightning casting harsh shadows on the flora and fauna.

Human models were used as well, principally for the ice-skating sequence; actress Jane Randolph and *Ice Capades* star Donna Atwood skated, and fell, for animator Frank Thomas.

The nature of the story, and the detail it required, made it clear that *Bambi* was not going to be a quick production, and before long Disney pushed it aside to take care of other matters, such as *Pinocchio, Fantasia,* and *Dumbo*. But he assigned Frank Thomas, Milt Kahl, Oliver Johnston, and Eric Larson to stay with *Bambi* all during this time, and, except for occasional breaks to work on other projects, notably training films during the

121

war, they kept *Bambi* in production from 1937 to 1942.

It was decided to use nonprofessional children to do the leading voices; two animators discovered the ideal voice for Thumper while visiting the home of a professor friend. His young son, Peter Behn, did a delightful job as the playful rabbit. There was one anxious moment, however, when some three years after the recording had been made, it was necessary to do some new scenes. They worried that Peter's voice might have changed, but luckily he was able to duplicate the pitch and quality exactly. A lady named Marion Darlington, who specialized in birdcalls, was also used on the sound track.

Thumper, as the most humorous character in the film, became a new Disney favorite, as had so many other supporting characters before him, but, like most of the others, he never appeared in another animated cartoon, although the character was adopted for Disney's popular comic books.

As real as Disney tried to be in the details of *Bambi,* the film also had a marvelous stylization, particularly in the use of color. The *New York Herald Tribune* noted: ". . . in *Bambi,* Disney does arbitrary and daring things with color to heighten the dramatic effects. There is a scene where Bambi and his mother venture out into an open field and then, alarmed by the approach of hunters, flee back to the forest. When they wheel and flee they are shown in a yellowish-white silhouette, a symbol of livid fear . . ." An even more notable example occurs when Bambi does battle with another deer in the forest. The entire scene is played in harsh, darkened colors, with reddish-black silhouettes prevailing (and appropriately discordant, pounding music on the sound track). The coming of autumn is shown in a swirl of brightly colored leaves before the camera.

The only effect in the film that doesn't come off is the forest fire, which is *too* stylized. The idea of giving the flames a sort of animated life goes against the grain of the film, and clashes with the meticulously drawn forest and the animals that the flames pursue. The only really impressive shot of the fire is the last one, as seen from the river's edge by the animals, the distant forest mountain ablaze.

The drama in *Bambi* is one of understatement, and its effectiveness is great. Dialogue, which is kept to a minimum, is used in a quiet way to contrast the vociferous nature of the film's climaxes. Man is never shown in the film, yet the simple statement by Bambi's mother, after a frenzied chase with dozens of deer running for shelter, that "man [pause] was in the forest" creates an impact no literal device could accomplish.

Similarly, the death of Bambi's mother, the introduction of the Great Prince of the Forest, Bambi's first meeting with Faline, are all done with a refreshing simplicity.

For some, this style was *too* understated. Indeed, *New York Post* critic Archer Winsten, who loved the film, pointed out:

> This picture is less occupied with the humors and slapstick of the ordinary Disney opus. It is a much more serious and elemental showing of nature. As such there is some question about its appeal to the very young. . . . This reviewer is of the opinion that, like many another work of art dealing with activities of the young, its greatest appeal will be for thoroughly adult minds.

Other adults, like the *Times*'s Bosley Crowther, found the film to have "a shade too much cuddly charm."

But for the most part people went to see *Bambi* knowing what to expect, for its spirit was that of the famous Salten book (even though there had been one omission, the character of Gobo, and several additions, namely the forest fire and the character of Flower), and the ads billed *Bambi* as "a Great Love Story."

Few were disappointed. *Bambi* did well in its initial release, both critically and monetarily (although the European market was still absent), and it has continued to delight audiences through several reissues.

It remains one of the Disney studio's loveliest works, dealing in qualities of nature and life that will keep it young and fresh forever.

SALUDOS AMIGOS

RELEASED BY RKO RADIO PICTURES ON FEBRUARY 6, 1943. Technicolor (with live-action sequences from a 16mm original). Production supervisor: Norman Ferguson. Story: Homer Brightman, Ralph Wright, Roy Williams, Harry Reeves, Dick Huemer, Joe Grant. Story research: Ted Sears, William Cottrell, Webb Smith. Musical director: Charles Wolcott. Art supervisors: Mary Blair, Herb Ryman, Lee Blair, James Bodrero, Jack Miller. Backgrounds for *El Gaucho Goofy* inspired by F. Molina Campos. Sequence directors: Bill Roberts, Jack Kinney, Hamilton Luske, Wilfred Jackson. Animators: Fred Moore, Ward Kimball, Milt Kahl, Milt Neil, Wolfgang Reitherman, Les Clark, Bill Justice, Vladimir Tytla, John Sibley, Hugh Fraser, Paul Allen, John McManus, John Engman, Dan MacManus, Joshua Meador. Backgrounds: Hugh Hennesy, Albert Dempster, Claude Coats, Ken Anderson, Yale Gracey, Al Zinnen, McLaren Stewart, Art Riley, Dick Anthony, Merle Cox. Music: Edward H. Plumb, Paul J. Smith. Foreign supervisor: Jack Cutting. Associates: Gilberto Souto, Alberto Soria, Edmundo Santos. Narrators: Fred Shields, Aloysio Oliveira. Running time: 43 minutes.

Songs: "Saludos Amigos" by Charles Wolcott and Ned Washington; other songs incorporated into film, although not written especially for the film: "Brazil" by Ary Barroso, English lyrics by S. K. Russell, "Tico Tico" by Zequinta Abreu, Aloysio Oliveira, Ervin Drake.

124

Voices: Clarence Nash (Donald Duck), Jose Oliveira (Joe Carioca), Pinto Colvig (Goofy).

Saludos Amigos is a combination travelogue, chamber-of-commerce goodwill film, and cartoon, and, considering the diversity, it comes off rather well. Along with *The Three Caballeros,* it is truly a film of its time, although it is eminently enjoyable today. But one must remember the context in which it was made in order to appreciate the film.

With Europe one large battleground, America in the 1940s turned to its southern counterpart and established a Good Neighbor Policy that took the country by storm. The Latin-American influence on the United States during the war was best personified by Carmen Miranda and her infectious songs, the meanings of which were obscure to most listeners, but the rhythms of which were delightful.

For Hollywood, the Good Neighbor Policy had yet another meaning: a way to beef up the distribution market and try to offset the loss of the European curcuit for the duration of the war.

Disney, like many others, was charmed by South America, and, under the auspices of the State Department, chartered a plane to visit several countries on the continent with some of his staff and produce a series of cartoons inspired by the colorful nations. Having done this, the government complained that each cartoon would only be valid in the country at hand, so Disney strung his four shorts together, with the aid of 16mm color footage that had been taken of himself and his staff during their trip. The result was a hybrid, too long to be called a short and too short to be called a feature. It received feature-film release and bookings, and was tremendously popular both here and in South America; its name was *Saludos Amigos*.

The film opens with the Disney staff boarding their plane in Los Angeles (the narrator coyly avoids the name of Disney or anyone else, referring to them as "a group of artists and musicians") for a trip to South

125

Walt Disney joins a band of musicians in Santiago while scouting material for *Saludos Amigos*.   *Movie Star News*

America. Then there is some travelogue footage, with frequent shots of Disney artists sketching picturesque scenes. We then join another typical American tourist at Lake Titicaca—Donald Duck.

This is the first of the animated sequences, with Donald acting as the typical tourist, dressing in a native costume, and having a native take his snapshot, etc. He rents a llama to travel along the mountainside, but while crossing a treacherous rope bridge over a deep valley, the llama gets stubborn. Donald gets excited, and soon the planks start to fall from the bridge. There is some frantic byplay with the llama, and, as Donald hangs onto the rope for dear life, the narrator says: "Above all, one should never lose one's temper." "Ahhh, shut up!" Donald shouts at the camera.

126

The Disney troupe travels on to Chile, where the artists are quite taken with the local airport that flies the mail over the perilous mountains to Mendoza. They create the character of Pedro, a little airplane, and we go into the second animated sequence. Pedro is the off-spring of a proud mama and papa plane. (He is first seen drinking gasoline out of a nipple at the end of a gas pump.) He goes to school to learn various things, but, most importantly, the flying route over the mountains from Santiago to Mendoza. One day, when his father has a terrible cold, it's up to Pedro to fly the mail.

He is very nervous, but, after a shaky takeoff, gets up in the air and does pretty well, managing to avoid a famous mountain, whose face is in the shape of a scowl, and which has always signified bad luck. He gets the mail in Mendoza, and is confidently flying home when he encounters a buzzard that leads him on a chase. Straying from his route, he has come far too close to the treacherous mountain, and runs into problems with frost and altitude. He is scared—the oil freezes in his cylinders. Just as he is about to cross the final hurdle, he sputters, apparently out of gas. Meanwhile, at the airport, his worried parents search through the fog for their baby, and, finally, hearing a sputter, realize he is on his way. Pedro lands, upside down, but he lands. "Don't ask me how he did it," says the narrator, who goes on to praise Pedro's performance in this most important service—making sure the mail goes through. Then a look in the pouch reveals its contents to be one post-card, which reads, "Dear Pancho, Having wonderful time, wish you were here" (all in Spanish). "Well," says the narrator, "it *might* have been important."

In the Pampas region Disney and his staff meet the gauchos, and are inspired to see what happens when an American cowboy is transplanted into this new setting. The result is the third segment, *El Gaucho Goofy*. This cartoon is done in the style of the *Goofy How To* series, the narrator citing the various clothing and equipment of the gaucho as poor Goofy tries to accustom himself, without much success. At one point, after Goofy has

127

Little Pedro wants to be an airmail plane just like his dad.
© Walt Disney Productions

captured a wild animal with the deadly bolas, the sequence is played again in slow motion (the narrator's voice also slowed down) to capture the beauty and grace of the action. Unfortunately, the slow motion reveals nothing but clumsiness as Goofy gets himself tangled up in the bolas, along with his horse.

Finally, we visit the Carnaval in Rio; the narrator explains the annual songwriting competition for the Carnaval theme. The winner this year is "Aquarela do Brasil" ("Watercolor of Brazil"), sung by Aloysio Oliveira. The Disney artists sketch a tropical bird and create the character of Joe Carioca, who takes Donald Duck on a tour of South America with the aid of a paintbrush that fills in the backgrounds as they go along. Joe teaches Donald the samba (to two of the composition's main themes, "Brazil" and "Tico Tico"), and the two of them go out and paint the town red for the finale of the film.

Saludos Amigos is a very disjointed film, but each of the four sequences is so enjoyable that it seems pointless to carp about construction, especially noting the way the film was put together "on order." Oddly enough, it is the cartoons that seem like interruptions to the live-action footage, instead of the other way around.

With hindsight, one can view Saludos Amigos as a dry run for Disney's full-length feature The Three Caballeros, which expanded on many elements first found in Saludos, particularly in the last two cartoons. El Gaucho Goofy, though typically fast and funny, like most of the 1940s Goofy outings, also has some hints of the slightly surreal kind of gag that fully blossomed in Caballeros. Here it is a running gag involved "wipe" dissolves that cut across the screen to bridge two scenes. Twice, with a horizontal and diagonal wipe, the background dissolves, but Goofy and his horse get squashed by the moving line!

The final sequence was, of course, the real blueprint for The Three Caballeros, with the invention of Joe Carioca, and the interpolation of the wonderful Latin songs into the film. But here, too, is a hint of the crazy kind of gag that permeated the later film, for although the animated paintbrush fills in the backgrounds for Joe and Donald as they samba along, at one point Donald walks right into the brush and is covered with blue paint.

Saludos Amigos opened in South America in late 1942 to tremendous acclaim and tremendous crowds. It wasn't released in the United States until February, at which time it was enthusiastically greeted. Howard Barnes called it "at once a potent piece of propaganda and a brilliant job of picture-making."

But John T. McManus in PM had a different outlook on the film.

Donald Duck is a typical American tourist at Lake Titicaca.
© *Walt Disney Productions*

. . . watching *Saludos,* I think most of us will experience the same general set of emotions, a mingled pride and sadness over the growing up of a beloved something we all foolishly hoped could stay young forever. For *Saludos*, as a whole, is not the fable-minded Disney child of before, stalking wild fantasy in its own wonderland; it is a fairly sophisticated young man of the Western world, exchanging bright and pointed pleasantries with our Latin-American friends, bringing our viewpoints into accord like a witty ambassador, and generally doing a job in hemisphere relations that no one before has managed to achieve. The great redeeming hope is that the child is not grown up for good, but only for the duration.

The war was, of course, a turning point for Disney in many ways, and McManus was one of the first critics to sense a definite change in the Disney style and outlook. The biggest change, however, was in the critical reception to his work, which was never to be the same again. Though critics kept hoping for another *Pinocchio,* Disney moved in new directions and lost some of the support he had enjoyed up to that time, particularly among highbrow critics.

But Disney's measure of success, as always, was in public reaction, and the best way to gauge that reaction was at the box office, which evidence led him to ignore the critics and continue to follow his own instincts.

Although *Saludos Amigos* has never been reissued, its material has been used on the Disney TV show, and all four cartoon segments were released separately as short subjects in 1955.

VICTORY THROUGH AIR POWER

RELEASED BY UNITED ARTISTS ON JULY 17, 1943. Technicolor. From the book by Major Alexander de Seversky. Scenes with Major de Seversky directed by H. C. Potter. Director of photography: Ray Rennahan, A.S.C. Art director: Richard Irvine. Technicolor color director: Natalie Kalmus. Associate: Morgan Padleford. Interior decorations: William Kiernan. Narrator: Art Baker. Animation supervisor: David Hand. Story director: Perce Pearce. Story adapters: T. Hee, Erdman Penner, William Cottrell, James Bodrero, George Stallings, Jose Rodriguez. Sequence directors: Clyde Geronimi, Jack Kinney, James Algar. Art directors: Herbert Ryman, Donald Da Gradi, Tom Codrick, Charles Philippi, Elmer Plummer, Don Griffith, Cliff Devirian, Glen Scott, Karl Karpe, Bill Herwig. Animators: Ward Kimball, John Lounsbery, Hugh Fraser, George Rowley, John Sibley, Norm Tate, Vladimir Tytla, Joshua Meador, Carleton Boyd, Bill Justice, Ed Aardal, John McManus, Oliver M. Johnston, Jr., Marvin Woodward, Harvey Toombs. Backgrounds: Albert Dempster, Dick Anthony, Claude Coats, Ray Huffine, Robert Blanchard, Joe Stahley, Nino Carbe. Music: Edward H. Plumb, Paul J. Smith, Oliver Wallace. Production manager: Dan Keefe. Film editor: Jack Dennis. Sound recording: C. O. Slyfield, Lodge Cunningham. Running time: 65 minutes.

Victory Through Air Power is a fascinating footnote to Disney's career. By 1942 he was busy making training films for the army, navy, and every conceivable division of the government; at the end of the war Disney estimated he had turned out some 300,000 feet of film for Uncle Sam.

But *Victory* was not another training film. Indeed, if anything, it went against the predominant thinking among the military hierarchy. Major Alexander de Seversky, a major figure in the history of aviation and a colleague of General Billy Mitchell, had written a book called *Victory Through Air Power*, outlining his ideas about strategic long-range bombing and how it could help win the war. It was cause for a great deal of comment, but the highest echelon among the military planners did not agree with the Major's philosophy.

132

Major Alexander de Seversky poses with one of the maps and models used in *Victory through Air Power*. © *Walt Disney Productions*

A German pilot in World War I soon discovered that using an ordinary machine gun cut off his own propellers!
© *Walt Disney Productions*

Disney was fascinated by Seversky's ideas, however, and felt so strongly about their importance to the war effort that he decided to illustrate them in a film that he would produce himself and release to theatres to win public support for the program. For a man whose financial standing was rather shaky, and whose studio was thriving on military assignments, it was a bold move.

The film opens with an introductory passage: "Our country in the past has struggled through many storms of anguish, difficulty, and doubt. But we have always been saved by men of vision and courage who opened our minds and showed us the way out of confusion." It goes on to show how one of these men, General Billy Mitchell, was "ignored and ridiculed," and it inserts a newsreel clip of Mitchell from 1934 defending his ideas. A title card concludes: "To the memory of Billy Mitchell and . . . other gallant airmen, this film is dedicated."

A book called *History of Aviation* is opened, and we follow the story of flight in this country—from the Wright brothers' historic moment at Kitty Hawk, through the first transcontinental flight, into World War I and the first use of aircraft for warfare, through the 1920s and a series of new aviation "firsts," up until the present day and our modern airships.

We then see a scrapbook of the achievements of Major de Seversky, his many contributions to the progress of aviation over the years. We join him in his office (in live action) as he recounts the background of World War II and the military strategy first used in Europe in 1939. Back into animation, we see how the Maginot Line and other so-called fortresses on land and sea were easily neutralized by Hitler, simply by flying over them; the analogy is made that Hitler created a "shield of air power," and this thought is visualized on a map of Europe.

The Battle of Britain was the turning point in Europe, for here at last Britain learned that in order to ward off attack it would have to gain control of its skies. Then, of course, came Pearl Harbor and our entry into the war.

Seversky then explains the difference between our supply lines and the enemy's: ours depend on various shipping routes that take us within range of enemy fire in many instances—this means we have to go to great lengths to avoid such zones and waste that much more time in delivery; Hitler's supply lines are all concentrated within the interior of his domain—his stronghold can be compared to a wheel, with the factories at the hub, sending supplies out through the various spokes.

The only way to weaken his strength, Seversky explains, is to attack the hub from above and stop his supply lines at their source.

The other problem we face is attacking Japan, and the only way to overcome it is by designing long-range bombers, which can take off from existing Allied air bases (such as those in Alaska) and fly toward their destination. New bombs are needed, and strategy must be employed to make optimum use of this power—hitting dams, for instance, the source of power for most of the munitions factories.

Finally, Seversky says, there must be one single air command to coordinate such actions around the world and ensure victory.

The final animated sequence shows Seversky's idealized air force in action, taking off for Japan, bombing the cities and factories and crippling their power. Then a giant eagle soars through the air, aiming for an octopus on the ground below; the eagle jabs at the head of the octopus, again and again, until it retreats and loses its grip on the map under it. The eagle triumphantly perches on top of the globe, and a zoom backward shows it to be the top of a flagpole flying the American flag in victory.

When Disney started making training and morale films for the government, he learned the real power of the motion-picture medium. But unlike so many producers of factual and educational films, Disney understood that an enthusiastic, *interested* audience would grasp and re-

135

tain much more than an audience that felt it was watching an illustrated lecture.

The same technique was applied to *Victory Through Air Power:* not a matter of sugarcoating the information, but merely presenting it in a simple, graphic manner, using the tools of an entertainment medium to instruct at the same time.

Victory Through Air Power is phenomenally powerful propaganda because it makes its points so crystal clear. When Seversky refers to a shield of air power, we see an actual shield atop a relief map òf Europe and see just how it works. When he talks about Hitler's wheel-like stronghold, the wheel is shown and the metaphor made real. The film is perfect propaganda because it leaves no room for argument; it *shows* you that what it says is true.

There is, of course, *some* sugarcoating to the film, and that is contained in its introductory sequence on the history of aviation. Much of this segment is treated in a lighthearted manner, and, although the gags are undeniably funny, one feels uneasy laughing in the midst of what is essentially a serious matter. (Fortunately, plans to include Donald Duck in the film were later scrapped.) Only here does the film go off target, by making the origin of airborne warfare during World War I a joke. (A German and a Frenchman, Fritz and Pierre, coexist peacefully in the sky, until one day one of them throws a brick at the other, and retaliation builds into full-scale war.)

Even with its jokes, this section of the film does provide a helpful background to the main topic at hand, and once Seversky enters the scene, jokes are forsaken, although there are still some very inventive animated touches.

Indeed, much of the film is done in a sort of limited animation style; backgrounds are sparse, and there are corner-cutting devices such as not bothering to animate the whirring propellers on some of the planes. Many of the points are illustrated with relief maps and abstract figures.

But, paradoxically, there are other points where the animation is unusually elaborate, such as the final sequence of our "dream Air Force" in action. At the airfield it is raining heavily, as the crewmen prepare the long-range bombers to go off on their missions. The rain does produce a satisfying dramatic effect, but it also would have been much simpler to animate the scene without it. Conclusion: Disney was willing to cut corners for the film, but not at the sacrifice of an important effect.

The live-action scenes are also well done, and though it might seem that these could have been shot by anyone, it is precisely that kind of thinking that sets most factual filmmakers apart from Disney. Disney hired successful stage and film director H. C. ("Hank") Potter to do the sequences with Seversky, largely because Potter was a flyer himself (then working for the Air Transport Command), and he already knew Seversky.

Potter knew that simply shooting Seversky at his desk, straight on, would be deadly, so instead he kept him moving constantly and broke up the action with a number of different angles, "luxuries" another less inspired director might have eschewed. In addition, says Potter:

We didn't want . . . to suddenly stop the animation and all of a sudden have Sasha [Seversky's nickname] standing there lecturing. What I did was to tie it in as much as possible by starting with an insert, of a map or a globe, or something, which would look like animation at first, and then you'd hear Sasha's voice and we'd pull the camera back, and he'd be standing in his office, talking. We made the transitions smoother that way.

Of the filming, Potter recalls:

Sasha had no experience as an actor, but essentially, he's a wonderful character. He has this very thick White Russian accent, and of course part of the

137

A visual symbol of the progress aviation has made since the turn of the century. © *Walt Disney Productions*

problem was to try and smooth out the Russian accent so that everybody would understand him. We got as much casual movement, wandering around the office set, as possible, which always bothered him, because he had to keep remembering all these moves.

We had to shoot the whole thing at night, at the Disney studio, because there was little or no sound-proofing, and Lockheed Airport was right next door, where they were making all the P-38s and Hudson bombers, so there were airplanes taking off all day long there, roaring over the studio. It was absolutely impossible to shoot during the day, so we started shooting at 10 at night, and worked until dawn. I remember one night Sasha couldn't hit the damn marks, and he stopped and said, "Hank, how can I remember the words, the expression, the meaning, the walking without limping [he had one wooden leg], and hit these marks, and think of what I am saying at the same time?" I said, "When you're flying air-planes, you're flying a plane, you're navigating, you're looking down at the ground to see if you're going where you're supposed to be going, you're listening to the radio, you're watching for other planes, and you're checking the instruments, all at the same time." I said, "Your motto should be 'Diwide the attention.'" He roared at that. He didn't have any marks from that point on, and every time we would start, the whole crew would holler at him, "Diwide the attention!"

Critical reaction to the film was mixed. Thomas M. Pryor in the *New York Times* enthused: "If *Victory Through Air Power* is propaganda, it is at least the most encouraging and inspiring propaganda that the screen has afforded us in a long time, Mr. Disney and staff can be proud of their accomplishment." Howard Barnes in the *Tribune* was more guarded, saying: "From a tech-nical standpoint, it is difficult to quarrel with the produc-tion. . . . It is the ideological content of the offering which is likely to give one pause." Other critics, like James Agee, were completely turned off by what they

139

considered the film's hard-sell approach.

Advertised as "Walt Disney's Full-Length Sensation," and touted in one comic-book handout as "The Newest, The Greatest Triumph in Screen History," *Victory Through Air Power* was not in the same league as *Pinocchio* or *Snow White* at the box office.

But it did have another kind of audience. Says H. C. Potter:

> The British Air Force thought this was the greatest thing that ever came down the pike, and the picture was much better known in England than it was here, in official circles, and early in the game. Walt told me this story, and swore this was what happened. When Churchill came over to the Quebec conference, they were trying to get Roosevelt interested in this long-range bombing idea, and Roosevelt didn't know what the hell they were talking about. Churchill said, "Well, of course, you've seen *Victory Through Air Power* . . ." and Roosevelt said, "No, what's that?" Air Marshal Tedder and Churchill worked on Roosevelt until Roosevelt put out an order to the Air Corps to fly a print of *Victory Through Air Power* up to Quebec. Churchill ran it for him, and that was the beginning of the U.S. Air Corps Long Range Bombing.

Which, of course, was Disney's real reason for making the film in the first place.

THE THREE CABALLEROS

RELEASED BY RKO RADIO PICTURES ON FEBRUARY 3, 1945. Technicolor. Production supervisor/director: Norman Ferguson. Sequence directors: Clyde Geronimi, Jack Kinney, Bill Roberts, Director (Pátzcuaro, Veracruz, Acapulco): Harold Young. Story: Homer Brightman, Ernest Terrazzas, Ted Sears, Bill Peet,

Ralph Wright, Elmer Plummer, Roy Williams, William Cottrell, Del Connell, James Bodrero. Brazilian and Spanish supervisor: John Cutting. Associates: Gilberto Souto, Aloysio Oliveira, Sidney Field, Edmundo Santos. Assistant production supervisor: Larry Lansburgh. Animators: Ward Kimball, Eric Larson, Fred Moore, John Lounsbery, Les Clark, Milt Kahl, Hal King, Franklin Thomas, Harvey Toombs, Bob Carlson, John Sibley, Bill Justice, Oliver M. Johnston, Jr., Milt Neil, Marvin Woodward, John Patterson. Special effects animation: Joshua Meador, George Rowley, Edwin Aardal, John McManus. Backgrounds: Albert Dempster, Art Riley, Ray Huffine, Don Douglass, Claude Coats. Layout: Donald Da Gradi, Hugh Hennesy, McLaren Stewart, Yale Gracey, Herbert Ryman, John Hench, Charles Philippi. Art supervisors: Mary Blair, Kenneth Anderson, Robert Cormack. Live-action sequences photographed by Ray Rennahan, A.S.C. Art director: Richard F. Irvine. Choreography: Billy Daniels, Aloysio Oliveira, Carmelita Maracci. Technicolor director: Natalie Kalmus. Associate: Morgan Padleford. Color consultant: Phil Dike. Process effects: Ub Iwerks. Process technician: Richard Jones. Music directors: Charles Wolcott, Paul J. Smith, Edward H. Plumb. Technical adviser: Gail Papineau. Film editor: John Haliday. Sound recording: C. O. Slyfield. Production manager: Dan Keefe. Running time: 70 minutes.

Songs: "The Three Caballeros" ("Ay Jalisco No Te Rajes") by Manuel Esperon, Ray Gilbert, Ernesto Cortezar. "Baia" ("Na Baixa Do Sapaterio") by Ary Barroso, Ray Gilbert. "Os Quindins De Yaya" by Ary Barroso. "You Belong to My Heart" ("Solamente Una Vez") by Agustin Lara, Ray Gilbert. "Mexico" by Charles Wolcott, Ray Gilbert.

Cast: Aurora Miranda, Carmen Molina, Dora Luz, Nestor Amarale, Almirante, Trio Calaveras, Ascencio Del Rio Trio, Padua Hill Players, and the voices of Sterling Holloway, Clarence Nash (Donald Duck), Jose
141

Joe Carioca, Panchito, and Donald Duck, *The Three Caballeros*.
© *Walt Disney Productions*

Donald shows off for the lovely bathing beauties south of the border.   © *Walt Disney Productions*

Oliveira (Joe Carioca), Joaquin Garay (Panchito), Fred Shields, Frank Graham. "Mexico" sung by Carlos Ramirez.

The Three Caballeros followed *Saludos Amigos* by two years (it would have been sooner, but war priorities made it difficult to get color prints), expanded on its themes and ideas, and resulted in a bright, fast-moving, and often brilliant mélange of sights and sounds. Somewhat like *Fantasia*, it was the cause of considerable controversy among critics in 1945, and only recently has become one of the most admired Disney features among film buffs.

The film opens with a spotlight on a giant gift-wrapped package; it's a birthday gift for Donald Duck, who excitedly opens it up and discovers, first, a movie projector. "Oh, boy," says Donald, "home movies!" as he snaps a reel of film into threading position and throws it onto the machine. The first film on the screen is *Aves Raras (Strange Birds)*, which tells principally of Pablo the Penguin, who never could get used to his Antarctic home and sailed for the South Seas. Another strange bird is the Aracuan, a crazy bird with a raucous song who walks out of the movie screen to shake hands with Donald and walks off *our* screen as well. (He and Donald were to meet again in the one-reel cartoon *Clown of the Jungle*.)

The next story is about Little Gauchito, who goes hunting and finds a flying burrito (a donkey), whom he enters in a local race, winning with ease, but having his scheme backfire when the crowd sees the donkey's wings.

Movies are over, and Donald opens his next gift, a book on Brazil. He flips open the cover only to find his old pal Joe Carioca inside. The volume is a giant pop-up book, and Joe paints a beautiful picture of his country for Donald by singing "Baia," as we see a beautiful panorama of Brazil, with its homes, soft skyline, mountains, jungle, a boat on the calm water, beautiful ancient churches, etc. Joe asks Donald if he's ever been to

143

Brazil; when Donald says no, Joe goes into a whole song and dance about it, splitting himself into a quartet, and eventually taking out a sledgehammer and crowning Donald, which shrinks the duck to Joe's miniature size (after all, he came out of a book) so he can go with him. They hop on a train, which appears on the next leaf of the pop-up book, and go to Brazil, where they meet Aurora Miranda, with whom Donald promptly falls in love. He joins Aurora and her musical friends in a long production number that combines live action and animation. She finally kisses Donald, which sends him into a whirlpool of fantasy—drums, tambourines, a montage of unreal colors, tinted footage of life dancers, a phantasmagoria of images. When he comes back down to earth, the whole background setting sways in time to the music, the lamppost and houses moving back and forth rhythmically. Finally the entire scene comes to a finale, and the book, still swaying, closes. Donald and Joe squeeze out of the binding and return to their normal size.

The last present is Mexico, represented at first by a sound track, whose variations are shown in the shapes of the instruments playing (illustrated as symmetrical forms emanating from the sound track's vertical line). At one point Donald gets caught in the sound track, and *his* image comes out of the track. But the music gets so wild that it finally explodes, sending a new visitor bursting forth—Panchito, a Mexican charro rooster.

He, Joe, and Donald sing "The Three Caballeros," full of wild, incredibly fast-moving gags. Then Panchito tells his friends about his country: of Mexican traditions, like the children's celebration of Christmas and the origin of the piñata. He encourages Donald to try to hit the piñata, and when he does a cascade of surprises are showered on him. A storybook provides the history of Mexico and live-action pictures of Mexico today. A magic sarape becomes the trio's flying carpet, taking them into the scenes of the storybook. They visit a fiesta where, in the midst of traditional dances, Donald starts to jitterbug with a lovely señorita. Then Panchito lassos Acapulco Beach and they travel there. Donald immediately goes after a bevy of bathing beauties, who play with him.

Dora Luz sings "You Belong to My Heart," sending Donald into another flight of fantasy. The girl appears in his eyes . . . he dances among the stars . . . everything he sees becomes a neon sign, then flowers, and wildly colored geometric figures . . . then silhouettes, gradually turning into shadows of his dream girl, who evolves back into a flower. After a burst of chorus girls, photographed from above, completes the number, there is quiet, and slowly a figure appears on a distant horizon. It is Carmen Molina, who marches forward to dance the famous "Jesusita," joined by a group of surrounding cactus plants, and playful Donald, who does his best to keep in step.

Finally, Donald plays a mock bullfight with his two friends, and they load the mock bull with fireworks. When Donald hits the bull head on, there is a tremendous explosion, as they sing a final chorus of "The Three Caballeros" and the fireworks in the sky spell out The End.

It is impossible to describe *The Three Caballeros* adequately on paper. First, there is simply so much going on, and second, there are no words to pinpoint many of the startling visual effects employed in the film. It is one long barrage of dazzling sights, accompanied on the sound track by some sixteen delectable songs, including several that became standards.

The film is full of visual puns, even in the "mildest" of its episodes, the story of Pablo the Penguin, in which the narrator (Sterling Holloway) tells us that "a blanket of fog rolled in," and we see literally that, or Pablo's little iceboat reaching the equator and bouncing off the hemisphere line. In the story of Little Gauchito, when the first-person narrator, telling of the race, says, "We passed them as if they were standing still," that's just what happens.

This is only a lethargic warm-up to what follows, particularly in the "Three Caballeros" number, where things happen so fast it is difficult to keep track of them. When a line of the song goes, "Through fair and stormy weather . . ." on the word "stormy," a sudden downpour erupts and flows over the brims of the singers' sombreros. When Panchito hits a high note and decides to hold it, Donald and Joe scurry around to find devices to shut him up, planting bushes that instantly grow around him, burning them down, putting out the fire with an avalanche of water, etc., all to no avail.

Donald's dream sequences are reminiscent of *Dumbo*'s "Pink Elephants" sequence in their imagination and constant evolution from one far-out concept to another, with perfectly logical transitions linking the bizarre visuals.

Much of this was too offbeat for some viewers, including at least one of the Disney staff, according to Ward Kimball, who refers to this film as "the only animation I can look back on with pride." Kimball told Mike Barrier of *Funnyworld:*

It's fun to look at today. Everything else I've done, I criticize, I say I should have done this or I should have done that, but on *Three Caballeros*, I had a lot of fun. When you see it now, it's kind of old hat, characters going out on the left and coming in from the right, with no hookups, sort of a magic animation.

There is a variety of styles within *The Three Caballeros;* not only Kimball's frantic no-holds-barred animation, but the soft, almost pastel quality of the Pablo and Gauchito segments, and the loveliness of Panchito's story of Mexican children at Christmas, which is shown as a series of tableaux.

The combination of live action and animation (the first time the studio had tried it to any great extent since the old *Alice in Cartoonland* efforts of the 1920s) was perfect. The synchronization of movement between the actors and the cartoon characters is right on target, and the illusion is such that you are willing to believe that Donald and the bathing beauties are really frolicking together, or that Donald is actually dancing with Aurora Miranda and her musicians.

Despite the episodic nature of the film and frequent shifts of locale, mood, and style, *The Three Caballeros* maintains its breezy pacing beautifully, allowing no lulls or feeling of superfluous material. The stream of music on the sound track is constant, and the whole film seems to have been laid out to one continuous rocking beat. It is difficult to leave a screening of the film without carrying this lilting music in your head.

Although the film was capitalizing again on the strong Latin-American bonds of the 1940s, it has little of the propaganda feeling of *Saludos Amigos,* although one is constantly fed a series of definitions, explanations of customs, and picture-postcard footage (both literal, as in Panchito's live-action storybook, and animated, as in the vision of Baia, which was obviously animated from detailed photographs).

The Three Caballeros was well under way in the mid-war years, but its production was constantly delayed by breaks during which the staff had to turn out government material; once completed, there was another long delay to get enough Technicolor prints to open the film. Said Disney in late 1944: "You have to stand in line now." Although the film was completed by October 1944, it did not open in New York until February 1945.

As with *Saludos,* Disney went right to the source for most of his material, hiring such prominent South American composers as Ary Barroso, Agustin Lara, and Manuel Esperon, and three leading female stars, Aurora Miranda of Brazil, and Dora Luz and Carmen Molina of Mexico. The musical aspect of the film paid off handsomely, for "You Belong to My Heart" and "Baia" became top song hits.

Building up the combination of live action and animation, *The Three Caballeros* was immodestly advertised as "the most startling advancement in motion picture technique since the advent of sound." Whereas it was warmly greeted by most mass-audience critics (although many professed to be confused by it all) and deemed a "socko feature production" by *Variety,* some of the more sophisticated reviewers were aghast at the animated mélange.

Under the headline WHAT HATH WALT WROUGHT?, *The New Yorker* called the film:

> . . . a mixture of atrocious taste, bogus mysticism, and authentic fantasy, guaranteed to baffle any critic now hopelessly enchanted with the word "Disney." . . . In the first place, a somewhat physical romance between a two-foot duck and a full-sized woman, though one happens to be a cartoon and the other pleasantly rounded and certainly mortal, is one of those things that might disconcert less squeamish authorities than the Hays office. . . . It might even be said that a sequence involving the duck, the young lady, and a long alley of animated cactus plants would probably be considered suggestive in a less innocent medium.

It was, however, a box-office success, although it has never been reissued (presumably because it is felt that, like *The Reluctant Dragon* and *Saludos Amigos,* it is too firmly moored to the 1940s). It has been relegated to second-class status among the Disney backlog, evidenced by frequent television exposure on the Disney TV show, making short subjects out of certain sequences, and availability for rental on 16mm. It is, ironically enough, the latter accessibility that has given the film its new-found reputation, and, once again, today's younger viewers, unconcerned by motivations, artistic pretensions, or critical guidelines for Disney's work, have found it to be a hugely entertaining, largely surreal endeavor, years ahead of its time in conception and execution, and more in tune with the free-form animation of today than that of the 1940s. (The film received its first theatrical reissue in 1976, but to the dismay of Disney buffs, it was badly cut to "featurette" length.)

RELEASED BY RKO RADIO PICTURES ON AUGUST 15, 1946. Technicolor. Production supervisor: Joe Grant. Directors: Jack Kinney, Clyde Geronimi, Hamilton Luske, Robert Cormack, Joshua Meador. Story: Homer Brightman, Dick Huemer, Dick Kinney, John Walbridge, Tom Oreb, Dick Shaw, Eric Gurney, Sylvia Holland, T. Hee, Dick Kelsey, Jesse Marsh, Roy Williams, Ed Penner, James Bodrero, Cap Palmer, Erwin Graham. Art supervisors: Mary Blair, Elmer Plummer, John Hench. Animators: Les Clark, Ward Kimball, Milt Kahl, John Sibley, Hal King, Eric Larson, John Lounsbery, Oliver M. Johnston, Jr., Fred Moore, Hugh Fraser, Judge Whitaker, Harvey Toombs, Tom Massey, Phil Duncan, Hal Ambro, Jack Campbell, Cliff Nordberg, Bill Justice, Al Bertino, John McManus, Ken O'Brien. Backgrounds: Claude Coats, Art Riley, Ralph Hulett, Merle Cox, Ray Huffine, Albert Dempster, Thelma Witmer, Jim Trout. Layout: A. Kendall O'Connor, Hugh Hennesy, Al Zinnen, Ed Benedict, Charles Philippi, Donald Da Gradi, Lance Nolley, Charles Payzant, John Niendorf. Effects animation: George Rowley, Jack Boyd, Andy Engman, Brad Case, Don Patterson. Musical director: Charles Wolcott. Associates: Ken Darby, Oliver Wallace, Edward H. Plumb. Process effects: Ub Iwerks. Color consultant: Mique Nelson. Sound: C. O. Slyfield, Robert O. Cook. Running time: 74 minutes.

Songs: "Johnny Fedora and Alice Blue Bonnet" by Allie Wrubel and Ray Gilbert; "All the Cats Join In" by Alec Wilder, Ray Gilbert, and Eddie Sauter; "Without You" by Osvaldo Farres, English lyrics by Ray Gilbert; "Two Silhouettes" by Charles Wolcott and Ray Gilbert; "Casey, the Pride of Them All" by Ray Gilbert, Ken Darby, and Eliot Daniel; "The Martins and the Coys" by Al Cameron and Ted Weems; "Blue Bayou" by Bobby Worth and Ray Gilbert; "After You've Gone" by Henry Creamer and Turner Leighton, "Make Mine Music," by Ken Darby and Eliot Daniel.

Voices: Nelson Eddy, Dinah Shore, Benny Goodman and Orchestra, The Andrews Sisters, Jerry Colonna, Andy Russell, Sterling Holloway, The Pied Pipers, The King's Men, The Ken Darby Chorus, and featuring Tatiana Riabouchinska and David Lichine.

After the release of *Fantasia*, Walt Disney was urged to adapt the same format to popular music. Disney did not commit himself to the idea, but in 1944 started formulating plans for just such a film. Initially, the feature was to run the full gamut of musical styles, and Leopold Stokowski was again to be involved. Plans changed, however, and though some classical pieces remained in the finished film, the accent was clearly on popular music. For "marquee value," he hired an array of popular singers and musicians.

The titles are done in a theatre-marquee and poster format, each poster bringing us closer to the theatre entrance. When the titles are completed, we go in the doors and our eyes fall upon a program, which reads, "A Music Fantasy in Ten Parts." Then the curtain opens and the first sequence begins.

A Rustic Ballad is "The Martins and the Coys," sung by the King's Men, a fast and straightforward cartoon of the hillbilly hit about an age-old mountain feud. A monumental shoot-out sends most of the two families up to heaven, where on neighboring clouds, they watch the precedent-breaking love match between young Henry Martin and Grace McCoy. They get married, but after a hoedown wedding ceremony, it turns out that the feud hasn't ended after all: Grace is a battle-ax supreme, who showers her husband with a flurry of rolling pins, crockery, etc. The angels above all have a good laugh.

Next is *A Tone Poem*, sung by the Ken Darby chorus, "Blue Bayou." This is one of the deliberately "arty" segments in the film, opening on a beautiful shot of the moon, with clouds passing across its face; this dissolves
150

into a view of the bayou, with a flamingo stopping to rest. He looks at his reflection in the water, dips into it, and the ripple is carried across the lake. When it stills, we see not the flamingo, but the moon again, in reflection. Then as the camera looks up, the flamingo and a companion fly off toward the moon as the song concludes.

For a change of pace, there is *A Jazz Interlude* with Benny Goodman and his orchestra, "All the Cats Join In," subtitled "A Caricature." A pencil draws the sequence's characters in a sketchbook, flipping the page for each new character or new scene. There are no backgrounds, except sparse details to indicate immediate backdrops like a sidewalk or a house. The pace is very fast as the song is illustrated in a vignette of a 1940s bobby-soxer going down to the malt shop with her boyfriend for a jitterbug session.

Next is *A Ballad in Blue*, "Without You," sung by Andy Russell. This segment tries to capture a mood with color and images that relate to the atmosphere the song describes. As the scene opens we are in a long, dark room, with just a hint of detail at the far end, lit by the natural light coming in from a tall window, revealing a handwritten note left on a chair nearby. As we move in closer, the rain outside crawls down the windowpane, and, taking on various colors, forms the backgrounds outside of roads, hills, trees, etc., then moving up to a starry blue sky, which in turn dissolves into a vision of trees against a far blue horizon. As the song comes to a close, we pull back into the room once more and the sequence ends as it began.

Jerry Colonna is featured in *A Musical Recitation* of "Casey at the Bat." It opens with a chorus singing the theme song, visualized by a series of old-fashioned lithographs reflecting the Gay '90s. Then we move into the ball park itself for the story of Casey, as sung and told by Colonna. The famous poem is injected with visual hyperbole in the form of endless sight gags (the ball sliding up the first baseman's foot right into his hand, the bat getting caught in one player's long waxed

151

These four instruments go on a surreal trip to the music of the
Benny Goodman quartet in "After You've Gone."
© Walt Disney Productions

moustache, etc.). At the climax of the story, on the third
strike, the line "the force of Casey's blow" is illustrated
by a tremendous gust of wind, shown over a scene of
the spectators in the stands. The gust turns the picture
into a blur, and it dissolves into a picture of birds singing in the trees (as the poem continues), bands playing
in the park, etc. But back in Mudville, we see Casey,
alone in the stadium as it begins to rain, going berserk,
chasing the ball all around the field with his bat.

Ballade Ballet features Tatiana Riabouchinska and
David Lichine, of the Ballet Russe, performing as Dinah
Shore sings "Two Silhouettes." A heart melts into two
cupids against a lacy background, which they open as a
curtain to reveal the silhouettes of the two dancers
against a pink background. They begin to dance, and the

152

backgrounds behind them change randomly. Soon the silhouettes are lifted out of conventional time and space and become part of the animation; during one of the ballerina's pirouettes, a cupid lifts her by the arms onto an animated ledge high above, where the dance continues. The sequence closes with the silhouettes in repose, and the two cupids closing the curtain and returning into the shape of a heart.

"Peter and the Wolf" is *A Fairy Tale with Music*, told by Sterling Holloway. It is the classic story that accompanied Prokofiev's music, with numerous additions and embellishments, such as specific names and identities for each of the animals (Sasha the bird, Sonja the duck, Ivan the cat) who accompany Peter on his premature hunting trip in the Russian forest.

Benny Goodman returns with his quartet (Cozy Cole, Teddy Wilson, Sid Wiess), this time for "After You've Gone," a surreal vision of the four instruments (clarinet, drums, piano, bass) engaging in a wild, chaselike battle. The clarinet and bass go at it in a boxing ring, engage in a chase over an endless, winding keyboard . . . the clarinet gets "hot," catches fire, and a river of music (notes, keys, clefs, etc.) puts it out, as the four instruments run off into infinity as the swinging improvisation draws to a close.

A Love Story is sung by the Andrews Sisters: "Johnny Fedora and Alice Blue Bonnet," the tale of two hats who fall in love in the window of a department store. They are separated when each is sold, and Johnny spends every moment on his buyer's head searching for Alice to no avail. He jumps around so much that he eventually is blown away and brought down to the point of being discarded. Just as he is about to be washed down a sewer, a man picks him up, cuts holes in his brim, and puts him on his horse. The new owner is an iceman.) And lo and behold, who should be next to him on the companion horse but Alice.

The finale is *Opera Pathetique*, featuring Nelson Eddy, who does all the voices for "The Whale Who Wanted to Sing at the Met." The story is told musically at first, then Eddy lapses into straight narration. Headlines tell of "Mystery Voice at Sea," and it is revealed that the voice belongs to a whale! Professors scoff, people don't believe it, but famed opera impresario Professor Tetti Tatti surmises that the whale must have swallowed an opera singer. He goes out to sea to harpoon the whale and rescue his latest discovery. A sea gull tells Willie the whale that Tetti Tatti is on his way, and, after much consideration, Willie decides to sing "Figaro" for his audition, doing tenor, baritone, and bass roles all at once. "He's swallowed *three* opera singers!" cries Tetti Tatti, determined to shoot him. But the three crewmen on board the ship are enjoying the music too much, and stand in his way. Willie serenades them, singing the entire sextet from *Lucia* himself.

At this point he dreams of his debut at the Met, standing on the stage, filling the entire house, the spotlight focused on his three tonsils. When he bows, he towers over the audience. The sailors, seals, and sea gulls are in attendance (the audience directly below the gulls wearing protection on their heads). This is followed by triumph after triumph. As Pagliacci he wears a huge clown's nose, and, instead of crying, spouts water, causing the orchestra members to wear raincoats, and the conductor to carry an umbrella. He plays in *Tristan und Isolde, Mephistopheles,* but his dream is curtailed when Tetti Tatti gets to the gun and harpoons poor Willie in the midst of a stormy sea.

The narrator urges us not to be too harsh on Tetti Tatti. "People aren't used to miracles," he explains, adding that "miracles never die." And, sure enough, as we make a tremendous ascent to Heaven through towering cloud formations, Willie is leading one hundred golden voices in song, and on the Pearly Gates hangs a sign reading "Sold Out."

It is pleasing that *Make Mine Music* ends on such a delightful note, for "The Whale Who Wanted to Sing at the Met" (later known as "Willie the Operatic Whale")

Willie the Whale treats his seagoing friends to an impromptu concert. © *Walt Disney Productions*

is surely one of the film's highlights, and tends to overshadow the film's very definite weaknesses.

Make Mine Music is a film of ups and downs, the ups being most of the popular material and the downs being the attempts to work with classical music, and/or become "artistic."

The Martins and the Coys is hardly a Disney classic, but it is certainly innocuous, whereas *Blue Bayou* and *Two Silhouettes* are embarrassing attempts at "culture." *Blue Bayou is* quite lovely, and actually a showcase for Disney's corps of effects animators, who really did raise their craft to a fine art (the sequence was originally set to "Clair de Lune" for use in *Fantasia*). But it has no point, and this is what offends the viewer—the knowledge that such a sequence is the result of conscious striving to "elevate" the standard cartoon sequence to a higher plane.

Two Silhouettes was unanimously chosen as the nadir of the film by its many critics, including some who thought the film as a whole had its moments. Brushing aside for the moment the (valid) criticism that the combination of live-action ballet and animation techniques negated both art forms, the sequence again seems to have no purpose, no direction, unlike, for instance, Norman McLaren's acclaimed short *Duo,* which presents a pas de deux in stroboscopic fashion. The very format of cupids and doilies spelled disaster for most viewers before the sequence was even under way.

One finds this artiness invading even some of the more pleasant sequences, such as *A Ballad in Blue,* which rests on the borderline between the two styles to be found in the film. Even when some of its abstracts start to "work," the effect is spoiled when the lyric "I pray . . ." cues the transformation of a tree into a cross.

Most disappointing of all is *Peter and the Wolf,* which at first glance would seem a most likely subject for Disney treatment. But there is an inherent problem with the piece; it was designed to be heard, not seen. The famous narration, keyed to special orchestration of the music, was intended to fascinate children by making them use their imaginations to visualize the story. Hence, *any* visual treatment destroys the essential meaning of the piece.

However, one must concede that it might be possible to do justice to Prokofiev's work. The problem here was that the Disney people went overboard. The charm of *Peter and the Wolf* is its simplicity, which is pummeled to death by naming every single solitary character in the story—Sonja the Duck, Mischa, Yascha, and Vladimir the hunters, Ivan the Cat, etc., etc., etc. The narration is no longer the classic one, but a more up-to-date and pointed kind, with sportscaster overtones ("Look out, Sacha!"). Here, for a change, the animation is quite pleasing, and it is the *concept* that fails.

What, then, are *Make Mine Music*'s moments? First,

the two Benny Goodman pieces, which seem, unlike most on the other musical compositions, to have actually *inspired* the Disney crew to match the music with something original and appropriate on the screen. "All the Cats Join In" is a delightful evocation of the bobby-sox generation, done in a striking format that even pokes fun at itself. The pencil that is drawing the characters can't keep up with the rapid pace of the action; it starts to draw a jalopy for the teen-agers, but they ride off with it before the pencil is through! It races ahead and draws a stoplight that forces the car to stand still while the finishing touches are added. The sequence ends as the jukebox explodes, sending records, musical notes, and other musical symbols flying in a million directions.

"After You've Gone" is perhaps the best surreal animation Disney ever did, buoyed by the sparkling sounds of the Goodman quartet. It moves very fast, its imagination unflagging in presenting the four humanized instruments on the lam in their nightmarish world. The same critics who condemned *Two Silhouettes* praised this segment as the highlight on the feature.

"Casey at the Bat" is also quite satisfying, in a more standard way, with all the accouterments of a typical 1940s Disney short subject—clever direction (one shot shows a close-up of a mitt as the ball is thrown into it), rapid-paced sight gags (a player on first base "leads" so energetically that it appears there are two of him running back and forth from the base to the midway point), and, in this case, a perfect choice for narrator-singer, Jerry Colonna.

"Johnny Fedora and Alice Blue Bonnet" is also very pleasing, with the smooth harmonies of the Andrews Sisters. The idea of telling the story from a hat's eye view, and minimizing the display of human faces, is a difficult one to maintain, and one can see definite stumbling blocks in the sequence, but, generally, it's quite well done.

Best of all is "The Whale Who Wanted to Sing at the Met." This is Disney doing what he does best, a com-

157

Walt Disney shows one of his singing stars, Dinah Shore, around the Burbank studio. © *Walt Disney Productions*

bination of fantasy and gentle satire—getting in spoofs not only of opera, but of human nature, and even a little joke at Nelson Eddy's expense. (When we first join Willie, he is singing "Shortnin' Bread," one of Eddy's popular hits.) The visions of Willie at the Met are simply priceless, topping each other with inventive gags (simply the *sight* of Willie made up as Pagliacci is hilarious), and including a generous helping of the most popular classical arias.

Appropriately enough, "Willie" has had the most exposure outside of the feature, playing independently as a short and being run many times on the Disney TV show.

When the film was released, in mid-1946, it met with widely mixed reaction. As Disney's first feature release since the war, it was highly anticipated (*The Three Caballeros* having been considered part of the general wartime atmosphere), and many critics became apologists for the film, feeling that even if it weren't top Disney, it would just be a short while before he was back in form.

Otis L. Guernsey, in the *Herald Tribune*, wrote: "*Make Mine Music* merely boils the pot without mixing in the ingredients of a masterpiece . . . [but] those who do not insist on the rare experience of a Disney masterpiece will have the delightful experience of a Disney potboiler, whose comedy, artistry, and fantasy make most of the live actor entertainments look drab and pedestrian by comparison."

The film provided the final break between Disney and the intellectuals who had made him their darling in the 1930s. Most expressive of this feeling is a review written by Hermine Rich Isaacs for *Theatre Arts* magazine:

Suppose you go to visit a friend. You know that he has a warm heart and is kind to animals, that his sense of humor is infectious, his professional skill beyond compare. But when you enter his house you find to your dismay that his walls are festooned with secondrate art; romantic scenes of white doves against lush blue backgrounds; vapid landscapes; valentine motifs, complete with lace cutouts, tinsel stars and hearts of assorted sizes. You discover that his furniture is carelessly assembled with little regard for harmony or any other concern except to fill space. You would not

159

Walt Disney goes over the score for "Casey at the Bat" with hammy Jerry Colonna. *Courtesy British Film Institute*

therefore cease to love the man, to laugh at his jokes or admire his skill; but you would have to admit with regret that his taste is deplorable. On similar internal evidence, this is the reluctant conclusion of a visitor to *Make Mine Music . . .*

After its initial release, *Make Mine Music,* like the other Disney omnibus features to follow, was cut down into ten segments that were released separately as shorts, some, like *Peter and the Wolf,* being given official rerelease, paired with a new feature. (*Peter* went out with *The African Lion* in 1955.) Most of the segments ended up on the Disney TV hour at one time or another as well.

Make Mine Music was a sharp disappointment to the millions who had eagerly awaited another Disney classic. They did not give up on him, however, and hoped that soon he would make another feature film to rate alongside his prewar achievements. For some, that film never came; others learned that Disney was simply changing and moving on to new areas where he hoped he could succeed as completely as he had with the animated feature.

SONG OF THE SOUTH

RELEASED BY RKO RADIO PICTURES ON NOVEMBER 1, 1946. Technicolor. Associate producer: Perce Pearce. Cartoon director: Wilfred Jackson. Photoplay director: Harve Foster. Screenplay: Dalton Raymond, Morton Grant, Maurice Rapf. Original story: Dalton Raymond, based on the *Tales of Uncle Remus* by Joel Chandler Harris. Photography: Gregg Toland. Film editor: William M. Morgan. Art director: Perry Ferguson. Costumes: Mary Wills. Special processes: Ub Iwerks. Sound director: C. O. Slyfield. Sound recording: Fred Lau, Harold Steck. Art treatment: Elmer Plummer. Technicolor color director: Natalie Kalmus. Associate: Mitchell Kovaleski. Music director: Charles Wolcott. Photoplay score: Daniele Amfitheatrof. Cartoon score: Paul J. Smith. Vocal director: Ken Darby. Orchestrations: Edward H. Plumb. Cartoon story: William Peet, Ralph Wright, George Stallings. Cartoon art directors: Kenneth Anderson, Charles Philippi, Hugh Hennesy, Harold Doughty, Philip Barber. Directing animators: Milt Kahl, Eric Larson, Oliver M. Johnston, Jr., Les Clark, Marc Davis, John Lounsbery. Animators: Don Lusk, Tom Massey, Murray McClellan, Jack Campbell, Hal King, Harvey Toombs, Ken O'Brien, Al Coe, Hal Ambro, Cliff Nordberg, Rudy Larriva. Background and color stylists: Claude Coats, Mary Blair. Background

Glenn Leedy and Bobby Driscoll listen to James Baskett as Uncle
Remus in *Song of the South*. © *Walt Disney Productions*

artists: Ralph Hulett, Brice Mack, Ray Huffine, Edgar
Starr, Albert Dempster. Effects animation: Joshua
Meador, George Rowley, Blaine Gibson, Brad Case.
Running time: 94 minutes.

Songs: "How Do You Do?" by Robert MacGimsey.
"Song of the South" by Sam Coslow, Arthur Johnston.
"That's What Uncle Remus Said" by Eliot Daniel, Hy
Heath, Johnny Lange. "Sooner or Later" by Charles
Wolcott, Ray Gilbert. "Everybody's Got a Laughing
Place," "Zip-a-dee Doo-Dah" by Allie Wrubel, Ray
Gilbert. "You'll Always Be the One I Love" by Sunny
Skylar, Ticker Freeman. "Let the Rain Pour Down,"
"Who Wants to Live Like That?" by Foster Carling.

Cast: Ruth Warrick (Sally), James Baskett (Uncle Remus), Bobby Driscoll (Johnny), Luana Patten (Ginny), Lucile Watson (grandmother), Hattie McDaniel (Aunt Tempy), Glenn Leedy (Toby), George Nokes, Gene Holland (The Favers Boys), Erik Rolf (John), Mary Field (Mrs. Favers), Anita Brown (maid), and the voices of James Baskett (Brer Fox), Nicodemus Stewart (Brer Bear), and Johnny Lee (Brer Rabbit).

Song of the South was advertised as "an epochal event in screen history." This would seem to be stretching things too far, but it was indeed an important film in the chronology of Disney's career, for it relied more on live-action dramatic footage than any previous film (*The Reluctant Dragon* having been mutually forgotten by both Disney and the press), and perfected the combination of animation and live action to a height of perfection, outdoing even *The Three Caballeros* in this respect.

The opening titles of the film are set against rustic engravings of the Old South. An introductory title states: "Out of the humble cabin, out of the singing heart of the Old South have come the tales of Uncle Remus, rich in simple truths, forever fresh and new."

The film's action begins with little Johnny being brought to live with his mother and grandmother at the latter's plantation. He doesn't understand that his parents are separating, and when his father says goodbye, Johnny is distraught. That evening, he decides to run away from home, but along the way he encounters Uncle Remus telling stories to some black children. When Remus hears that Johnny is running away from home, he decides to use psychology to lure him back. He tells Johnny he was thinking of running away too, and would like to go with him, but first they must stop at his cabin for some provisions. While there, he tells Johnny a story. As he starts to describe what kind of day it was when the story took place, the camera dollies in, and as he begins to sing "Zip-a-dee Doo-Dah," the background around his head (now in close-up) bursts

163

away to reveal a brilliantly blue sky, with Uncle Remus walking through an animated countryside, singing. As he ambles along, the birds flutter around him, and all the local animals get into the spirit of things.

Then he encounters Brer Rabbit, who is boarding up the entrance to his home in the Briar Patch and "never comin' back." As he goes off, he is spotted by Brer Fox, who has left a trap for him. The trap catches Brer Rabbit by the foot and has him dangling upside down from a tree limb. The Fox comes running after his prey from his hilltop hideout, but meanwhile Brer Bear walks by. Brer Rabbit uses Tom Sawyer-like psychology to convince Brer Bear that he's earning a dollar a minute for hanging there acting as scarecrow. Since he has plenty of money by now, he offers to let Brer Bear take his place, which the oafish Bear is happy to do. By the time Brer Fox reaches the trap, the Rabbit is on his way down the road; Brer Fox convinces Brer Bear that he's been made a fool of, and the two of them start fighting, as Brer Rabbit goes on his way, laughing uproariously.

The moral, Uncle Remus tells Johnny, is "You can't run away from trouble—there ain't no place that far." Johnny takes the hint and returns home to his worried mother, who has the impression that Uncle Remus led him astray in the first place.

Without many friends, without a father, and under the thumb of his overprotective mother, Johnny soon comes to rely on Uncle Remus more and more as a companion. One day he meets up with two rowdy brothers who bully their little sister and her pet dog. To save the dog from being drowned, Johnny adopts it himself, and becomes friendly with Ginny, the little girl. But he doesn't know how to handle the two brothers.

Uncle Remus tells him the story of Brer Rabbit and the Tar Baby, which picks up where the last tale left off. The Fox and Bear fashion a human figure out of tar, and leave it sitting by the side of the road. Brer Rabbit comes by, sings "How Do You Do?" to the fellow, and becomes annoyed that he doesn't answer back. After several attempts, he punches the Tar Baby in the nose,

Brer Fox has the last laugh on Brer Rabbit . . .
© *Walt Disney Productions*

. . . and shares the laugh with Brer Bear at the dinner table.
© *Walt Disney Productions*

and becomes entangled in the gooey mess, a sitting duck for Brer Fox and Brer Bear; the Fox wants to roast him, while the Bear wants to "knock his head clean off."

Again, Brer Rabbit uses psychology. He says he'll welcome roasting, hanging, or whatever, but "please, whatever you do, don't throw me in the briar patch." He makes them believe that there would be no worse fate than that, so the Fox falls for it, and hurls him into the midst of the thorny field. Brer Rabbit makes sounds of pain from underneath, but then springs up laughing hysterically. "I was born and raised in the Briar Patch," he sings mockingly. The lesson: it shows you what happens when you get mixed up in somethin' you got no business getting mixed up in.

Johnny uses the same idea when the two nasty brothers threaten to tell his mother that he's taken their dog. Johnny tells them to go ahead, but whatever they do, not to tell their *own* mother. They fall for it, and get a whipping from their mother for having treated the dog so badly in the first place. After that, they do tell Johnny's mother, who once again blames Uncle Remus for encouraging the boy.

Johnny's mother decides to give him a birthday party, to enliven his spirits. He insists on inviting Ginny, even though she comes from a poor family, duly noted by Mother. When she is late, Johnny goes to get her, and on the way her brothers taunt her and push her into a mud puddle, spoiling her new dress. Ginny cries uncontrollably, upset not only about the dress, but too ashamed to go to Johnny's party. Uncle Remus comes upon the scene, and, instead of sharing her sorrow, starts laughing. The youngsters ask him why, and he says he's thinking about his Laughing Place.

This leads to the next story, as Brer Rabbit has been captured once again by the Fox and Bear. He starts singing, "Everybody's Got a Laughing Place," as he is about to be cooked. Brer Bear asks him what he's talking about, and Brer Rabbit explains that it's a secret place he knows about. Not wanting to be fooled again, the Fox and Bear make the Rabbit lead them to this laughing place, which turns out to be a giant beehive. As Brer Bear is chased about by the angry insects, he hollers to the Rabbit, asking what's the big idea. "I didn't say this was *your* laughing place," Brer Rabbit replies, "this is *my* laughing place," and, indeed, he can't stop laughing at the sight of Brer Fox and Brer Bear running frenziedly about.

The story succeeds in cheering up Johnny and Ginny, but then Johnny's mother arrives and blames Uncle Remus for keeping the children from their party. She demands that he never speak to Johnny again.

Heartbroken and convinced that he's a good-for-nothing, Uncle Remus decides to go away. When Johnny sees him riding away in his carriage, he runs after him, across a field where a bull is grazing. The bull runs after Johnny and knocks him unconscious. That night, Johnny's father is sent for, but even his presence can't bring Johnny out of his delirium. They plead with Uncle Remus to come to see the boy, and he does, soothing the youngster's anxieties and helping him back to normal. Johnny's father and mother now realize how important it is that they stay together.

Soon all is right with the world. Johnny is no longer dependent upon Uncle Remus and can appreciate him as a friend. He romps along with Ginny and his black friend, singing "Zip-a-dee Doo-Dah," conjuring up the cartoon animals that previously only Uncle Remus had been able to bring to life. Seeing them prancing along, Remus can't believe his eyes, and calls for them to wait, running to join them at the crest of the hill as they all join hands and walk into the sunset on what is *truly* a beautiful day.

The critics were virtually unanimous in their appraisal of *Song of the South*. Bosley Crowther wrote that "the ratio of 'live' to cartoon action is approximately two to one, and that is approximately the ratio of its mediocrity to its charm." *Time* thought that "it could have used a much heavier helping of cartooning," claiming that except for the two youngsters, "the live actors are bores."

Even *Variety* concurred. "Story of misunderstood Johnny gets away to an ambling start, and only picks up . . . when the live Uncle Remus segues into the first cartoon sequence . . . the rest of the story, including the confused and insufficiently explained estrangement of the parents, overbalances the three cartoon sequences, and could be cut . . . these cartoon sequences are great stuff."

There is no denying that it is the cartoon segments that make this film. They have a joy, a cheerfulness about them that is absolutely irresistible, and, of course, they are populated with delightful songs, such as the Academy Award winner "Zip-a-dee Doo-Dah," and "Everybody's Got a Laughing Place." The color in these sequences is probably the most bright and vivid ever seen in motion pictures, a quality characteristic of most of Disney's 1940s cartoon output.

The combination of live action and animation is startling, and the transitions used to link them are ingenious, from the first, with a literal burst of blue introducing the live Uncle Remus walking down an animated path, to later, more intricate dissolves. In the first such sequence Brer Rabbit dances about Uncle Remus's feet, casting a shadow as he does! It is virtually impossible to tell where the live film ends and the animation begins, with such later highlights as Uncle Remus lighting the pipe of an old bullfrog who is sitting by the stream fishing.

The cartoon sequences also stand out because they are from the pen of Uncle Remus (Joel Chandler Harris), and rate among the most memorable in American folklore. Their little morals, in showing how brains can always outwit brawn, are cunning, and a treat to watch as Brer Rabbit tries them out on his adversaries.

More than one critic wondered why Disney didn't simply call his film *Uncle Remus* and make total use of these marvelous tales. Of course, this was not Disney's idea at all; he was looking for a new kind of entertainment form, and he believed *Song of the South* was it. In interviews given at the time of the film's release, he

With cartoon storyboards for a background, Disney shares some Uncle Remus with his two discoveries, Luana Patten and Bobby Driscoll. *Courtesy British Film Institute*

indicated that he planned to make most of his films a blend of live action and animation from that time on, including *Alice in Wonderland*.

Song of the South also, being Disney's deepest plunge into live filming, presented him with his first "contract players." Disney was justifiably proud of Bobby Driscoll and Luana Patten, two extremely winning and talented young children, and, just like every other studio in town, signed them to contracts and built them up as his own personal stars over the next few years with considerable success.

Not that they are the only good things about the live sequences. James Baskett, who was then a regular character on the Amos 'n' Andy radio show, is ideal as Uncle Remus, eliciting just the right kind of warmth and humor, and later poignancy, from the character. He and Hattie McDaniel contribute one of the film's most delightful moments, when she sings "Sooner or Later" as she feeds him some of her apple pie.

But not everyone found this kind of setting "charming," particularly some liberal reviewers and Negro organizations. *Time* commented that Uncle Remus was "bound to enrage all educated Negroes, and a number of damnyankees." They were correct. The NAACP, though noting the "remarkable artistic merit" of the film, deplored "the impression it gives of an idyllic master-slave relationship which is a distortion of the facts." The National Urban League called the film "another repetition of the perpetuation of the stereotype casting of the Negro in the servant role, depicting him as indolent, one who handles the truth lightly."

A Disney spokesman, quoted in *PM*, noted that the film did not depict slavery, since it took place after the Civil War, and that Disney "was not trying to put across any message, but was making a sincere effort to depict American folklore, to put the Uncle Remus stories into pictures."

The Disney spokesman also pointed to a review written by Herman Hill in a Negro newspaper, the *Pittsburgh Courier,* reading in part: "The truly sympathetic handling of the entire production from a racial standpoint is calculated . . . to prove of inestimable good in the furthering of interracial relations."

Indeed, protest was not widespread among the American public (certainly not in the South, where the *Atlanta Journal*'s film critic rated the film alongside *Gone With the Wind*), who flocked to see the film and made it a major Disney money-maker, both in its initial release and on reissue in 1956.

It was only in the 1960s, when civil rights became a major concern of the entire United States, that it became clear that *Song of the South* and films of that kind would be touching sensitive spots if shown again. Even the reissue of *Gone With the Wind* in 1967 sparked some (relatively minor) protest among certain Negro groups who objected to the depiction of slavery and southern plantation life.

In February 1970, prompted by one exhibitor's request to make the film available, the Disney company announced, in the pages of *Variety*, that the film was "permanently" withdrawn and would not be shown again.

But by late 1971 Disney executives had second thoughts, probably noting a change in black attitudes, with more tolerance toward the inescapable facts of history, and a more objective acceptance of formerly taboo Hollywood products of the 1930s and 1940s. In January 1972 *Song of the South* was reissued to overwhelming nationwide reaction; reportedly it was one of the most successful reissues in the company's history.

So *Song of the South* is off the shelf once more, and it is a good thing, for, no matter what one's political leanings or racial attitudes, one cannot deny a film's existence. It is difficult to condemn a film of this kind, Uncle Tom accusations notwithstanding, for in spite of its syrupy story line and occasional flaws, *Song of the South* has some of the most delightful moments Disney ever captured on film. It generates a feeling of happiness and peace, and these are commodities that never go out of style—indeed, they are much too scarce nowadays.

FUN & FANCY FREE

RELEASED BY RKO RADIO PICTURES ON SEPTEMBER 27, 1947. Production supervisor: Ben Sharpsteen. Live-action director: William Morgan. Cartoon directors: Jack Kinney, Bill Roberts, Hamilton Luske. Authors: Homer Brightman, Harry Reeves, Ted Sears, Lance Nolley, Eldon Dedini, Tom Oreb. *Bongo* based on an original story by Sinclair Lewis. Directing animators: Ward Kimball, Les Clark, John Lounsbery, Fred Moore, Wolfgang Reitherman. Character animators: Hugh Fraser, Phil Duncan, Judge Whitaker, Arthur Babbitt, John Sibley, Marc Davis, Harvey Toombs, Hal King, Ken O'Brien, Jack Campbell. Backgrounds: Ed Starr, Claude Coats, Art Riley, Brice Mack, Ray Huffine,

Willie the Giant helps concoct a posed still with the principals of *Fun & Fancy Free:* Mickey, Goofy, Donald, Charlie McCarthy, Luana Patten, Edgar Bergen, and Mortimer Snerd.
© *Walt Disney Productions*

Lumpjaw antagonizes happy-go-lucky Bongo in the first half of *Fun & Fancy Free.* © *Walt Disney Productions*

Ralph Hulett. Layout: Donald Da Gradi, Al Zinnen, Ken O'Connor, Hugh Hennesy, John Hench, Glen Scott. Effects animation; George Rowley, Jack Boyd. Musical director: Charles Wolcott. Musical score: Paul J. Smith, Oliver Wallace, Eliot Daniel. Live-action cameraman: Charles P. Boyle. Film editor: Jack Bachom. Process effects: Ub Iwerks. Sound supervision: C. O. Slyfield. Sound recording: Harold J. Steck, Robert Cook. Technicolor color director: Natalie Kalmus. Associate: Morgan Padleford. Running time: 73 minutes.

Songs: "Fun & Fancy Free" by Bennie Benjamin, George Weiss. "Lazy Countryside" by Bobby Worth. "Too Good to Be True," "Say It with a Slap" by Eliot Daniel, Buddy Kaye. "Fee Fi Fo Fum" by Paul J. Smith, Arthur Quenzer. "My Favorite Dream" by William Walsh, Ray Noble. "I'm a Happy-go-lucky Fellow" by Leigh Harline, Ned Washington. "Beanero" by Oliver Wallace. "My, What a Happy Day" by Bill Walsh and Ray Noble.

Cast: Edgar Bergen, Dinah Shore, Luana Patten, Charlie McCarthy, Mortimer Snerd, and the voices of Anita Gordon (The Singing Harp), Cliff Edwards (Jiminy Cricket), Billy Gilbert (The Giant), Clarence Nash (Donald Duck), The Kings Men, The Dinning Sisters, The Starlighters.

Fun & Fancy Free was one of the bread-and-butter movies Disney made after the war to get material into release as quickly as possible, and regain his studio's lost momentum. As such, it is a pleasant enough film, but hardly outstanding. Its greatest notoriety derives from the fact that it is one of the few Disney feature films to include his short-subject stars Mickey Mouse, Donald Duck, and Goofy.

The film opens in a stream, with Jiminy Cricket sailing along on a leaf singing "I'm a Happy-go-lucky Fellow" (originally written and recorded for *Pinocchio*). He goes ashore, and in his wanderings enters a home and finds a

173

doll and teddy bear seated together, looking rather glum. To cheer them up, he puts on a record, *Bongo*, "A Musical Story sung by Dinah Shore."

Bongo the Wonder Bear is a circus star, who rides a unicycle, even on a tightrope, juggles, and dives one hundred feet into a wet sponge. Offstage, however, he is shackled and mistreated by his trainers. During a train ride to the next town, Bongo works up the courage to hop off on his unicycle and flee into the woods. Being a circus animal, he isn't used to the forest and revels in discovering nature's beauty, singing, "I Love to Hang Around a Lazy Countryside."

Bit by bit he tries to accustom himself to nature's ways, and while hunting for food he comes upon a lovely female bear. He absolutely flips, and a dream sequence illustrates his reverie in the form of a heart-themed sequence. All seems idyllic until a ferocious bear, Lumpjaw, arrives on the scene to compete with Bongo for his mate. She turns around and slaps Bongo. He is bewildered. She slaps him again, and he walks away heartbroken. She tries once more, but this time she accidentally slaps Lumpjaw, turning him from a devil into an angel. This leads to an explanation, via song, "[A Bear Likes to] Say It with a Slap," which tells that this is how bears express their love. When Bongo finally figures this out, he runs back to his girl to save her from the clutches of Lumpjaw. This isn't so easy, and he is forced to do battle with the bear; the fight takes them over the river, through a canyon, down a waterfall, into the mountains. After a logrolling climax, Lumpjaw goes sailing down the river and Bongo claims his mate for a happy ending.

Having thus cheered up the dolls, Jiminy notices on the bureau an invitation sent to the dolls' owner, Luana Patten, inviting her to a party being given that evening by Edgar Bergen, Charlie McCarthy, and Mortimer Snerd at the house across the way. He hops over to see what's going on, and joins Edgar and friends, being careful to stay in the background.

The party is charming, and Edgar decides to add to

the fun by telling a story. "I think I'll go out and wind the sundial," Charlie says, trying to escape. But he is held back, and Edgar spins the tale of Happy Valley, which is called that because a Singing Harp spreads joy across the land with her songs. One day a great shadow is cast over the valley, and the Harp disappears. Happy Valley deteriorates into a woeful state. "All was misery," says Bergen. "Just like the eighth grade," adds Charlie.

An example of the local destitution is shown in the plight of three starving farmers, Mickey, Donald, and Goofy. Mickey slices bread for them from their remaining loaf . . . slices so thin they are transparent! Narrator Bergen pays tribute to the fact that Donald doesn't complain, doesn't crack under the pressure. "Shut up!" Donald shouts hysterically, "I can't stand it!" He becomes desperate and suggests killing their pet cow for dinner, but Mickey convinces him it would be much better to sell it. He does, and receives in payment some magic beans. At this point the story becomes "Jack and the Beanstalk," with Mickey, Donald, and Goofy as our collective hero.

The beanstalk grows up into the sky, and the trio set out for the beautiful castle that rests on a cloud in front of them. They encounter Willie the Giant, try to avoid him, and then outsmart him, and make him so angry he locks them up in a treasure chest with the Singing Harp, whom he kidnapped some time ago. He accidentally drops Mickey during this procedure, so while the Harp sings Willie to sleep, Mickey tries to secure the key to the chest and free his friends. He succeeds, but wakes the Giant in the process, and there is a mad chase down the beanstalk; when they get to the bottom, they chop it down and send Willie to an untimely end.

That's the end of the story, but Mortimer is unhappy because they killed the Giant. Bergen tries to explain that he needn't be sad, that it was only a story. At that point the house shakes as the animated Willie lifts up the roof of the house, asking directions! Bergen faints, the Giant apologizes for intruding, and continues down

175

into the Hollywood valley, peeking in buildings, and picking up the Brown Derby to use for a hat.

Fun & Fancy Free is a sometimes uneven blend of elements, but it does have some moments. Jiminy Cricket (drawn with much bolder face lines than when he appeared in *Pinocchio*) has a bright opening tune, and adds some wry comments throughout the film. In the final segment, with Edgar Bergen and company in live-action footage, the camera periodically cuts to the animated Jiminy helping himself to some of the party food.

Bongo, based on a story by Sinclair Lewis, is an innocuous but unaccountably weak featurette. Its story could have been told in five minutes, so the additional footage used is comprised of aimless action and "mood" songs. It is animated much in the style of the Disney shorts, with occasional exceptions when Bongo strolls through the countryside and we see impressive views of a picture-postcard mountain and lake, with a shimmering reflection, lush green countryside, etc. (Incidentally, two of the forest animals who become friendly with Bongo are early incarnations of Chip 'n' Dale, who made their short-subject debut just around this time.)

The countryside idyll, and the dream sequence with a heart motif (one giant heart explodes into a thousand smaller cupids, hearts, etc. . . . Bongo and his girl nestle under a heart-shaped sun in the cotton-candy clouds, when they are swept away by a waterfall that takes them down through a heart-shaped hatch in the bottom of a cloud, etc.), is very nice, but it is impossible to become involved with the characters or the story, because they are *so* rambling and easygoing. This was apparently a general reaction, for several times, both at the time of the feature's release and in subsequent reissues of the short alone, the Disney company tried to build up the character of Bongo, to no avail.

The live-action footage with Edgar Bergen, Luana Patten, and Bergen's famous dummies is quite amusing,

176

and provides a good framework for the forthcoming cartoon, with Charlie McCarthy's wisecracks bringing Bergen down to earth several times when he becomes a bit too sanctimonious in narrating the story.

The Happy Valley segment, which had originally been planned as an extended Mickey Mouse cartoon called *Mickey and the Beanstalk,* is a nice variation on the classic fairy tale, with some particularly bright touches. As usual, most of the big laughs come from Donald Duck's doings, as in the climax when Mickey is trying to get the key into the treasure-chest keyhole. Inside, Donald pushes Goofy aside and walks toward the hole declaring, "Let me have it, Mickey," at which instant the key plunges in and knocks him flat with a funny "honk" sound effect.

The voice of Willie the Giant is amusingly essayed by Billy Gilbert, whose presence is especially noted when Mickey tries to engineer the escape, and succeeds, but accidentally opens the Giant's package of snuff, causing him to "erupt" in a mad sneezing fit—Gilbert's famed specialty.

But again, this sequence is hardly of feature-film caliber, looking more like just what it is: an elongated short subject.

The final live-action sequence, and punch-line gag of the Giant coming to Bergen's house (and donning the Brown Derby afterward), adds a nice offbeat touch to the otherwise standard finish of the story.

With *Fun & Fancy Free*'s theatrical release, most critics welcomed Disney back to his home territory, but noted that he seemed to be "coasting" with such half-hearted fare. It was true, and it was not until the "Wind in the Willows" sequence of *Ichabod and Mr. Toad* that Disney impressed his admirers with the kind of inventiveness they expected of him.

In the 1960s Disney animated a new framework for this feature, with his new character Ludwig von Drake and his pet flea Herman taking the place of Edgar Bergen et al. when the Happy Valley sequence was run on the Disney TV show. *Bongo* was reissued theatrically in

1971, where once again it failed to make an impression with audiences.

MELODY TIME

RELEASED BY RKO RADIO PICTURES ON MAY 27, 1948. Technicolor. Production supervisor: Ben Sharpsteen. Cartoon directors: Clyde Geronimi, Wilfred Jackson, Hamilton Luske, Jack Kinney. Story: Winston Hibler, Harry Reeves, Ken Anderson, Erdman Penner, Homer Brightman, Ted Sears, Joe Rinaldi, Art Scott, Bob Moore, Bill Cottrell, Jesse Marsh, John Walbridge. "Little Toot" by Hardie Gramatky. Folklore consultant: Carl Carmer. Directing animators: Eric Larson, Ward Kimball, Milt Kahl, Oliver Johnston, Jr., John Lounsbery, Les Clark. Character animators: Harvey Toombs, Ed Aardal, Cliff Nordberg, John Sibley, Ken O'Brien, Judge Whitaker, Marvin Woodward, Hal King, Don Lusk, Rudy Larriva, Bob Cannon, Hal Ambro. Backgrounds: Art Riley, Brice Mack, Ralph Hulett, Ray Huffine, Merle Cox, Dick Anthony. Layout: Hugh Hennesy, A. Kendall O'Connor, Al Zinnen, Don Griffith, McLaren Stewart, Lance Nolley, Robert Cormack, Thor Putnam, Donald Da Gradi. Effects animation: George Rowley, Jack Boyd, Joshua Meador, Hal McManus. Color and styling: Mary Blair, Claude Coats, Dick Kelsey. Musical directors: Eliot Daniel, Ken Darby. Associate: Paul J. Smith. Special arrangements: Vic Schoen, Al Sack. Technicolor color director: Natalie Kalmus. Associate: Morgan Padleford. Live-action photography: Winton Hoch, A.S.C. Special processes: Ub Iwerks. Film editors: Donald Halliday, Thomas Scott. Sound director: C. O. Slyfield. Sound recording: Robert O. Cook, Harold J. Steck. Running time: 75 minutes.

Songs: "Melody Time" by George Weiss and Bennie Benjamin. "Little Toot" by Allie Wrubel. "The Lord Is Good to Me," "The Apple Song," "The Pioneer Song" by Kim Gannon and Walter Kent. "Once Upon a Wintertime" by Bobby Worth, Ray Gilbert. "Blame It on the Samba" by Ernesto Nazareth, Ray Gilbert. "Blue Shadows on the Trail," "Pecos Bill" by Eliot Daniel, Johnny Lange. Also featuring "Trees," poem by Joyce Kilmer, music by Oscar Rasbach, and "The Flight of the Bumble Bee" by Rimsky-Korsakov.

Cast: Roy Rogers, Luana Patten, Bobby Driscoll, Ethel Smith, Bob Nolan, Sons of the Pioneers, and the voices of Buddy Clark, The Andrews Sisters, Fred Waring and his Pennsylvanians, Frances Langford, Dennis Day, with Freddy Martin and his Orchestra featuring Jack Fina.

Melody Time was the last of Disney's musical mélanges, and certainly the best. In its choice of material, presentation, and artistic style it managed to avoid most of the pitfalls of its predecessors and emerge as a solidly enjoyable outing.

The opening titles are shown as sheet music. At the conclusion of the titles, a brush and palette appear, and the brush paints a comic masque (voiced by Buddy Clark) who introduces the first number. Thereafter, he is not seen, but heard, introducing each sequence as the brush paints a title logo and voice credit.

Frances Langford sings "Once Upon a Wintertime," which is done as a greeting-card-come-to-life, with deliberately exaggerated characters and backgrounds, as the song is illustrated with a boy and girl going skating, having a quarrel, and ending as he saves her from drowning, for a happy reconciliation. The actions of the boy and girl are duplicated by a pair of young rabbits who go through the same cycle. The whole sequence is shown as a flashback, as we see a double-hinged picture frame of the couple, much older and married, in a Victo-

Luana Patten and Bobby Driscoll listen as Roy Rogers and the Sons of the Pioneers spin the tale of Pecos Bill in *Melody Time*. *Movie Star News*

rian living room.

Bumble Boogie is a jazz interpretation of "The Flight of the Bumble Bee" with Freddy Martin and his Orchestra, featuring Jack Fina at the piano. Our host describes it as an "instrumental nightmare," and that it is, with a bumblebee caught in a surreal musical world, chased by piano hammers across an endlessly winding musical staff, repeatedly encountering blockades and such, all with musical motifs.

Next is the story of *Johnny Appleseed*, with Dennis Day doing the voices of Johnny, the Old Settler, and Johnny's Angel, in telling the story of this famous folklore hero who follows his guardian angel's advice to "get on the wagon rollin' west," and finds his purpose in life as he travels around the land planting apple trees, which bring so much pleasure to people in so many ways.
180

When it comes time to die, the Angel awakens him from a nap, and he leaves his "mortal husk" behind as the two of them march off to Heaven, where, Johnny is told, there aren't yet any apple trees. That's why, the narrator explains, when he sees a majestic group of clouds in the sky, they aren't clouds at all, but apple blossoms.

The Andrews Sisters sing the story of *Little Toot,* a young tugboat who wants to be as successful as his Dad, but keeps getting into mischief and disgracing his poor father. As punishment, Little Toot is sent out beyond the twelve-mile limit, but while out there one night, a ship becomes lost in a storm, and Little Toot brings it in, against all odds, safely to port, making himself a hero and reinstating his Dad for a happy ending.

"Trees," sung by Fred Waring and his Pennsylvanians, is the film's only nod to "art," in a sweeping mosaic of images illustrating Kilmer's famous poem, showing trees in light, shadow, night, rain, sunshine, sunset, etc., with a provocative punch line as the tree, atop a mountain at the end of the storm, is shown, in backlighting courtesy of the sun, to be a cross!

Blame It on the Samba, with Ethel Smith and the Dinning Sisters, reunites Donald Duck and Joe Carioca, who are (literally) blue, until the last member of the trio, The Aracuan Bird, cooks up a dose of the samba that gradually restores their color and perks them up. The Aracuan Bird mixes a giant cocktail in a huge glass, which reveals inside Ethel Smith at the organ. Donald and Joe dive in and join her, dancing on and around her and the organ. Then the backgrounds begin to change behind them, with increasing rapidity, until they return to the Café de Samba for a bright finale.

The last segment in the film is *Pecos Bill,* which opens with lovely views of the desert at night, as Bob Nolan and the Sons of the Pioneers sing "Blue Shadows." After this haunting panorama, we see, in long shot, Roy Rogers, the Sons, and young Bobby Driscoll and Luana Patten gathered around a campfire in the midst of this animated desert. When Bobby asks Roy why coyotes

181

Johnny Appleseed tests out a prime specimen.
© Walt Disney Productions

howl at the moon, Roy answers by telling the tale of Pecos Bill, a famous tall tale about a boy who was raised by coyotes until he could outdo every animal in the land at their own game. He finds his match in a wonder horse, Widowmaker, and the two are inseparable pals, until Bill meets the beautiful Slue Foot Sue, a heck of a cowgirl, and falls madly in love with her. They decide to get married, and on her wedding day Sue determines to ride the stubborn Widowmaker, who hasn't liked her from the start. He gives her a hard time, and finally throws her; she lands on her bustle, which bounces her into the air. Every time she lands, she bounces higher, and no one, not even Bill, can catch her. Pretty soon she's bouncing up into outer space, toward the moon, from which she never returns. Heartbroken, Bill returns to the coyotes, and every night howls at the moon for his poor Slue Foot Sue.

Melody Time is an extremely winning film, and if it hasn't the brilliance of Disney's more coherent animated features, it does have a number of points to recommend it. For one thing, there is a very noticeable move away from literalism in all the segments of the film, encompassing various styles of drawing. *Once Upon a Wintertime* strives for a greeting-card effect, and, in keeping with that style, uses unreal colors, using what would look interesting or attractive, not necessarily what would look natural. There is a good ice-floe sequence, but even here there is only the impression of a rushing river, whereas a few years earlier in a Disney feature it would have been detailed down to the last bubble.

This is also true of *Johnny Appleseed*, where the trees have no detail, no leaves (in the style adopted by most cartoon producers during the 1950s); Johnny's cabin is *blue*, and the rolling hills in the background are done in an impressionistic, rather than realistic, style.

Bumble Boogie is a successful attempt to duplicate the feel of the surreal "After You've Gone," which was the best-received segment of *Make Mine Music*, and, again, it is short, sweet, and full of marvelous surreal cartoon images that make it a unique Disney work, not a literal transformation of live action into animated form.

Trees is done in Disney's consciously arty method of animation, although unlike such former endeavors as "Blue Bayou," it at least has a theme to work with and some sense of direction. Many of the images *are* beautiful, and some of the visual ideas are quite striking: the reflection of the sun breaking through a rainstorm turns out to be a drop of water from which the camera

183

pulls *way* back to move into the next scene. Similarly, a close-up of the colorful sky becomes a multicolored leaf when the camera pulls back and reveals a flurry of leaves swirling about.

Blame It on the Samba revives the style and feel of *The Three Caballeros,* and rather well, although not going to some of the extremes of that feature. Still, there are many complex ideas in the brisk-moving sequence, starting when Donald and Joe dance with Ethel Smith as she and the organ float around a full 360 degrees, then joining her in the jungle where she plays conga drums that illuminate on every beat, and continuing to samba as the backgrounds change behind them in a window-shade format of dissolves.

Pecos Bill marks the first encounter between Disney and the famous American tall tales, and it is a felicitous collaboration. The best moments in *Pecos Bill* are those that bring to life the marvelous exaggerations: Bill roping a cyclone, igniting his cigarette with a bolt of lightning, digging the Rio Grande as an irrigation ditch, etc. In fact, one wishes there were even more of such material in the segment, for this, one feels, is what cartoons are all about—to present precisely this kind of visual hyperbole that captures the viewer's imagination with its very impossibility. (Disney knew when he had a good thing, and went on to animate Paul Bunyan and other famous folklore heroes.)

The feature is filled with good songs, notably the score for *Johnny Appleseed,* well sung by Dennis Day, "The Lord Is Good to Me," "The Apple Song," sung by Johnny's angel and amusingly illustrated as he comes to each new apple invention, and "The Pioneer Song." The "Blue Shadows" segment of *Pecos Bill* is also quite lovely, the Western harmonies perfectly matching the beautiful views of nighttime on the prairie.

What *Melody Time* lacks is unity. The paintbrush format and Buddy Clark's introductions are a poor substitute for cohesion, and, though one can enjoy the various segments, there is a feeling, when *Pecos Bill* brings the film to an abrupt conclusion, that something is

184

missing. *Fantasia* was episodic, too, but one felt that it was cut from a whole cloth, as it were. There was never a feeling of fragmentation.

But Disney was counting on the appeal of his seven cartoon segments carrying the film without undue stress on format, and he was right in this respect. Bosley Crowther echoed most of the critical faction when he dubbed the film "a gaudy grab-bag show in which a couple of items are delightful, and the rest are just adequate fillers-in." Once more, there was that cry for the genius that Disney had shown once upon a time.

As with the other omnibus features, *Melody Time* did not receive reissue as a complete feature; instead, the segments were cut up and rereleased separately, *Johnny Appleseed* having the longest life outside of this feature in theatres and on the Disney TV show. Two of the segments, *Trees* and *Bumble Boogie*, were reissued together as a new short subject called *Contrasts in Rhythm*.

SO DEAR TO MY HEART

RELEASED BY RKO RADIO PICTURES ON JANUARY 19, 1949. Technicolor. Director: Harold Schuster. Screenplay: John Tucker Battle, based on the book *Midnight and Jeremiah* by Sterling North. Photoplay art director: John Ewing. Director of photography: Winton C. Hoch, A.S.C. Editors: Thomas Scott, Lloyd L. Richardson. Musical score: Paul J. Smith. Vocal director: Ken Darby. Orchestrations: Edward H. Plumb. Music editor: Al Teeter. Photoplay set director: Mac Alper. Special process shots: Ub Iwerks. Sound director: C. O. Slyfield. Sound recording: Max Hutchinson, Robert O. Cook. Technical director: Larry Lansburgh. Technicolor color director: Natalie Kalmus. Associate: Morgan Padleford. Associate producer: Perce Pearce. Cartoon director: Hamilton Luske. Cartoon story treatment: Marc Davis, Ken Anderson, William Peet. Cartoon art treatment: John Hench, Mary Blair, Dick Kelsey. Cartoon layout: A. Kendall O'Connor, Hugh Hennesy, Don Griffith, Thor Putnam. Cartoon backgrounds: Art Riley, Ralph Hulett, Jim Trout, Dick Anthony, Brice Mack, Ray Huffine. Animators: Eric Larson, John Lounsbery, Hal King, Milt Kahl, Les Clark, Don Lusk, Marvin Woodward. Effects animation: George Rowley, Joshua Meador, Dan McManus. Running time: 84 minutes.

Songs: "So Dear to My Heart" by Ticker Freeman and Irving Taylor. "Ol' Dan Patch," "Lavender Blue (Dilly Dilly)," "Stick-to-it-ivity" by Eliot Daniel and Larry Morey. "It's Whatcha Do with Whatcha Got" by Don Raye and Gene DePaul. "County Fair" by Robert Wells and Mel Torme.

Cast: Burl Ives (Uncle Hiram), Beulah Bondi (Granny Kincaid), Harry Carey (judge), Luana Patten (Tildy), Bobby Driscoll (Jeremiah Kincaid), Raymond Bond (storekeeper), Walter Soderling (villager), Mat Willis (horse trainer), Spelman B. Collins, and the voices of John Beal, Ken Carson, Bob Stanton, and The Rhythmaires.

There has been a lot of talk about nostalgia, but if a working definition were needed, one could point to *So Dear to My Heart* as a personification of the word. It is one of Disney's finest live-action films, brimming with period (1903) atmosphere and detail, rich characterizations, and moving performances. Although cast in the same mold as *Song of the South,* it is a much better film, and, unlike its predecessor, is essentially live action, with a few brief animated sequences. Indeed, if anything, it is the cartoon material that seems intrusive, not the live action.

The film opens in an attic, as the camera moves in on an old scrapbook. The pages turn, showing drawings of the country locale of the story, with mementos of the

Beulah Bondi and Burl Ives worry about Bobby Driscoll's latest mischief in *So Dear to My Heart.* © *Walt Disney Productions*

period: cutouts, a Christmas card, an old calendar, an old-fashioned valentine, each one leading into a short animated vignette, as a chorus sings the theme song of the picture. The final picture dissolves into a live-action establishing shot of the farm where our first-person narrator lived as a small boy, the Kincaid homestead, with Granny plowing the field outside.

The off-screen voice reminisces about what it was like, as we go down the main street, visit the general store, and witness the arrival of the famed trotting horse Dan Patch, who is taken for a short trot to stretch his legs during a break in a long railroad trip. The chorus sings "So Dear to My Heart," as this introductory segment concludes with a shot of the Kincaid house at night, where the story begins.

187

The family sheep is about to give birth, and Jeremiah goes out to the barn with Granny to witness the event. There are twins, one white and one black. The mother shuns the black sheep, and, seeing this, Jeremiah decides to adopt it himself. Granny doesn't like the idea, but when she sees how sincere the boy is, she gives in.

In the next scene Jeremiah pastes a picture of the lamb (named Danny, after Dan Patch) in his scrapbook. The scrapbook is full of wise sayings, and an owl who accompanies most of them comes to life and sings to Jeremiah that "it's what you do with what you got that counts," explaining that there's nothing wrong with being a black sheep.

Except, of course, that over the next few months Danny grows up and becomes quite mischievous. Jeremiah's strongest ally in defending the sheep to Granny is Uncle Hiram, the town blacksmith and handyman. He puts the idea in the boy's head that he might train Danny and take him to the county fair to compete. Granny is dead set against the idea, but that night the owl in Jeremiah's scrapbook comes to life again to sing to him of "Stick-to-it-ivity," illustrating his point with the stories of Columbus, who crossed the sea in spite of a brutal storm, and Robert Bruce, who was inspired to go into battle in Scotland after several defeats when he saw the doggedness of a spider trying to spin his web.

Jeremiah is inspired to earn his own money to go to the fair, and is told by the local storekeeper that honey is scarce, and he would gladly pay ten cents a pound for it. Jeremiah and his young girl friend Tildy spot a honeybee in the nearby field and follow it "home" into the swamp, where they discover a busy hive that yields (with Hiram's assistance) some seventeen dollars' worth of honey.

All looks well for the county fair trip, until one night when Danny runs away. Despite a severe thunderstorm, Jeremiah goes out into the night to look for Danny, and Granny has to drag him home. She gives him a stern lecture, telling him that he no longer loves the lamb as he once did, that his only reason for now wanting to go to

188

Bobby Driscoll and "Danny" receive a special award from Judge Harry Carey. © 1964 Walt Disney Productions

the fair is self-gratification. She is particularly shocked when she warns him that the Lord may not spare Danny during the night, and he refuses to accept it. She tells him how ashamed she is of his attitude.

The next morning Jeremiah is up at the crack of dawn, and soon returns with the lamb, safe and sound. But he announces that he isn't going to the fair, because last night he promised God that if He spared the lamb, he wouldn't go. Granny, fighting back tears, tells the boy that she too made a promise to God, that if He spared the lamb they *would* go, and since she has known Him longer than Jeremiah, He won't mind him overlooking his favor in deference to hers.

A souvenir program from the fair in Jeremiah's scrapbook comes to life, and introduces the wondrous event. Before the competition Granny tells the boy that no matter what happens, he must come out of that arena proud, in the tradition of the Kincaids. When the judge comes around to Jeremiah and his lamb, the boy is forced to admit that his pet has no pedigree, unlike his competitors. To make matters worse, as the judge is leaving, Danny butts him in the rear. Sure enough, another sheep wins the Blue Ribbon. But as Jeremiah is leaving the arena, the judge makes another announcement. He declares that Danny is something special: a lamb with no special background, who has been made a prize animal by love and care. "It's what you do with what you got that counts," he explains, in presenting Danny and his owner with the Award of Special Merit, being given for the first time in forty years.

When the ecstatic group returns home, Hiram emerges from the train and "clears the way" for Danny in the same way that Dan Patch's owner had done for the famous horse. The whole town is out to greet their famous son, and his return is cause for celebration. We dissolve back to the scrapbook in the attic, and the film ends as it began.

So Dear to My Heart is a truly lovely film; its characters and their emotions are real and vivid, and this is what makes the film a special experience.

Although one seldom thinks of directors exerting their own style and influence on a Disney film, this was an instance of selecting the ideal man for the job.

Says Harold Schuster today:

At my first meeting with Walt Disney he told me that he had run *My Friend Flicka* at his home, and that Mrs. Disney and his two daughters had liked it so much that they had run it many times. He said that he felt I was the right director for *So Dear to My Heart* and that he would like me to read the book. After reading the book and the first draft screenplay I was

190

very enthusiastic over the project; also, the idea of working with Walt Disney appealed to me greatly. I told him so and how I felt, which seemed to please him. I was under contract at 20th Century–Fox at the time, so things were arranged with my home studio, and I was on my way.

During the preparatory period I worked with the writer, John Battle, on the screenplay, had meetings with Walt and Perce Pearce, the producer, on a wide variety of subjects including story, sets, music, casting, etc. Also during this period I made trips to the location, which was in the San Joaquin valley, near the town of Visalia. Also in Sequoia National Park where some of the sets were built. This whole area is very lush with olive, grape, and cotton farming, one of the loveliest valleys in the world. At Walt's suggestion I brought my first assistant, Jasper Blystone, over from 20th. He wanted to have as many pros with me as possible, as from what I gathered, they had lost production time on *Song of the South*.

Casting was simplified by the fact that Bobby Driscoll and Luana Patten were already under contract, and ideal for the two juvenile roles. Of the former, *Time* wrote: "Bobby Driscoll is a rarity among child actors; when relaxed, he is an attractive kid, and when called upon to act, he is not at all repellent." Schuster suggested using Beulah Bondi, having worked with her before. A test was made of Burl Ives, as this was his first film, and, like Bondi, he proved to be ideal. Choosing Harry Carey to play the judge was a sentimental decision for Schuster, who had worked with John Ford and shared with the director a warm affection for this marvelous character actor. Alas, Carey did not live to see the film's release; he died in late 1947 at the age of sixty-nine.

As was now standard practice, elaborate storyboards were drawn for each scene, and careful thought was given to the transitions from live action to animation and back again. These are extremely well handled in the

191

Beulah Bondi, Walt Disney, and director Harold Schuster discuss a scene on location. *From the private collection of Harold Schuster*

film, most memorably in the first animated segment, where Danny the lamb is shown romping through various pages of the scrapbook. He reaches a fence and starts to leap over it, when the camera cuts to live action and the live animal bursts through Granny's screen door.

The animated sequences themselves are quite charming, although, with hindsight, one wonders just how necessary they were. In the film they serve the function of instilling certain attitudes in the young hero, but these points probably could have been settled in another manner if Disney had so desired. But just at this point he wasn't ready to abandon cartoons entirely. (Indeed, one might speculate that the success of this predominantly live-action film might have given Disney enough confidence to proceed with his first *all* live-action endeavor.) And Disney explained: "I saw the cartoon characters as figments of a small boy's imagination, and I think they were justified." The cartoon segments are done in a stylized method not seen before; the earliest scenes try to maintain the idea of an old-fashioned scrapbook come to life, with great success. The longest animated sequence is tied to the song "Stick-to-it-ivity." When the owl talks about Columbus facing a bitter storm, the visual style is that of a children's storybook, with the howling wind given a human face. In the tale of Robert Bruce there is a different kind of stylization, the major battle scene depicted in abstract figures, harshly shown with contrasty shadows and directional lighting, concluding with Bruce standing triumphant atop the castle he has taken, holding his gleaming sword against the bright blue sky.

The songs, considering their direct function to the story, are quite pleasant in conveying their message. But the film's true musical highlight is an extended scene where Burl Ives comes calling on Beulah Bondi and sings "Lavender Blue," duetting with her on "Billy Boy."

More than anything else, however, the film oozes with atmosphere, this the result of having chosen such a perfect location, and making optimum use of it (although one establishing shot of the Kincaid home at night employs an animated sky). One hazard was carefully avoided; shooting started much later in summer than had been planned, and the countryside had begun to dry up. So every night twenty-seven "greens men" worked diligently watering the soil and plants that they might look fresh and green for the camera in the morning.

Says Schuster:

Some of the interior sets were built on the location in conjunction with the exteriors, mostly because there was only the one small stage at the studio. The Grundy store was one of these. They found an old, and I mean old, hardware store near the town of Porterville. It was closed, and the various wares

193

inside were bought lock, stock, and barrel, and moved into the Grundy store. Both the barn and Granny's house were built on the location. The railroad station was already there as were the railroad tracks. We rented the old engine and cars from Paramount, who had used them for *Union Pacific*.

Walt would come up sometimes on weekends, we would have Sunday breakfast, and talk over the rushes. He was a very enthusiastic gentleman, and a joy to be around. His suggestions were always presented as suggestions only. He left the reins firmly in my hands.

This was a method that may have come as a surprise to Disney's staff of animators and cartoon directors, who were well accustomed to Disney's involvement with every phase of production. But Disney realized, early on, that the only way live-action filming would get done would be if he stayed out of the director's way and confined his ideas to the preparation stages or post-production. This made him extremely popular with visiting directors, who without exception found assignments on the Disney lot to be rewarding experiences, especially after having dealt with the production heads of other Hollywood studios.

Asked if he felt there was a conscious effort to duplicate the feel of *Song of the South*, Schuster replies:

As far as I know there was no conscious effort to form *So Dear to My Heart* into any previous mold. Any resemblance to *Song of the South* would only reflect the Disney studio's general attitudes about what constituted entertainment. In the sense that Walt's selection of screen subjects remained consistent with his beliefs, one might agree that *Song* and *So Dear* were generically members of the same family.

The reviews of *So Dear to My Heart* were among the most favorable Disney had received in several years.

Variety called it "a first-rate job of sentimental story-telling," and Howard Barnes in the *New York Herald Tribune* declared that "Walt Disney has finally found a gracious and engaging formula for blending real drama with the pictorial imagination of an animated cartoon."

The film's only problem was one of timing, coming as it did at the tail end of a cycle of Hollywood films based on turn-of-the-century nostalgia: *Meet Me in St. Louis, State Fair, Centennial Summer*, etc., a fact that was noted by most of the reviewers.

So Dear to My Heart held another drawback for the Disney company, in that it wasn't as easy a film to "sell" as most previous efforts; there were no characters to build up, or sources to boast of (even though it had been adapted from Sterling North's *Midnight and Jeremiah*, which had been a popular book). Its simple story, simply told, made it less marketable than, say, *Song of the South*, and, as a result, it never made as much money in its initial release or in reissue as other Disney features.

But it was a source of personal satisfaction for Disney. He told one reporter: "*So Dear* was especially close to me. Why, that's the life my brother and I grew up with as kids out in Missouri. The great racehorse, Dan Patch, was a hero to us. We had Dan Patch's grandson on my father's farm."

It remains today one of his loveliest films.

ICHABOD AND MR. TOAD

RELEASED BY RKO RADIO PICTURES ON OCTOBER 5, 1949 (originally reviewed in the trade press as *The Adventures of Ichabod and Mr. Toad*). Technicolor. Production supervisor: Ben Sharpsteen. Directors: Jack Kinney, Clyde Geronimi, James Algar. Directing animators: Franklin Thomas, Oliver Johnson, Jr., Wolfgang Reitherman, Milt Kahl, John Lounsbery, Ward

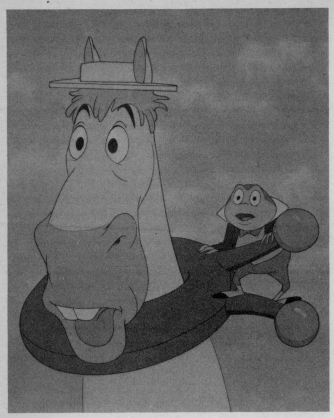

Cyril and Mr. Toad express wide-eyed wonderment at one point of *The Wind in the Willows*. © *Walt Disney Productions*

Kimball. Story: Erdman Penner, Winston Hibler, Joe Rinaldi, Ted Sears, Homer Brightman, Harry Reeves. Character animators: Fred Moore, John Sibley, Marc Davis, Hal Ambro, Harvey Toombs, Hal King, Hugh Fraser, Don Lusk. Backgrounds: Ray Huffine, Merle Cox, Art Riley, Brice Mack. Layout: Charles Philippi, Tom Codrick, Thor Putnam, Al Zinnen, Hugh Hennesy, Lance Nolley. Effects animation: George Rowley, Jack

Boyd. Music director: Oliver Wallace. Vocal arrangements: Ken Darby. Orchestrations: Joseph Dubin. Film editor: John O. Young. Color and styling. Claude Coats, Mary Blair, Donald Da Gradi, John Hench. Special processes: Ub Iwerks. Sound director: C. O. Slyfield. Sound recording: Robert O. Cook. Music editor: Al Teeter. Based on "The Legend of Sleepy Hollow" by Washington Irving and "The Wind in the Willows" by Kenneth Grahame. Running time: 68 minutes.

Songs: "Ichabod," "Katrina," "The Headless Horseman" by Don Raye, Gene DePaul. "Merrily on Our Way," music by Frank Churchill and Charles Wolcott, lyrics by Larry Morey and Ray Gilbert.

"Ichabod" narrated by Bing Crosby. "Willows" narrated by Basil Rathbone, with the voices of Eric Blore (Mr. Toad), Pat O'Malley (Cyril), Claud Allister (Water Rat), John Ployardt (prosecutor), Collin Campbell (Mole), Campbell Grant (Angus MacBadger), Ollie Wallace (Winky).

In the late 1940s Disney admirers were seriously worried that the filmmaker was slipping into a pattern of mass-audience mediocrity. The first film to really reassert Disney's staff as the leading exponents of animated film was *Ichabod and Mr. Toad*, the awkwardly named feature film (originally titled *Two Fabulous Characters*) comprised of two half-hour sequences: Kenneth Grahame's *The Wind in the Willows* and Washington Irving's *The Legend of Sleepy Hollow*.

The film opens on a stained-glass window and moves inside to a colorful library, dollying closer and closer to the bookshelf, where we see one volume with Mr. Toad stamped in gold on the red spine. The book comes off the shelf and opens to the title page; we flip through the first few pages, in storyboard style, as narrator Basil Rathbone sets the scene for the story.

It seems that Toad Hall has been in uproar ever since

Ichabod Crane runs head on into the Headless Horseman in *The Legend of Sleepy Hollow.* © *Walt Disney Productions*

J. Thaddeus Toad has adopted a horse (named Cyril) and carriage. The two go prancing along singing "We're merrily on our way to nowhere in particular," when the fun-loving Toad spies an automobile for the first time. "A motorcar!" he exults, "what have I been missing!" His eyes become a whirlpool as he drifts off into flights of fancy, imagining himself to *be* a motorcar. His friends, Rat and Mole, lock him up for the night, for his own good, but he escapes, and the next morning is arrested for having stolen a car.

In court all seems hopeless until the bartender, Winky, is called on to testify. Only he can tell the truth, knowing that Toad did not steal the car, but traded Toad Hall for it to a bunch of crafty weasels. But when Winky gets on the stand, he says that Toad *did* steal the car! Toad is convicted and sentenced to prison.

That Christmas, Cyril helps Toad escape from jail, and sets about, with his friends, to prove himself innocent. They discover that he was framed, since Winky and the weasels have taken the deed of Toad Hall for their own. Toad and his comrades go to the Hall to recapture the deed, and engage in a slam-bang fight for the valuable scroll, eventually emerging victorious. Toad is cleared, and his friends relax, now that Toad has "reformed" his ways. Then they look out the window and see Toad and Cyril riding Toad's latest discovery, an airplane.

The camera then moves into an adjoining library and Bing Crosby assumes the narration as *The Legend of Sleepy Hollow* comes off the shelf and opens to a map that sets up the locale of our story. Ichabod Crane is the new schoolmaster in town; he likes his job, because he can depend on free dinners from the mothers of his students. He also wins over the young ladies of the town by giving them singing lessons.

When he first spies a beautiful young lass named Katrina Van Tassel, Ichabod falls hopelessly in love, and she returns the favor. But the town's self-styled Don Juan, a burly fellow named Brom Bones, isn't giving up Katrina so easily. He can't make any headway over the
200

effortlessly charming Mr. Crane, until he discovers Ichabod's Achilles' heel: he is wildly superstitious.

At a Halloween party given by Katrina, Brom tells the story of the Headless Horseman, and frightens the wits out of poor Ichabod, who has to ride home late that night, alone, through Sleepy Hollow. His imagination runs wild, and before long he sees the Horseman, laughing satanically as he holds a jack-o'-lantern in one hand. Ichabod runs for his life, toward the wooden bridge that means safety, but before he can get across, the Headless Horseman throws the jack-o'-lantern straight for Ichabod's head.

There is a dissolve to the following morning; all that's left at the scene of the incident is a smashed pumpkin, and Ichabod's hat lying on the ground. It was rumored that Ichabod merely moved away and started life anew in a nearby town, married to a local widow, but the residents of Sleepy Hollow know better, as they reprise Brom Bones's song: "Don't try to figure out a plan; You can't reason with a Headless Man!"

Ichabod and Mr. Toad is one of Disney's most beguiling animated features; *The Wind in the Willows* in particular has some of the finest work the studio ever did.

This opening sequence is a marvel of perfection, first in the casting of the voices. Basil Rathbone's crisp narration provides a nice contrast to the veddy-British tinge of the others. Eric Blore simply *is* Mr. Toad, the wild-eyed, whimsical hero of the tale. (Indeed, the choice was so natural that Disney thought of it back in 1941, when the project was first announced.) Pat O'Malley and the others provide first-rate support.

The fanciful air of Kenneth Grahame's story, written in 1908, is perfectly captured by Disney with a multitude of subtle touches and skillful direction. When Rat lectures Toad on his foolishness, Toad holds his hands over his ears, and the sound track becomes muffled. Intrigued with the effect, Toad tries it out continually during his friend's tirade.

The trial is perhaps the highlight of the film. The prosecuting attorney is shown most frequently as a flowing cape, leaving the witness box after a successful questing. Toad acts as his own counsel, striking hilarious poses as a British barrister, complete with wig and monocle (which he nonchalantly polishes during his speech). When Winky gets on the witness stand, he absentmindedly begins to polish the rail, as he would his bar.

The jail and subsequent breakout segment is masterfully done. Full of remorse, Toad cries, creating a puddle on the floor of his cell. Each teardrop landing in the puddle conjures up a picture of one of his friends. Then Cyril gets in to see him, disguised as his mother; he whispers his scheme to Toad, as the camera moves in to watch Toad's eyes widen and start turning into whirlpools, growing larger and larger. Suddenly there is a cut to clouds of smoke, which clear to reveal escape whistles blowing in the night. A succession of images follows: a bobby on the telephone, searchlights on the prison walls, bobbies riding into the streets on bicycle, in the nighttime fog, etc., before we see Toad running ahead of them, excited and confused. He jumps onto a train about to pull out of the station, and dives off when it goes over a river trestle.

The battle for the repossession of the deed is cunningly choreographed, with Toad, Rat, and Mole doing their best to outwit the band of weasels—people running back and forth, over and under each other, etc.

Key points in the story are told via newspaper headlines. When Toad escapes in search of an automobile, narrator Rathbone says: "He was determined to get a motorcar, even if he had to beg, borrow, or—" and the sentence is finished with the flash of a morning headline: TOAD ARRESTED. After the fracas with the weasels, Toad emerges holding the deed, and another newspaper flashes before the camera, reading: TOAD EXONERATED/GOOD NAME CLEARED.

The Legend of Sleepy Hollow lacks this kind of invention, for it has a totally different feel, exemplified by the choice of Bing Crosby as narrator. Easygoing Bing wastes no time in making his mark on the film, referring to its hero as "old Icky" and telling the story in both words and music (nicely kidding himself when, as Ichabod giving voice lessons, he warbles "boo-boo-boo-boo").

The gags come fast and funny throughout the film, with dozens of throwaways, in depicting Ichabod's lack of dedication to the teaching profession (either daydreaming about food, or later, daydreaming about Katrina), and more broadly in his competition with Brom Bones for Katrina's attention.

Naturally, the showiest part of the film is Ichabod's ride home at night, which is masterfully done. Clouds close in on the moon above; trees seem to close in on him as he passes them entering the forest. His whistle is eerily echoed . . . the wind blows the leaves about . . . there are strange cries in the night . . . fireflies form "eyes" inside a tree hollow . . . crickets seem to be chirping his name, and the frogs seem to be saying "headless horseman, headless horseman."

Ichabod tries to convince himself that all of this is innocent, and is relieved when his eyes betray most of these incidents for what they really are. Then, suddenly, he sees it: a black figure in a scarlet cape, perched upon a formidable black stallion pawing the air in defiance, backlit against the sky, the Horseman laughing wickedly, sparks flying from his horse's hooves, brandishing a sword in one hand and a jack-o'-lantern in the other. It really is a frightening vision, and gives impetus to the frantic chase scene that follows, with Ichabod scrambling for the wooden bridge.

Together, these sequences form a most engaging feature, with, as the saying goes, something for everyone. The half-hour length seems ideal for each of the stories, with neither a feeling of abruptness nor a hint of padding to reach that length. And somehow the two tales seem to complement each other quite well, providing an interesting contrast, notable in style and execution, and more obviously in the change of narrator.

Although there was some mild carping about toying with Kenneth Grahame's original (with the addition of Cyril and Winky to the plot), the reaction to *Ichabod and Mr. Toad* was generally favorable, *Time* magazine particularly praising the first half, saying, "This lighthearted, fast-moving romp has inspired some of Disney's most inventive draftsmanship and satire." (No one pointed out one mild economy measure, in the artists' using the model of Grace Martin from the *Martins and Coys* sequence of *Make Mine Music* for Katrina in *Sleepy Hollow*. Both bore a close resemblance, as well, to Slue Foot Sue in *Pecos Bill*.)

Both sequences have proved to be hardy Disney perennials, in single reissue and television exposure.

CINDERELLA

RELEASED BY RKO RADIO PICTURES ON FEBRUARY 15, 1950. Production supervisor: Ben Sharpsteen. From the original story by Charles Perrault. Directors: Wilfred Jackson, Hamilton Luske, Clyde Geronimi. Directing animators: Eric Larson, Ward Kimball, Norman Ferguson, Marc Davis, John Lounsbery, Milt Kahl, Wolfgang Reitherman, Les Clark, Oliver Johnston, Jr., Franklin Thomas. Story: Kenneth Anderson, Ted Sears, Homer Brightman, Joe Rinaldi, William Peet, Harry Reeves, Winston Hibler, Erdman Penner. Character animators: Marvin Woodward, Hal Ambro, George Nicholas, Hal King, Judge Whitaker, Fred Moore, Hugh Fraser, Phil Duncan, Cliff Nordberg, Ken O'Brien, Harvey Toombs, Don Lusk. Backgrounds: Dick Anthony, Merle Cox, Ralph Hulett, Brice Mack, Ray Huffine, Art Riley, Thelma Witmer. Layout: A. Kendall O'Connor, Thor Putnam, Charles Philippi, Tom Codrick, Don Griffith, McLaren Stewart, Lance Nolley, Hugh

Hennesy. Effects animation: George Rowley, Joshua Meador, Jack Boyd. Music directors: Oliver Wallace, Paul J. Smith. Orchestrations: Joseph Dubin. Film editor: Donald Halliday. Color and styling: Claude Coats, Mary Blair, Donald Da Gradi, John Hench. Special processes: Ub Iwerks. Sound director: C. O. Slyfield. Sound recording: Harold J. Steck, Robert O. Cook. Music editor: Al Teeter. Running time: 74 minutes.

Songs: "Bibbidi Bobbidi Boo," "So This Is Love," "A Dream Is a Wish Your Heart Makes," "Cinderella," "The Work Song," "Sing, Sweet Nightingale" by Mack David, Jerry Livingston, Al Hoffman.

Voices: Ilene Woods (Cinderella), William Phipps (Prince Charming), Eleanor Audley (stepmother), Rhoda Williams, Lucille Bliss (stepsisters), Verna Felton (Fairy Godmother), Luis Van Rooten (King, Grand Duke), James MacDonald (Jacques, Gus), Don Barclay, Claire DuBrey.

Disney had not made a full-length animated feature since *Bambi*. His various pastiches were often well received, but even at their best critics felt that they came nowhere near the heights reached by his initial feature-length efforts.

For his return to this field, Disney chose *Cinderella;* it was hoped that the obvious family relationship to *Snow White* would create audience excitement that had been lacking from the multiepisode cartoons of late.

This return to the fairy-tale genre also provided a challenge to the Disney staff to come up with fresh angles to a timeworn tale. They succeeded remarkably well.

Every child knows the story of Cinderella, who is abused by her cruel stepmother and ugly stepsisters, whose fairy godmother transforms her into a ravishing beauty so she can attend a royal ball, where she completely captivates the Prince. At the stroke of midnight

The birds and the mice get together to make Cinderella's ball gown. © *Walt Disney Productions*

Cinderella's ugly stepsisters have their own way of keeping Cinderella from going to the ball. © *Walt Disney Productions*

she must flee from the ball or be seen as a scullery maid once more. Running off, she drops one glass slipper. The Prince is determined to find the girl he loves, and tests the slipper on each maiden in the kingdom, until he is reunited with Cinderella for a happy ending.

The task facing the Disney staff was similar to that of *Snow White:* to provide enough secondary characters and diversionary sequences to surround this simple and familiar tale. The major inventions along this line were Cinderella's animal friends: Jacques and Gus the mice; the bluebirds; Bruno the dog; and their collective enemy, Lucifer the cat.

The animals figure importantly throughout the film, beginning with the very first scene (after the traditional storybook opening): the little birds awaken Cinderella and help her get up and get dressed, as she sings "A Dream Is a Wish Your Heart Makes." In the midst of this cheery scene, we see the mice waking up too. Jacques is awakened by the singing; he stretches a yawn, licks his hair, brushes it back (it falls back into disarray immediately), and finds, to his annoyance, that his tail has become knotted during the night.

Noise from the hallway sends Cinderella and her friends down the stairs, where they find a mouse caught in one of the traps. He is scared, but Cinderella and her other mouse friends assure him that he is welcome; the chubby rodent says his name is Octavius, but Cinderella rechristens him Gus.

Meanwhile, in the kitchen, the cagey cat Lucifer is making things difficult for Bruno, an extremely easygoing dog. Cinderella tells the cat to live and let live, and goes upstairs to awaken her stepmother and stepsisters.

To get their morning meal the mice must distract Lucifer long enough to sneak out into the yard and bring back provisions. It works, but on the way back Gus takes too much at once, and spills his food, catching Lucifer's eye and leading to a mad chase. The frightened mouse seeks refuge in a teacup, which Cinderella then brings to one of her sisters, with disastrous results. Cinderella is summoned by her stepmother, who accuses her of deliberately playing a wicked joke on the girl.

Throughout the rest of the film, the actions of the humans and the animals are perfectly integrated this way, with one scene leading into another naturally. One can imagine the endless work by story men to achieve this perfectly rounded result.

Other new characters to the tale are the King and Grand Duke. They are upset because the King's son is still single, and apparently has no interest in women. They decide to hold a ball, inviting every eligible female in the kingdom, in the hope that the Prince will find one to his liking.

When Cinderella sadly realizes that she has no time to make a dress for the ball, her animal friends decide to make one for her. This is easily the highlight of the film, an absolutely enchanting sequence that begins with the birds singing "Cinderella" (or, as they pronounce it, "Cinderelly"), bemoaning her fate in this household. This is followed by a parody, as one of the birds sings, "We can do it, we can do it," urging her comrades to help in fashioning a ball gown. Then, as the birds and mice go to work gathering remnants from the sisters' rooms and putting them together, they hum the tune of "A Dream Is a Wish Your Heart Makes."

That night, as the stepmother and two stepsisters are about to leave the house, Cinderella descends the stairway, looking radiant in a beautiful gown. The sisters, ugly and garishly dressed, pounce on Cinderella, recognizing the origin of the various materials, and rip the dress to shreds!

She runs out into the backyard, crying, and there is met by her fairy godmother, who cheers her up as she sings "Bibbidi Bobbidi Boo." A pumpkin turns into a glowing coach with a wave of the fairy's wand; the mice become noble horses; a horse becomes a stylish coachman; and the dog a footman. A new gown materializes, complete with glass slippers, and Cinderella is off to the ball—warned that the spell will last only until midnight.

At the ball the Prince has been stifling yawns all evening, but he suddenly perks up when he first catches sight of Cinderella. He asks her to dance, and they become the center of attraction; the Prince then takes her out into the courtyard. The King is beside himself with joy at his son's sudden awakening. Just then the clock strikes twelve, and Cinderella breaks away. The Prince, distraught, runs after her, and, when she drops one of her slippers on the palace staircase, scoops it up. The King's horsemen chase after Cinderella's carriage, but by the time they get close, the twelfth chime has struck, and the coach is again a pumpkin, the horses mice.

The King is fast asleep, dreaming happily about his future grandchildren, when the Grand Duke awakes him with the bad news. The King orders the Duke to search every house in the land until he finds the slipper's rightful owner.

When Cinderella hears this, she is ecstatic, and her stepmother senses what has happened. She locks Cinderella in her room, in the attic of the house. The mice vow to get the key back, and actually succeed in sneaking the instrument out of the stepmother's pocket. Then, however, they face a long journey up a flight of stairs, pushing a key that is twice their size! When they finally reach the top, all seems well until Lucifer arrives, blocking their way, and trapping Gus. The others go to get the lazy dog Bruno, and for once the canine asserts himself and does battle with Lucifer, allowing the mice to open the door and free Cinderella.

During this fracas the Duke has arrived and tried the slipper on the two stepsisters, to no avail. He is about to leave when Cinderella appears for her turn. The Duke walks toward her with the slipper, and the quick-thinking stepmother trips him, sending the slipper shattering on the floor. All seems lost, but Cinderella calmly announces that it's all right—she has the matching slipper!

The picture dissolves to a royal wedding scene, with Cinderella's pet horse leading the others driving the royal coach, with the mice, dressed in their finery, throwing rice at the happy couple. "And they lived happily ever after," as the storybook closes for The End.

It is easy to dismiss *Cinderella* as an unremarkable Disney product, but those who do so obviously haven't seen it recently.

It is a work of genuine charm, thanks to skillful characterizations and storywork, and, most importantly, an especially winning score. Songs can literally make or break a film like this, and, in this case, as with most other Disney animated features, the songs enhance the qualities already present and help to establish others that might not be clear otherwise.

Cinderella is a likable enough character, especially in her dealings with the animals who share her household. But our fondness for her is crystallized in scenes such as the one where she sings "Sing, Sweet Nightingale." In the parlor the stepmother is giving vocal lessons to her two tin-eared daughters; their screechy bursts of song are unbearably bad. Inside Cinderella is washing the floor. As she begins to sing her tune, soap bubbles rise in the air echoing her voice. Each bubble reflects her face in a different color scheme, until a group of bubbles creates a chorus to bring the song to life. It's a lovely and imaginative scene.

The sequence of the birds and mice making Cinderella's dress simply would not work without the key musical numbers that give it direction and tempo. The high-pitched voices of the various animals bring to the rendition an endearing quality that makes it especially memorable.

Similarly, the jovial nature of the Fairy Godmother is perfectly expressed as she sings the bouncy "Bibbidi Bobbidi Boo." Every song in the score makes a definite contribution to the film—none seems arbitrarily inserted into the narrative.

Visually, *Cinderella* is not a flamboyant film, but it does have a full quota of inventive ideas. The stepmother's face is always seen in the shadows, particularly striking when her beady eyes are highlighted. The Fairy Godmother materializes out of twinkling stars in the sky, in a very pleasing special effect. And the romantic aura of Cinderella and Prince Charming dancing at the ball is evoked by creative use of color and backlighting, particularly when they walk out into the garden.

Admittedly, these are mild innovations when compared to the startling discoveries of *Pinocchio* or other earlier films, but the facile style of *Cinderella* makes it no less entertaining.

The film's strongest point is its ability to elicit emotional response from its audience. These are more scenes calculated to traumatize a viewer in *Cinderella* than in practically any other feature, a surprising statement when one considers the horrific elements of other Disney films, but still true. The most sophisticated audience would have difficulty not reacting audibly when the stepmother trips the Grand Duke, and the glass slipper—Cinderella's only hope, it seems—smashes to bits on the floor. By the same token the scene where the stepsisters rip Cinderella's dress to shreds is a terrifying real display of wickedness, on a level more likely to strike a responsive chord with children than many a more elaborate "horror" scene.

The sequence of the mice trying to bring the key upstairs is another example of involving an audience. We see the staircase from the mice's point of view, each step a tremendous hurdle to overcome. We suffer and strain with them as they push the key up the steps, one by one, and we feel the satisfaction they enjoy at reaching the top—when *suddenly* Lucifer's evil face appears to spoil the whole thing.

The greatest part of *Cinderella*'s success lies in its ability to get hold of its audience this way and make them feel they are experiencing the entire film. It is a quality many other filmmakers have tried to achieve without success.

In following this idea through to its logical conclusion, however, there is one thing missing from *Cinderella*, and that is retribution for the evil stepmother and stepsisters. It would not have had to be major (as it was in the Grimm version of this tale, wherein their eyes were pecked out by angry birds!)—it could have been as simple as a shot of their humiliation at seeing Cinderella marrying the

211

The Fairy Godmother steps in to make things right.
© *Walt Disney Productions*

Prince. But the lack of *any* such sequence does seem curious, and must send a lot of toddlers out of movie theatres asking their beleaguered parents what ever happened to the wicked ladies.

With *Cinderella* Disney hoped to return to the full-length animated feature story on a yearly basis, a schedule he found he could maintain for but a very brief time. Indeed, the film was advertised as being "six years in the making," although much of that time was taken up by preliminary ideas and discussions.

Comparisons to *Snow White* were inevitable, and the Disney people decided that it was a healthy association. The key advertising copy began: "Not since *Snow White and the Seven Dwarfs* a picture like this . . ."

Bosley Crowther in the *New York Times* reported that "although [*Cinderella* is] no chef d'oeuvre, it is well worth the love and labor spent," which seems as good a description as any.

The public, however, responded as it hadn't for any Disney feature since *Bambi,* going to see *Cinderella* in such numbers that the animated film became one of the year's top-grossing films, and Disney's biggest money-maker in many a year, grossing over $4 million in its initial release (two subsequent reissues have brought the total up to more than twice that amount with another go-round in spring 1973) proving that what the Disney name alone could not do, the pairing of the Disney name with a story of universal appeal could. He took the hint and chose similarly famous tales for his next two cartoon endeavors, *Alice in Wonderland* and *Peter Pan.*

As before, Disney knew that his best measuring stick was the box office, the only real reflection of what his audience wanted to see.

TREASURE ISLAND

RELEASED BY RKO RADIO PICTURES ON JULY 19, 1950. Technicolor. Producer: Perce Pearce. Director: Byron Haskin. Screenplay: Lawrence E. Watkin, from the novel by Robert Louis Stevenson. Photography: F. A.

Young, B.S.C. Editor: Alan L. Jaggs. Music: Clifton Parker, played by the Royal Philharmonic Orchestra. Conductor: Muir Mathieson. Production executive: Fred Leahy. Production manager: Douglas Peirce. Assistant director: Mark Evans. Matte artist: Peter Ellenshaw. Production designer: Thomas Morahan. Location directors: Russell Lloyd, Alex Bryce. Location cameramen: L. Cave Chinn, Stanley Sayre. Camera operator: Skeets Kelly. Continuity: Joan Davis. Technicolor color consultant: Joan Bridge. Makeup: Tony Sforzini. Hairstyling: Vivienne Walker. Sound engineer: Jack Locke. Sound editor: Kenneth Healey Ray. Running time: 96 minutes.

Cast: Bobby Driscoll (Jim Hawkins), Robert Newton (Long John Silver), Basil Sydney (Captain Smollett), Walter Fitzgerald (Squire Trelawney), Denis O'Dea (Doctor Livesey), Ralph Truman (George Merry), Finlay Currie (Captain Bones), John Laurie (Pew), Francis de Wolff (Black Dog), Geoffrey Wilkinson (Ben Gunn), David Davies (Arrow), Andrew Blackett (Gray), Paddy Brannigan (Hunter), Ken Buckle (Joyce), John Gregson (Redruth), Howard Douglas (Williams), and, as Silver's pirates, Geoffrey Keen (Israel Hand), William Devlin (Tom Morgan), Diarmuid Kelly (Bolen), Sam Kydd (Cady), Eddie Moran (Jack Bart), Harry Locke (Haggott), Harold Jamieson (Scully), Stephen Jack (Job Anderson), Jack Arrow (Norton), Jim O'Brady (Wolfe), Christ Adcock (Pike), Reginald Drummond (Vane), Gordon Mulholland (Durgin), Patrick Troughton (Roach), Leo Phillips (Spotts), Fred Clark (Bray), Tom Lucas (Upson), Bob Head (Tardy).

There are few adventure tales greater than Robert Louis Stevenson's *Treasure Island;* what is more, it's a story overflowing with cinematic possibilities. These were realized most vividly in Walt Disney's live-action version of the classic tale, filmed in England in 1949.

There could hardly have been a more perfect choice for Disney at this stage of his producing career. Both he

Long John Silver (Robert Newton) befriends Jim Hawkins (Bobby Driscoll) when they first meet at the tavern.
© *Walt Disney Productions*

Long John's eyes widen when he sees the treasure stashed away by wily old Ben Gunn; Squire Trelawney is interested too.
© *Walt Disney Productions*

and RKO, his distributing company, had "frozen" pounds in England from film revenues there; they could not be spent except *in* England. Solution: make a film there. But Disney, despite his international popularity, had always been considered as American as Uncle Sam. Solution: take advantage of the British location and resources to make a British-based film that would still have universal appeal (like Stevenson's book) and retain some American identity factor by casting Bobby Driscoll as Jim Hawkins.

Everything meshed perfectly. Disney appointed veteran Perce Pearce as his producer, a job he was to maintain on most subsequent overseas ventures, and hired cameraman-turned-director Byron Haskin to pilot the film.

The resulting film is less Disneyesque than any other up to this point, largely because of the subject itself, but also because Disney had less to do with the actual making of the film than any other before. He visited the English location several times during filming, but only briefly, and took a hands-off attitude toward director Haskin and screenwriter/adaptor Lawrence Watkin.

Where the Disney touch is most evident, aside from certain changes in the Stevenson plot, is in the actual appearance of the film. It was budgeted at $1,800,000, a considerable sum for a film with no stars even today. The settings, interior, exterior, and artificial, are all on a lavish scale befitting the atmosphere of the story. The film was photographed by subsequent Academy Award–winner Freddie Young, who brought out all the rich possibilities in every shot. And Tom Morahan, the film's production designer, injected as much color into the production as possible without becoming garish; the opening sequences, on the seacoast and at the inn where Jim lives and works, are properly stark, but never devoid of color.

The first shot of the film shows waves crashing against a rocky shore on a gray and windy day. The camera travels up a craggy coastal road to the Admiral Benbow Inn, where Black Dog enters the deserted establishment
216

and leaves his message for Captain Billy Bones with young Jim Hawkins. Then the dying captain gives Jim a treasure map, and the adventure is on.

The script is faithful to Stevenson's book for the most part; introductory material about Jim's parents is eliminated, and other matters condensed from time to time. But basically the story is the same one young boys have thrived on for years, with Jim accompanying Doctor Livesey and Squire Trelawney on a treasure hunt aboard the schooner *Hispaniola*, where they discover that their one-legged cook, Long John Silver, is actually the head conspirator in a devilish scheme to mutiny and claim ownership of the map. Battles between the two factions, mysterious characters coming in and out of the narrative, bargains and doublecrosses fill out the rest of the story in the scramble for buried riches on Treasure Island.

But central to the book, and emphasized in the film, is the relationship between young Jim and Long John Silver. Jim is rather mature for his age, and is beyond the fairy-tale stage of hero-worshiping pirates. But he is still a boy, and he relishes the opportunity to go to sea on a great adventure. He *does* get taken in by Long John's facade of good humor and courtliness, but this is not due so much to Jim's naïveté as to Silver's convincingness.

Long John is a very magnetic character; a completely unscrupulous man who remains in his most wicked moments totally beguiling, to Jim as well as to us. His sense of humor and irony almost never desert him, and it is the knowledge that his facade is not entirely phony that makes him so irresistible.

For his part Silver develops a genuine admiration for Jim as well. Even when he holds the boy prisoner in his makeshift fortress on Treasure Island, he shows concern for his welfare, and tells his motley crew that Jim is "more of a fighter than any two of you."

Their mutual regard is put to several difficult tests during the course of the story: Jim has given his word to Silver, while his prisoner, that he will not try to escape,

217

Disney and Robert Newton toast a visitor to the set of *Treasure Island*, Lady Tedder, wife of the British chief of the Air Staff.
Courtesy British Film Institute

and given the chance, refuses to renege on Long John.
Similarly, when Long John and his men finally arrive at the treasure site and find it barren, Silver hands Jim a gun so that the two of them can escape the wrath of the crew.

But screenwriter Watkin builds on Stevenson's foundation for an original finale to the scenario. The last reel of the film has more twists and turns than one can keep track of, especially in the hot and cold relationship between the boy and the pirate. After Jim and his friends, with the repentant Silver in tow, discover the treasure in Ben Gunn's cave, Long John tries to escape with the money in a rowboat. Jim finds him, and Silver aims his gun at the boy, threatening to shoot him if he doesn't give the boat a shove. Jim stands motionless, but Silver is unable to shoot him, even though it may

218

mean his own demise. Just then the rest of the party realize what has happened and come to capture the scoundrel; and now Jim cannot bear to see Long John taken off. He suddenly moves forward and pushes the rowboat out to sea. From out on the horizon, too far off to be fired on, Long John waves back appreciatively to Jim Hawkins for the conclusion of the film.

Although this changes Stevenson's finale (in which Silver escapes, without Jim's help or knowledge, with only a small sack of coins), it is most assuredly in keeping with the spirit of the author's work, and enhances the already fascinating relationship between these two characters.

This effect is also brought about by the actors playing the lead roles. There was anticipatory criticism of Bobby Driscoll, an American, playing the British Jim Hawkins, but he carried it off masterfully, certainly much better than the affected and stiffened Jackie Cooper in MGM's 1934 version of the story.

The film, however, belongs to Robert Newton, as Long John Silver. Rereading Stevenson, one finds that Newton *is* Long John, and the "hamminess" that many found overbearing in the performance is really as much Stevenson as it is Newton.

Director Byron Haskin explains:

In orchestrating the cast of thirty-six speaking parts, Long John was very near the top in flamboyant playing. I would rate the performances as beginning with the least offensive, the doctor. He was the measuring stick by which the others were to be judged. On up the scale came the squire, etc. Handling such an unwieldy number was one of the greatest tasks of making the film. By the time Newton's manners were to be considered I could do little more than let him "rip," in the language of the period. I cast Ralph Truman in the role of George Merry, however, giving him full scope to out-ham Newton whenever he could. At times, Newton, by contrast, looked downright underplayed!

"Anyhow," he concludes, "the film was a children's story, told by Stevenson to children. Kids don't go in much for subtleties."

Indeed, Newton was so powerful as Long John that he found himself locked into the characterization, repeating it for Haskin in an Australian-filmed feature, *Long John Silver,* a TV series of the same name, and similar roles such as the title part in *Blackbeard the Pirate.* Newton's trouping may have been ham, but his performance remains in the memory long after everything else about the film has been forgotten.

Not that there aren't other outstanding qualities to the movie; the entire cast is filled with skilled British actors giving life to the fictional characters created by Stevenson. Walter Fitzgerald as the bumbling, loose-tongued Squire Trelawney, Finlay Currie (who appeared in virtually every film Disney made in England) as the dying Billy Bones, Geoffrey Wilkinson as the slightly lunatic Ben Gunn, all add color to the fast-paced proceedings.

The film also has the look of authenticity, thanks not only to skillful art direction, but ample use of "glass shots," whereby artificial backgrounds and extensions are painted onto glass in front of the camera lens, yielding an amazingly lifelike result. When Jim Hawkins arrives in the port town of Bristol, the sky is filled with the masts and riggings of dozens of ships in the harbor—all paintings giving the illusion of reality. This intricate work was done by a man named Peter Ellenshaw, who had worked on such famous British fantasies as *The Thief of Bagdad,* and who later joined the Disney staff.

An actual sailing ship was chartered for the duration of the filming, as well, for matching with studio-built interiors and establishing shots at sea. There were three camera units at work on the film, one shooting out on the ocean (under the direction of Russell Lloyd), one shooting exteriors, and another shooting interiors at Denham Studios.

Director Haskin had served as cinematographer on

other seagoing films, notably *Captain Blood* and *The Sea Wolf* at Warner Brothers. He was to go on to make some of the most memorable science-fiction films of the 1950s for George Pal. Haskin brought a good sense of pacing and, to use his word, orchestration to the film, and made the most of a first-rate script. Adapter/scenarist Lawrence E. Watkin, best known as the author of *On Borrowed Time,* subsequently did the scripts for Disney's three British-made swashbucklers in the 1950s.

Perhaps the film's most famous scene occurs when young Jim tries to recapture the ship from Long John's two motley crewmen on board. One passes out of his own accord, but the other comes stalking Jim, causing the youngster to climb into the crow's nest as a place of refuge. The mutineer, Mr. Hand, climbs the rigging, to be greeted at the top by Jim aiming a pistol (given him by Silver!) at the pirate. Hand is sure Jim is bluffing, and suddenly tosses a knife into the boy's shoulder, inciting Jim to pull the trigger and send his adversary plummeting to a watery death.

This is not the only example of full-blooded violence in the film; another sequence uses jump-cutting to make a sailor's death (by gunshot in the forehead) doubly dramatic. Credit goes to Haskin for bringing out the full potential of each situation.

Reaction to the film was the same in England and in America; intellectual critics chastised Disney for what they felt was diluting the original. (A British headline read: "Yo Ho Ho and a Coca-Cola.") John Mason Brown wrote in *Saturday Review:* "Mr. Disney's movie . . . is meant for those who have never read *Treasure Island* or who have forgotten it long ago."

But *Time* magazine captured the essence of the film perfectly. "It is played so broadly by British actors in stock company style that even the youngest fan can follow the adventures of the cast's only U.S. actor, Bobby Driscoll, as cabin boy Jim Hawkins."

The film did not perform as well as had been hoped at the box office, and eventually was shown on the Disney television show instead of being reissued. It seems an unfortunate fate for what is one of Disney's all-time best live-action films, a truly outstanding adventure tale, of which there are far too few.

ALICE IN WONDERLAND

RELEASED BY RKO RADIO PICTURES ON JULY 28, 1951. Technicolor. Production supervisor: Ben Sharpsteen. Directors: Clyde Geronimi, Hamilton Luske, Wilfred Jackson. Animating directors: Milt Kahl, Ward Kimball, Franklin Thomas, Eric Larson, John Lounsbery, Oliver Johnston, Jr., Wolfgang Reitherman, Marc Davis, Les Clark, Norman Ferguson. Story: Winston Hibler, Bill Peet, Joe Rinaldi, Bill Cottrell, Joe Grant, Del Connell, Ted Sears, Erdman Penner, Milt Banta, Dick Kelsey, Dick Huemer, Tom Oreb, John Walbridge. Character animators: Hal King, Judge Whitaker, Hal Ambro, Bill Justice, Phil Duncan, Bob Carlson, Don Lusk, Cliff Nordberg, Harvey Toombs, Fred Moore, Marvin Woodward, Hugh Fraser, Charles Nichols. Effects animation: Joshua Meador, Dan MacManus, George Rowley, Blaine Gibson. Color and styling: John Hench, Mary Blair, Claude Coats, Ken Anderson, Don Da Gradi. Layout: Mac Stewart, Hugh Hennesy, Tom Codrick, Don Griffith, Charles Philippi, Thor Putnam, A. Kendall O'Connor, Lance Nolley. Backgrounds: Ray Huffine, Ralph Hulett, Art Riley, Brice Mack, Dick Anthony, Thelma Witmer. Musical score: Oliver Wallace. Orchestrations: Joseph Dubin. Vocal arrangements: Jud Conlon. Running time: 75 minutes.

Songs: "Very Good Advice," "In a World of My Own," "All in a Golden Afternoon," "Alice in Wonderland," "The Walrus and the Carpenter," "The Caucus Race," "I'm Late," "Painting the Roses Red," "March of the Cards" by Bob Hilliard and Sammy Fain.

" 'Twas Brillig" by Don Raye and Gene DePaul. "A Very Merry Un-birthday" by Mack David, Al Hoffman, and Jerry Livingston. "We'll Smoke the Blighter Out," "Old Father William," "A E I O U" by Oliver Wallace and Ted Sears.

Voices: Kathryn Beaumont (Alice), Ed Wynn (Mad Hatter), Richard Haydn (Caterpillar), Sterling Holloway (Cheshire Cat), Jerry Colonna (March Hare) Verna Felton (Queen of Hearts), Pat O'Malley (Walrus, Carpenter, Tweedledee and Tweedledum), Bill Thompson (White Rabbit, Dodo), Heather Angel (Alice's sister), Joseph Kearns (Doorknob), Larry Grey (Bill), Queenie Leonard (bird in the tree), Dink Trout (King of Hearts), Doris Lloyd (The Rose), James Macdonald (Dormouse), The Mello Men (Card Painters), Don Barclay, Pinto Colvig (flamingoes), Ken Beaumont (card painter), Ed Penner (Baglet), Larry Grey (card painter), Queenie Leonard (flower).

Disney first thought of doing *Alice in Wonderland,* in a way, in the 1920s, for the general theme of Lewis Carroll's fable was the basis for his *Alice in Cartoonland* series, with a live girl playing in a cartoon world. But the idea of a bona fide adaptation of the classic story into a feature-length film occurred to Disney many times in the ensuing years. In 1933 there was discussion about Mary Pickford starring in such a feature, combining live action and animation. In 1945 the studio announced that Ginger Rogers was going to star in the film. After *Song of the South,* Disney said that he intended to build the film around his new star, Luana Patten. (He formally registered the title with the MPAA in 1938.)

Finally, in 1946, he decided to go ahead with the film as an all-cartoon feature. Initially, the studio declared that it would be drawn in the style of the famous Sir John Tenniel illustrations. Disney explained: "When you deal with such a popular classic you're laying yourself wide open to the critics."

But before long, as the feature took shape, it became

223

clear that simply bringing the Tenniel drawings to life was both impractical, and not what Disney-lovers would expect. So the artists and animators consulted Tenniel's work and came up with free translations of his characters, close enough to the originals to be identifiable, distinctive enough to be recognized as Disney creations.

And for the first time since the classic animated features of the early 1940s, a full-length live-action film was shot for the animator to consult (featuring most of the actors who supplied the film's voices). The resulting cartoon feature took five years to complete at an estimated cost of $3 million.

Unlike the other Disney features derived from classic books, *Alice* does not open on a storybook. Rather, it begins with a view of Big Ben, pulling back to reveal Alice and her older sister sitting under a shady tree by a stream. As her sister reads, Alice daydreams, lying in the grass, and suddenly discovers before her a quaint White Rabbit singing "I'm Late," as he runs into a nearby hole.

Alice follows, and falls down the rabbit hole, floating through space, passing all kinds of distorted objects and settings, and unreal color patterns. When she finally lands, it is on her head, and she turns rightside up to follow the rabbit, who has gone through a doorway.

From this point on, it is Lewis Carroll's story, with all the familiar elements: Alice trying to get herself the right size to pass through the keyhole of the door, encountering Tweedledee and Tweedledum, who tell the story of the Walrus and the Carpenter, and meeting such unusual characters as an opium-smoking caterpillar and the Cheshire Cat.

She attends a Mad Tea Party with the Mad Hatter and March Hare, and wanders off to meet the Queen, who invites Alice to participate in a most unscrupulous game of croquet, after which Alice is put on trial, and forced to escape this insane world back through the keyhole . . . at which time she wakes up and finds the whole episode has been a dream.

Alice is the most episodic of Disney's full-length story
224

The Mad Hatter pours, after a fashion, at his un-birthday party
© Walt Disney Productions

features, and as such has more trouble maintaining pace and continuity than most. The Walrus and Carpenter story, for instance, although faithful to Carroll, seems extraneous and bothersome in that it keeps Alice from moving on and proceeding with her adventures. Of course, most of her encounters are essentially obstacles to Alice, but they are taken care of with more dispatch than this.

The caterpillar, for instance, asks Alice, "Whoo R U?," blowing those letters into the air as he puffs away. She valiantly attempts to hold a conversation with him, but his non sequiturs make it impossible. When she reaches the point of exasperation, Alice tries to tackle the stubborn fellow, only to be left holding his skin while he, having turned into a butterfly, flutters away.

Directing animator Ward Kimball feels that the film

Alice, suddenly enlarged, scolds the egotistical Queen in Wonderland.   © *Walt Disney Productions*

degenerated into a loud-mouthed vaudeville show. There's no denying that there are many charming bits in our *Alice,* but it lacks warmth and an overall story glue. *Alice* suffered from too many cooks—directors. Here was a case of five directors each trying to top the other guy and make his sequences the biggest and craziest in the show. This had a self-cancelling effect on the final product.

For example, I was in charge of the animation for the Mad Tea Party, Tweedledee and Tweedledum, and the Cheshire Cat, but because all of the other sequences in the show tried to be "mad," the result was that the only real "mad" thing in the whole picture, in my opinion, turned out to be the Cheshire Cat! Why? Because compared to the constant, all-out, wild gyrations of the other characters, he played it real cool. His quiet, underplayed subtleties consequently stole the show!

The Cheshire Cat is, unquestionably, one of the most memorable things about the film. He first appears as a toothy smile, the rest of his body gradually materializing around it, as he sings an offhand rendition of "Jabberwocky." He playfully asks Alice, "Can you stand on your head?" as his body swings aside and hops on top of his head, perched atop a tree.

As great as the Cat is visually, however, it and all of *Alice*'s other characters benefit tremendously from their voices, and for this film Disney chose very formidable actors to supply them. It is one of the first times in Disney animated features where the viewer is thinking about the actor while watching the character on screen, an unhealthy trend that resurfaced in the 1960s.

For the most part the idea worked to *Alice*'s advantage, however. Sterling Holloway is delightfully coy as the Cheshire Cat, Richard Haydn is ideal as the Caterpillar, and in the Mad Tea Party sequence, Ed Wynn and Jerry Colonna are hilarious as the Mad Hatter and the March Hare, respectively.

Disney shows some sketches to Kathryn Beaumont, the voice of Alice. *Courtesy British Film Institute*

229

What one remembers specifically about the Tea Party are those two delightful voices and "A Very Merry Unbirthday," more than the visuals, although there are some very funny gags, as when the White Rabbit stumbles in and makes the mistake of mentioning that his watch is broken. The Hatter takes it in hand, opens it up, and, with the Hare, gives the watch a lightning-paced going-over that involves pouring every conceivable item on the table into the tiny timepiece. Finally, when the Hare hands him some mustard, the Mad Hatter stops dead in his tracks, looks at the mustard and comments, "Don't let's be silly!"

One of the best visual scenes in the film involves the march of the cards, heralding the Queen's arrival. Here colors flash on the screen and the cards form a succession of geometric figures as they march along, with various imaginative camera angles heightening the effect. The scene concludes with a ready-made card game; the cards shuffle themselves and deal out to nonexistent players.

The climactic sequence with the Queen is quite funny, also benefiting from a particularly strong voice characterization by Vejna Felton.

The film's other visual highlight is the flower sequence, where Alice finds herself wandering among oversized and strongly individualistic flowers, which take on various personality traits (a snooty society woman with a laced bodice, two drunken buttercups, etc.) in an especially colorful and beautifully designed scene.

In all, *Alice in Wonderland* is a very flashy and generally entertaining film, but it lacks that essential thread that made Disney's best features hang together, and, moreover, it lacks *warmth*. Of course, *Alice* is not *Snow White* or *Cinderella*, and one shouldn't demand the same things of it. Yet Disney's best animated features have always communicated something to their audience that would leave the viewer with an afterglow, feeling he had just undergone an experience, as opposed to watching a cartoon. *Alice* has no such aftereffects. Once over, it can be dismissed, and though one wouldn't have wanted Disney to turn the story into a Grimm's fairy tale,

230

there should have been some way to give the audience more empathy with its heroine.

The critics, as Disney had anticipated, had their knives sharpened in readiness for *Alice*. The *New Yorker* wrote:

> In Mr. Disney's *Alice* there is a blind incapacity to understand that a literary masterwork cannot be improved by the introduction of shiny little tunes, and touches more suited to a flea circus than to a major imaginative effort. . . . Possibly nobody is going to create a visualization of *Alice* that won't do violence to the nostalgic imagery of the piece that remains in the mind's eye of those who grew up on Tenniel's illustrations. But even granting a certain latitude for variations in approach, [the film is] a dreadful mockery of the classic.

Even *Life* magazine, one of Disney's staunchest supporters, noted that "the leering loony faces he has concocted will be a shock to oldsters brought up on the famous John Tenniel illustrations."

For the most part critical reaction has played a small role in shaping the popularity of Disney's films, but somehow, either because of the bad reviews or simply because *Alice* did not have the appeal of the more universal Grimm's fairy tales and such, *Alice in Wonderland* did not perform as well as the box office as Disney had expected. Accordingly, it was one of the few cartoon features he allowed to be shown on his TV program, and consequently it has never been reissued theatrically. An amusing postcript concerns the fact that the film, available for 16mm rental, became spectacularly popular with college audiences in the late 1960s for its "mind-blowing" surrealism and natural links to the drug culture. Although Disney did not discourage such identification with *Fantasia* when it was reissued at this time, the company decided that it was unwise to become too closely identified with this sector of the audience and withdrew *Alice* from 16mm distribution.

Another sidenote concerns the fact that when *Alice*

was about to be released, a small New York distribution company cleverly picked up the rights to a French puppet film of *Alice in Wonderland* made by Louis Bunin, and scheduled it to open at the same time as the Disney cartoon. The Disney company tried to obtain and injunction to withhold the rival film for eighteen months, claiming that the public would be misled by competitive advertising, but the motion was denied and the Bunin film opened, to generally bad reviews. It failed to affect the outcome of the Disney film either way.

Oddly enough, *Alice in Wonderland*'s enduring success has been its score, with two song, "I'm Late" and "A Very Merry Un-birthday" becoming standards and perpetuating the film even though it has long been out of distribution.

THE STORY OF ROBIN HOOD

RELEASED BY RKO RADIO PICTURES IN JUNE 26, 1952. Technicolor. Producer: Perce Pearce. Director: Ken Annakin. Screenplay: Lawrence E. Watkin. Director of photography: Guy Green, B.S.C. Ecitor: Gordon Pilkington. Art directors: Carmen Dillon, Arthur Lawson. Music: Clifton Parker, played bzy the Royal Philharmonic Orchestra. Conductor: Muir Mathieson. Production manager: Douglas Peirce. Unit manager: Anthony Nelson-Keys. Assistant director: Peter Bolton. Matte artist: Peter Ellenshaw. Camera operator: Dave Harcourt. Technicolor color consultant: Joan Bridge. Location directors: Alex Bryce, Basil Keys. Location cameramen: Geoffrey Unsworth, Bob Walker. Makeup: Geoffrey Rodway. Hairstyling: Vivienne Walker. Sound director: C. C. Stevens. Sound editor: Wyn Ryder. Running time: 83 minutes.

Cast: Richard Todd (Robin Hood), Joan Rice (Maid Marian), Peter Finch (Sheriff of Nottingham), James Hayter (Friar Tuck), James Robertson Justice (Little John), Martita Hunt (Queen Eleanor), Hubert Gregg (Prince John), Bill Owen (Stutely), Reginald Tate (Hugh Fitzooth), Elton Haytes (Allan-a-Dale), Antony Eustrel (Archbishop of Canterbury), Patrick Barr (King Richard), Anthony Forwood (Will Scarlet), Hal Osmond (Midge the Miller), Michael Hordern (Scathelock), Clement McCallin (Earl of Huntingdon), Louise Hampton (Tyb), Archie Duncan (Red Gill), Julian Somers (posse leader), Bill Travers (posse man), David Davies (forester), and, as the Merrie Men, Ivan Craig, Ewen Solon, John Stamp, John Brooking, John Martin, Geoffrey Lumsden, Larry Mooney, John French, Nigel Neilson, Charles Perry, Richard Graydon, Jack Taylor.

Having formed RKO—Walt Disney British Productions Ltd., and succeeded in filming a most creditable live-action feature, Walt Disney decided to continue making films in England, with Perce Pearce as his producer. They decided to continue in the action-adventure genre, and chose as their next project Robin Hood.

This time out, in addition to using an all-British crew, Disney hired a British director as well, a young man who had made an impressive start at Rank studios with such films as *Trio* and *Quartet*, Ken Annakin. At the time he joined the production, some preparatory work had already been done by Disney and Pearce with their cameraman, Guy Green, and art director, Carmen Dillon. As on *Treasure Island*, three separate shooting units were established, one doing action work on exterior location, and two doing interiors at Denham Studios.

Disney spent part of the summer in England, working closely with Annakin. The director recalls:

I remember talking about the original Errol Flynn *Robin Hood*, and I looked at it, just to get an idea

233

what had been done before, because I never like to do anything twice. Walt didn't seem very worried about seeing the original, and in fact, I doubt if he ever did. His approach is always that the film is a Disney picture, and therefore, because of his attitudes and his approach, the picture is bound to be different from anything else made on that subject before.

That was exactly what happened, of course; the Disney film adheres to the Robin Hood legend, yet it is a work unto itself. One is hard pressed to make comparisons between the Disney *Robin Hood* and earlier versions, not because one is better than another, but simply because each one is different.

The film opens on a storybook, which dissolves into a city scene, where a strolling minstrel sings a ballad of Robin Hood. He reappears throughout the film, as a narrative device, and adds a unique flavor to the period piece.

The story is as everyone remembers it. King Richard leaves his domain to go on a crusade, appointing his brother Prince John to reign during his absence. The Prince, in turn, appoints a new sheriff of Nottingham to carry out the new laws he has in mind. Before long, the happy kingdom becomes a dictatorship, where the people are driven mercilessly and taxed beyond endurance.

At a public archery tournament young Robin Hood and his father show up the Sheriff's bowmen; the angered Sheriff has Robin's father killed. To avenge his death Robin takes to the woods with others who have been wronged by the new rulers, and forms his band of Merrie Men. They are soon joined by John Little, redubbed Little John, and jovial Friar Tuck.

Robin and his Men soon become public heroes, much to the consternation of the Prince and Sheriff, who are unable to capture these "bandits." The "bandits" then prove their loyalty to the King when it is discovered that the good Richard is being held hostage in Austria for a

Robin (Richard Todd) and Maid Marian (Joan Rice) realize that they still love each other. © *Walt Disney Productions*

At one point Robin is forced to hold Maid Marian captive in Sherwood Forest. James Hayter is Friar Tuck; Michael Hordern is at extreme left. © *Walt Disney Productions*

235

ransom of 100,000 marks.

The Queen is to deliver the ransom money, but the Prince has his men dress as Robin Hood's cohorts and steal the money, to turn the Queen against Robin. Robin manages to foil this plot, but he then learns that the Prince has locked Maid Marian in his castle to keep her from exposing this scheme. Robin returns to the castle for a fight to the death with the Sheriff of Nottingham, and rescues Maid Marian. Soon afterward Robin's forest hideout is visited by a mysterious stranger, who reveals himself to be King Richard! He expresses his thanks to Robin and the Men, and then dubs the bandit leader the Earl of Locksley, and orders Maid Marian to marry the newly created nobleman for a resoundingly happy ending.

The Story of Robin Hood is an eminently satisfying film. It takes all the familiar elements of the story—the confrontation between Robin and Little John on a wooden bridge over a stream, the archery tournament, the climactic duel—and plays them out with such gusto that one forgets ever having seen them before.

There are delightful variations as well. Robin and his Men communicate with each other by shooting whistling arrows throughout the forest—different arrows producing different pitches, and thus signifying different things.

Robin's relationship with Maid Marian is newly expanded. They are shown at the beginning of the film as youthful sweethearts; then they are separated for a long time, before they meet again, with Marian in the charge of the Queen, and Robin as the bandit/hero who tries to rekindle their romance.

A particularly delightful scene invented for this scenario has Robin and his Men sneaking into town during a public meeting to raise funds for the King's ransom. The Sheriff has made a magnanimous gift, claiming that he has donated every cent he has. Meanwhile, the Merrie Men discover a strongbox in the Sheriff's quarters filled to the brim with gold coins and precious trinkets. They open the box, bring it into the town square, and dump its contents into the public kitty. As the Sheriff turns pale, Robin, disguised in the crowd, shouts, ''Three cheers for the Sheriff!''

The performances are uniformly fine, with an impressive roster of talented players; James Robertson Justice as Little John and Peter Finch as the wicked Sheriff stand out. Richard Todd, in the first of his three assignments for Disney, is ingratiating as Robin Hood, and plays his scenes with Joan Rice quite nicely for an attractive and believable romance.

This is an extremely good-*looking* film as well. The locations are beautiful, with lush green countrysides; the sets are truly formidable and realistic.

The seemingly effortless pacing and knowing use of camera angles and cutting is doubly impressive when one considers certain background facts. For instance, Annakin has vivid memories of the difficulties in shooting Technicolor at that time.

It was the very elaborate three-strip system, with a very immobile camera. When you wanted to reload the camera in its very heavy blimp, you had to have it lifted on chains, and it took the first-class Technicolor crew a minimum of eleven minutes to reload the camera. After every single shot the camera had to be opened and the gate had to be examined; the prism was the great thing because this was the light splitter which gave the registrations on the three strips.

For this reason, if you were making a big picture like *Robin Hood,* you had to be very certain that you were not wasting setups or wasting shots, because it was a big industrial process every time to set up your camera.

Annakin's prescreening of the Errol Flynn *Robin Hood* was probably responsible for the decision to find a new approach to the inevitable climactic battle between Robin and the Sheriff. In the earlier version there is the justly famous duel between Flynn and Basil Rathbone on the castle steps. In this film the duel takes the two adversaries all around the castle, climaxing in a chillingly exciting encounter with the drawbridge. As Robin tries to escape, the Sheriff starts to pull the bridge upright. Robin climbs to the top, hoping to squeeze out before it closes shut. The Sheriff, trying to stop him, gets caught and is crushed by the closing platform, a grisly but satisfying end for this most nefarious of villains.

The use of storyboards was new to Annakin, "but it appealed to my logical brain very, very much," and prompted ingenious scenes such as the first meeting between Prince John and the Sheriff of Nottingham after King Richard has left, played on the balcony of the castle against a brilliant but ominous orange sky at sundown.

At the time of its release *The Story of Robin Hood* was greeted with muted enthusiasm. One British critic opined: "The most that can be said for it is that it is unmemorable," whereas the *New York Times*'s A. H. Weiler found it "an expert rendition of an ancient legend that is as pretty as its Technicolor hues, and as lively as a sturdy Western."

Time has been kind to the film, as so many inferior films in this genre have followed it; today it seems better than ever. As for comparisons with other versions, it holds its own quite well. Douglas Fairbanks's 1922 *Robin Hood* is an excellent film, but the enormity of the settings and the scope of the production tend to dwarf the characters somewhat. The 1938 Warner Brothers epic, filmed in color, is strongly personality-oriented, with the brilliant playing of Errol Flynn, Basil Rathbone, Claude Rains, and a first-rate cast dominating the action.

Disney's *The Story of Robin Hood* strikes a happy medium, leaning heavily on strong characterizations, but placing them against a colorful and sumptuous tableau that gives the film a fine period flavor. The studio's subsequent animated feature film, released in 1973, put a much greater emphasis on comedy.

PETER PAN

RELEASED BY RKO RADIO PICTURES ON FEBRUARY 5, 1953. Adapted from the play by Sir James M. Barrie. Directors: Hamilton Luske, Clyde Geronimi, Wilfred Jackson. Directing animators: Milt Kahl, Franklin Thomas, Wolfgang Reitherman, Ward Kimball, Eric Larson, Oliver Johnston, Jr., Marc Davis, John Lounsbery, Les Clark, Norman Ferguson. Story: Ted Sears, Bill Peet, Joe Rinaldi, Erdman Penner, Winston Hibler, Milt Banta, Ralph Wright. Color and styling: Mary Blair, Claude Coats, John Hench, Donald Da Gradi. Backgrounds: Ray Huffine, Art Riley, Albert Dempster, Eyvind Earle, Ralph Hulett, Thelma Witmer, Dick Anthony, Brice Mack. Layout: Mac Stewart, Tom Codrick, A. Kendall O'Connor, Charles Philippi, Hugh Hennesy, Ken Anderson, Al Zinnen, Lance Nolley, Thor Putnam, Don Griffith. Character animators: Hal King, Cliff Nordberg, Hal Ambro, Don Lusk, Ken O'Brien, Marvin Woodward, Art Stevens, Eric Cleworth, Fred Moore, Bob Carlson, Harvey Toombs, Judge Whitaker, Bill Justice, Hugh Fraser, Jerry Hathcock, Clair Weeks. Effects animation: George Rowley, Blaine Gibson, Joshua Meador, Dan MacManus. Musical score: Oliver Wallace. Orchestrations: Edward H. Plumb. Vocal arrangements: Jud Conlon. Running time: 76½ minutes.

Songs: "The Elegant Captain Hook," "What Makes the Red Man Red?," "You Can Fly, You Can Fly, You Can Fly," "Your Mother and Mine" by Sammy Cahn and Sammy Fain. "A Pirate's Life" by Oliver Wallace and Erdman Penner. "Tee-Dum Tee-Dee" by Oliver Wallace, Ted Sears, and Winston Hibler. "Never Smile at a Crocodile" by Frank Churchill and Jack Lawrence.

Voices: Bobby Driscoll (Peter Pan), Kathryn Beaumont (Wendy), Hans Conried (Captain Hook, Mr. Darling), Bill Thompson (Mr. Smee), Heather Angel (Mrs. Darling), Paul Collins (Michael Darling), Tommy Luske

239

(John), Candy Candido (Indian chief), Tom Conway (narrator), Don Barclay, Roland Dupree.

James Barrie's *Peter Pan* seemed like an ideal subject for Walt Disney—and Disney knew it as early as 1935. In 1939 he arranged with the Great Ormond Street Hospital in London (to whom Barrie bequeathed ownership of the play) to produce an animated film of the classic show, which had been filmed once before in 1925.

Although random thoughts were given to the project throughout the 1940s, it wasn't until the last year of that decade that production finally began, with another live-action film being made for the animator's benefit. The film, which was released in early 1953, cost some $4 million.

The film opens on a shining star in the sky, panning down to a view of London at twilight, then gradually into the neighborhood of the Darling residence. The narrator introduces the family, whom we first see as silhouettes against the window shades.

Mr. Darling, upset by his children's harping on Peter Pan, the hero of older sister Wendy's bedtime stories, decides that it is Wendy's last night in the nursery, and the last night for Nana, the nurse-dog, as well. He ties Nana outside as he and Mrs. Darling go out for the evening.

But as they leave, Mr. Darling making sarcastic remarks about the existence of this character, the camera swings up to the roof and there, silhouetted in the moonlight, is Peter himself. He and Tinker Bell creep into the nursery to reclaim Peter's shadow, which Wendy has captured and locked up. In the ensuing commotion the children wake up, and Peter, hearing that Wendy is going to leave them, offers to take her to Never-Never-Land, where she won't have to grow up, and where she can continue to tell stories about him. Tinker Bell, jealous of the attention Peter is paying to Wendy, doesn't like the whole idea.

Nevertheless, Peter, Wendy, and her younger

brothers Michael and John all think wonderful thoughts, get sprinkled with pixie dust, and fly off into the night, "the second star to the right and straight on till morning."

The rest of the film takes place in Never-Never-Land, where Captain Hook does his best to capture the elusive Peter, Tinker Bell tries very hard to sabotage any plans that involve Wendy, and Michael and John frolic with Peter's Lost Boys, who get homesick when Wendy sings of "Your Mother and Mine."

Hook kidnaps Princess Tiger Lily in the hope of luring Peter, and does so, but Peter manages to rescue the Indian maiden and foil Hook at the same time. Undaunted, Hook captures Tinker Bell and plays on her jealousy to get her to reveal Peter's hideout, where he plants a time bomb. Tinker escapes just in time to save Peter from the blast, but not before Hook's crew have captured Wendy, Michael, John, and the Lost Boys and taken them captive aboard their ship.

Peter meets Hook on his own territory, and after a battle in the ship's rigging, the unfortunate Captain falls overboard into the jaws of a crocodile who acquired one of his hands long ago and has been waiting for the rest of him ever since. The determined crocodile chases the frantic Hook off to the horizon.

Tinker Bell covers the entire ship with pixie dust, so it can sail back to London. When Mr. and Mrs. Darling come home that night, and Wendy and the boys try to tell them of their adventures, they go to the window and point to Peter's ship, which can be seen in the form of a cloud sailing in front of the moon. Mr. Darling looks at it and says gently that he seems to remember having seen it himself, long, long ago.

It is difficult to find fault with *Peter Pan;* it is one of Disney's brightest, most straightforward animated features, a film in which everything clicks. One is tempted to say that it lacks the innovative brilliance of a *Pinocchio* (which is perfectly true), but it seems unfair to criticize the film for what it isn't, when it *is* such an

241

Tinker Bell interferes with Peter as he is about to open a deadly
package from Captain Hook. © *Walt Disney Productions*

Peter fights it out with Captain Hook as Wendy and Mr. Smee
look on. © *Walt Disney Productions*

unpretentious, delightful endeavor.

In some ways the Disney version of *Peter Pan* was revolutionary. It was the first enactment of the Barrie play where Peter was not played by a girl . . . to show Tinker Bell and the Crocodile . . . to be able to have Nana be a real dog (onstage it was always an actor) . . . and not to ask the audience to revive Tinker Bell after the explosion by clapping hands.

The latter decision was the most momentous for the Disney staff, the others having been taken care of rather simply. Even in the silent film with Betty Bronson, this timeworn but effective technique, with Peter beseeching the audience to prove it believes in fairies by applauding, was included. Yet Disney seemed to sense that this was, after all, a stage-play innovation, and not really appropriate for his film. The fact that the film works well without it, and remains faithful to its source, proves him to have been correct.

The actual design of Tinker Bell was another problem, since the sprite had always been shown as merely a beam of light (even in the silent film). Existing character sketches trace Tinker Bell's development from inception in 1938 to the design finally used; in the 1940s the Disney artists considered modeling her after the current conception of female attractiveness, an idea that would have proved disastrous, if employed. Disney claimed in a magazine article that the final decision on Tinker Bell's looks was cemented by the popularity of Marilyn Monroe, after whose figure Tinker was modeled. Some critics, determined to find the worst in Disney, found his use of an amply endowed nymphet for the role of Tinker Bell to be suggestive.

As with *Alice in Wonderland*, much publicity was generated by the unique Disney procedure of filming a live-action movie for animators to study. Explaining its use, director Hamilton Luske told Aline Mosby of UPI:

Cartoonists, just like artists, must have living models to draw from. Otherwise, they'd be drawing what they think certain characters would do in a situa-

243

tion, not what they really would do. We could, of course, have the live models act out a scene on a stage. But then the animators would have to trust their memories when they go back to their drawing boards. A film is easier, as it can be run over and over for the artists. And they can correct any mistakes in a scene before the drawing is made.

Hans Conried, who did the voice of Captain Hook, was also hired to portray him in this film. He recalls:

Usually they had pantomimists and/or dancers, but they felt that I could play the part. Now when I say I worked two and a half years, I don't say that I worked constantly, but over that period they would say "Have you got two weeks?", "Have you got four days?", "Have you got a week?" I was in costume, and they had an elemental set, and I would go through the business making my physical action coincide with the sound track, which was already finished. Usually, in dubbing, which I've done a lot of for foreign actors, you have to make your sound coincident with his latent action, but here you make your physical action coincident with the sound track. That was lots of fun; it was a very friendly, familial surroundings at Disney, particularly in those days.

Dancer Roland Dupree appeared as Peter in the live-action film, with June Foray, Margaret Kerry, and Connie Hilton as mermaids.

Students of the musical film would do well to study *Peter Pan*, not only to hear the beautiful choral arrangements by Jud Conlon, but to observe how masterfully the musical element of the film integrated into the story. When the children ask Peter how they get to Never-Never-Land, he tells them it's easy, and begins to talk the lyrics of "You Can Fly." The kids join him, speaking rhythmically, but naturally, and almost, but never quite, bursting into song; the actual singing is taken up by the chorus, as the children fly out of the nursery window and into the night. Throughout the rest of the film, songs are introduced, and sometimes sung, in fragments, or so naturally that one is hardly aware they have begun. Even in the midst of Wendy's tender song "Your Mother and Mine," action is continuing, as Captain Hook's crew gathers outside the hideout to cpature the Lost Children.

Visually, the film is also rather straightforward, with bright splashes of color and sharply defined drawings, except in the scenes of London, which are the lushest in the film. When the children fly out the nursery window and sail over London, there is an absolutely stunning view of the city below—virtually a full-scale relief map, tinted in dark blue, seen through the clouds! The opening and closing scenes of the film also boast beautiful views of the city, with the memorable shot of the stardust ship sailing in front of the moon.

There is as much adventure as anything else in *Peter Pan,* with most of the humor deriving from the broadly funny activities of Captain Hook and his crew, but the film does have many small touches as well: Michael sprinkling pixie dust on Nana so she too can fly to Never-Never-Land (and fly she does, except that she is tied to the doghouse and cannot break away, so as she floats in the air, she waves goodbye to Michael) . . . Captain Hook, preparing to meet Tinker Bell, sprucing up, and screwing in a special golden hook . . . Michael's teddy bear confounding a live bear about to pounce on the children in the forest . . . and the Crocodile himself, a sly, smiling creature whose presence is made known by a constant tick-tock caused by an alarm clock he swallowed long ago.

In all, *Peter Pan* is a brisk and entirely winning adaptation of the Barrie play. There was some fear that the memorable television version of *Pan* with Mary Martin in the 1950s might eclipse the Disney film as being the "definitive" version, especially with its melodic score, but *Pan* has outlived the TV show and become one of Disney's all-time top-grossing films. Aside from that, it is pointless to compare the two versions, which are totally different in scope and medium, and both of which succeed on their own terms.

THE LIVING DESERT

Released by buena vista on november 10, 1953. Print by Technicolor (from 16mm). Associate producer: Ben Sharpsteen. Director: James Algar. Screenplay: James Algar, Winston Hibler, Ted Sears. Photography: N. Paul Kenworthy, Jr., Robert H. Crandall. Additional photography: Stuart V. Jewell, Jack C. Couffer, Don Arlen, Tad Nichols. Narrator: Winston Hibler. Animation effects: Joshua Meador, John Hench, Art Riley. Musical director: Paul J. Smith. Orchestrations: Edward H. Plumb. Film editor: Norman Palmer. Special processes: Ub Iwerks. Sound director: C. O. Slyfield. Sound recording: Harold J. Steck. Running time: 73 minutes.

With the success of the True-Life nature short subjects, Disney became the recipient of endless wildlife film submitted by naturalist-photographers around the country. Some particularly fascinating footage was shot by N. Paul Kenworthy, Jr. He had studied insect life on the great American desert as part of a doctoral thesis for UCLA, and this film was the result. Its highlight was a breathtaking sequence of a wasp battling it out with a tarantula, attempting to paralyze its enemy by stinging it in exactly the right spot.

Disney was intrigued enough to hire Kenworthy and assign him to return to the desert for more footage. He accepted other free-lance material, and had his staff assemble it into the first feature-length subject in the nature series, *The Living Desert*.

He saw no reason why the same material that had

received audience enthusiasm in his short subjects couldn't be adapted to a feature format, using real-life footage but presenting it in an entertaining manner.

The format of *The Living Desert* is one that became the standard for all successive True-Life features. It opens with the impressive True-Life logo, a gleaming globe turning within a frame, set against a sky-blue background. After the title credits, the film is introduced by a series of background pictures painted by an animated paintbrush on camera.

In *The Living Desert* the brush paints the North American continent, and illustrates the presence of trade winds in the Pacific and their effect. The brush then goes back over the continent, turning it into a relief map to illustrate how the winds are blocked from moving further east by the Rocky Mountains. This phenomenon creates the desert that we are about to explore.

The narrator for the films is Winston Hibler, a veteran on the Disney staff. The decision to have him narrate the series was not accidental, to be sure. He has a pleasant midwestern kind of speech that imbues the films with a reassuring air of homeyness; when his voice is first heard, it is clear that this won't be a college lecture, but, instead, an interesting talk.

Hibler co-wrote the script for *Desert* with director James Algar and Ted Sears. They like to indulge in flowery dramatics (the introduction tells us that this is "a drama as old as time itself," etc.), but somehow these phrases *work* as spoken by the unpretentious Hibler.

The scenarists display a reverence for the ways of God, as personified by Nature, with a capital N. Near the beginning of the film's animal footage, Hibler explains that "nature knows neither villain nor hero," so the ensuing battle between rattlesnake and tarantula is a question of might versus might, cunning versus cunning, not a good-guy bad-guy confrontation.

But this reverence does not carry over to specifics in the rest of the film, for much of the material in *The Living Desert* is played for laughs. One of the film's first

247

shots is of the bubbling vats found near desert geysers. Hibler calls the scene "a symphony of the mud puddles," a well-edited series of gurglings with appropriate music and sound effects. The outstanding use of sound effects in the films should be particularly mentioned, for though most of the footage was shot silent, it is sometimes hard to tell, so beautifully are the actual sounds of nature dubbed in.

From that point on there are numerous "gag" sequences throughout the film. Hibler even refers to a roadrunner seen early in the proceedings as "comedy relief" in the animal world of the desert. The narration is full of cute references; the chickwalla is called a "second-story man" as he scrounges through other animals' homes. A skunk is dubbed "Sweet William."

Worst of all is the musical humor. A millipede moves along to railroad music on the sound track. A burrowing snake inspires a ballet. And in two sequences stop and reverse motion are added so that the courtship of two tarantulas is set to a tango, and the mating of two scorpions is done in the form of a square dance (with Hibler doing the calls, using special material: "Stingers up for the stingaree, but watch out gal, you don't sting me . . ."). An owl observing the scene seemingly cocks his head in time to the music.

It was this Disneyesque touch that gave the series a bad name with many critics. It wasn't that these sequences weren't funny or clever; it was just that they didn't belong in what was being touted as a factual film. Bosley Crowther commented: ". . . Mr. Disney and his writers and editors are inclined to do with nature pictures pretty much what they have always done with cartoons." This was a far cry from the predictions of Richard Dyer McCann, who, during the film's preparation, had said that the film "may well be the biggest single step toward a new kind of maturity in American motion pictures," referring to widespread acceptance of documentary films. The real shame is that this kind of treatment was unnecessary, as later films in the series proved. Viewing the films with youngsters in the

A hawk and a rattlesnake engage in a fierce battle in *The Living Desert*. © *Walt Disney Productions*

The little kangaroo rat is fascinated by the movements of the sidewinder, but not so intrigued that he doesn't know enough to get out of the way. © *Walt Disney Productions*

audience demonstrates that this audience does not get restless during the film's "straight" moments. The sheer majesty and excitement of the actual footage is enough to rivet their attention to the screen.

In *The Living Desert* this is largely due to the close-up camera work. There are, to be sure, panoramic views of the desert, but these are used mostly as establishing shots before getting into the actual meat of the sequences, which are played with the camera at ground level so that we can become involved in the action of the animals, and not remain aloof observers.

Desert also has some of the best footage ever shot for the series. One segment concerning bats opens inside a cave just as the sun is setting. As if on cue, hundreds upon hundreds of the winged animals suddenly swarm out of the cave, literally blackening the sky as they go out for their nightly prowl.

The battle of the rattlesnake and the tarantula, and the later fight between a rattlesnake and a hawk, are both tremendously exciting, the effect of the latter augmented by the fact that the scene was intercut with several different camera angles. A less violent, but no less fascinating, scene has a little kangaroo-rat burrowing into the ground when a vicious sidewinder slithers along. The rat isn't afraid of the snake, only annoyed, and tries to shoo him away by kicking sand in his face, repeatedly hopping forward to see if the job is done, then leaping backward on the chance that the snake might strike. He is so persistent that the venomous snake actually gives up and goes away!

The final portion of the film has a series of impressive scenes. A dry spell is broken by a sudden cloudburst, at first a welcome relief for the desert, but then too much of a good thing. As the camera shows an apparently peaceful spot set between some craggy rocks and hills, there is a thunderous sound in the distance, and suddenly a "wall of water" rumbling toward the lens—it's a flash flood caused by the downpour. This instant river swallows everything in its path, but eventually it leaves its canyonlike place of origin to spread out over the vast desert, where the combination of expanse and the heat of the sun dries it up rather quickly.

It leaves behind one aftereffect, however, a new life for the flora of the desert. That evening the desert comes alive with night-blooming flowers (filmed in time-lapse photography) that blossom into desert beauty, only to close up with the first rays of the sun.

As the sun sets at the end of that day, narrator Hibler tells us that on the desert "there are no endings, only new beginnings."

The Living Desert's popularity and box-office success (it was released as a package with *Stormy*, a live-action short, and the animated *Ben and Me*), capped by the Academy Award for the year's best documentary feature, was a source of special satisfaction for Disney. He had been discouraged from doing the initial True-Life shorts, even by people within his organization, and when he embarked on a feature enterprise, he met with resistance from RKO, his distributor. It was this dispute that led to the formation of Disney's own distribution company, Buena Vista, an idea that had been in the back of brother Roy Disney's mind for some time.

What Disney was *not* prepared for was the anger of critics around the country for tampering with what was supposedly factual film; the scorpion dance in particular was the target of considerable attack. Though Disney had long since learned to ignore most criticism, he and his staff apparently did take heed in this case, for after the next feature, such gimmicky and "cute" material was virtually eliminated from the True-Life series.

In a 1967 filmed interview with the BBC's Philip Jenkinson, series director James Algar said that "there wasn't much of that material in the films," which "were done as outright straight reports of how an animal's life is led." But he also gave an indication of the naïveté of many viewers when he reported that "I have had people ask how we possibly get animals to move in time to music. The answer is evident to anyone who works with such films . . . we put the music to the action." It was

251

precisely the fear that children would grow up thinking that scorpions moved in time to square-dance music that caused many critics to lambaste Disney for imposing his "touch" on the material in the film.

The real crime is that such critics, who still mention the series in a derogatory light, never bothered to recheck the series later on, when the viewpoint started to change. Nor did they stop long enough to weigh the relative merits and liabilities of the film. For with all its faults, *The Living Desert* is still a magnificent film, with some of the most remarkable action ever caught on film. Its success opened the door for acceptance of such material with an audience that otherwise might have forever shunned documentary films.

And today, some twenty years after its release—twenty years in which the documentary film has undergone many changes in attitude and technique—*The Living Desert* retains all its power and magnitude. Because of the material it deals with, and the excellence of its photography, it will undoubtedly stay that way for many years to come.

THE VANISHING PRAIRIE

RELEASED BY BUENA VISTA IN AUGUST 17, 1954. PRINT by Technicolor (from a 16mm original). Associate producer: Ben Sharpsteen. Director: James Algar. Screenplay: James Algar, Winston Hibler, Ted Sears. Photography: Tom McHugh, James R. Simon, N. Paul Kenworthy, Jr., Cleveland P. Grant, Lloyd Beebe, Herb Crisler, Dick Borden, Warren Garst, Murl Deusing, Olin Seawall Pettingill, Jr., Stuart V. Jewell. Narrator: Winston Hibler. Musical director: Paul J. Smith. Orchestrations: Edward H. Plumb, Joseph Dubin. Production manager: Erwin Verity. Animation effects: Joshus Meador, Art Riley. Film editor: Lloyd Richardson. Special processes: Ub Iwerks. Sound director: C.

252

O. Slyfield. Sound recording: Harold J. Steck. Music editor: Al Teeter. Running time: 75 minutes.

As soon as the footage for *The Living Desert* was completed, Disney sent his photographers out again to tackle a new topic, the American prairie. Once again this material was supplemented by footage purchased from freelance cameramen who shot film on their own and submitted it to Disney. Another two years was needed to complete the second True-Life feature, but since work had begun while the first film was in the editing stages, Disney was able to release *The Vanishing Prairie* in 1954, less than a year after his initial success.

The magic paintbrush this time paints a picture of the United States to show how it is divided into three regions by the Rocky Mountains on the West and the Mississippi River toward the east, creating a natural boundary for the great American prairie, a region that, we are told, is dying a slow death.

The brush paints examples of cave drawings made by Indians that depict animals that once existed on the prairie, but that are now extinct.

As the spring thaw comes to the prairie today, life begins its new yearly cycle. Birds return to the region and alight on the streams and ponds—except that some are still partially frozen, causing the winged creatures to make some very slippery landings. Grebes, whooping cranes, and grouse all appear during the first days of spring.

A buffalo gives birth to a calf, removing the membranous sac and eating it, then massaging the newborn to build its circulation. The mother then helps its child as it tries to stand and walk. Finally on its own, the calf takes its place among the other buffalo in the herd.

Prong-horn antelope and big-horn sheep (who are amazingly surefooted along mountain paths) roam freely. But the deer is victimized by the mountain lion, which kills the weaker animal for one reason only: food for its young.

Prairie dogs build underground homes, with levees

Two buffalo meet head on in this scene from *The Vanishing Prairie*. © *Walt Disney Productions*

This prairie dog can't figure out where all the buffalo have come from. © *Walt Disney Productions*

around the entranceways to protect them from enemies and from the elements. A coyote, the prairie dog's greatest enemy, tries to invade his underground home, but the little animal is too fast, leading the coyote on an underground chase that results only in frustration.

Another enemy of the prairie dog is the falcon, who swoops down from above to catch its prey.

Even kindred animals fight each other, and one vicious buffalo battle incites a massive stampede. But fighting is forsaken when disaster strikes. A lightning bolt sets the prairie ablaze, the fire spreading with amazing rapidity until flames cover everything in sight. Nature provides relief in the form of a cloudburst, but soon there is too much of a good thing as a flash flood results, routing the prairie dogs from their homes.

Before long, however, the prairie returns to normal, the elements under control and life continuing in its everyday pattern. The narrator explains that we have seen examples of a life that is quickly going out of existence—actually a ''look into the past.''

Like *The Living Desert*, *The Vanishing Prairie* is a dazzling collection of sequences, brilliantly photographed and edited for maximum results. And like its predecessor, *The Vanishing Prairie* won the Academy Award for the year's best documentary feature film.

It also brought Disney into conflict with the state censorship board in New York—a confrontation no one dreamed would ever happen. That Walt Disney, the purveyor of the screen's finest family entertainment, should ever have censorship problems was the target of many a snicker in 1954—and a cause of considerable embarrassment for the New York board of censors.

The board decided to ban *The Vanishing Prairie* from New York State because of the sequence showing a buffalo giving birth. Disney was stunned by the decision. ''The birth scene would never have appeared on the screen if I believed it might offend an audience,'' he said, adding, ''it would be a shame if New York children had to believe the stork brings buffaloes, too."

After considerable comment, and a complaint lodged by the American Civil Liberties Union, the board reversed its decision and the film was allowed to be shown intact. The *New Yorker*'s critic wrote: ". . . Mr. Disney shows us the birth of a buffalo calf—an episode that, I understand, caused the state censors (who themselves must at one time have been born) a bit of uneasiness. I lived through the scene, and I suspect you will, too."

Generally speaking, the film was well received by most critics, although there were still complaints about such sequences as two bighorn sheep locking horns to the tune of "The Anvil Chorus." But there was less of this material in *Prairie* than there had been in *Desert,* and criticism was proportionately milder.

The film espouses the same themes as earlier True-Life films: the endless cycle of life, the inevitability of nature (one animal must be killed so that another may survive, etc.). The life-styles of the various animals are well presented, giving each species a feeling of individuality in the viewer's mind.

The miracles of life are presented in a straightforward manner, most notably the birth scene, which in its utter simplicity is absolutely fascinating. There is no attempt to doctor the sequence or impose human viewpoints on the animals' actions.

Though the Disney company usually tried to keep their photographers' techniques a secret, Hollywood correspondent Joe Hyams presented a revealing article on how a great deal of the film was made. Tom McHugh shot most of the buffalo footage over a long period of time. Patience was the key ingredient in getting the footage he wanted. In order to get close to the animals, he covered himself and his camera with an old buffalo hide and wandered into the midst of the herd. When he found a buffalo who was carrying a calf, he simply stayed by its side until the birth took place.

For the stampede he set up a series of cameras along the path the buffalo were sure to follow, stringing trip wires across the road. When the animals ran through, they set off the cameras and provided one of the film's most impressive sequences. Indeed, the film is full of ingenious photography, such as the scene of the hawk attacking the prairie dog; the camera is at ground level, with the dog in tight close-up, as the hawk swoops down right into the lens, missing its target by a hair. For some scenes three to five cameramen shot the same action, providing a variety of angles for the editor to assemble.

The sequences of the prairie dogs' homes were artificially prepared by creating a controlled situation, a replica of the prairie earth "sliced in half," bordered on one side by a dark plate glass, much like ant farms. After giving the animals plenty of time to get accustomed to the new surroundings, the photographers were able to shoot their footage through the glass and simulate what must actually happen on the prairie.

An estimated 120,000 feet of 16mm film was shot and edited down to the 30,000 used in the release print of the film. Only in this fashion could the Disney staff present such truly outstanding material—by giving its photographers the opportunity to *wait* and get exactly what they were after.

In its recent reissue *The Vanishing Prairie* showed that, like the other films in this series, it retains its full dramatic impact for audiences of all ages to marvel at an existence they otherwise might never have a chance to observe.

20,000 LEAGUES UNDER THE SEA

RELEASED BY BUENA VISTA ON DECEMBER 23, 1954. Technicolor, CinemaScope. Director: Richard Fleischer. Screenplay: Earl Felton, based on the novel by Jules Verne. Photography: Franz Planer, A.S.C. Special effects photography: Ralph Hammeras, A.S.C. Under-

A view of the fantastic, futuristic submarine *Nautilus*.
© *Walt Disney Productions*

water photography: Till Gabbani. Editor: Elmo
Williams, A.C.E. Art director: John Meehan. Set
decorations: Emile Kuri. Costumes: Norman Martien.
Music: Paul J. Smith. Orchestrations: Joseph S. Dubin.
Production manager: Fred Leahy. Second unit director:
James Havens. Assistant directors: Tom Connors, Jr.,
Russ Haverick. Matte artist: Peter Ellenshaw. Special
processes: Ub Iwerks. Special effects: John Hench,
Joshua Meador. Diving master: Fred Zendar. Produc-
tion development: Harper Goff. Sketch artist: Bruce
Bushman. Technicolor consultant: Morgan Padleford.
Makeup, hairstyling: Lou Hippe. Sound director: C. O.
Slyfield. Sound recording: Robert O. Cook. Running
time: 127 minutes.

Song: "A Whale of a Tale" by Al Hoffman and Norman
Gimbel.

Cast: Kirk Douglas (Ned Land), James Mason (Captain Nemo), Paul Lukas (Professor Aronnax), Peter Lorre (Conseil), Robert J. Wilke (first mate of *Nautilus*), Carleton Young (John Howard), Ted de Corsia (Captain Farragut), Percy Helton (diver), Ted Cooper (mate of *Lincoln*), Edward Marr (shipping agent), Fred Graham (Casey Moore), J. M. Kerrigan (Billy), Harry Harvey (shipping clerk), Herb Vigran (reporter).

20,000 Leagues Under the Sea was Disney's most ambitious live-action film to date, and it remains one of the most successful he ever made.

Disney knew that no amount of money, technical wizardry, or inventiveness could take the place of a good story. And he was certain that Jules Verne's futuristic tale of a despotic sea captain and his fantastic submarine was a story worthy of a major production. Consequently, no expense was spared in putting this story on the screen. Since Disney had no full-time live-action crew on the payroll, the personnel were hand-picked from the Hollywood hopper.

Ironically, the man chosen to direct the film was Richard Fleischer, the son of Disney's onetime rival Max Fleischer, who had started in short subjects and shown tremendous promise with modest low-budget films like *Narrow Margin* and *So This Is New York*.

Planning *20,000 Leagues* entailed more complex work than any live film Disney had yet tackled. Compared to the logistics of shooting, the screenplay must have been relatively simple, although director Fleischer recalls that "it was a very difficult book to translate to the screen, because there wasn't really any story."

Characters and their interplay were developed, with appropriate thought given to limited comedy relief from the tense dramatics of the story line. For the first time Disney decided to hire well-known names to head his cast, and he made an ideal selection with Kirk Douglas as the swaggering sailor Ned Land, James Mason as the Machiavellian Captain Nemo, Paul Lukas as the distinguished professor, and Peter Lorre as his aide-de-camp.

Art director John Meehan was imported from Paramount studios, where he had won Academy Awards for his work on *The Heiress* and *Sunset Boulevard*. His creations, particularly the main lounge of the submarine, replete with velvet chairs, divans, rococo ornaments, and a pipe organ, are largely responsible for the film's success.

Veteran cameraman Franz Planer had the double challenge of working in the newly developed CinemaScope process, and trying to create believable and sufficient lighting in sets that were built with viewable ceilings (in order to emphasize the submarine's interior settings).

The submarine itself, the *Nautilus*, was built to scale, two hundred feet long, shaped as Verne had described it, as an undersea monster, its headlights appearing as "eyes" in the dark waters.

Although most underwater filming was done on location, a special sound stage was built at the studio to house a giant tank for more intimate and complex shots. Most of the seagoing material was shot off the coast of Nassau in the Bahamas, where the fifty-four-man crew spent eight weeks filming. Aware that the story of how the film was made could be in some ways as interesting as the film itself, Disney assigned a second unit to make a documentary about the filming of *20,000 Leagues*. The resulting hour-long film, shown on the Disney TV show as *Operation Undersea,* won an Emmy award as the year's best individual program.

The plot of the film has to do with the strange reports of a sea monster attacking ships in the Pacific in 1868. The armed frigate *Abraham Lincoln* is sent out to sea to find and destroy this monster; aboard the ship are harpooner Ned Land, Professor Pierre Aronnax, a specialist on sea creatures, and his assistant Conseil. The *Lincoln* does indeed find the monster, but is attacked and sunk; Land, Aronnax, and Conseil withstand the crash and are rescued by the "monster," which turns out to be a submarine.

Its commander, Captain Nemo, is a misfit genius who

has harnessed some of the world's greatest discoveries, but is bound to use them to destroy mankind. The Professor welcomes the opportunity to learn from the *Nautilus*'s expeditions, but Ned Land's only thought is of escape, and gradually he wins Conseil to his way of thinking. When the sub makes a stop at a tropic island, Ned sends a flurry of bottles with notes in them out to sea on the chance that one might be spotted.

The *Nautilus* is heading for Vulcania, the island headquarters of Nemo and his men. Along the way the submarine is attacked by a giant squid; Ned rescues Nemo from the clutches of the sea beast and earns his gratitude.

Prodded by the Professor, Nemo decides to make peace with the world and share the fantastic secrets he has learned—of atomic energy, electricity, and other wonders. But when they reach Vulcania, warships are waiting in ambush, having received Ned's message. Infuriated, Nemo determines that no one shall learn his secrets; he plants a deadly explosive on the island, returns to the submarine, and holding Ned, the Professor, and Conseil captive, orders the *Nautilus* to make a final trip to the ocean floor. He has been shot while planting his bomb, and this will be his last voyage.

Ned manages to break loose, and rescues his comrades just in time to flee the submerging vessel. As they float to safety, they see the results of the bomb, which completely destroys the island, the warships, and everything in sight, as the *Nautilus* goes down for the last time.

20,000 Leagues Under the Sea is fantasy at its best, with the Disney production team making the unbelievable come to life, in order to project a convincing tale against real-life backgrounds. The sumptuous mounting and careful attention to detail contribute immeasurably to the overall effect.

James Mason is compelling as Captain Nemo, wavering on that fine line between genius and madman, playing Bach's "Toccata in D Minor" on his pipe organ one moment, and planning a murderous attack the next. The balance of the cast fills the various roles to perfection, Douglas's byplay with Nemo's pet seal and Lorre's unique personality providing gentle but welcome comedy relief.

In fact, everything about the film seems unmistakably *right*. It was obviously the result of tremendous effort, and director Richard Fleischer recalls one instance of Disney's insistence upon perfection, no matter the cost.

The fight with the octopus was very difficult, more a mechanical problem than anything else. The first time we tried it, the monster just didn't work; it got waterlogged, and started to sink. It wasn't engineered properly, and it couldn't do all the things we needed it to do. It looked very phony anyway. After we spent a lot of money on it, and a lot of time, Walt and I finally decided to stop this sequence, go on to something else, and give us a chance to redo this animal.

I was talking to the writer, and we realized that the concept was wrong. When we first did the sequence it was done on a flat, calm sea at sunset, and everything was very clear; you could see the mechanics of this thing too clearly. We came up with the idea that this should be done at night, during a storm at sea, so we had spray, and waves, and great excitement and obscuring action so that you don't see all the flaws. It made it a hundred times more expensive to do that way, but when we presented the idea to Walt, he said, "You're absolutely right, do it that way."

Another frequent problem was getting fish to swim by the camera; most of them carefully avoided the production areas. In more than one instance this problem was solved by having animated fish "swim" in front of the lens (particularly notice in the first scene of Paul Lukas standing with Mason in the picture-window nose of the submarine).

Such perfectionism, made possible by the resources of the Disney studio, was responsible for *20,000*

The inside of the *Nautilus* is also something to see. Here Captain Nemo treats his captives to a sumptuous dinner. James Mason, Kirk Douglas, Peter Lorre, and Paul Lucas. © *Walt Disney Productions*

A highlight of the film has Captain Nemo battling a giant squid atop his submarine. © *Walt Disney Productions*

Leagues Under the Sea becoming one of the great films of its kind, as well as one of Disney's biggest grossing films. It would be some time before Disney would top this achievement in the field of live-action films.

DAVY CROCKETT, KING OF THE WILD FRONTIER

RELEASED BY BUENA VISTA ON MAY 25, 1955. TECHnicolor. Producer: Bill Walsh. Director: Norman Foster. Screenplay: Tom Blackburn. Photography: Charles P. Boyle. Editor: Chester Schaeffer. Art director: Marvin Aubrey Davis. Set decorations: Emile Kuri, Pat Delaney. Costumes: Norman Martien. Music: George Bruns. Orchestrations: Edward H. Plumb. Unit production manager: Henry Spitz. Assistant director: James Judson Cox. Matte artist: Peter Ellenshaw. Special artwork: Joshua Meador, Art Riley, Ken Anderson. Special processes: Ub Iwerks. Makeup: Lon Philippi. Sound: C. O. Slyfield, Robert O. Cook. Running time: 93 minutes.

Songs: "The Ballad of Davy Crockett" by Tom Blackburn, George Bruns. "Farewell" by Davy Crockett, George Bruns.

Cast: Fess Parker (Davy Crockett), Buddy Ebsen (George Russel), Basil Ruysdael (Andrew Jackson), Hans Conried (Thimblerig), William Bakewell (Tobias Norton), Kenneth Tobey (Colonel Jim Bowie), Pat Hogan (Chief Red Stick), Helene Stanley (Polly Crockett), Nick Cravat (Bustedluck), Don Megowan (Colonel Billy Travis), Mike Mazurki (Bigfoot Mason), Jeff Thompson (Charlie Two Shirts), Henry Joyner (Swaney), Benjamin Hornbuckle (Henderson), Hal Youngblood (opponent political speaker), Jim Maddux (first congressman), Robert Booth (second congressman),

Eugene Brindel (Billy), Ray Whitetree (Johnny), Campbell Brown (Bruno).

The phenomenal success of Davy Crockett caught everyone by surprise, including Walt Disney. The character was developed as a subject for some "Frontierland" episodes on the Disneyland TV show, and as Disney later told it: "We had no idea what was going to happen to 'Crockett.' Why, by the time the first show finally got on the air, we were already shooting the third one and calmly killing Davy off at the Alamo. It became one of the biggest overnight hits in TV history, and there we were with just three films and a dead hero."

Where there's a will, there's a way, however, and Disney did his best to keep Davy alive. First of all there was that song, an innocuous little tune called "The Ballad of Davy Crockett," which before long was on the lips of every young boy in America. Then came the merchandising boom, headed by coonskin caps and followed by a wide assortment of unrelated products.

Finally it was decided to take advantage of the Crockett boom and splice the three one-hour programs into a feature film for theatrical release, just in time for summer vacation. Here is where Disney's policy of turning out quality TV programming paid off, for the finished product, trimmed to ninety minutes, hardly betrays its television origin—a neat trick that few other producers could have pulled off. Disney also had the foresight to film his series in color.

The resulting feature film is an episodic but well-paced entertainment. Special animation involving Davy Crockett's *Journal,* and a colorful relief map of the country, provide transitions between segments, accompanied by special lyrics to the Davy Crockett theme song.

The opening segment deals with Davy the Indian Fighter, an unorthodox civilian volunteer scout whom the British grow to find invaluable. Assigned to track down the savage Chief Red Stick, he does, but instead of killing him, wins his admiration and respect.

He and his sidekick Georgie Russel then help a small

265

Davy Crockett engages in hand-to-hand combat with Chief Red Stick (Pat Hogan). © *Walt Disney Productions*

Davy (Fess Parker), Georgie (Buddy Ebsen), and Thimblerig (Hans Conried) survey the territory ahead of them.
© *Walt Disney Productions*

town get rid of a thieving troublemaker called Bigfoot Mason. Davy becomes a local hero, and is encouraged to run for office. When he receives word that his young wife has died suddenly, he decides that he has nothing tying him down anymore, and agrees.

Once in the Nashville legislature, he is approached by his former General, Andrew Jackson, who is running for President and wants Davy to run for Congress on the same ticket. When elected, Davy goes around the country on speaking tours, bolstering the legend created by his friend Georgie's pulp fiction about their exploits. Then he discovers that Jackson has used his absence to try to put through a bill taking land away from the Indians. He returns to Congress just in time to head off a vote, register his disgust, and resign.

He and his sidekick then take off for new adventure in Texas, encountering a sly dandy named Thimblerig along the way. They arrive at the Alamo and find a rapidly deteriorating situation. Leader Jim Bowie is injured and cannot leave his bed; he tells Crockett in confidence that they are running out of food and ammunition. Later, when Davy tells the men that things look bleak and they are free to go, everyone stays to finish the fight. The Mexicans break into the fort and fight hand to hand. The men put up a valiant fight, knowing it is their last. Our final view of Davy Crockett shows him swinging his rifle to ward off attackers, as the ballad tells us he did not die, because his spirit lives on.

There are several indications in this film that the Disney people did not expect Davy to become a national hero all over again. Though he is an admirable man, he is violent when he has to be, as in the hand-to-hand fights, as well as the initial Indian battle, where he is seen bayoneting various red men, hollering "Give it to 'em, boys!" and such. He is also shown to have a not inconsiderable ego ("We'll give 'em the old Crockett charge," he announces at one point), perfectly willing to play on his fame during the speaking tour.

After Davy became the idol of millions, writers Tom Blackburn and Norman Foster (the latter also directed) were more careful to make him a pious and fault-free character.

It is also interesting to note that a film made under the aegis of Walt Disney shows Davy Crockett being "used" by the President of the United States! Those who find nothing but pablum in Disney's product ought to look again.

The film itself is fairly well made, although occasional economies are apparent. Throughout the film Georgie will say to Davy, "Hey, look at that," and there will be an insert of a bear, alligator, or other animal obviously snipped from a Disney nature reel. There is a glass shot of the Capitol building in Washington, but on the other end of the scale authentic locations are used for the legislature and Jackson's colonial home, which adds a nice feeling of reality to the otherwise fictitious doings.

It is easy to see where the three segments begin and end, but basically the editing job is smooth. One jarring note is the character played by Hans Conried, Thimblerig, whose appearance is insufficiently explained in the feature-film version of the story.

It has been reported that Buddy Ebsen was originally being considered for the role of Davy. Then one day some Disney people were screening a science-fiction film called *Them!,* and took a fancy to a young actor who had a brief but prominent scene. They tested him and decided that here was their Davy Crockett. Overnight Fess Parker became a star.

There is something about Parker that projects sincerity to an audience, and obviously he was a perfect choice to play Davy. Subsequent roles for Disney showed him to be a competent and likable actor, but one of limited range. Director Norman Foster later recalled: "I found if I didn't do something to get adrenaline in his system, he would get slower and slower. He seemed to lack vitality. I told him to take vitamin pills."

Buddy Ebsen provided a perfect counterpart for

Parker's dry, understated manner with his affable and often boisterous performance as Georgie Russel. It is his exuberance, not Parker's, that puts over a scene, such as the one where the two scouts save some British soldiers from an Indian ambush by giving the appearance of having the redskins "surrounded," purely by verbal tricks.

Obviously, Davy Crockett was too good a thing to let go with just a one-shot TV exposure and feature-film follow-up. He would be heard from again the following year.

LADY AND THE TRAMP

RELEASED BY BUENA VISTA ON JUNE 16, 1955. TECH-nicolor, CinemaScope. Associate producer: Erdman Penner. Directors: Hamilton Luske, Clyde Geronimi, Wilfred Jackson. Directing animators: Milt Kahl, Franklin Thomas, Oliver Johnston, Jr., John Louns-bery, Wolfgang Reitherman, Eric Larson, Hal King, Les Clark. Story: Erdman Penner, Joe Rinaldi, Ralph Wright, Donald Da Gradi, based on an original story by Ward Greene. Animators: George Nicholas, Hal Am-bro, Ken O'Brien, Jerry Hathcock, Erick Cleworth, Marvin Woodward, Ed Aardal, John Sibley, Harvey Toombs, Cliff Nordberg. Don Lusk, George Kreisl, Hugh Fraser, John Freeman, Jack Campbell, Bob Carl-son. Backgrounds: Claude Coats, Dick Anthony, Ralph Hulett, Albert Dempster, Thelma Witmer, Eyvind Earle, Jimi Trout, Ray Huffine, Brice Mack. Layout: Ken Anderson, Tom Codrick, Al Zinnen, A. Kendall O'Connor, Hugh Hennesy, Lance Nolley, Jacques Rupp, McLaren Stewart, Don Griffith, Thor Putnam, Collin Campbell, Victor Haboush, Bill Bosche. Effects animation: George Rowley, Dan McManus. Music score: Oliver Wallace. Orchestrations: Edward H.

Plumb, Sidney Fine. Vocal arrangements: John Rarig. Film editor: Donald Halliday. Sound director: C. O. Slyfield. Sound recording: Harold J. Steck, Robert O. Cook. Music editor: Evelyn Kennedy. Special processes: Ub Iwerks. Running time: 75 minutes.

Songs: "He's a Tramp," "La La Lu," "Siamese Cat Song," "Peace on Earth," "Bella Notte" by Sonny Burke and Peggy Lee.

Voices: Peggy Lee (Darling, Peg, Si, and Am), Barbara Luddy (Lady), Larry Roberts (Tramp), Bill Thompson (Jock, Bull, Dachsie), Bill Baucon (Trusty), Stan Freberg (Beaver), Verna Felton (Aunt Sarah), Alan Reed (Boris), George Givot (Tony), Dallas McKennon (Toughy, Professor), Lee Millar (Jim Dear), The Mello Men.

For his first animated feature since *Peter Pan,* Disney chose a story by Ward Greene called *Lady and the Tramp*. He later explained: "We were free to develop the story as we saw fit, which is not the case when you work on a classic. Then you must adhere rigidly to the sequences conceived by the author, which are familiar to your audience. Here, as the characters came to life and the scenes took shape, we were able to alter, embellish, eliminate and change to improve the material." Although the statement was made as a publicity release, it does make clear the advantage the Disney staff enjoyed with this film.

The result is a well-thought-out, enjoyable cartoon feature, not as compelling as many earlier works, but certainly more handsome than some, due in large part to Disney's decision to make the film in CinemaScope. Thus, an added emphasis was given to the layout and design departments to create a succession of picturesque backgrounds against which the story could be played.

The film opens on a panoramic view of a quaint New England town in the early part of the century during a

270

Lady and Tramp meet in a kiss when they both nibble on the same strand of spaghetti at Tony's. © *Walt Disney Productions*

Trusty and Jock try to divert the driver of the paddy wagon carrying Tramp away. © *Walt Disney Productions*

snowfall. Darling (the human heroine) opens her Christmas package to find a female puppy inside, a gift from her husband Jim Dear. They name her Lady, and in a filmic transition we see her grow up.

She lives in an exclusive section of town with her canine friends Jock (a Scottish terrier) and Trusty (a basset hound devoid of the sense of smell) on the same block. When they chance to encounter a dog from the wrong side of the tracks (Tramp), they treat him with disdain.

Darling gives birth to a baby; at first Lady is apprehensive, because she has been ignored in all the excitement, but when the baby arrives, Jim Dear and Darling apologize and introduce her to the new member of the family. Unfortunately, they must go away for a few days, and Darling's Aunt Sarah comes to mind the baby. She takes an instant dislike to Lady, heightened when her scheming Siamese cats make a shambles of the living room and foist the blame on Lady. Aunt Sarah buys a muzzle for the perplexed dog.

At this Lady breaks loose, but she soon finds herself in unfamiliar territory, being chased by some tough street dogs. Luckily, Tramp is nearby, and he rescues her, taking her to the zoo where he persuades an industrious beaver that the muzzle would be of value to him in hauling logs. The beaver obligingly cuts through the muzzle and sets Lady free.

Then Tramp takes Lady around town, showing the sheltered pet his freewheeling view of life and romancing her over spaghetti dinner at the back entrance to Tony's restaurant.

The next morning Lady awakens to her responsibility, to return home and look after the baby; Tramp is unable to persuade her to stay footloose and fancy free. On their way home he goads her into joining him for a quick spree through a chicken coop, and she is trapped by a dogcatcher. In the dog pound she meets some other canines who tell her that Tramp is a bit of a rogue and a ladies' man; Lady is totally disillusioned.

Aunt Sarah comes to claim Lady, and chains her to

her doghouse in the backyard. When Tramp comes to apologize, she refuses to listen to him. Then she sees a slimy neighborhood rat coming up the side of the house and into the baby's room. She breaks her chain and, with Tramp, gets upstairs into the room to save the child; Tramp engages in a vicious scrap with the rodent, emerging triumphant, by knocking over the baby's crib in the process. Sarah comes in, doesn't see the rat, and thinks that Tramp has attacked the child!

She has the dogcatcher come to take him away. Just then, Jim Dear and Darling arrive home and discover what has happened. Jock and Trusty decide not to waste any time in going after the dogcatcher to stop him; using Trusty's nonexistent sense of smell, they try to track down the wagon, and miraculously they do, racing after it with Jim Dear and Darling not far behind in a cab. They succeed in stopping the wagon and saving Tramp, but in the excitement the wagon overturns, crushing poor Trusty.

The next scene, however, shows that Trusty has only suffered a broken leg, as he and Jock come to pay a Christmas visit to Lady, Tramp, and their growing brood of children—three little ladies, and one little tramp. The film ends on the same snowy panorama with which it began.

Though *Lady and the Tramp*'s story may not be much, its varied assets—highlight sequences, the songs, some of the visuals—are strong enough to make the film a most congenial piece of fluff.

The story is told from a dog's-eye view, the humans never really shown in much detail, although they figure prominently in key sequences. Animation buff Mike Barrier has pointed out that there is a conflict, however, between two approaches in the film: part of the time the situations stress the fact that these are dogs, and at other times an attempt is made to give them human characteristics. It is as if the Disney staff considered both angles, saw that both could work, and then didn't have the heart to reject one set of gags in favor of the other, resulting in a combination of both.

Most of the film's best sequences are built around songs, and the film's score is particularly delightful, as written by Peggy Lee and Sonny Burke, and in several cases, sung by Miss Lee, who does the voices for Darling, the Siamese cats, and Peg. When Tramp takes Lady to dinner at the back door of the Italian restaurant, the owner, Tony, and his cook, Joe, do their best to make it a special occasion. (They admire Lady, and the restaurateur tells Tramp: "You take-a Tony's advice and settle down with this one.") After serving a meal of spaghetti and meat balls, they serenade the canine couples with a love song, "Bella Notte," accompanying themselves on accordion and violin. During the song Lady and Tramp nibble at the same strand of spaghetti, bringing their lips together in a kiss.

When the song speaks of "stars in her eyes," we see stars in Lady's eyes, and the camera pans up between two tenement buildings toward the moon, partially obscured by laundry strung between the two buildings. Then an off-screen chorus picks up the song for another verse as we see a series of romantic vignettes with Lady and Tramp throughout the evening (admiring the moon from a lover's lane where humans are doing the same thing).

Later, when Lady is thrown into the dog pound, she meets a colorful assortment of dogs, including a cockney bulldog, an aristocratic Russian wolfhound, and the saucy Peg, who fills Lady in on her boyfriend by singing "He's a Tramp."

This sequence also has a curious but very engaging spoof of prison films, with one dog working on a tunnel and another being taken off to the gas chamber. ("Poor Nutzy is taking the long walk," another dog comments sadly.) Though such humor is momentarily jarred amidst the general straightforwardness of the rest of the film, it does add a nice touch to the now jaunty proceedings.

There is also humor inherent in the felines' song, which begins, "We are Siamese if you please/We are Siamese if you don't please . . ." Though their subsequent actions are a bit hard to take, the coyness of the two slithery cats in this song makes the scene a delight.

Another comic highlight is the attempt to convince the beaver of the muzzle's value to him, thanks in large part to Stan Freberg's amusing voice characterization for the animal. When he does bite the muzzle off, and tries to use its teeth to pull a log downhill for him, he gets tangled up and soon finds himself tumbling down the hill in a state of utter disarray. When the log miraculously lands right in place at his dam, however, and he looks up, unharmed, he smiles the smile of a satisfied customer.

There are other, smaller, visual ideas in the film, such as the scene near the beginning where Lady, her first night in the house, insists on sleeping on the bed with Jim Dear and Darling. Jim finally gives in, warning, "But tonight only." The pictures dissolves to show Lady's growth while she continues sleeping, an ingenious way to show considerable passage of time and establish an important point (Jim and Darling's pampering of Lady) with an absolute minimum of effort.

There is an amusing dreamlike sequence where Tramp tells Lady what life will be like for her when the baby arrives and her masters' attention will be drawn away from her, and another nice transitional scene of months passing until the baby's birth (with Lady walking through the transparent pages of a calendar to show passage of time).

The climactic sequences have considerably more atmosphere than the rest of the film, with its pastel colors and meticulous backgrounds. The fight with the rat takes place during a rainfall, with flashes of lightning outside, and especially dramatic cutting to heighten the emotional impact (in addition to which, the rat itself is designed to be especially disgusting).

The subsequent chase through the streets for the dog-catcher's wagon takes place after the rainfall, on muddy streets lit only by the moon and occasional streetlamps casting reflections in the puddles scattered about. It is one of the most visually impressive sequences in the film.

The use of CinemaScope is especially skillful, without being ostentatious, as it was in many live-action films at this time. Ward Kimball wrote about the experience of first using 'Scope in an article for *Films in Review:*

> Our layout men, whose work is analogous to that of set designers, had to re-scheme the staging of all action to suit backgrounds twice as long as those we had been using. In doing so they soon made a discovery: in CinemaScope, *cartoon characters* move, not the backgrounds. Because there is more space, the characters can move about without getting outside the visual angle. They can also move about more in relation to each other. In CinemaScope cartoon characters no longer perform in one spot against a moving background, *but are moved through the scenes.*
>
> Fewer separate scenes and fewer cuts [are] needed, since the action takes place in continuous, unbroken movement across one wide vista, where formerly numerous cuts back and forth had to be employed. Also, panoramic backgrounds are fewer and more figures can be shown simultaneously.

If there is a criticism to be made about the animation in the film, it is that this film represents the height of literalism in Disney's work. *Sleeping Beauty* was more elaborate than *Lady and the Tramp,* but, because it was a fairy tale, offered more opportunity for visual invention.

Though *Lady* does have its share of pictorial ideas, the film as a whole seems to be striving for a goal of realism in its setting, backgrounds, movements, and detail work. From one point of view this is something to marvel at, an achievement Disney was able to carry out better than any other animation studio. From another standpoint it takes a lot of the fun out of animation. Where is the wonderful visual hyperbole of *Dumbo,* the boundless imagination of *Fantasia*, the surrealism of *The Three Caballeros*, or even the stylistic vision of reality of *Bambi?*

One of *Lady and the Tramp*'s biggest laughs with a small-fry audience comes at the beginning of the dog-pound sequence, where four scruffy mongrels howl out a pitiful version of "Home, Sweet Home." The incongruity of the situation, plus the amusing rendition, make it one of the solid gag points in the film. But there is little of such material in *Lady;* it tries to compensate with a full quota of charm, more likely to appeal to older audiences.

Much of the "charm" was lost on critics, however, who gave the film a surprisingly negative reaction. The *New Yorker* thought the story was handled "with a sentimentality that Albert Payson Terhune might have found excessive," and found the leading characters singularly unappealing. The critic also seemed bent on attacking CinemaScope, which, he said, "gives them [the dogs] the dimensions of hippos." The same quixotic streak ran through Bosley Crowther's review in the *New York Times*, in which he noted that CinemaScope made the film's "flaws" more apparent, adding that "the artists' work is below par." (One begins to wonder if these critics saw the same film everybody else did—"dimensions of hippos"? "flaws"?) Meanwhile *Variety*, in a generally favorable review, commented: "Curiously, in making a hero out of the jaunty Tramp, the writers worked in a fight with a rat that recalls to mind the terror of the bat episode in *Lost Weekend*. This is for kids?"

So once more Disney's accolades were to come not in the form of reviews, but from the public, which made the film a substantial hit. It was accompanied in general release by the first "People and Places" subject in CinemaScope, *Switzerland*.

The film received a major shot in the arm on Disney's own TV show, where Peggy Lee explained how the score came about, and demonstrated some of the songs from the movie with Sonny Burke and the Mello Men.

Recently Miss Lee expressed her warm memories of the film by saying: "Walt Disney was such a wonderful man to work with—so enthusiastic and full of ideas, just brimming."

In its two theatrical reissues, *Lady and the Tramp* has continued to please audiences, and though it is easy to cite its shortcomings and complain about how it *should* have been done, it shares with most of Disney's animated features a total likability that, at least at the time of viewing, seems to transcend all other considerations. It is only later that one is able to pinpoint faults.

Lady and the Tramp cost an estimated $4 million and took over three years to produce. Disney wanted to go one step further for his next animated endeavor, and he envisioned *Sleeping Beauty* as the screen's ultimate cartoon feature.

THE AFRICAN LION

RELEASED BY BUENA VISTA ON SEPTEMBER 14, 1955. Technicolor (from 16mm). Associate producer: Ben Sharpsteen. Director: James Algar. Photography: Alfred G. Milotte, Elma Milotte. Writers: James Algar, Winston Hibler, Ted Sears, Jack Moffitt. Narrator: Winston Hibler. Music: Paul J. Smith. Orchestrations: Joseph Dubin. Production manager: Erwin Verity. Special processes: Ub Iwerks. Film editor: Norman Palmer, A.C.E. Animation effects: Joshua Meador, Art Riley. Sound director: Robert O. Cook. Music editor: Evelyn Kennedy. Running time: 75 minutes.

The African Lion is a stunning film. Every time it produces an obvious highlight sequence, one settles back to relax, but before long there is another equally

The African lioness with her cubs. © *Walt Disney Productions*

Disney toasts Elma and Alfred Milotte as they embark on their
journey to Africa. (Note the beverage used—Donald Duck orange
juice.) *Courtesy British Film Institute*

exciting piece of film to top the one before it.

Alfred and Elma Milotte, who had filmed the first True-Life short subject, and launched the entire series, spent three years in Africa and exposed 100,000 feet of film for this feature, a far cry geographically from their initial venture.

The time was well spent, for *African Lion* abounds with thrilling and beautiful scenes. What is more, it conforms to the True-Life formula without resorting to the much criticized gimmickry of earlier True-Life features. This not only doesn't diminish the interest in its subject matter, but it actually enables the audience to become *more* involved. This is not to say that there isn't room for lighter moments in these documentaries; there is some very amusing footage of playful baboons in *African Lion,* and narration that brings the animals' lives and characteristics into focus for a young audience, explaining, for instance, that a giraffe is "three times as tall as a tall man" or observing that "the king of beasts is a helpless male compared to his mate."

A foreword declares that "the story is nature's own, the actions of her creatures, completely spontaneous."

The film opens with the paintbrush filling in a picture of the African continent, then filling in the various sections as narrator Winston Hibler points out the various regions and their characteristics. The lion's life-style is considered in the cyclical format used throughout these films; with each season we not only examine the lion, but his compatriots in the jungle, and the physical characteristics of the region.

The film's high points stand out in one's memory: an antelope leaping through the air in a mad chase . . . a beautiful shot of a pride of lions sleeping under a picturesque tree whose branches bend over under them . . . a cheetah racing after a gazelle at eighty miles per hour before making his kill (the camera following laterally, catching the excitement of the chase perfectly) . . . a lioness stalking her prey, and trying to ward off the scavengers (a jackal, a vulture, and a hyena) who want to distract her long enough to get at the meat and tear it apart . . . elephants digging impromptu wells during the dry season . . . a rhino inexorably stuck in the mud, struggling to get out (which he can't do) . . . terrible dust storms . . . fantastic shots of a locust invasion, showing how their wings filter sunlight to produce incredible visual effects.

The lion family is shown under various conditions, with the female providing for the male and her cubs, killing other animals only to supply food for the family.

The film ends with the coming of tropical rains that begin the new yearly life cycle.

The Milottes considered this their favorite film, and expressed unending gratitude to Walt Disney for enabling them to pursue such a lengthy project without economic pressure or interference. Appropriately, *The African Lion* received accolades. Bosley Crowther called it "the purest of the Disney nature films," and in retrospect, Pauline Kael, while condemning the series as a whole, singled out *African Lion* as a choice item for children's viewing.

Ironically, though the earlier features, which had earned the series wide disfavor, won two Academy Awards, this one was bypassed in favor of *Helen Keller in Her Story,* an independent production.

An interesting sidenote to the film in an incident that occurred during filming in Africa. (The Milottes traveled through Kenya, Uganda, Tanganyika, South Africa, and Zululand to collect their footage.) The Milottes are documentarians in the truest sense of the word, and they attempted to remain passive observers as much as possible in filming their wildlife studies. But after shooting the sequence of a rhinoceros stuck in a deep mudhole, they decided that it was more important to be compassionate human beings than merely zoological filmmakers, and, with considerable effort, dislodged the animal from the mud. The rhino showed its appreciation by charging after Alfred Milotte, who scrambled into his trailer, which soon shook with a resounding thud from the crash of the animal's horn against the side. So much for humanity.

281

PERRI

RELEASED BY BUENA VISTA ON AUGUST 28, 1957. TECHnicolor. Producer, narrator: Winston Hibler. Directors: N. Paul Kenworthy, Jr., Ralph Wright. Screenplay: Ralph Wright, Winston Hibler, based on a novel by Felix Salten. Photography: N. Paul Kenworthy, Jr., Joel Colman, Walter Perkins, William Ratcliffe, James R. Simon, John P. Hermann, David Meyer, Warren E. Garst, Roy Edward Disney. Music: Paul J. Smith. Song arrangements: Carl Brandt. Orchestrations: Carl Brandt, Franklyn Marks. Production manager: Louis Debney. Special processes: Ub Iwerks, A.S.C. Film editor: Jack L. Atwood. Special art effects: Peter Ellenshaw, Joshua Meador. Sound: Robert O. Cook. Music editor: Evelyn Kennedy. Running time: 75 minutes.

Songs: "Break of Day" by George Bruns, Winston Hibler. "And Now to Sleep (Lullaby of the Wildwood)" by George Bruns, Winston Hibler, Ralph Wright. "Together Time" by Paul J. Smith, Gil George, Ralph Wright, Winston Hibler.

Perri was Walt Disney's first "True-Life Fantasy," a genre that he hoped would provide his staff with the best of all possible worlds. By making no bones about the "fantasy" angle of the film, it was felt that the Disney nature-film staff could now do what they had tried to hold in check in the bona fide True-Life films— manipulate the documentary footage to their hearts' content and fashion it into a story.

The perfect subject for such treatment was found in Felix Salten's book *Perri,* and the Disney staff had the advantage of what they had learned from their previous experience with Salten, in *Bambi.* Indeed, the format and overall atmosphere of *Perri* owes a great deal to the earlier animated feature.

The film opens with a biblical quotation ("To everything there is a season . . ."). First we see a

Perri herself. © *Walt Disney Productions*

A scene from the winter fantasy. © *Walt Disney Productions*

beautiful starlit sky, with the sun gradually rising and brightening the landscape (this done with animation), then a slow dissolve to live action with beautiful scenes of the sky, greenery, and morning life in the forest, as an off-screen chorus sings "Break of Day." The theme of the film, we are told, is the endless stream of life, season by season.

The seasons are identified by such names as Time of Beauty, Time of Beginnings, Time of Hunting, Time of Peace, etc. Throughout this progression, we follow the life of Perri, a young female squirrel, from birth, when she is first exposed to the laws of survival (a marten killing her father as her mother tries to move her offspring away to a safe place), to maturity, and the continuing fight for life against the squirrels' forest enemies: the winter of hibernation, the spring and mating season when she meets Porro, a climactic forest fire, and the inevitable happy ending, when she and Porro settle down as a new yearly life cycle begins.

With each seasonal change, after we catch up with Perri and watch her development, we see other animals as well, and their various life styles in the forest. Most of the key sequences involve animals trying to ward off predators, often without success. As the narrator explains, "Death is a necessary evil; some die that others may survive."

When Perri hibernates for the winter, the film presents a winter fantasy, a surrealistic dream sequence with Perri and other animals frolicking in the snow against a beautiful deep-blue sky. Glimmering snowflakes converge in the form of rabbits; Perri and the other animals leave glittering trails as they fly through the air. Then the enemy weasel appears and tries to stalk his prey, to no avail, for this is, after all, a fantasy. When he catches a rabbit, it disintegrates into a flurry of snowflakes once more. Finally, an owl is angered at all the commotion and takes off after the weasel (flying directly into the camera). The entire scene is played against an ethereally lovely setting of snow and sky, each unreal in the beauty of its colors.

Aside from this flashy sequence, the major difference between this film's technique and that of a True-Life film is the actual use of film. There are numerous first-person shots, of a hawk swooping down to catch Perri, perched atop a tree, of Perri herself as she edges out onto a very unsteady branch to escape a marten, and at the top of a tree as it is cut down and falls to the ground.

Some scenes, like the one near the beginning where a marten chases the mother squirrel, are tremendously exciting, because there is a variety of angles intercut to give the sequence a genuine feeling of movement. There are, throughout the film, superbly edited pieces of action made possible by the kind of preplanning impossible in the factual nature films. There are also subtle optical effects that would be considered cheating in a nonfiction film, such as using slow motion to make a too brief close-up of Perri linger on screen a few seconds longer.

All this was made possible by the same kind of patience and skill that went into the True-Life films. Nine cameramen, led by True-Life veterans N. Paul Kenworthy, Jr., and Ralph Wright, spent two complete life cycles in the Uintah National Forest of Utah to get appropriate footage for all four seasons, as well as winter material from Jackson Hole, Wyoming. Some shots were spontaneous, but most of the film's impressive camera work was the result of hard work and careful planning. Many camera platforms were constructed as high as fifty feet in the air to get treetop footage.

Some 200,000 feet of 16mm film were exposed, and then edited down to 8,000 feet for the finished film, an incredible ratio of 25 to 1. The result, however, is a truly dazzling accomplishment. With that much material to choose from, Winston Hibler and his staff were able to pick precisely the actions they wanted to express. There is not a wasted second on screen, and the diversity of the footage is put to work, especially in such lovely sequences as the lullaby scene, strongly reminiscent of *Dumbo*'s "Baby of Mine," with assorted families clinging to their mothers as they prepare for sleep.

Although the film is carefully scripted, and filmmaking

tricks were imposed on the actuality in the forest, *Perri* does not really invent much that does not exist. If the plot points are fictitious, the actions of the animals are not, and in depicting the mating season and the fight for survival against natural enemies, *Perri* paints an exciting and accurate picture of animal life in the forest. Though the word "sex" is never uttered, and the mating season is referred to as "Together Time," the film still takes a healthier and more open view of the mating ritual than any other contemporary film aimed at children, as well as a good many supposedly made for adults in this preliberated screen era.

As always, the music is an essential part of the film's success, and Paul Smith's score is, as might be expected, first-rate. The lovely choral arrangements of the film's three songs are also outstanding in creating a mood of beauty and happiness.

Generally speaking, *Perri* was well received, although most critics had moments of uncertainty about the integrity of combining fictional ideas with factual footage; most were more critical, however, of the sentimental nature of the film.

John Beaufort wrote:

Mr. Disney's effort to combine pictorial record with narrative fiction is not, unfortunately, an unqualified success. The producer's assertion that "fantasy never impairs reality" will certainly not get by the naturalists unchallenged. There is, furthermore, a cloying and cheapening coyness to some of the basic concepts. Such arch phrases as "time of beginning . . . time of alone . . . together time, etc." are decidedly hard to take.

Archer Winsten in the *New York Post* thought the film fine for children but warned that "there is an element of baby-food mush that could be considered a hindrance to some adults."

On the whole Disney's experiment was warmly greeted, more so by the public than by the critical community. For future endeavors, the producer decided to eschew all classifications, and in later fictional animal films Disney decided to simply let the material speak for itself.

OLD YELLER

RELEASED BY BUENA VISTA ON DECEMBER 25, 1957. Technicolor. Director: Robert Stevenson. Screenplay: Fred Gipson, William Tunberg, from a novel by Gipson. Photography: Charles P. Boyle. Editor: Stanley Johnson. Art director: Carroll Clark. Set decorations: Emile Kuri, Fred MacLean. Costumes: Chuck Keehne, Gertrude Casey. Music: Oliver Wallace. Orchestrations: Clifford Vaughan. Second unit director: Yakima Canutt. Assistant director: Robert G. Shannon. Matte artist: Peter Ellenshaw. Makeup: Pat McNalley. Hairstyling: Elaine Stone. Sound supervision: Robert O. Cook. Sound recording: Frank McWhorter. Music editor: Evelyn Kennedy. Running time: 83 minutes.

Song: "Old Yeller" by Oliver Wallace, Gil George, sung by Jerome Courtland.

Cast: Dorothy McGuire (Katie Coates), Fess Parker (Jim Coates), Tommy Kirk (Travis Coates), Kevin Corcoran (Arliss Coates), Jeff York (Bud Searcy), Beverly Washburn (Lisbeth Searcy), Chuck Connor (Burn Sanderson), and Spike (Old Yeller).

Having enjoyed major success with nature films involving animals, and equal success on television with the "Mickey Mouse Club," where the emphasis was on children, Walt Disney reasoned that combining these two sure-fire elements would result in widely popular film fare. *Old Yeller* was to be the first of innumerable Disney projects about a boy and his dog. With the many spin-offs that have followed, this film is still one of the best of its kind.

The setting is Texas in 1869. Jim Coates is forced to leave his family for three months to go on a cattle drive, hoping to earn enough money so that he can settle down for good. Fifteen-year-old Travis becomes the head of the household during his absence, dedicating himself to the regimentation of farm life. When his playful younger brother falls in love with a stray dog who wanders onto the farm and causes temporary havoc, he is irritated, but his mother reminds him that little Arliss is lonely, and craves the friendship of the dog.

Before long, the yellow dog wins over the whole family, proving to be a brilliant watchdog and protector as well as a friend. A cowboy comes to the farm one day and explains that the dog is his; he's been tracking it for a long time. But when he sees how attached young Arliss is to the canine, he softens and "trades" with the youngster for it, acquiring a horned toad in the deal.

Travis takes Yeller with him on an expedition to trap some wild pigs; he follows the advice of a shiftless neighbor, Bud Searcy, and sits in a tree, trying to rope the pigs from above. When he falls into the midst of the pack, Yeller fights off the vicious animals as best he can. Travis's leg is badly hurt and bleeding at the end of the fracas, but Yeller is even worse off. Eventually, both boy and dog heal, but Yeller is kept in confinement for several weeks to make sure he hasn't caught rabies from the pigs.

One evening when it seems that the danger has passed, Travis notices Yeller acting strangely, becoming insanely vicious for no good reason. He suddenly realizes what has happened, and with cold determination shoots the dog.

From that time on he is disconsolate. Bud Searcy's daughter Lisbeth gives Travis one of Yeller's little pups (the mother is the dog owned by Lisbeth in the story), but Travis rejects it cruelly, Just then, Father comes

Pa (Fess Parker) tries to explain to Travis (Tommy Kirk) that we have to face up to some things we don't like—such as Yeller's death. © *Walt Disney Productions*

home; his wife explains what has happened, and he has a talk with his son, telling him that we can't control life, as much as we'd like to, that we should always try to look for a brighter side to things. Travis tells him he's trying, but it's very difficult. When he returns to the farm from Yeller's grave, however, he meets the puppy again, and sees in it for the first time a glimmer of Yeller himself. He brightens and adopts the dog as his own, for a happy ending.

Old Yeller is a lovely film, under the able guidance of Robert Stevenson, who treats his subject with the dignity and understatement that brings out all the emotion inherent in the story. In less skilled hands the same material could have been cloying and phony; this film never sinks to that level.

The rigors of farm life and interfamily relationships in such an environment are beautifully portrayed. The performances are first-rate. Fess Parker has relatively little to do in the film, but he communicates the warmth and sincerity that had become his hallmark by now (many ob-

Tommy Kirk and Kevin Corcoran with Old Yeller.

servers noting the similarities between his personality and that of Gary Cooper). Dorothy McGuire is fine as the mother, and little Kevin Corcoran is his usual self, having established the character of Moochie on TV, which overlapped into most of his subsequent screen roles for Disney. In many ways the outstanding performance of the film is that of Tommy Kirk, complete with Texas accent. His subsequent comedy roles in Disney films never gave him the scope of this characterization, and he carries off the full range of intense emotion with uncanny skill. Knowing that he was capable of this makes it all the more sad to watch him in the bumbling comedy parts he played later on.

The film's vignettes are told in a compact, straightforward manner, with Yakima Canutt's second-unit direction lending excitement to the few action scenes in the narrative. One nice touch of Stevenson's occurs when little Arliss has to face the cowboy stranger to bargain with him for ownership of Yeller. The shot of the boy walking up to the cowboy is shown from the youngster's point of view, looking up at the very tall man—a charming idea that works perfectly.

Old Yeller was well received by the critics, and, released at Christmastime, grossed an incredible $8 million in domestic showings alone. It was the phenomenal success of this film and a few follow-ups that convinced Disney for good that if his studio was to prosper, it had to concentrate its energies on modest live-action endeavors and relegate animation to a sideline activity.

SLEEPING BEAUTY

Released by buena vista on january 29, 1959. Technicolor, Technirama. Production supervisor: Ken Peterson. Supervising director: Clyde Geronimi. Sequence directors: Eric Larson, Wolfgang Reitherman, Les Clark. Directing animators: Milt Kahl, Franklin Thomas, Marc Davis, Oliver Johnston, Jr., John Lounsbery. Story adaptation: Erdman Penner, from the Charles Perrault version of "Sleeping Beauty." Additional story: Joe Rinaldi, Winston Hibler, Bill Peet, Ted Sears, Ralph Wright, Milt Banta. Production design: Donald Da Gradi, Ken Anderson. Backgrounds: Frank Armitage, Thelma Witmer, Albert Dempster, Walt Peregoy, Bill Layne, Ralph Hulett, Dick Anthony, Fil Mottola, Richard H. Thomas, Anthony Rizzo. Layout: McLaren Stewart, Tom Codrick, Don Griffith, Erni Nordli, Basil Davidovich, Victor Haboush, Joe Hale, Homer Jonas, Jack Huber, Ray Aragon. Color styling: Eyvind Earle. Character styling: Tom Oreb. Character animation: Hal King, Hal Ambro, Don Lusk, Blaine Gibson, John Sibley, Bob Carlson, Ken Hultgren, Harvey Toombs, Fred Kopietz, George Nicholas, Bob Youngquist, Eric Cleworth, Henry Tanous, John Kennedy, Ken O'Brien. Effects animation: Dan MacManus, Joshua Meador, Jack Boyd, Jack Buckley. Music adaptation: George Bruns, adapted from Tchaikovsky's "Sleeping Beauty Ballet." Choral arrangements: John Rarig. Film editors: Roy M. Brewer, Jr., Donald Halliday. Sound supervision: Robert O. Cook. Music editor: Evelyn Kennedy. Special processes: Ub Iwerks, Eustace Lycett. Running time: 75 minutes.

Songs: "Once Upon a Dream" by Sammy Fain, Jack Lawrence. "Hail the Princess Aurora" by Tom Adair, George Bruns. "I Wonder" by Winston Hibler, Ted Sears, George Bruns. "Skumps" by Tom Adair, Erdman Penner, George Bruns. "The Sleeping Beauty Song" by Tom Adair, George Bruns.

Voices: Mary Costa (Princess Aurora), Bill Shirley (Prince Phillip), Eleanor Audley (Maleficent), Verna Felton (Flora), Barbara Jo Allen (Fauna), Barbara

Sleeping Beauty (Briar Rose) sings, as her forest friends listen attentively. © 1970 Walt Disney Productions

Maleficent kidnaps Prince Phillip so he won't be able to rescue Sleeping Beauty. © Walt Disney Productions

Luddy (Merryweather), Taylor Holmes (King Stefan), Bill Thompson (King Hubert), Candy Candido (Goons).

Walt Disney envisioned *Sleeping Beauty* as his masterpiece, the ultimate in animated filmmaking. The project was first considered in 1950, when preliminary work was begun on a small scale. The next few years saw the story take shape. In 1954 the project was laid aside for two years, while the Disney staff concentrated on the Disneyland park and the studio's two television series. Work resumed in earnest in 1956, and consumed the next three years. By the end of that time the cost of the seventy-five-minute film had mounted to $6 million, making it the most expensive animated cartoon of all time.

The fantastic effort and phenomenal expense do show up on the screen; it is unquestionably Disney's most elaborate cartoon film, the visuals on screen enhanced by the wide-screen Technirama process and the aural stereophonic sound system. The critical question, beyond that of choice of subject matter, was the wisdom of allowing an animated film to become so elaborate, many feeling that this concerted effort to reproduce reality on a grand scale was the height of nonart. It was a question even Disney had to face, much as he disdained the opinions of critics, once the film was released and digested by the public.

Curiously, just as critical lambasting of many of Disney's earlier feature films seems hollow and unimportant today, when the films stand on their own and provide consummate entertainment, so the criticisms of *Sleeping Beauty* seem slightly irrelevant over a decade after its initial release. One can imagine reviewers going to see the film in 1959, ears abuzz with the scandalous news that $6 million had been spent, minds agog with thoughts on other recent Disney features to use for comparison, all subjected to the promotional assault prepared by the Disney company to ensure the film's success.

Times have changed since 1959, more so than one

might imagine at first glance. When *Sleeping Beauty* was reissued in 1971, it came at a time when children's and so-called family entertainment had sunk to a new low on television and in theatres. Viewed in this context, it is difficult to dismiss it as second-rate Disney, or over-produced, or any of the other descriptions leveled at the film. Its imagination and its florid animation style are a welcome breath of fresh air after a brief perusal of Saturday-morning kiddie fare on the tube.

Not that *Sleeping Beauty* looks good only in comparison to the current competition. But seen in the light of the seventies, it seems much better than anyone gave it credit for in 1959. The so-called heavy-handedness just isn't there, and, at seventy-five minutes, it makes its point and provides more entertainment than most other, lengthier, films of this kind.

Disney knew the risk he was taking in producing another well-known fable like *Sleeping Beauty*. "[It] was tough," he told Bob Thomas, "because it had many of the elements we had already used in *Snow White* and *Cinderella*. You've got to give the creators new things to work with so they'll be able to keep their enthusiasm up. You're in trouble if they start saying, 'Haven't we done this before?' "

Indeed, they *had* done this before, and entirely new approaches to the story had to be conceived. The basic story is elementary. Celebrating the birth of a daughter (their first), the King and Queen hold a royal celebration, but neglect to invite a bad fairy, who, offended at the rebuff, casts a curse on the child that will cause her to prick her finger on a spindle when she turns sixteen and die. A good fairy is able to alter the curse so that death becomes sleep. Despite all precautions, the prophecy is fulfilled on the Princess's sixteenth birthday, and she falls into a deep sleep, awakened (in the story) one hundred years later by an adventuresome Prince who kisses her and breaks the spell.

As in *Cinderella* and *Snow White,* the Disney staff's challenge was to provide enough diversions and additions to stretch the story to feature film length without
296

letting the seams show.

In the Disney script three good fairies named Flora, Fauna, and Merryweather take the royal child with them into the forest where they raise her in seclusion as a normal child, keeping her out of sight of the evil witch named Maleficent. She had been promised since birth to Prince Phillip, but she does not know her own identity; thus, when the two accidentally meet in the forest and fall in love, they are unaware that they are already engaged to be married. When, on Princess Aurora's sixteenth birthday, she is discovered by Maleficent and put to sleep, the Good Fairies place the entire kingdom under a spell so as to rescue Aurora without anyone knowing what has happened. The Fairies discover that Maleficent has already kidnapped the Prince, but they help him escape, and do battle with the fiery witch. After a spectacular battle, in which Maleficent takes the form of a dragon, the Prince emerges victorious, finds Aurora, and awakens her with a kiss. The kingdom is brought to life once more in the midst of its celebration for Aurora's sixteenth birthday and her impending marriage to the Prince.

The embroidery is neat and effective. The three fairies provide gentle comedy relief, trying to live in the forest as normal women, without the aid of their magical powers. They finally summon up their magic on Aurora's birthday in order to create a dress for her, leading to a running gag of whether it should be pink or blue; the two fairies in disagreement continue to change the color back and forth right through the last scene of the film.

Further comedy is provided by Aurora's father, King Stefan, and Prince Phillip's father, King Hubert, who eagerly anticipate the joining of their families in marriage. A prolonged comedy scene involving them is built around "The Skump Song," as they toast each other's happiness and engage in a teasing sort of rivalry.

Horror and suspense is provided by Maleficent, her pet raven, and her "goons," comic/evil characters who waddle around her castle as protectors (their amusing

Flora, Fauna, and Meriwether help Phillip escape; here they are confronted by Maleficent's pet raven. © *Walt Disney Productions*

mumbles having been recorded by Candy Candido). Maleficent is evil personified, not only in the design of her face and costume, but in the black magic she conjures up, from a nightmarish vision of her prophecy, at Aurora's birth, to the flaming reality of her countenance as a dragon battling the Prince in the climactic scenes.

Aurora herself, called Briar Rose during her stay with the Fairies, is, as might be expected, pleasant, attractive, and largely nondescript, which just about sums up the Prince as well. Conscious of this, the film's creators find ways of providing additional points of interest in all their scenes. Virtually every scene of the Prince (until the final battle) is stolen by his horse, Samson, who is far more amusing than his stoic master.

The romantic scenes between Briar Rose and Phillip are abetted by an attractive song ("Once Upon a

Dream''), a sequence of them dancing, their bodies reflected in a stream among picturesque forest settings, and a whole flock of cute animals who are Briar Rose's friends. One has no time to get involved with either Briar Rose or Phillip, which is as it should be.

The visual aspect of the film is quite staggering. After the traditional storybook opening, we join the royal celebration of the Princess's birth, heralded by the song ''Hail the Princess Aurora.'' The pageant is shown from a lateral point of view, with five or six rows of people marching through the street—guards, jesters, spectators, banners flying, flags waving. This dissolves into the interior of the palace, seen from afar. From high up in the great hall, the camera slowly pans forward and downward to the center of activity. As it does, the camera passes through innumerable layers of columns, banners, arches, and such, a fantastic conglomeration of detail for what is essentially an establishing shot. (Its closest ancestor is the equally stunning shot of the village at morning in *Pinocchio*.)

Throughout *Sleeping Beauty*, detail is piled upon detail, with never-ending backgrounds, and a brilliant panorama of layout for each setting. Effects animation is brought into play in the opening sequence, when Flora and Fauna bestow their good wishes on the Princess, and these graces are envisioned in dreamlike visions. Then, when Maleficent describes her curse, we view it as a whirlpool of nightmarish scenes, swirling through the air as a montage shows us the fate that is to befall her.

Many critics found such details ''oppressive,'' but it is difficult to pin this word on the film. There is no denying that *Sleeping Beauty* is much ado about nothing, while a film like *Dumbo* took its simple story and, through a general brightness and unpretentiousness, made every inch count without seeming ''heavy.'' Yet *Sleeping Beauty* is only ''heavy'' in terms of the amount of effort put into the construction of the visuals. As entertainment, it moves very briskly, with an abundance of humor, romance, song, and suspense, skillfully intertwined so none of these elements seem out of proportion with the whole.

This time around, Disney was determined to have his human characters as realistic as possible. Once again, a live-action film was shot for the animators' use (with Helene Stanley, who had posed for Cinderella, repeating in the role of Sleeping Beauty, Ed Kemmer as the Prince, and Jane Fowler as the witch), and Disney insisted on perfection. "I had only one general suggestion for our animators [regarding the characters]," he explained. "Make them as real as possible, near flesh-and-blood . . . That is why we used living models more carefully than ever before, in order to give the artists inspiration, to help them shape the anatomy of movement and expression of the cartoon figures."

This, like Disney's other goals, was fully achieved in *Sleeping Beauty*, for unlike the two former princes in *Snow White* and *Cinderella*, Prince Phillip seemed to come to life, his climactic battle with Maleficent seeming chillingly real—too real for some observers, in fact. Bosley Crowther in the *New York Times* called the fight "the noisiest and scariest go-round he has ever put into one of his films . . . the question is whether he has fouled [the film] as a safe entertainment for little kids." The sight of a fire-breathing dragon filling the Technirama screen with searing flames aimed at Our Hero was indeed a considerable jolt for many small fry—and adults as well. The mood of the scene is heightened by George Bruns's electrifying music, adapted from Tchaikovsky. Though the score for the film is generally pleasant, it is this extended piece of music, accompanying the Prince's battle to reach Briar Rose, that really dazzles.

The flaw in *Sleeping Beauty* is the limit of its appeal. The problem is not that the dragon sequence is too scary for youngsters, but that it comes so late in the film. There is little else of an exciting nature in the narrative, and very little outright comedy for a red-blooded child to sink his teeth into. There are no patently comic creations in the film (like the dwarfs in *Snow White*, or the mice in *Cinderella;* the three fairies are a shallow substitute) to relieve the "ickiness" of the story for young boys who like to think they are beyond the stage of fairy tales but are still too young for the nuances of characterization that dot this film's comedy-relief personalities.

In short, *Sleeping Beauty* is a very good film, but more so for older audiences than for young children. The visual grandeur and the intricacy of the animation are lost on the tiny tots, who only want to see lots of color and movement, and be provided with some fun. The songs are lovely, based on Tchaikovsky themes that are certain to appeal to adults; but there is no "Heigh Ho" or "Cinderelly" to capture the fancy of eager kids. Girls might enjoy the situations of the three fairies trying to fashion a ball gown, but for young boys, it's hardly the thing.

To Disney's credit, he was aware of a possible barrier against this sector of his audience. "We had to find out what we had and whether it would please the public," he said. "I'm never sure myself what they're going to buy."

With *Sleeping Beauty*'s astronomical cost, the Disney organization decided to take no chances on losing their collective shirt, so in addition to a massive promotional campaign for the film, *Sleeping Beauty* was premiered at road-show prices around the country, even though there was no reserved-seat policy. To ward off criticism that $2.40 (the admission price in New York) was a lot to pay for a seventy-five-minute movie, a wide-screen short, *Grand Canyon,* was paired with the feature to round out the program.

The elaborate screen and sound processes were amply touted. This particular wide-screen process, Technirama 70, was based on a special system of film running through the camera horizontally, exposing two 35mm frames simultaneously. This unusual film is then printed normally on standard 35mm film and shown with an anamorphic lens for the wide-screen, extra-dimension effect. The promotion campaign had to combat some rather unenthusiastic reviews that, even in praising the film, compared it unfavorably with earlier Disney products.

In London, C. A. LeJeune wrote in the *Observer:*

Once upon a time, a couple of generations ago, Walt Disney, still a simple barnyard artist and the happy contriver of the Silly Symphonies, astonished the world and delighted most of it with his first full-length cartoon in color, *Snow White and the Seven Dwarfs.* Even where we criticized, we felt that Disney had the root of the matter in him. Here was a splendid new way of telling fairy stories, which should grow even better as the years went on.

Twenty-one years have passed since *Snow White,* and now Walt Disney Inc., master of many enterprises, presents us with Snow White's sister *Sleeping Beauty.* The two films have a great deal in common, apart from the marked family resemblance between the heroines, and the question naturally arises, has Disney's work developed from that time to this time? So far as techniques are concerned, yes, undoubtedly. In all that affects the imagination, regrettably but definitely no.

Still, *Sleeping Beauty* managed to gross $5.3 million in its initial release—helpful money for the depleted Disney coffers, but not enough to make it a success, official or otherwise. (It must be remembered that much of that money was accumulated from admission fees double those of most other Disney films.) The same year a modest comedy called *The Shaggy Dog,* produced for less than $1 million, earned back an astounding $9 million—and that without reserved-seat prices.

It proved to Disney that times indeed had changed since *Snow White,* that the fairy tale was no longer a viable format (except in the case of reissues, where he was bringing back films with established reputations), especially at his studio, where the well had apparently run dry for new variations on old themes. Animated cartoons were still feasible, but, obviously, they would have to rely on the same formulas that were making his live-action movies so successful—stories involving boys, dogs, and other animals.

As always, Disney took his cue from public response. *Sleeping Beauty* marked the end of an era at the Walt Disney studio.

THE SHAGGY DOG

RELEASED BY BUENA VISTA ON MARCH 19, 1959. DIRECtor: Charles Barton. Screenplay: Bill Walsh, Lillie Hayward, suggested by the novel *The Hound of Florence* by Felix Salten. Associate producer: Bill Walsh. Photography: Edward Colman. Editor: James D. Ballas. Art director: Carroll Clark. Set decorations: Emile Kuri, Fred MacLean. Costumes: Chuck Keehne, Gertrude Casey. Music: Paul J. Smith. Orchestrations: Joseph Mullendore. Assistant director: Arthur J. Vitarelli. Special titles: T. Hee, Bill Justice, Xavier Atencio. Animal supervision: William R. Koehler. Sound: Robert O. Cook, Harry M. Lindgren. Music editor: Evelyn Kennedy. Running time: 104 minutes.

Cast: Fred MacMurray (Wilson Daniels), Jean Hagen (Frieda Daniels), Tommy Kirk (Wilby Daniels), Annette Funicello (Allison D'Allessio), Tim Considine (Buzz Miller), Kevin Corcoran (Moochie Daniels), Cecil Kellaway (Professor Plumcutt), Alexander Scourby (Dr. Mikhail Andrassy), Roberta Shore (Franceska Andrassy), James Westerfield (Officer Hanson), Jacques Aubuchon (Stefano), Strother Martin (Thurm), Forrest Lewis (Officer Kelly), Ned Wever (E. P. Hackett), Gordon Jones (Captain Scanlon), John Hart (police broadcaster), Jack Albertson (reporter), Mack Williams (Betz), Paul Frees (psychiatrist), and Shaggy. Opening narration by Paul Frees.

Tommy Kirk, as the shaggy dog, drives to the heroine's rescue.
© *Walt Disney Productions*

Now a hero, Fred MacMurray poses with the shaggy dog, along with Forrest Lewis, James Westerfield, Kevin Corcoran, Tommy Kirk, Tim Considine, and Jean Hagen. © *Walt Disney Productions*

Though essentially just a low-budget comedy, shot in black and white, *The Shaggy Dog* is an important film in the chronology of Walt Disney's output. It was the first live-action comedy he ever made, and it was the first of his films to star Fred MacMurray. Its astounding success (grossing over $9 million in its first release) led to important changes in Disney's production outlook in the years that followed.

The story has a misfit teen-ager (Tommy Kirk) visiting a nearby museum and inadvertently taking with him (in his pants cuff) a ring which through an ancient spell transforms him into a large shaggy dog, identical to the one owned by neighbor Franceska Andrassy. Since the boy's father is allergic to dogs, he spends most of his time as a canine in the neighboring house, causing considerable confusion as he changes back and forth from boy to dog. While in the house, however, he overhears Franceska's father talking with an associate, and realizes that they are spies, planning to steal government missile plans. As the boy/dog convinces his father of his identity and is then discovered by the spies, a mad chase ensues, with Franceska being kidnapped by her own father, who hops aboard a motorboat to escape. The dog goes after it and saves Franceska when she is thrown overboard. When the police arrive and the enemies are caught, however, the dog is now a boy again, and the *real* dog gets the credit for everything.

On this slim story line the film is built, with various twists and turns and isolated gag sequences that have little to do with the story at hand.

The Shaggy Dog is a curious film. By rights, it should be fast paced, broad entertainment, but, instead, it takes its own sweet time, never pushing for laughs, and ambling through 104 minutes of running time. There isn't even a final punch line, just a fade-out. In some ways this relaxed attitude is preferable to that of later Disney films where things are driven home so hard as to be obnoxious. Yet on the other hand, there is an almost lethargic manner to much of the film that kills many obvious opportunities.

Disney later revealed that the story was being originally considered as a TV series, and the film most definitely has its genesis in TV situation comedy. Father, as played by Fred MacMurray, is a total idiot, and, although he is said to be a postman, he is never once shown working. Any hope of believability is tossed away in the scene where bumbling MacMurray goes to the police and tells them that his son is a dog, prompting a scene with a psychiatrist that Bosley Crowther pointed out "comes straight from *Harvey*."

The characters are purposely treated that way by director Charles Barton, a veteran of innumerable movies and, of course, TV situation comedies. He gets some nice moments out of this formula (such as husband and wife kissing each other good morning, blithely unaware that they have missed each other by a foot or two), but the film's most solid laughs involve simple sight gags of the sheep dog performing human tasks like brushing his teeth, gargling, wearing pajamas, and driving a car. It is this material that formed the foundation of the film's premise, and one wonders why it wasn't put to more extensive use.

Most critics were agreed that the premise of the comedy was a good one, but, in *Time*'s words, "Disney tells his shaggy-dog story so doggedly that he soon runs it into the pound." The premise alone was enough to draw millions of kids and adults into theatres around the country, and Disney realized that this combination of situation comedy and fantasy was one well worth pursuing (along with another idea, that of designing imaginative main titles, in order to capture the audience right away).

Of the film's star, *Variety* noted: "It's a pleasure to see such a master of timing and emphasis as Fred MacMurray back in comedy again, even though he is somewhat limited in his material. Where he has a good line, he shows that he has few peers in this special field of comedy." The romantic comedies that had made MacMurray a star in the 1930s were no longer being done in Hollywood, and of late he had drifted into routine

Westerns. His expertise in *The Shaggy Dog* not only reaffirmed his comic prowess, but convinced Disney that here was someone he should hold onto for future projects. The Disney-MacMurray relationship became a most fruitful one in years to come.

The final thing that the Disney people learned from this film was that repetition, and the obvious, were the surest laugh-getters of all. Running gags involving Forrest Lewis as a perplexed policeman paid off so well in this film that it was decided to use the actor again in *The Absent Minded Professor*. And from that film, elements were borrowed and repeated in the next comedy. It got to the point where audiences, particularly youthful ones, anticipated with glee the same faces and reactions they had enjoyed in earlier Disney comedies every time they went to the theatre. This preconditioning became a staple of Disney's product throughout the 1960s.

In case anyone thought that this film's success was a fluke, it was reissued in 1967 on a double bill with *The Absent Minded Professor,* where it did smash business all over again. And in 1976 the Disney studio revived the formula in a successful sequel called *The Shaggy D. A.*

DARBY O'GILL AND THE LITTLE PEOPLE

RELEASED BY BUENA VISTA ON JUNE 26, 1959. TECHnicolor. Director: Robert Stevenson. Screenplay: Lawrence E. Watkin, suggested by the Darby O'Gill stories by H. T. Kavanagh. Photography: Winton C. Hoch. Editor: Stanley Johnson. Art director: Carroll Clark. Set decorations: Emile Kuri, Fred MacLean. Costumes: Chuck Keehne, Gertrude Casey. Music: Oliver Wallace. Orchestrations: Clifford Vaughan. Assistant director: Robert G. Shannon. Special photographic effects: Peter Ellenshaw, Eustace Lycett. Animation effects: Joshua Meador. Technical adviser: Michael O'Herlihy. Makeup: Pat McNalley. Hairstyling:

Ruth Sandifer. Sound: Dean Thomas, Robert O. Cook. Running time: 93 minutes.

Songs: "The Wishing Song," "Pretty Irish Girl" by Oliver Wallace, Lawrence E. Watkin.

Cast: Albert Sharpe (Darby O'Gill), Janet Munro (Katie O'Gill), Sean Connery (Michael McBride), Jimmy O'Dea (King Brian), Kieron Moore (Pony Sugrue), Estelle Winwood (Sheelah), Walter Fitzgerald (Lord Fitzpatrick), Denis O'Dea (Father Murphy), J. G. Devlin (Tom Kerrigan), Jack MacGowran (Phadrig Oge), Farrell Pelly (Paddy Scanlon), Nora O'Mahony (Molly Malloy).

Darby O'Gill and the Little People is not only one of Disney's best films, but is certainly one of the best fantasies ever put on film. The key to its success is its convincingness; Disney knew this, and decided to carry out the theme of credibility to the last degree. Publicity stills of the producer "conferring" with King Brian of the Leprechauns were issued, stories of lengthy negotiations before permission was secured from the Little People were planted. And, as a finishing touch, a title on the film itself reads, "My thanks to King Brian of Knocknasheega and his leprechauns, whose gracious cooperation made this picture possible—Walt Disney."

Darby O'Gill is a roguish old storyteller who works as a caretaker on the governor's estate. When a younger man comes to take his place, and move into his house, Darby asks for time to break the news to his daughter Katie. That night Darby chases a runaway horse to the top of a haunted hill, where the horse suddenly rears, turns flaming colors and backs the frightened man into a well. Darby tumbles down into the land of leprechauns, where King Brian explains that he has brought him there as a favor, so Darby won't have to make embarrassing explanations to his daughter.

The King asks Darby to play his violin, and the resulting celebration climaxes with the leprechauns

Find the special effects: that's Darby O'Gill playing for the leprechauns. © *Walt Disney Productions*

opening the wall of their mountain home to ride outside and paint the town red. Darby manages to escape through the opening, and when Brian tracks him to his home, he gets the leprechaun into an all-night drinking session, until it is morning and the King's powers to return home are gone. Darby says he won't let the King go until he is granted three wishes.

Brian agrees, but tricks Darby into wasting two of his wishes. The third, Darby tells him, will be when he sees Katie and the new caretaker Michael McBride united in marriage. Brian tries to fix things in that direction, but the courtship is disrupted when Katie learns from meddlesome Pony Sugrue that Michael is taking her father's job away. That evening she goes after a runaway horse to the top of the same haunted hill, and, when the horse acts up, she falls and hits her head against the rocks.

Katie lies near death, and Darby hears the cry of the banshee, a sure sign that the worst is near. Then, from the sky, comes the dreaded Costa Bower, the Death Coach. It lands in front of Darby's house, and the headless driver asks for her. Darby, in anguish, tells Brian that his third wish is to be taken away in Katie's place. Brian reluctantly agrees, and the minute Darby steps into the coach Katie begins to recover. Then, up in the flying coach, Brian tricks Darby into making a fourth wish—and everyone knows that a fourth wish always cancels out the previous three. Darby is suddenly home again, and Katie is well.

Michael challenges his rival, Pony Sugrue, to a fight, in return for the trouble he has caused between himself and Katie, and, having licked him, wins Katie's hand in marriage. Darby drives them off in his carriage for the finale.

Darby O'Gill and the Little People was more than twenty years in the making. Disney had his eye on the original stories in the mid-1940s, and in the summer of 1946 sent several artists to Ireland for background material. In 1947 he hired Lawrence Watkin to work on a script for the film. In December 1948 Disney himself visited Ireland, and announced that the film, then called *The Little People*, would be made soon. When he saw the Broadway hit *Finian's Rainbow,* with Albert Sharpe as the canny Irishman, he knew he had his star player.

Yet the project was constantly being set aside in favor of more immediate tasks. The twenty years were not wasted, however, for it is likely that the detail and meticulous handling the film received could not have resulted from a standard one to two year preparation period. Here was a case of Disney knowing exactly what he wanted, and having the patience to wait for the best results.

The special effects are breathtaking, and in the instance of the Death Coach, absolutely terrifying. The coach travels down from the skies in a winding route, becoming more horrifying as it gets closer and we see the color-negative image of the coach and four being driven by a headless man.

310

Michael McBride (Sean Connery) and Katie O'Gill (Janet Munro) are off in Darby's horse cart to be married. © *Walt Disney Productions*

Yet the most impressive effects in the film are the ones that inspire the least immediate reaction, namely the scenes with the leprechauns. Disney's idea was to make these sequences *so* realistic that they would seem absolutely natural, and, indeed, after a while, one finds oneself believing completely that Darby is really talking to a twenty-one-inch king! The scene of Darby standing in the great hall of Knocknasheega, playing the violin as the little people dance gaily around him, is an example of this movie magic. There cannot possibly be any trickery here—he's really standing there surrounded by leprechauns!

There are many other subtle effects throughout the film, such as the delightful scene where King Brian talks to Michael and then Katie in their sleep, trying to bring the couple together. He climbs up Katie's bedpost and talks to her; when she involuntarily answers him, she wakes herself up, and he instantly disappears. Then when she goes back to sleep, he materializes once more and continues his conversation.

The film is also full of Peter Ellenshaw's exquisite matte shots, showing the village, the local scenery, and the haunted hill—all responsible for making it seem as if the film were really shot in Ireland, when the entire picture was made in California on the Albertson and Rowland Lee ranches and on two large sound stages at the Disney studio.

Color control is also magnificent in this film, dictated down to the smallest detail. In the opening scene, for instance, when a magistrate drives up in a horse-drawn carriage, the high wheels of the coach are painted bright yellow—a minor point, to be sure, yet just one of hundreds of factors that combine to make *Darby* such a visual delight.

The performances are also a joy, with a handpicked cast largely imported from the Dublin stage, and such troupes as the Abbey and Ulster theatres. *Variety* wrote: ''Sharpe's performance is a gem. He benefits from the combination of being lovable, yet humanly frail and prone to greed and pride . . . but embellishes the role with a refreshingly individual manner of expression that should endear him." Jimmie O'Dea is every bit his match as King Brian, striking the perfect blend of charm and deviousness that characterizes the leprechauns in general.

With this film Disney signed Janet Munro to a contract, and her fresh beauty and ingratiating charm became a solid asset for several Disney films over the next few years. Her screen partner, Sean Connery, impressed no one at this time, and it was several years before he became a superstar with the James Bond series.

Lawrence Watkin's screenplay is little short of brilliant, deriving humor, horror, romance, and *humanity* from the basic situations, giving voice to breezy Irish wit but also leaving room for sentimentality. The question of whether the leprechauns are real or just a figment of Darby's imagination is nicely handled throughout the film, with a satisfying conclusion implying that if someone believes in something, that's all that really counts—*not* what others may think.

This was Robert Stevenson's first major film for Disney, and on the strength of it earned the director many plum assignments from the studio in years to follow. Though most Disney features are a team effort, there can be no denying that without a good director at the helm, seemingly surefire elements can fizzle out. Stevenson brought to his films a skill and taste that always got the most out of every given situation, instead of merely recording the action on film. It is no coincidence that many of Disney's best live-action films bear his name.

As with many of Disney's best films, this production, with its visual beauty, great performances, lilting music (which propels so much of the film's action), and genuine wit, has more appeal to older audiences than it has for children, especially very young children. The *New York Times*'s A. H. Weiler reported that "a large, restless contingent of small fry at yesterday's initial showing of the picture . . . seemed more entranced by the cavortings of Donald Duck and Pluto in an old short called *Beach Picnic* than in the adventures of Darby and his ilk." There was also concern that many, especially younger, viewers would have difficulty cutting through the heavy Irish accents. There was so much concern, in fact, that when *Darby* didn't do as well as anticipated at the box office, Disney had the film dubbed for reissue!

Critical reaction to the film was mild at best, the *New York Herald Tribune* echoing the lukewarm response by calling it "an innocent diversion." This kind of assessment, coupled with the film's disappointing box-office take, must have been a bitter pill for Disney to swallow, having lavished so much love and care (not to mention money) on the production. It is certainly a sad comment on mass taste to note that a beautiful film like this should fail to attract half the audience that rushed to see *The Shaggy Dog*. It also answers the question of why the following years saw so few Disney films the caliber of *Darby* and so many in the spirit of *The Shaggy Dog*.

POLLYANNA

RELEASED BY BUENA VISTA ON MAY 19, 1960. TECHnicolor. Director, screenplay: David Swift, based on the novel by Eleanor H. Porter. Associate producer: George Golitzen. Photography: Russell Harlan. Editor: Frank Gross. Art directors: Carroll Clark, Robert Clatworthy. Set decorations: Emile Kuri, Fred MacLean. Costumes: Walter Plunkett. Assistants: Chuck Keehne, Gertrude Casey. Music: Paul J. Smith. Orchestrations: Franklyn Marks. Assistant director: Joseph Behm. Matte artist: Peter Ellenshaw. Special effects: Ub Iwerks. Sequence consultant: Donald Da Gradi. Dialogue coach: Leon Charles. Makeup: Pat McNalley, Hairstyling: Ruth Sandifer. Sound: Robert O Cook, Dean Thomas. Music editor: Evelyn Kennedy. Running time: 134 minutes.

Cast: Hayley Mills (Pollyanna), Jane Wyman (Aunt Polly), Richard Egan (Dr. Edmund Chilton), Karl Malden (Reverend Paul Ford), Nancy Olson (Nancy Furman), Adolphe Menjou (Mr. Pendergast), Donald Crisp (Mayor Karl Warren), Agnes Moorehead (Mrs. Snow), Kevin Corcoran (Jimmy Bean), James Drury (George Dodds), Reta Shaw (Tillie Lagerlof), Leora Dana (Mrs. Paul Ford), Anne Seymour (Mrs. Amelia Tarbell), Edward Platt (Ben Tarbell), Mary Grace Canfield (Angelica), Jenny Egan (Mildred Snow), Gage Clarke (Mr. Murg), Ian Wolfe (Mr. Neely), Nolan Leary (Mr. Thomas), Edgar Dearing (Mr. Gorman), Harry Harvey (editor), William Newell (Mr. Hooper).

Critics who went to see *Pollyanna* expecting a sloppily sentimental, tear-jerking film were astonished to discover a beautifully acted, intelligently scripted film of genuine warmth, one of the best live-action films Disney ever made. It marked the American debut of the remarkable young Hayley Mills, daughter of actor John Mills, and, more surprisingly, the feature-film debut of director/scenarist David Swift. It also boasted a star cast unusual for a Disney film, and many behind-the-scenes technicians imported from other studios especially for this picture. Obviously, *Pollyanna* was earmarked as something special, and that's exactly what it turned out to be.

The story is basically the familiar one written by Eleanor H. Porter. Orphaned Pollyanna comes to live with her wealthy Aunt Polly in Harrington, circa 1912. She immediately starts upsetting things in the very proper household and throughout the town, with her uncanny knack for seeing the bright side of things (in what she calls "the glad game," always finding something to be glad about), with which she overpowers some of the town's leading malcontents.

Her first friend in town is Jimmy Bean, a carefree youngster from the town orphanage. Together they engage in various adventures.

Pollyanna first goes to visit crotchety old Mrs. Snow,

Hayley Mills, Jane Wyman, and Anne Seymour in *Pollyanna*.
© *Walt Disney Productions*

Pollyanna plays with one of the prisms in the home of Mr.
Pendergast (Adolphe Menjou). © *Walt Disney Productions*

a hypochondriac invalid who feels sorry for herself. Pollyanna is the first person who doesn't sympathize with the old woman, and eventually wins her over with her honesty and friendliness.

Then she and Jimmy meet the hermitlike Mr. Pendergast, who catches them trespassing on his property, but instead of scolding them, becomes another friend, interesting the youngsters in glass prisms, and the colorful light they spread around his home.

Pollyanna then works her magic on the town preacher, Reverend Ford. Every Sunday his hellfire-and-brimstone sermons (usually recommended by Aunt Polly, who for all intents and purposes runs the entire town) give everyone indigestion. The young girl finds him rehearsing a sermon one afternoon, and he confesses to her that he feels he isn't reaching his congregation. She tells him that her father, a missionary, taught her a valuable lesson, which he inscribed on a charm: When you look for the bad in mankind, you will surely find it. He is dumbfounded with the shock of discovery, and that Sunday he comes to church a new man, telling the congregation that he intends to spend future sermons exploring the *joy* in the Bible—and he also vows to get to know his people much better.

Finally, Pollyanna plays matchmaker for Aunt Polly and young Dr. Chilton, who had once been sweethearts several years ago. Since then, Aunt Polly has become more and more spinsterish, and her niece is determined to do something about it.

One thing that comes between Polly and Dr. Chilton is the subject of the town orphanage, which Aunt Polly sponsors. A new one is needed, and Chilton organizes a bazaar to raise money for it. At first, most of the townspeople are afraid to oppose Polly Harrington openly, but bit by bit enthusiasm grows, especially when meek Reverend Ford decides to take a stand and support the event.

Pollyanna is forbidden to go, but Jimmy Bean helps her climb through her window, down a tree, in order to attend. She has the time of her life, and even wins a doll—her very first. Going home that night, she climbs the tree and is almost inside when she drops her doll; reaching for it, she falls to the ground with a scream.

The next day it becomes clear that her legs are paralyzed. Dr. Chilton arranges to take her to Baltimore for immediate surgery, but he tells Aunt Polly that surgery cannot do anything for Pollyanna's state of mind. For the first time she is sullen, and she rejects the glad game as being stupid. But then an amazing thing happens. People, hundreds of them, gather on the front lawn and knock on Aunt Polly's door. They say that they are friends of Pollyanna, and they want to wish her well. Dr. Chilton brings her downstairs, and she sees just how much she has meant to so many people in town. Mrs. Snow is no longer an invalid, Reverend Ford is now part of the community, and Mr. Pendergast is even going to adopt Jimmy Bean. And Aunt Polly realizes that all this time she has given everything to Pollyanna, and to the town, but love, and that's more important than anything. As Pollyanna is taken to the train, the whole town comes to see her off, and as the train pulls out of the station, a sign is hung from the station platform: Harrington—The Glad Town.

Pollyanna is a lovely film in every respect. Its sentiment is derived from natural situations, and it never descends into bathos. The characters are all three-dimensional in situations where they might have been played as stereotypes. Aunt Polly, for instance, is not wicked, but a woman with a flaw—she has become cold and unloving. None of the other transformations are miraculous, because the people had goodness in them all along—even Mr. Pendergast, who clearly has a gleam in his eye even while bawling out little Jimmy Bean. It just took Pollyanna to bring out the goodness inside these people. Contrast this with the earlier version of the film made in 1920 with Mary Pickford. It too is most enjoyable, but it's largely played for comedy, and the characters surrounding Mary, especially Aunt Polly, *are* caricatures. This doesn't take away from the comic aspect of the film; it just makes it less real.

The settings of the film are appropriately realistic. Most of the exteriors were filmed in Santa Rosa, California, and in the Napa Valley, doubling quite nicely for early century New England. Actual settings such as the train station, with a period locomotive, add to the flavor. The interiors, from the church (apparently real) to the sumptuous home of Aunt Polly, are ideal in carrying out the goal of realism.

Scenes like the opening one, in which the main titles are superimposed over shots of Jimmy Bean rolling a hoop through the picturesque town, are delightful in capturing the nostalgic feeling for such lovely period settings.

Both the art director, Robert Clatworthy, and the costume designer, Walter Plunkett, were hired for the picture from other studios, bringing with them a skill for creating exactly the kind of colorful stylishness required for the film. *Pollyanna* has a rich, quality look unique among Disney films of this period.

Publicity releases declared that *Pollyanna* boasted "the most important star cast in the history of the Disney studios," and this was not exaggeration. The large cast was obviously handpicked, resulting in a fantastic array of first-rate character portrayals, with Karl Malden, Adolphe Menjou (whose last film this was), and Agnes Moorehead standing out. Even the character bits were filled by such reassuringly familiar faces as Ian Wolfe, Edgar Dearing, and Harry Harvey, screen veterans all.

Variety called the film "a personal triumph for Hayley Mills," echoing the sentiments of most reviewers. Walt Disney happened to be watching a British film called *Tiger Bay* to see John Mills, whom he was considering for the leading role in *Swiss Family Robinson*. At the same time he was amazed at the performance of Mills's daughter in this, her first film, and he immediately signed her to a contract. Wrote the London *Observer:* "It is sheer joy to watch and listen to her, and since she seems to have the gift of touching off the talents in her fellow actors, *Pollyanna* turns out to be a very charming and amusing film, with a spring freshness that is never mawkish.''

The film also marked another equally impressive debut; it was the first feature film for director/writer David Swift, who had worked for Disney in the late 1930s, starting as office boy and working up to becoming assistant animator to Ward Kimball. He left in the 1940s, and made his mark the following decade when he created the successful TV series ''Mr. Peepers.'' After considerable work in television, Disney gave him his first chance at doing a feature, and he did a remarkable job.

Someone once asked Samuel Goldwyn how long a movie should be. ''How long is it good?'' Goldwyn replied. *Pollyanna* is one of the longest films Disney ever released, yet its length is justified by the carefully crafted script that constantly provides new angles to the story, maintaining a high level of interest at all times. Swift's scenario is full of marvelous touches, both humorous and poignant. When preacher Karl Malden is shown delivering one of his typical sermons, he walks quietly to the pulpit, looks heavenward, then downward meditatively, and suddenly shouts at the top of his lungs, ''Death comes unexpectedly!'' He goes on to deliver what is, in essence, a hilarious double-talk lecture keyed to this phrase.

Swift, as director, lingers over the bazaar, including as many details as possible to create a complete aura of what a small-town fair might have been like in 1912. A highlight comes when a group of girls dressed as the American flag sing ''America'' from the bandstand, with Pollyanna taking a solo.

There are other little moments—items that go by rather quickly on the screen, yet contribute to the film's overall flavor. For instance, when Jimmy Bean takes Pollyanna fishing for the first time, he sticks his face underwater to watch the fish, a shot viewed by the audience from below the surface! The whole plot device of the kids' fascination with prisms is a lovely visual idea, as well as a means of providing a bond between the children and Mr. Pendergast.

In every respect *Pollyanna* is an excellent film, and it received generally outstanding notices. Arthur Knight wrote in the *Saturday Review*: "*Pollyanna* has the feeling for Americana, the nostalgic glow of a simpler, gentler way of life that has characterized most of the Disney live-action features. . . . There is warmth here. . . . More fundamental, there seems to be a genuine belief that the art of positive thinking, as practiced by Eleanor H. Porter's little heroine, is every bit as applicable today as when the 'glad game' was first invented."

Time magazine, in a curiously backhanded yet favorable review, called the film "the best live-actor movie Disney has ever made," qualifying that remark by calling it "a Niagara of drivel and a masterpiece of smarm."

Yet again, for the third time in a year, a high quality, high cost Disney film did not do especially well at the box office. *Pollyanna*'s gross of $3,750,000 fell far short of the $6 million goal, and Walt Disney thought he knew why. "I think the picture would have done better with a different title," he explained. "Girls and women went to it, but men tended to stay away because it sounded sweet and sticky." He may have been correct.

In any event the film has been shown on the Disney television show, the mark of failure in theatrical release. Again, it seems a shame.

SWISS FAMILY ROBINSON

Released by buena vista on december 10, 1960. Technicolor, Panavision. Producer: Bill Anderson. Director: Ken Annakin. Screenplay: Lowell S. Hawley, based on the novel by Johann Wyss. Photography: Harry

Waxman. Additional photography: Paul Beeson. Editor: Peter Boita. Art director: John Howell. Assistant art directors: John Hoestli, Peter Murton. Set decorations: Jack Stephens. Costumes: Julie Harris. Music: William Alwyn. Conductor: Muir Mathieson. Second unit director: Yakima Canutt. Associate producer: Basil Keys. Production manager: Bill Hill, Assistant director: Rene Dupont. Matte artist: Peter Ellenshaw. Special effects: Dan Lee, Walter Stones. Production designer: John Howell. Sketch artist: John L. Jensen. Makeup: Bill Lodge, Charles Nash. Hairstyling: Eileen Bates. Sound: Leslie Wiggins, John S. Dennis, Gordon K. McCallum. Running time: 128 minutes.

Song: "My Heart Is an Island" by Terry Gilkyson.

Cast: John Mills (father), Dorothy McGuire (mother), James MacArthur (Fritz), Janet Munro (Roberta), Sessue Hayakawa (pirate chief), Tommy Kirk (Ernst), Kevin Corcoran (Francis), Cecil Parker (Captain Moreland), Andy Ho (pirate), Milton Reid (pirate), Larry Taylor (pirate).

Ken Annakin recalls:

While we were in the mountains near Zermatt shooting *Third Man on the Mountain,* I remember Bill Anderson saying to me that *Swiss Family Robinson* was the subject Walt was toying with as our next picture. I read the book. It was very old-fashioned, and I wondered what Walt's approach was going to be. Bill Anderson and I returned to Burbank and we sat down with Walt. He said "Well now, let's throw the whole book out the window. Let's just keep the idea of a Swiss family emigrating, trying to emigrate to America. They get shipwrecked, but they are able to save all the things in the ship. They then make a life on an idyllic island, I think you ought to think of all the things you might like to do, all the animals you could use in an entertaining way. Let's make it a

Mother (Dorothy McGuire) and Father (John Mills) relax as Francis (Kevin Corcoran) enjoys the local recreation in *Swiss Family Robinson*. © *Walt Disney Productions*

James MacArthur and Tommy Kirk, set ashore at a cove on the island, discover pirates up to no good. © *Walt Disney Productions*

wonderful show for the whole family, with all ideas possible.''

And that's exactly what they did. Filmed on a grand scale, the resulting film was thought a bit overpowering by some critics, but audiences flocked to see it, loved it, and made it one of the biggest hits in Disney history.

The main titles appear over sequences of a storm at sea. Stranded alone on the ship, when the storm dies down, the Robinson family decides to build a raft and flee for shore, taking with them as many supplies and animals as they can.

Mother is the most upset about being stranded, but when her husband and three sons complete their tree house and present it to her, she is delighted. They find life a dream on the island. "Everything we need," says Father blissfully, "right at your fingertips." Mother corrects him, however; there are no girls, and she questions the idea of her two grown sons not knowing any more of life than this island. So the two boys, Fritz (the eldest) and Ernst, take off to sail around the coast and make sure that this really *is* an island.

They wreck their boat on the rocks, but, coming ashore, discover a band of pirates holding two prisoners, a sea captain and his grandson. They manage to rescue the boy and set off into the forest in an effort to find their way back to the family overland. The boys can't understand why their companion can't keep up with them—until they discover that "he" is really a girl, at which point they fall over themselves trying to help her. Their journey home is long and tortuous, and back at the tree house Mother, Father, and young Francis don't know if they will ever see the boys again. Happily, they do make it back, just in time for Christmas, and the girl, Roberta, is welcomed as if she were one of the family.

Some friction develops, however, as the two boys begin to rival for her attention, the younger Ernst growing explosive at his older brother's cool self-assurance.

But they all realize that the pirates will be coming
324

after them, and they prepare a fantastically elaborate series of traps, as well as a hilltop fortress. Then they sit back and wait for the pirates to come. Fritz tells Roberta of his dream, to go on to New Zealand and help shape the new world there. Ernst wants to return to England and continue his schooling, and Roberta tells him that her grandfather can get him into one of the finest universities. They forget about the impending attack, and the whole family participates in a wild animal race. Just as they get going, however, the pirates are spotted coming in to shore; the family retreats to the fortress.

As the pirates come ashore, the booby traps are set off one by one: a bridge collapses under the pirates' feet, a barrage of arrows is launched by automatically operated crossbows, they are pelted with coconut bombs, and, when they climb up the hill, are greeted by an avalanche of logs and rocks, not to mention some concealed tiger pits. The pirates continue on, however, and things start to look bleak, when Roberta's grandfather comes into the cove with his ship. At this, the pirates flee, and all is safe once more.

The captain offers to take the whole family back to England with him, but now there are second thoughts. Ernst goes to attend the university, but Roberta decides to stay with Fritz. He declares that he doesn't want to go to New Zealand; he'd rather stay on the island, and, as it turns out, so would Mother, Father, and Francis. They *do* have everything they could ever want, after all.

Swiss Family Robinson is a hugely entertaining film, and a beautiful one as well, with eye-filling scenery everywhere the camera turns. It was filmed on the island of Tobago, which turned out to be a perfect choice.

Disney and his collaborators sensed the key ingredient for this film's success right from the start: create a paradiselike situation, and have the family give the audience the vicarious pleasure of doing exciting, amusing things everyone would love to be able to do. This is the film's great appeal.

For instance, the tree house, a fantastically elaborate

John Mills and friends on location for *Swiss Family Robinson*. Note that although this is outdoor shooting, on a beautiful day, lights and reflectors are still necessary. © *Walt Disney Productions*

affair, was built in a giant tree just as it is seen on screen. It has an elevator, a stove, running water, a skylight, all the comforts of home. The swimming hole, complete with Tarzanlike vines to swing on, ready-made sliding ponds, and the cool water itself, is another dream spot (although not so dreamy for the crew; this location, because it was surrounded by foliage, got only three hours of sunlight a day, and took an inordinate amount of time to film).

The friendly animals also provide a lot of fun. Who wouldn't love to ride an ostrich in a race, or sit atop an elephant in the crashing surf. Most of all, who wouldn't love to live in such an absolutely *beautiful* place?

Of course, all this beauty, and diversity, and ingenuity on screen required a tremendous amount of effort off screen. The entire film took twenty-two weeks to shoot at a cost of $4.5 million.

The first thing was to find a good location: Jamaica, Puerto Rico, Trinidad, and the Galapagos islands were scouted before Tobago was discovered. It was ideal for filming purposes, with one hitch: there were no animals to be found. Thus, a menagerie was assembled—colorful tropical birds, gulls, ostriches, snakes, tigers, zebras, baby elephants, monkeys—and flown to the island, along with appropriate trainers.

The director recalls:

There were fourteen trainers in all, and about 4:00 each day, they would come to me and say, ''Mr. Annakin, can you tell me what attitude you want from my animal tomorrow,'' and then they would discuss it and put in last-minute work each night trying to get the desired results. One afternoon at 3:30 our flamingos took off from Tobago and headed south to British Guiana! We couldn't do anything about this, but fortunately the animal handler was right, and they returned the next day at feeding time.

It took five months to build the necessary sets and incidental objects on the island, including the wreckage,

327

which was built on scaffolding at sea, with divers participating. "It was absolutely real shooting," says Annakin, "something which appealed to me very much because of my documentary beginnings. I liked shooting exteriors. I think it gives much more satisfaction to the audience in the end, and in this case I wanted to keep very much away from the original version that was made by RKO (in 1940), which we ran at Disney. It was a good picture, but you could feel the restrictions of them having to work in a tank."

But Annakin and the crew had to pay the price for realism; it took ten days to shoot the sequence of floating the animals and supplies ashore. "The lines were always getting crossed. You'd find a pig or a cow was tied with a barrel underneath, he'd suddenly turn upside down, and the continuity girl on the camera raft would suddenly shriek, and someone would have to dive in to put the animal right so it wasn't hurt."

Every move, every shot was calculated in advance; Annakin, Bill Anderson, Disney, a sketch artist named John Jensen, and stuntman-turned-second-unit-director Yakima Canutt worked together on storyboards, first deciding what they would like to do and then deciding if it *could* be done. Disney was concerned that there should be something happening every minute, particularly in the climactic pirate attack. He would examine the storyboards and comment: "That works, that works, yeah, that works, although there is a little hole here; we need a bit of action here. Devise some action here." And they would.

The performers almost seem to take a back seat to this spectacular action in considering such a film, but in reality they can be taken for granted only because they are all so smoothly professional. John Mills strikes just the right note of adverturism, tempered with humor and a genuine feeling of enjoying the whole escapade. Dorothy McGuire is warm and real as the mother who worries every step of the way. Equally realistic are the two battling brothers, played by James MacArthur and Tommy Kirk, and the girl they fight over, Janet Munro.

328

The only sour chord is struck by Kevin ("Moochie") Corcoran, whose cuteness and sense of mischief did him well in earlier endeavors, but here seem merely obnoxious. What is more, though his actions are supposed to be funny, it is he who causes many of the worst crises the family faces. One is yearning for John Mills to give the kid a good whipping.

Sessue Hayakawa as the pirate chief has the film's single most memorable shot. As he leads his clan up the hill to the family's fortress, a coconut bomb rolls down into his hand. He picks it up, examines it, can't figure out what it is, and, shrugging, tosses it over his shoulder, where it explodes!

This is part of the massive pirate attack for which many critics took Disney to task, saying that he had soft-soaped the menacing angle by making it a slapstick travesty. This, however, was the intention of Disney and the entire staff, in keeping with the fun of the rest of the film, and at least one critic took it in the proper spirit. Wrote Arthur Knight in the *Saturday Review:*

> Although Lowell Hawley's screenplay takes considerable liberty with the original classic . . . everything is at once so genial and so generous that it would take a stern soul indeed to mourn the absence of Johann Wyss' incessant preachments and homilies. . . . By casting it with seasoned and attractive players . . . Disney has avoided the one-dimensionality that afflicts most children's films. And by playing it tongue-in-cheek—including a pirate attack in which everyone is blown up but nobody dies—director Ken Annakin has dodged both the cloying sweetness and the bloody horror of earlier Disney efforts in this field.

Other reviewers generally found the film to be first-rate family entertainment, the *New York Times* calling it a "grand adventure yarn," and *Time* declaring it "good Disney and bad culture," although that magazine shared some others' reservations about the finale, calling it "a regular Donald Duck comedy in live action."

Yet no complaints were heard from youthful audiences, who adored the film and went to see it in droves. Any apprehensions the Disney higher echelon had about the film's rather high budget were dispelled by its box-office returns. It held its own in a recent reissue as well, and brought the worldwide gross up to nearly $30 million, making it one of Disney's top all-time grossers.

Even so, it would be some time before the Disney company would invest this much time, effort, and money in a live-action film. (This was one of the studio's few recent wide-screen endeavors, a definite asset to the eye-popping action and scenery.) Still, it was nice to see that kind of all-out effort by so many people pay off so nicely.

ONE HUNDRED AND ONE DALMATIANS

RELEASED BY BUENA VISTA ON JANUARY 25, 1961. TECHnicolor. Production supervisor: Ken Peterson. Directors: Wolfgang Reitherman, Hamilton Luske, Clyde Geronimi. Art director, production designer: Ken Anderson. Directing animators: Milt Kahl, Marc Davis, Oliver Johnston, Jr., Franklin Thomas, John Lounsbery, Eric Larson. Story: Bill Peet, based on the book *The Hundred and One Dalmatians* by Dodie Smith. Backgrounds: Albert Dempster, Ralph Hulett, Anthony Rizzo, Bill Layne. Layout: Basil Davidovich, McLaren Stewart, Vance Gerry, Joe Hale, Dale Barnhart, Ray Aragon, Dick Ung, Homer Jonas, Al Zinnen, Sammy June Lanham, Victor Haboush. Layout styling: Don Griffith, Erni Nordli, Collin Campbell. Color styling: Walt Peregoy. Character styling: Bill Peet, Tom Oreb. Character animation: Hal King, Cliff Nordberg, Eric Cleworth, Art Stevens, Hal Ambro, Bill Keil, Dick 330

Pongo arranges for Roger and Anita to meet; it isn't subtle, but it works. © 1964 Walt Disney Productions

Lucas, Les Clark, Blaine Gibson, John Sibley, Julius Svendsen, Ted Berman, Don Lusk, Amby Paliwoda. Effects animation: Jack Boyd, Ed Parks, Dan MacManus, Jack Buckley. Music: George Bruns. Orchestrations: Franklyn Marks. Film editors: Donald Halliday, Roy M.

Brewer, Jr. Sound supervision: Robert O. Cook. Music editor: Evelyn Kennedy. Special processes: Ub Iwerks, Eustace Lycett. Running time: 79 minutes.

Songs: "Cruella de Ville," "Dalmatian Plantation," "Kanine Krunchies Commercial," words and music by Mel Leven.

Voices: Rod Taylor (Pongo), Lisa Davis (Anita), Cate Bauer (Perdita), Ben Wright (Roger Radcliff), Fred Warlock (Horace), J. Pat O'Malley (Jasper, miscellaneous dogs), Betty Lou Gerson (Cruella de Ville; Miss Birdwell), Martha Wentworth (Nani; goose; cow), Tom Conway (collie), George Pelling (Great Dane), Micky Maga (Patch, a puppy), Barbara Beaird (Holly, a puppy), Queenie Leonard (cow), Marjorie Bennett (cow).

Like most of Disney's films at this time, *One Hundred and One Dalmatians* opens with a brightly inventive title sequence. A series of dots spread before the camera and evolve into 101 dogs who all start barking at once! This leads into the main title, and each successive card or credit brings with it a unique concept. The Dalmatian spots become musical notes when composer George Bruns's name appears. The layout is splashed onto the screen when that department is credited, and gradually colored in as color credits appears. A typewriter clicks out the original story credit, etc.

Many live-action films have suffered from overly imaginative title sequences, when the rest of the film was unable to maintain the same level of ingenuity. *One Hundred and One Dalmatians,* on the other hand, is merely off to a flying start.

The opening shot is of London from the air. A jaunty British voice narrates in the first person, and, as we come into the hero's apartment, we see that it's the dog who is talking, not the man, as one would presume. In fact, Pongo refers to songwriter Roger as "my pet." He decides that Roger is spending too much time with his work and needs a mate—and so, incidentally, does he.

When he gazes out the window and sees a beautiful female Dalmatian, being walked by an equally lovely girl, he instantly gets Roger to take him out for a walk, and Pongo tries to arrange a meeting of the two duos in the park. It works out badly, with the humans getting tangled up in the dog leashes and falling in a brook. Despite this mishap, it's love at first sight, for both humans and canines, and the picture dissolves to a wedding ceremony, with Roger and Anita inside the church, and Pongo and Perdita taking the same silent vows outside.

Married life is hectic but most pleasant, with a housekeeper who loves the dogs as much as Roger and Anita. Just as Perdita is about to give birth, a schooldays chum of Anita's named Cruella de Ville shows up, insisting that she must have the puppies when they arrive. Cruella is a flighty and impossible character, but Roger senses evil in her as well, and even writes a song about her expressing his feelings.

When the puppies—fifteen of them—arrive, and Cruella comes to claim them, Roger stands firm and refuses, upsetting the wealthy woman, who is used to having things her own way. A short time later, while Roger and Anita are out walking their dogs, two cockney crooks force their way into the house and steal all fifteen puppies, locking up the distraught housekeeper.

The police are unable to find any clues, although Roger and Pongo are convinced Cruella is behind the evil deed. That evening Pongo tells his mate that "the humans have tried everything; now it's up to us dogs." He makes use of The Twilight Bark to send a relay of signals out of London into the countryside, where the Colonel, an aging dog of military bearing, takes on the search with his aides, a horse called The Captain and a cat named Tibbs. They find the puppies locked up in the long-deserted de Ville mansion, along with a passel of other young Dalmatians. There are ninety-nine in all; it seems that Cruella has been storing them up to make herself a magnificent fur coat!

Tibbs decides to effect an escape plan, while Jasper

and Horace (the crooks) are engrossed in a TV show. By now Pongo and Perdita have arrived on the scene, and Pongo goes inside to ward off the thugs while the Colonel and Tibbs take the puppies back to their barn headquarters. Jasper and Horace track them there, however, necessitating a sudden retreat; Pongo and Perdita must now keep track of ninety-nine cold, tired little pups in a blinding snowstorm, as they make their way back to London.

A collie comes to their aid with a place to stay overnight, and a tip that a truck is going to London in the morning. That morning, however, Cruella joins in the chase, discovers the dogs in the back of the truck, and embarks on a wild run over icy, mountainous roads, trying to knock the truck off the road. In the end Cruella's car is driven off the road by her own henchmen! They all end up on a snowy hill, their cars in a hundred pieces, with Cruella calling them idiots for bungling the job.

Back in London, Roger and Anita are in deep sorrow when the dogs arrive; there is a joyous reunion, and the realization that there are 101 Dalmatians in all. They decide to keep them all, and perhaps move to the country. Roger suggests: "We'll have a Dalmatian plantation," and turns the rhyme into a song. They all join in singing, as the camera moves back into the London night, the music waking up the entire city.

One Hundred and One Dalmatians is Disney in his element, a thoroughly delightful film that many considered to be his best animated feature in years. Unlike some of his 1950s endeavors, this cartoon is not weighed down by attempts to duplicate reality. In fact, it revels in the stylistic exaggeration of reality, best exemplified by the character of Cruella de Ville. Her design is a caricature; her body is a thin line, encased in a huge, billowing white fur coat. Her face is bony and angular, suggesting the canniness of her personality, and her hair is a shock of black and white moplike strands. She carries at all times a mile-long cigarette holder and leaves behind her a trail of smoke wherever she goes. Even her

One of Disney's most colorful villainesses of all time, Cruella de Ville. © 1961 Walt Disney Productions

Pongo, Perdita, and the puppies watch their favorite TV star, Thunderbolt. © 1961 Walt Disney Productions

car is an exaggeration—a long, long luxury limousine that careens down the city streets and screeches to a halt in front of the Radcliffs' home. Cruella is doubly striking, of course, in contrast to Anita, who is drawn much in the classic style of Disney heroines.

But this is the joy of *One Hundred and One Dalmatians:* it is real enough to be believable and engrossing, but at all times retains its identity as an animated cartoon, to be enjoyed and laughed at.

The film is full of ingenious visual ideas, a prime one being the similarities between dog and owner. The human Roger is drawn with an oversized nose and angular chin to accentuate the parallel between his face and Pongo's. When Pongo scours the sidewalk outside his window for likely prospects to meet, he sees a parade of dog-walkers who match their pets' looks to a tee: a droopy female artist-type walking her droopy dog, whose floppy ears match her mistress's hairdo, a pampered French poodle whose owner's furs match her natural fur, etc.

The settings are also on the borderline between reality and invention. The opening view of London is much more stylized and caricatured than the similar opening shot in *Peter Pan,* for instance. This formula meshes nicely with the attitude toward the characters themselves.

The personality of virtually every supporting character is conveyed visually as much as through dialogue: the Colonel has a proud but absentminded look about him that helps to solidify his C. Aubrey Smith–like character. The Collie who helps the Dalmatians during their long wintry trek not only sounds reliable and authoritative (thanks to Tom Conway's voice), but looks that way. Jasper and Horace are hilariously seedy; one look at them is enough to know that they'll bungle the job.

One of the key plot points in the climax is visual. In order to pass by Cruella unnoticed, and climb aboard the truck to London, the puppies cover themselves with soot, so they no longer look like Dalmatians. The scheme is foiled when a drop of water from a rooftop splashes on one of the dogs and reveals his identity.

The delightful visual aspect of the film is matched by a witty script. The songs, which are really incidental and not large-scale production numbers, are fun, especially "Cruella de Ville," in which Roger takes out his venom in a set of saucy lyrics.

There are some amusing jibes at television throughout the film. At home the puppies are captivated by the canine TV star Thunderbolt, who invariably foils his human adversaries. The show is sponsored by Kanine Krunchies, represented by a hilariously silly commercial. Later, Jasper and Horace pass the time at the lonely mansion by watching "What's My Crime." The guest crook signs in, and a panel, aided by a loquacious moderator, tries to identify him. When the show is over, the host asks the crook if he can come back next week, but the firm hand of his jailer seems to indicate that it won't be possible. (Incidentally, in one scene the puppies watch a clip from Disney's *Flowers and Trees* on the TV set.)

There are warm, realistic touches to the film that give depth to the characters and heighten the audience involvement in their lives. When the puppies arrive, several at a time, the fifteenth appears not to survive. But Roger takes the infant pup and massages its heart, stirring it back to life. He and Pongo happily dance a jig in celebration of the event. Later, when the housekeeper discovers the puppies gone, she screams in horror and runs out into the London streets, crying in anguish.

In short, everything *works* in *One Hundred and One Dalmatians*, bringing the picture together into a briskly paced, cohesive whole with nary a dull spot in sight. *Time* magazine called it "the wittiest, most charming, least pretentious cartoon feature Walt Disney has ever made . . . one of the nicest things that have happened so far this year to dog's best friend." Joseph Morgenstern in the *New York Herald Tribune* noted that "it is in the province of sophisticated humor that Mr. Disney is a

337

late arrival, and a welcome one. *One Hundred and One Dalmatians* comes up with some engaging spoofs of the British spy thriller genre, and does it without for a moment compromising its appeal for the young. . . . In their flight the pups are aided by a shaggy dog who sounds like Colonel Blimp, a Ronald Colman collie, a sturdy village Labrador whose accent slips occasionally and a whole animal underground stationed strategically throughout the countryside.''

Howard Thompson in the *Times* declared that Cruella "makes the *Snow White* witch seem like *Pollyanna*. . . . Imagine a sadistic Auntie Mame, drawn by Charles Addams and with a Tallulah Bankhead bass. . . . Even with a lady Lucifer hell-bent for their hides, the Dalmatians are a friendly lot worth knowing.''

One Hundred and One Dalmatians was made possible (or perhaps "more feasible") because of a then revolutionary development called Xerography. Put simply, the Xerox system made it possible for Disney animators to copy initial drawings many times over, eliminating the necessity to draw 101 separate dogs for those mass scenes. ("Of course," commented cartoon director Chuck Jones, "only the Disney studio would think of doing a hundred and one spotted dogs. We have trouble doing *one* spotted dog.") Even so, the animation staff of approximately three hundred worked on the film for three years, bringing the cost of the feature to $4 million.

Coupled with the Xerox process, however, was a new drawing style that seemed appropriate to this film, less so to later ones. For the first time Disney animators used a rough-line technique that most closely resembled their rough sketches before undergoing the finishing processes. It was, of course, that smooth, polished style that had won Disney the reputation for slickness in his work of recent years; this was apparently a blacklash reaction that, in some observers' eyes, went too far in the opposite direction.

This naturally had no bearing on the film's entertainment value, and certainly had nothing to do with block-
338

ing its success, which was considerable. Indeed, the film was a bigger hit than Disney's more ambitious *Sleeping Beauty* of several years back, and proved its worthiness to take its place alongside the other Disney cartoon classics when it was reissued in 1969 to a huge and enthusiastic audience.

THE ABSENT MINDED PROFESSOR

RELEASED BY BUENA VISTA ON MARCH 16, 1961. ASSOCIATE producer: Bill Walsh. Director: Robert Stevenson. Screenplay: Bill Walsh, based on a story by Samuel W. Taylor. Director of photography: Edward Colman, A.S.C. Editor: Cotton Warburton, A.C.E. Art director: Carroll Clark. Set decorations: Emile Kuri, Hal Gausman. Costumes: Chuck Keehne, Gertrude Casey. Music: George Bruns. Orchestrations: Franklyn Marks. Second unit director: Arthur J. Vitarelli. Assistant director: Robert G. Shannon. Special effects: Peter Ellenshaw, Eustace Lycett, Robert A. Malley, Joshua Meador. Sequence consultant: Donald Da Gradi. Makeup: Pat McNalley. Hairstyling: Ruth Sandifer. Sound supervision: Robert O. Cook. Sound mixer: Dean Thomas. Music editor: Evelyn Kennedy. Running time: 97 minutes.

Songs: "Medfield Fight Song," special lyrics to "Sweet Betsy of Pike" by Richard M. Sherman and Robert B. Sherman.

Cast: Fred MacMurray (Ned Brainard), Nancy Olson (Betsy Carlisle), Keenan Wynn (Alonzo Hawk), Tommy Kirk (Bill Hawk), Ed Wynn (fire chief), Leon Ames (President Rufus Daggett), Wally Brown (Coach Elkins), Alan Carney (first referee), Elliott Reid (Shelby Ashton), Edward Andrews (defense secretary), David Lewis (General Singer), Jack Mullaney (air force captain),

339

Nancy Olson and Fred MacMurray go for a ride in his Model T (over an aerial shot of the Walt Disney studios in Burbank, in this publicity still). © *Walt Disney Productions*

The Medfield basketball team springs into action, thanks to Flub-ber. © *Walt Disney Productions*

Belle Montrose (Mrs. Chatsworth), Forrest Lewis (Officer Kelly), James Westerfield (Officer Hanson), Ned Wynn (youth), Gage Clarke (Reverend Bosworth), Alan Hewitt (General Hotchkiss), Raymond Bailey (Admiral Olmstead), Wendell Holmes (General Poynter), Don Ross (Lenny), Charlie Briggs (Sig), Wally Boag (TV newsman), Leon Tyler (basketball player #18), Gordon Jones (rival basketball coach), Paul Frees (voice of army alert, pilot on radio, radio announcer).

The film opens with Professor Ned Brainard working an experiment, as he lectures his class. He mixes a potion and sets off an explosion, at which time the main titles appear.

The Prof is to be married that night; he's missed his own wedding twice before, but he can't resist playing around in his lab for a while before the big event. This time there's a big explosion that knocks him out cold. Next morning, when he wakes up, he notices that a metal container is sailing up into the air. It contains a gooey substance that floats, and he calls it Flubber (flying rubber). He hopes his fiancée Betsy will forgive him for missing the wedding when she hears about this great discovery, but she's too angry to listen, and he's too bumbling to make a coherent explanation.

That night he rigs up his old model T with flubber and gets the thing to fly! He tries to show Betsy, but she refuses, going to the Medfield basketball game with his rival, Shelby Ashton. At the game Medfield is being pummeled by a team twice its size. The star player, Bill Hawk, can't play because Brainard flunked him, and Bill's father, Alonzo Hawk, shifty president of the Auld Lang Syne Finance Company, has bet heavily against Medfield, certain that they will lose. During half time, Brainard irons flubber onto the soles of the team's sneakers, and during the second half they spring into action—literally. They hop all over the court, making basket after basket, and blocking every shot by the opposing team for a tremendous victory. The Prof tries to explain to Betsy that this was his doing, but she thinks he's trying to take credit for the team, and belittles him. She just doesn't understand.

After he drops Betsy off, Shelby drives home, and is suddenly pursued by a strange otherworldly force. It's Brainard, flying his car above Shelby's, bouncing on the roof, honking his horn, and eventually causing him to crash into a police car, leaving him with a thoroughly outlandish alibi.

Unfortunately, Alonzo Hawk has been up late that night, and has seen Brainard's car flying. He catches on immediately, and tries to make a deal, but Brainard says no. The Prof then calls Washington, but gets only a runaround. Representatives of the three armed forces are intrigued, however, and they come to Medfield to see a demonstration. Meanwhile, Hawk switches cars on Brainard, leaving him with a duplicate Model T. When the Professor tries to get his car to fly, it won't budge, and he is made to look like a fool. Betsy pities him, and at last believes what he says.

She and Ned determine to get the car back from Hawk, but first they must take care of Hawk himself. They get him to try on some flubberized shoes, and, on the sidewalk outside his home, he starts to bounce up in the air. He's crazy about it, as he bounces higher and higher; when he asks how they get it to stop, they tell him they don't know, and leave him there in a most unusual predicament. Then they go off to his warehouse, and foil his henchmen in order to retrieve the flubberized car.

He and Betsy then fly to Washington, but instead of a warm greeting, they are treated as an Unidentified Flying Object. Then the army, navy, and air force men hear of it and come to his rescue. Brainard is received as a hero at the White House. And he actually gets married to Betsy; as they fly off in his car, the "Just Married" sign on the back has been changed to read "Finally Married."

Disney staffer Ward Kimball has recalled that Walt's greatest pleasure in making live-action movies was when he could produce some cartoonlike effect on the screen.

Thus, the fantasy of a flying car and bouncing basketball players must have appealed to his imagination—as he knew it would to millions of others.

The Absent Minded Professor cannot really be called one of Disney's *best* films, but it surely is one of his biggest audience-pleasers. Everything is tailored toward getting laughs on the broadest possible basis, and one cannot argue with success.

The key effects sequences are quite well done. The car footage is done with a combination of live action wires (such as shots of the car taking off, and bouncing on other cars), miniatures (which are the least convincing), matte and process work. By intercutting these various types of shots, the overall effect is rather good. There are nice individual touches, too, such as Brainard driving the car into a cloud to avoid an army bomber during the Washington finale.

The filmmakers decided that such trickery could only be carried off in a black-and-white film, a decision repeated for *Son of Flubber*. A few short years later, the Disney technicians surpassed even these effects for *Mary Poppins*, in color. The basketball game goes on at some length, and, although the shots of the kids bouncing high in the air are really amazing, they start to wear thin. There are some good variations, though, such as one play shown entirely in the eyes of the referee, whose openmouthed face follows the team bounce by bounce across the court. Undercranking (to make the movements faster) and even frame-cutting are ingredients in this sequence.

The scene of Keenan Wynn, as Alonzo Hawk, bouncing on the flubberized shoes is one of the most impressive in the film, because it is shot outdoors, where you realize trickery is at a minimum; there is also a marvelous shot from his point of view of Brainard and Betsy standing on the ground, with the camera bouncing high in the air.

There are other striking moments: while the Professor is bouncing atop Shelby's car, the victim's eyes widen

343

into a look of unspeakable horror, accentuated by the fact that he's wearing a dark makeup that offsets the whites of his eyes. Later, when Brainard is being chased by Alonzo Hawk, he gets through an alleyway by driving his car on the other side of a building!

The script itself is really rather obvious, with few surprises; indeed, the film's major laughs come from the anticipation of what is about to happen. This is based largely on typecasting, including the police officer from *The Shaggy Dog*, Forrest Lewis, and a partner, played by James Westerfield; snooty Alan Hewitt (who has been in countless Disney films ever since) as an army officer; Elliott Reid as the snobby intellectual; Edward Andrews as the hypocritical soft-soaping government official, etc.

Keenan Wynn is, of course, thoroughly despicable as Alonzo Hawk, but there is a nice piece of irony in one sequence where he's bouncing up and down uncontrollably. Fire engines come to his rescue, and who should be playing the fire chief but Ed Wynn—Keenan's father, as well as the venerable Fire Chief of radio fame.

The most important casting of all, however, was that of Fred MacMurray, and he is inspired in the lead role. He plays his part with such utter conviction that you believe him completely—his naïveté, his absentmindedness, his determination, and even his occasional stupidity.

This was not the last Disney film to poke fun at the government, which also came in for a ribbing in the sequel to this picture. Some have found a parallel between Professor Brainard's rejection and runaround from the government and Disney's own career, in which he repeatedly had to do things on his own, without the support of others. In any event the satire is healthy, and yet another example of nonsugary content, however innocuous, in Disney films.

The Absent Minded Professor won rousing reviews from critics. *Time* called it "the season's kookiest science-fiction farce. . . . Flubber provides fuel for a very funny piece of hyperbolic humor in the grand
344

American tradition of Paul Bunyan . . .'' The *New York Times* called it "remarkably bouncy entertainment." *Variety* went a bit deeper.

On the surface, *The Absent Minded Professor* is a comedy-fantasy of infectious absurdity, a natural follow-up to Walt Disney's *The Shaggy Dog*. But its mass appeal goes deeper than that. For beneath the preposterous veneer lurks a comment on our time, a reflection of the plight of the average man haplessly confronted with the complexities of a jet age civilization burdened with fear, red-tape, official mumbo-jumbo and ambitious anxiety. Deeply rooted within the screenplay is a subtle protest against the detached, impersonal machinery of modern progress. It is an underlying theme with which an audience can identify. It is the basic reason why the film is going to be an enormously popular attraction . . .

The wordage may have been a bit erudite for Disney, but the sentiment was definitely true, resoundingly reaffirmed by the studio's other comedies of the 1960s.

The Absent Minded Professor was launched by a special hour program on the Disney TV show featuring MacMurray explaining "Serendipity," defined as "the art of happy accidents." The film took off at the box office for astronomical results, so much so that Disney decided that a sequel was warranted. The original showed its staying power in 1967 when it did big business all over again on a double bill with *The Shaggy Dog*.

Incidentally, *Time* magazine supplied, for interested readers, the special effects department's recipe for flubber: "To one pound of salt water taffy add one heaping tablespoon polyurethane foam, one cake crumbled yeast. Mix till smooth, allow to rise. Then pour into saucepan over one cup cracked rice mixed with one cup water. Add topping of molasses. Boil till it lifts lid and says 'Qurlp.' "

BABES IN TOYLAND

RELEASED BY BUENA VISTA ON DECEMBER 14, 1961.
Technicolor. Director: Jack Donohue. Screenplay: Joe
Rinaldi, Ward Kimball, Lowell S. Hawley, based on the
operetta by Victor Herbert and Glenn McDonough.
Photography: Edward Colman. Editor: Robert Stafford.
Art directors: Carroll Clark, Marvin Aubrey Davis. Set
decorations: Emile Kuri. Costumes: Bill Thomas, Chuck
Keehne, Gertrude Casey. Music: George Bruns, based
on Herbert's musical score. Orchestrations: Franklyn
Marks. Libretto: Mel Leven. Choral arrangements: Jud
Conlon. Choreography: Tommy Mahoney. Special effects: Robert Mattey. Animation sequences: Eustace Lycett, Joshua Meador, Bill Justice, Xavier Atencio.
Makeup: Pat McNalley. Hairstyling: Ruth Sandifer.
Sound: Robert O. Cook, Dean Thomas. Music editor:
Evelyn Kennedy. Running time: 105 minutes.

Songs: "I Can't Do the Sum," "Just a Toy,"
"Floretta," "Castle in Spain," "We Won't Be Happy
Till We Get It," "Lemonade" "Just a Whisper Away,"
"March of the Toys," "Toyland" by Victor Herbert.
"The Workshop Song," "The Forest of No Return,"
"Slowly He Sank into the Sea" by George Bruns, Mel
Leven.

Cast: Ray Bolger (Barnaby), Tommy Sands (Tom
Piper), Ed Wynn (The Toymaker), Annette Funicello
(Mary Contrary), Henry Calvin (Gonzorgo), Gene
Sheldon (Roderigo), Tommy Kirk (Grumio), Mary
McCarty (Mother Goose), Kevin Corcoran (Boy Blue),
Brian Corcoran (Willie Winkie), Ann Jilliann (Bo Peep),
Marilee and Melanie Arnold (The Twins), Jerry Glenn
(Simple Simon), John Perri (Jack-Be-Nimble), David
Pinson (Bobby Shaftoe), Bryan Russell (The Little
Boy), James Martin (Jack), Ilana Dowding (Jill), Bess
Flowers (villager).
346

This lavish, colorful, Disneyized version of the Victor Herbert classic opens with a puppet named Sylvester J. Goose talking to the audience through the part in a stage curtain. He is followed by Mother Goose, who invites us all to join her in Mother Goose Village. The curtain opens, and the camera moves into an unbelievably bright and colorful setting, where the storybook characters are celebrating the impending marriage of Tom Piper to Mary Contrary.

The villainous Barnaby is jealous, however, and has his two henchmen, Gonzorgo and Roderigo, kidnap Tom and do away with him. Instead of killing the boy, they sell him to a gypsy camp to make extra money on the deal. The next day, when Mary learns of Tom's demise, Barnaby plays on her sorrow to ask her hand in marriage. She refuses, but that night realizes that she is in dire financial straits, and next day agrees to marry the leering rogue. At a prewedding celebration that night a gypsy troupe comes to entertain, and a gypsy hag sings a song—at the end of which "she" removes her wig to reveal none other than Tom! He and Mary are reunited, and the marriage with Barnaby is called off.

When Mary's younger brothers and sisters wander off into the Forest of No Return, Mary and Tom go after them and end up in Toyland, where they offer to help the harried Toymaker meet his Christmas deadline. The Toymaker's inventor helper Grumio concocts a ray gun that can shrink anything to miniature size. Barnaby invades the toy factory, uses the ray gun to put Tom out of the way and have the Toymaker marry him to Mary. Tom takes advantage of his new size to activate the toy soldiers and lead them into battle against Barnaby. They emerge victorious, Grumio's new ray gun returning Tom to normal size. Back in the village it's celebration time once more as Tom and Mary are finally wed.

Babes in Toyland is filled to the brim with gimmicks, ranging from minor (animated stars bursting out of Tom's head when he is bopped with a sledgehammer by the two henchmen) to major (talking/singing/dancing trees in the Forest of No Return), an endless procession of songs, staged in a variety of fashions to avoid repetition from one to the next, and a large cast performing in the most colorful settings ever devised for a live-action Disney film.

Unfortunately, all these elements combined cannot overcome some basic and serious flaws that hamper the picture.

First, there is no heart to the film. The viewer feels no emotion for any character on the screen, and when there is no empathy with a hero or heroine, a film is off to a bad start. Besides a lack of charisma on the part of the main characters, there is no menace to the villains. The whole film is played in an *opera comique* style that keeps everything at the most superficial level. Barnaby is simply not a villain; there is never any feeling of danger in any of his schemes, and the tone of the picture is such that even the supposedly scary sequence, with the living trees, is sugarcoated to keep it from ever getting *too* frightening.

In trying to keep the film at the level of fluffy entertainment, the filmmakers forgot to breathe life into the whole production.

For older viewers there is an air of contrivance about the film. Every movement, every gag, every gimmick has a preplanned, mechanical look about it that in its very calculatedness leaves the viewer cold.

That the film has these shortcomings is a shame, because it also has the kind of imagination and potentiality that indicates what it *could* have been. Some of the musical numbers are excellent. When Ray Bolger sings "Castle in Spain" to Annette Funicello, he goes into an elaborate dance number involving a fountain of dancing waters that, at one point, match his movements precisely. "I Can't Do the Sum" has Annette sitting down at a table trying to balance her books. As she sings of her problem, four other Annettes hop out of her skin to join her in the song, each one tinted a different color. Later, she looks in a full-length mirror while singing, and as she walks away the four Annettes walk out of the mirror to join her. As she sings of the confusion

Ray Bolger, Mary McCarty (with Sylvester the Goose), Marilee and Melanie Arnold, Kevin and and Brian Corcoran, and Annette Funicello listen to Henry Calvin and Gene Sheldon tell the story of Tommy Sands's demise. © 1961 Walt Disney Productions

Tommy Sands, Kevin Corcoran, Annette Funicello, and toymaker Ed Wynn examine the rubble after an explosion in the toy factory. © 1961 Walt Disney Productions

of figures, assorted numbers fly in the air around her head. The gypsy hag number provides Tommy Sands with his best moment in the film, in an amusing and effective performance of the song.

One of the film's true highlights involves its two best performers, Henry Calvin and Gene Sheldon, performing a quasi-Laurel and Hardy act as Barnaby's thick-witted henchmen. They are easily the funniest thing in the film, and their number "Slowly He Sank into the Sea" is a comic gem, with Calvin singing the (fictitious) saga of Tom's death at sea as Sheldon dances about him; with every chorus the puddle at their feet, from Sheldon's crocodile tears, grows deeper and deeper.

Would that the same could be said for the rest of the cast. Ray Bolger has no business playing a villain, even though he does a creditable job; his broad rendition of the role renders the part thoroughly unbelievable. Annette Funicello and Tommy Sands may well be the dullest romantic team ever depicted on the screen, and the overemphasis on them, and their uninspired renditions of the Victor Herbert songs really bog down the film and kill its interest for the adolescent audience that rejects such "mush." As for Ed Wynn, a little of him goes a long way, although he does contribute some of the film's more humorous moments. Tommy Kirk is saddled with another idiotic role as Wynn's assistant.

The Toyland finale, with the wooden soldiers attacking Barnaby, is good, although curiously not as exceptional as one would expect from Disney. The sequence is fairly short, and the animated trickery rather routine, considering the special effects that have preceded it (Bolger's piggy bank, which projects alluring dollar signs in the air, sending his henchmen floating after them; night "falling" at Toyland, literally; the living trees). The material in this sequence is not on a par with, say, George Pal's Puppetoons, which were used to such good effect in *Tom Thumb* a few years earlier.

The reviews of *Babes in Toyland* reflected these failures in the film's conception. *Variety* deemed it "great for the moppets . . . but some of the more mature patrons may be distressed to discover that quaint, charming *Toyland* has been transformed into a rather gaudy and mechanical 'Fantasyland.' What actually emerges is *Babes in Disneyland.''* Time commented: "*Babes in Toyland,* Walt Disney's first live-action musical, is a wonderful piece of entertainment for children under five, but children over five who plan to see it will be well advised to take some Berlitz brushup lessons in baby talk." Paul V. Beckley summed up his review in the *New York Herald Tribune* by saying that "the whole film has the character of frosting without any cake underneath."

Oddly enough, even though this was Disney's Christmas release, and was well promoted with an hour-long special on the Disney TV show giving behind-the-scenes glimpses of the making of the film, it did not do all that well at the box office. Considering its cost and potential, it grossed just $4,600,000 in domestic release, or a little more than half what the *Shaggy Dog* pulled in.

Babes in Toyland was filmed only once before, by Hal Roach in 1934, with Laurel and Hardy as the stars, and Charlotte Henry and Felix Knight as the romantic leads. It hasn't the color or special effects of the new version, but it is everything the Disney film should have been: charming, funny, frightening, and truly memorable.

The film was just a case of Disney trying to outdo himself, and channeling his energy in the wrong direction. It was his first live-action musical, and he profited by the experience. A few years later he turned out a little something called *Mary Poppins.* Remember?

THE SWORD IN THE STONE

RELEASED BY BUENA VISTA ON DECEMBER 1963. Technicolor. Production supervisor: Ken Peterson. Director: Wolfgang Reitherman. Art director: Ken Anderson. Directing animators: Franklin Thomas, Milt

Kahl, Oliver Johnston, Jr., John Lounsbery. Story: Bill Peet, based on the book by T. H. White. Character animators: Hal King, Eric Larson, Cliff Nordberg, Hal Ambro, Dick Lucas. Character design: Milt Kahl, Bill Peet. Backgrounds: Walt Peregoy, Bill Layne, Albert Dempster, Anthony Rizzo, Ralph Hulett, Fil Mottola. Layout: Don Griffith, Basil Davidovich, Vance Gerry, Sylvia Cobb, Dale Bernhart, Homer Jonas. Effects animation: Dan MacManus, Jack Boyd, Jack Buckley. Music: George Bruns. Orchestrations: Franklyn Marks. Film editor: Donald Halliday. Sound supervision: Robert O. Cook. Music editor: Evelyn Kennedy. Running time: 75 minutes.

Songs: "A Most Befuddling Thing," "Blue Oak Tree," "Mad Madame Mim," "That's What Makes the World Go Round," "Higitus Figitus," "The Legend of the Sword in the Stone" by Richard M. Sherman, Robert B. Sherman.

Voices: Ricky Sorenson (Wart), Sebastian Cabot (Sir Ector), Karl Swenson (Merlin), Junius Matthews (Archimedes), Alan Napier (Sir Pelinore), Norman Alden (Kay), Martha Wentworth (Madame Mim, Granny Squirrel), Ginny Tyler (little girl squirrel), Barbara Jo Allen (scullery maid), Richard and Robert Reitherman, and The Mello Men.

The Sword in the Stone was welcomed as Disney's first animated cartoon feature in two years. Though it was fairly well received and moderately successful at the box office, few could resist commenting how different this film seemed from the earlier animated endeavors, not only in drawing style, but in the whole atmosphere of the film, which was telling a medieval tale with a bit too much of its head in the 1960s. In fact, the opening title music is incongruously jazzy in nature, before settling down to more appropriate period music for the storybook introduction.

One of *The Sword in the Stone*'s tableaux, illustrating the legend of King Arthur and the sword that made him king.
© *1962 Walt Disney Productions*

Wart, the boy-king, and his mentor, Archimedes.
© *1962 Walt Disney Productions*

A volume of *The Sword in the Stone* by T. H. White is opened to the first page, with a troubadour singing the background of the story, illustrated by a series of tableaux, explaining the sword imbedded in the stone, which would determine the next king—whoever would be able to pull the sword out of its rigid position.

We next meet Merlin the Magician, and his pet owl Archimedes, in their forest retreat. Merlin forsees a visitor coming to join him; it turns out to be young Wart, who is running after an arrow lost in a hunting expedition by his knight, Kay. Wart drops in on Merlin, who announces with a flourish that he is now going to assume responsibility for Wart's education. He returns to the castle to live with Wart, and immediately takes the boy out for a series of unusual adventures.

Merlin turns the boy into various animals, to get an idea of how they live, and to prove his general theory that brains always conquer brawn. First he changes Wart into a fish, precipitating an exciting battle with a killer pike, in which Wart is forced to use his brains (with a little help from Archimedes). Then he becomes a squirrel, which gets awkward when a female squirrel falls in love with him and refuses to accept his rejection. Finally, he becomes a bird, and as such is chased by a hawk into the cabin of Madame Mim. When she learns that he is one of Merlin's friends, she decides to do away with him. Just then, Merlin shows up, and challenges Madame Mim to a wizard's duel, in which the two opponents can turn themselves into anything at all in order to destroy the other. Mim plays dirty, but Merlin is too crafty to fall for her tricks. When she becomes a fire-breathing dragon, it looks as if all is lost, but Merlin uses his brains, and becomes a germ, which spreads a disease throughout the dragon's system and kills her.

These adventures have done Wart no good in his duties as a squire, however, and just before the big jousting match, he realizes he has forgotten to bring Kay's sword. Running off to find a replacement, he spots the sword in the stone and pulls it out easily. When the others see the fabled sword, they ask where he got it, and refuse to believe his story. They return to watch Wart pull the sword from the stone once more, and awed by the spectacle, dub him their king.

Merlin leaves, and Wart, now King Arthur, is uncomfortable on the throne. But Merlin returns to him to remind the boy that *knowledge* is the real power. Wart understands at last.

The Sword in the Stone is a good film, but it falls far short of greatness. One would think that with a story as good as T. H. White's, transference to the realm of animated cartoon would have been relatively simple. But instead of playing up the wonder and awe of Merlin and the boy he takes under his wing, the Disney screenplay does everything it can to bring them down to earth. Merlin's magic is a matter-of-fact thing, and the life to which Wart aspires is treated in a mundane fashion.

Most distressing of all is the attempt to make the jokes "relevant" to the 1960s, with Merlin constantly dropping throwaway lines about seeing into the future. At the end, when Merlin returns to visit the new King Arthur, he announces that he's just been to Bermuda, and he sports sunglasses, a flowered shirt, and shorts. The final gag in the film is a spoof of a then-current television commercial! This only cheapens the film, instead of making it funnier or more appealing. It also leaves it in danger of dating badly in years to come.

In addition to the obvious, there *is* considerable wit in *The Sword in the Stone,* both in Merlin's dialogue, and especially in that of his pet owl, Archimedes. But in the opening portion of the film, there is an overreliance on dialogue that would tend to make many young viewers restless. It is well into the film before there is a purely visual sequence, such as Merlin using magic to have all the dirty dishes in the castle wash themselves, or shrinking his belongings and having them find their way into his traveling case when he goes to join Wart. Most of the visual humor in this part of the film is in the manner of little touches, such as Merlin pouring his tea down his beard, accentuating his absentmindedness.

The film's real highlight is the wizard's duel. Here is

the kind of sequence that remains in one's memory (more than can be said for the rest of the film), with a whole series of ingenious visual ideas as Madame Mim continually tries to top Merlin by changing herself into progressively more vicious animals, concluding with her pièce de résistance, a fire-breathing dragon. Even her dirty pool is shown visually, with Merlin using his wits to avoid her trickery.

The scenes in which Wart becomes various animals hark back most closely to the Disney of yore, as well as providing more movement and excitement than any other segments in the film. The sequence where Wart, as a fish, is pursued by a shark, has genuine thrills; its conception and timing are superb, making the most of the situation. Meanwhile, the squirrel sequence provides some truly charming moments, as the determined female squirrel pursues her potential mate. There is an amusing punch line as Merlin, who has turned himself into a somewhat older squirrel, finds an older female coming after *him!*

There are the obligatory "beauty shots" throughout *Sword,* scenes played in the reflection of a stream, the stylized tableaux at the beginning of the film, and inventive visual concepts such as the rickety tower of the castle where Merlin is sent to live.

But *The Sword in the Stone* more closely resembles the Disney live-action product of this era than the classic animated cartoons that one associates with the studio. Like so many of the live movies, it provides thoroughly pleasant entertainment for seventy-five minutes, but it leaves the audience with nothing to take out of the theatre. It's difficult to remember very much about the film even when one tries, unlike most of the good Disney cartoon features, which have an indelible stamp on the memory.

Most reviewers were grateful for even half-steam Disney animation at this point, and the film, released at Christmastime, garnered generally favorable reviews. Judith Crist in the *Herald Tribune* found it "a thorough delight. . . . The songs are bright and singable, the art work lovely and the plot charming in its twists and turns." Howard Thompson in the *Times* called it "a warm, wise and amusing film. . . . The humor sparkles with real, knowing sophistication—meaning for all ages—and some of the characters on the fifth-century landscape of Old England are Disney pips . . ."

Not that these critics were wrong. The film *is* charming, and enjoyable, but it lacks the spark that set so many other Disney films out of the ordinary. Stanley Kauffmann in *The New Republic* wrote a dissenting opinion: "A huge coast-to-coast malted milk made of pasteurized Arthurian ingredients. Every element in it, pictorial and musical, is derivative of earlier and better Disney pictures, and the whole has a factory-line feeling devoid of joy."

Proof of the pudding came at the box office. The film grossed $4½ million, not bad by any means, but hardly up to par for a Disney Christmas release. More interestingly, the film has left no traces; its characters have not evolved into Disney "classics" that are worthy of merchandising or following up on the printed page. In discussions of Disney's work the film is seldom, if ever, mentioned. Despite a recent reissue, the film has never achieved the lasting affection audiences feel for other Disney cartoon features.

MARY POPPINS

RELEASED BY BUENA VISTA ON AUGUST 29, 1964. TECHnicolor. Coproducer: Bill Walsh. Director: Robert Stevenson. Screenplay: Bill Walsh, Donald Da Gradi, based on the *Mary Poppins* books by P. L. Travers. Photography: Edward Colman. Editor: Cotton Warburton. Art director: Carroll Clark, William H. Tuntke. Set decorations: Emile Kuri, Hal Gausman. Costume and design consultant: Tony Walton. Costume designer: Bill Thomas. Costumers: Chuck Keehne, Gertrude Casey. Consultant: P. L. Travers. Music supervisor, arranger, conductor: Irwin Kostal. Choreography: Marc Breaux, Dee Dee Wood. Assistant directors: Joseph L. McEveety, Paul Feiner. Makeup: Pat McNalley. Hairstyling: La Rue Matheron. Sound supervision: Robert O. Cook. Sound mixer: Dean Thomas. Music editor: Evelyn Kennedy. Dance accompanist: Nat Farber. Assistant to the conductor: James MacDonald. Live-action second unit director: Arthur J. Vitarelli. Animation director: Hamilton Luske. Animation art director: McLaren Stewart. Nursery sequence design: Bill Justice, Xavier Atencio. Animators: Milt Kahl, Oliver Johnston, Jr., John Lounsbery, Hal Ambro, Franklin Thomas, Ward Kimball, Eric Larson, Cliff Nordberg, Jack Boyd. Backgrounds: Albert Dempster, Don Griffith, Art Riley, Bill Layne. Special effects: Peter Ellenshaw, Eustace Lycett, Robert A. Mattey. Running time: 140 minutes.

Songs: "Spoonful of Sugar," "Jolly Holiday," "I Love to Laugh," "Chim-Chim-Cheree," "Feed the Birds (Tuppence a Bag)" "Step in Time," "Stay Awake," "Sister Suffragette," "A Man Has Dreams," "The Life I Lead," "Let's Go Fly a Kite," "Fidelity Fiduciary Bank," "The Perfect Nanny," "Supercalifragilisticexpialidocious" by Richard M. Sherman, Robert B. Sherman.

Cast: Julie Andrews (Mary Poppins), Dick Van Dyke (Bert; Mr. Dawes, Sr.), David Tomlinson (Mr. Banks), Glynis Johns (Mrs. Banks), Ed Wynn (Uncle Albert), Hermione Baddeley (Ellen), Karen Dotrice (Jane Banks), Matthew Garber (Michael Banks), Elsa Lanchester (Katie Nanna), Arthur Treacher (Constable Jones), Reginald Owen (Admiral Boom), Reta Shaw (Mrs. Brill), Arthur Malet (Mr. Dawes, Jr.), Jane Darwell (The Bird Woman), Cyril Delevanti (Mr. Grubbs), Lester Matthews (Mr. Tomes), Clive L. Halliday (Mr.

Bert and Mary Poppins get an assist from some animated friends.
© 1964 Walt Disney Productions

Mousley), Don Barclay (Mr. Binnacle), Marjorie Bennett (Miss Lark), Alma Lawton (Mrs. Corry), Marjorie Eaton (Miss Persimmon).

There really is one word to describe *Mary Poppins,* and that is supercalifragilisticexpialidocious. To attempt a more complete assessment would exhaust a library full of adjectives.

Many regard *Mary Poppins* as Walt Disney's crowning achievement, and that it may well be. Certainly it was the biggest hit in the history of the studio, both critically and financially; it is the kind of movie that will continue to play forever. And in most regards, it *does* have the feeling of a masterwork; that is to say, the film is really the culmination of thirty-five years' work, for no amount of enthusiasm or capability could take the place of the experience of the Disney staff, under the guidance of Walt himself, that worked together to make this film. Of equal importance, however, is the fact that Disney deliberately went out and hired "new blood" to work with his veteran staff, in what was obviously a perfect blend of veteran know-how and youthful imagination.

The film begins quietly, on a panoramic view of London at dawn (the year is 1910); in our aerial view of the city, over which the titles appear, we get our first glimpse of Mary Poppins, sitting atop a cloud with her umbrella and carpetbag. Gradually zeroing in on a particular neighborhood, we see a one-man band entertaining some people outside the local park. This is Bert, a happy-go-lucky fellow who says hello to us and gives us a brief tour of the street, which houses Admiral Boom, a precise military man who fires his rooftop cannon at eight every morning and every evening at six. Then we see the Banks home, where a frustrated nanny is walking out, fed up with the two "incorrigible" Banks children.

That evening, Mr. Banks, a very precise man, places an advertisement in the newspaper for a very strict governess. His children compose their own ad for a

Dick Van Dyke, Julie Andrews, Matthew Garber, and Karen Dotrice in *Mary Poppins*. © 1963 Walt Disney Productions

Richard (*left*) and Robert (*right*) Sherman, the brother-songwriting team responsible for *Mary Poppins*'s delightful score, pose on the set of the film with its two stars. © 1963 Walt Disney Productions

nanny, which Banks regards as foolish and tears up, tossing the pieces into the fireplace. The fragments of paper miraculously fly up the chimney and into the sky, where they are transmitted to Mary Poppins. The next morning a group of nannies waiting outside the house are suddenly blown away by a strong gust of wind, leaving the path clear for Mary Poppins to float down from the sky, her umbrella providing a natural parachute.

The children soon discover that Mary Poppins, who describes herself as "practically perfect," is a very unusual woman. For their first game she tells the children that they must clean up their room; their dour expressions turn to smiles when Mary actually turns the chore into a game, with the toys and clothes arranging themselves at the snap of a finger.

Out for a walk they find Bert drawing chalk paintings on the sidewalk. When one picture of a lovely countryside captures the children's fancy, Mary, Bert, and the youngsters hop into the picture, and suddenly find themselves in a magical world of make-believe. As the kids go off to the merry-go-round, Bert and Mary stroll along and stop at an outdoor café where Bert dances with their penguin waiters. Later they join Jane and Michael on the merry-go-round, as the horses break loose for a jaunt in the country. First they become part of a hunting party, and then join a horse race, which Mary wins! Asked for her reaction, she says that it's supercalifragilisticexpialidocious, joined in song by a group of local buskers. Just then, it starts to rain, "melting" the drawings and causing the foursome to return home.

Every day brings new adventures. The children go with Mary to see her Uncle Albert, who rises to the ceiling every time he starts to laugh—and, unfortunately, he can't stop laughing. They join him for tea, and find his laughter so contagious that soon they too are floating near the roof. To Mr. Banks's complaint that the children are having nothing but fun and not learning anything, Mary suggests that he take them to the bank with him. That evening, however, she sings to the children of the old bird woman who sits on the steps of a building near the bank, selling food for the birds at tuppence a bag. When the children go to the bank the next day, Father wants Michael to open an account with his tuppence, but the boy wants to feed the birds instead. A misunderstanding with the chairman of the bank, aging Mr. Dawes, attracts attention, and confusion starts a run on the bank. The children run away as fast as they can, getting lost in a dingy part of town; they are discovered by Bert, who explains his sooty condition by telling them of his life as a chimney sweep. He and Mary take them to the London rooftops to meet the fraternity of chimney sweeps, who revel in a boisterous song and dance.

That night their father is called to the bank, where he is fired. Suddenly a change comes over him. His eyes are opened for the first time, as he realizes that in his effort to be precise, and run his life as the bank is run, he has been cold and unloving. He tells off the board of directors of the bank, and disappears into the night. The next morning he appears from the basement of the house, having repaired a kite that the children broke earlier that week. They are astonished at the change in their father, who insists that they run to the park and fly their wonderful kite. For the first time he really *is* their father. Her work done, Mary Poppins bids the children good-bye, and flies off into the sky for new adventures.

Mary Poppins is a film rich in detail, but its universal appeal is due to the fact that it blends so many elements together: there is wit in the subplot of Mrs. Banks's suffragette movement, and individual jokes (when Banks is fired at the bank, the ceremony is marked by turning his umbrella inside out and punching a hole in his bowler hat); there is whimsy in the presence of Admiral Boom, who keeps his house "ship-shape" (which is to say, exactly like a ship!); there is fantasy in the key sequences like the long excursion into the cartoon world of Bert's painting; there is sentiment in the basic theme of making Mr. Banks realize his neglect of his children, as well as in specific ideas such as the Bird Woman; and, of course, there is music.

There is so much in the film that the result is almost overpowering. The whole long "Jolly Holiday" segment is a brilliant set piece in itself. Mary and Bert stroll along through cartoon fields, stopping at a roadside barnyard where the animals join in a musical tribute to Mary. At the outdoor café, four busy penguins wait on the couple, prompting Bert to get up and imitate their funny walk. This segues into a soft-shoe dance routine featuring Bert and the four animated penguins. Then, at the merry-go-round, when the horses break loose, Mary, Bert, Jane, and Michael find themselves riding to hounds along with a host of cartoon horsemen. The finale is the animated horse race, into which our live-action friends intrude, followed by a prize ceremony when Mary wins the race.

This whole sequence is filled to overflowing with fantastic detail. There is one astounding shot where we see Mary and Bert walking over a mill bridge, their images reflected in the water below; on top of this comes a family of animated ducklings, rippling through the live-action reflection! In this early part of the segment Bert presents Mary with a cartoon bouquet, which flies away in a hundred directions (it was comprised of colorful little birds); later, at the end of the horse race, a cartoon judge gives Mary a live-action bouquet, for a neat parallel.

Even the transitions opening and closing the sequence are ingenious. When the foursome jumps into the sidewalk, they raise a cloud of chalk dust. At the end, when it begins to rain, the cartoon backgrounds start to blur around the live-action characters in the foreground, signaling their return to reality.

To record every magical moment of the film on paper would be to reproduce a detailed account of the entire script. But it is important to note that there is no repetition in *Mary Poppins;* its wonders emerge from an apparently bottomless bag of tricks. On the one hand there is the brilliantly exuberant chimney-sweep segment (which critic Judith Crist said showed "why movies were invented"), not only choreographed to perfection, but *designed* and arranged cinematically to a tee. Then there is the uncommonly beautiful and haunting sequence where Mr. Banks is called to his office at night to be fired. There has been a buildup to this, where Bert has explained to the children that their father, for all his gruffness, is a good man. He has also asked them to consider how lonely he is; when they need help, they can go to him, but he has no one to go to. With this thought freshly planted, we see Banks walking to the bank that night, all alone, through the deserted park, the empty lamplit streets, and through the cavernous bank entrance itself. The segment accentuates once again the reason for *Mary Poppins*'s success: it has humanity, as well as fantasy, in its makeup.

One of the amazing things about this film is its total stylization. Nothing in it is real; every square inch is designed, and designed with a purpose in mind. Even the opening panorama of London, one soon discovers, is a painting, which is artfully blended into live action when the camera closes in on the neighborhood where the Bankses live. Some of the design ideas are flamboyant, such as the rooftops where the chimney sweeps perform; some are more subtle, but just as vital, such as the ominous conference room where the bank board of directors waits to fire Mr. Banks.

The color, needless to say, is dazzling, particularly in the "Jolly Holiday" sequence, which also features some of the most delightfully executed cartoon animals to appear in any Disney film. The barnyard chorus that sings "It's a Jolly Holiday with Mary" is sheer joy.

The songs, written by the Sherman brothers, are without qualification their best ever, in turns witty, sentimental, formularized, and unique. Mr. Banks's patter songs are a direct descendant of Rex Harrison's from *My Fair Lady,* but there are no antecedents for the joyful "Spoonful of Sugar" or the haunting "Chim-Chim-Cheree." Every song in the film suits its context perfectly and conveys emotions and ideas otherwise unexpressed in dialogue.

As good as the songs are, however, it is the delivery

365

that puts them over. Reading the lyrics of "Feed the Birds (Tuppence a Bag)," one finds a simplistic and cloying piece of material that is transformed into a song of depth and meaning by Julie Andrews's beautiful rendition and the tasteful arrangements of Irwin Kostal. The entire score is given 200 percent performances by Julie Andrews, Dick Van Dyke, and the other players.

Which brings us to the cast of the film. Again, it is impossible to say too much in praise of the entire troupe. The character of Mary Poppins is supposed to be enigmatic. When performing some nifty feat of magic, like sliding *up* a banister, she does it with nonchalance. In any discussion of herself, she uses the term "practically perfect." And when confronted with questions or pleas about the things she can do (as when the children try to relive their day's adventure in the chalk drawing), she denies knowledge of what they are talking about. Yet she *is* sweet, and she *does* bowl everyone over with her charm and sense of fun.

Julie Andrews captures every nuance of the character; those who scoffed at her Academy Award for the performance, explaining it off as a sentimental gesture, or a backhanded insult at Jack Warner (who decided not to use her in the film of *My Fair Lady*), ought to look at her work in *Poppins* once again. It truly is inspired.

Dick Van Dyke has never been better. He has never had a better vehicle for his talents, which are more considerable than many TV viewers might think. He captures the carefree nature of Bert to perfection, with particular highlights coming in his two big dance scenes, with the cartoon penguins and with the chimney sweeps. But he also conveys a warmth and genuine friendliness that goes beyond the geniality of a good song-and-dance man. He has the rare ability to talk to children (as he does in several key scenes of the film) without ever talking down to them.

Cute children have murdered many a promising film, but there is a difference between children who *are* cute and children who *act* cute. Watch the two youngsters as they read their rhyming advertisement for a nanny in the early part of this film; they are as appealing as any child performers who ever worked on the screen. Both Karen Dotrice and Matthew Garber had proven their worth in Disney's *Three Lives of Thomasina* earlier that year; *Mary Poppins* reaffirmed their talent.

David Tomlinson and Glynis Johns are perfectly suited to their roles as the children's parents. Tomlinson never makes the father a villain; even children can see that he is merely cold and aloof, not wicked. His extroverted performance is exactly what the role calls for, and his delivery of the patter songs is a treat. Glynis Johns's role is relatively small, but she is the kind of performer who lights up a screen the minute she appears. She makes every minute count, and her amusing suffragette song is most enjoyable.

The supporting cast could not possibly be improved. Two veteran scene stealers, Arthur Treacher and Reginald Owen, make their admittedly minor roles stand out. Ed Wynn is, as always, Ed Wynn, in a role tailormade for him, as the man who can't stop laughing.

What is there to say of Robert Stevenson's direction and the work of his many collaborators? It is very seldom that a movie shows so much thought and imagination and planning in the execution of every square inch of film. All that can be said is that everything works beautifully.

Is there, then, *anything* wrong with *Mary Poppins?* Well, the film, like Mary herself, is practically perfect. It misses perfection just by a hair. Its largest flaw is overlength. While millions of children have sat in rapt attention through the whole film, few people could help but squirm at one point or another through the two hours and twenty minutes. Though it would be a shame to touch this film, it does seem likely that some trimming could have made the film just a little bit better by sharpening its impact. Probably the easiest thing to cut would have been the whole Ed Wynn laughing sequence, but this might have been retained if some judicious cutting had been done in several existing sequences. In any event the length is not fatal to *Mary*

Poppins; just something that takes a little bit away from its overall strength.

Another point applies more to film buffs and adults than to children, but it is worth noting. In the "Spoonful of Sugar" sequence, stop-motion live-action photography is used, and even played backward, with the children, and Mary Poppins, superimposed on top. This is responsible for a scene of Jane snapping her fingers and watching her toys, strewn all over the floor, leap back onto the shelf in perfect array.

Though the average viewer would not understand how this movie magic had been accomplished, even an untrained eye can see the graininess of the stop-action film, and the contrast of the players matted in on top. The point is, this is the only sequence in the entire film where one is *aware* of special effects. Even a trained eye is stumped for the rest of the film, and what is more, the viewer doesn't *care* about how the other tricks were accomplished. The illusion is complete, because one is willing to let oneself believe what he sees on the screen. The "Spoonful of Sugar" sequence merely reminds the astute viewer that he is watching some sort of special effect.

Some will say this is carping, and perhaps it is. But it in no way changes the fact that *Mary Poppins* is an outstanding film. Such was the opinion of nearly every critic who saw the movie. Not since the early days of animation had Disney received such laudatory reviews. Critics found that two anticipated brickbats would have to be laid aside; first, the film had not destroyed P. L. Travers's character, although there was some change in the transition from book to film; second, the film was not an icky piece of sentiment—indeed, such qualities were nicely restrained.

So, Hollis Alpert in *Saturday Review* called it "one of the most magnificent pieces of entertainment ever to come from Hollywood." Bosley Crowther wrote that ". . . as Mary Poppins says, 'Practically perfect people never permit sentiment to muddle their feelings.' But being not practically perfect, I find it irresistible."

Judith Crist wrote in the *New York Herald Tribune:*

> The performers surpass even the technical wizardly
> of the film. . . . Miss Andrews is superb at song and
> dance and comedy and the heart of the matter (Too
> beautiful to be Mary Poppins? This is a carp by the
> old-in-heart who don't know that Mary Poppins is
> young and beautiful because anyone beloved by
> children is). And Dick Van Dyke's Bert reveals that
> this young performer's gifts have never been truly ex-
> ploited before—obviously because they're limitless.
> Watch the final cast credits for further proof.

Miss Crist refers to the fact that Van Dyke plays a second role in the film, which is not revealed until the end.
He renders a hilarious performance as the very, very old
chairman of the bank board of directors, Mr. Dawes, Sr.

Time commented:

> Although she [Mary] pokes her pretty fingers into a
> world of sticky sweetness, she almost invariably pulls
> out a plum. All speeches and cream, with a voice like
> polished crystal, she seems the very image of a prim
> young governess who might spend her free Tuesdays
> skittering off to Oz. To make a good show better, Dis-
> ney employs all the vast magic-making machinery at
> his command. The sets are luxuriant, the songs lilting,
> the scenario witty but impeccably sentimental, and
> the supporting cast only a pinfeather short of perfec-
> tion.

The public responded to *Mary Poppins* as it had to no
previous Disney film. Bolstered by these enthusiastic
reviews, as well as the most high-powered promotional
campaign ever launched by the studio, the film earned
an unbelievable $31 million in domestic release and a
reported total of $45 million from worldwide showings.
It is impossible to tell how much additional revenue was

realized from the sale of records, sheet music, and the hundreds of licensed items that accompanied the film. (Another huge amount is anticipated from the film's 1973 reissue.)

But when one speaks of *Mary Poppins*'s "success," the financial end of it seems secondary in importance. What really counts, and what will continue to count in future years, is the fact that it pulls together so brilliantly all the elements that Disney had employed throughout his career, without including any of the producer's less endearing traits (fondness for destructive animals, for instance) or excesses.

The film won an astounding thirteen Academy Award nominations, winning in five categories: Best Actress, Film Editing, Original Score, Song, and Special Visual Effects. It was Disney's most formidable evening in thirty-five years in Hollywood.

If he had made no other film in his lifetime, *Mary Poppins* would earn Walt Disney the gratitude of the world. As it happens, it was instead the pinnacle of an already fantastic career.

THE JUNGLE BOOK

RELEASED BY BUENA VISTA ON OCTOBER 18, 1967. Technicolor. Director: Wolfgang Reitherman. Directing animators: Milt Kahl, Franklin Thomas, Oliver Johnson, Jr., John Lounsbery. Story: Larry Clemmons, Ralph Wright, Ken Anderson, Vance Gerry, inspired by the Rudyard Kipling *Mowgli* stories. Character animation; Hal King, Eric Larson, Walt Stanchfield, Eric Cleworth, Fred Hellmich, John Ewing, Dick Lucas. Background styling: Albert Dempster. Backgrounds: Bill Layne, Art Riley, Ralph Hulett, Thelma Witmer, Frank Armitage. Layout: Don Griffith, Basil Davidovich, Dale Barnhart, Tom Codrick, Sylvia Roe-
370

mer. Effects animation: Dan MacManus. Music: George Bruns. Orchestrations: Walter Sheets. Production manager: Don Duckwall. Film editor: Tom Acosta, Norman Carlisle. Sound: Robert O. Cook. Music editor: Evelyn Kennedy. Running time: 78 minutes.

Songs: "I Wanna Be Like You," "Kaa's Song," "My Own Home," "That's What Friends Are For," "Colonel Hathi's March" by Richard M. Sherman, Robert B. Sherman. "The Bare Necessities" by Terry Gilkyson.

Voices: Phil Harris (Baloo the Bear), Sebastian Cabot (Bagheera the Panther), Louis Prima (King Louis of the Apes), George Sanders (Shere Khan, the tiger), Sterling Holloway (Kaa, the snake), J. Pat O'Malley (Colonel Hathi, the elephant), Bruce Reitherman (Mowgli, the man-cub), Verna Felton, Clint Howard (elephants), Chad Stuart, Lord Tim Hudson, J. Pat O'Malley (vultures), John Abbott, Ben Wright (wolves), Darleen Carr (girl).

The Jungle Book was the last animated cartoon feature that bore Disney's personal stamp. For the second time in a row he decided to base a cartoon feature on a well-known book (in this case a collection of stories), although the adaptation was, predictably enough, quite freewheeling.

It deals with Mowgli, an Indian boy abandoned at birth, who is raised as a wolf cub, after being discovered by Bagheera, the panther. Ten years later Bagheera decides to return Mowgli to his people when he learns that the tiger Shere Khan is coming back to his home territory. Their trip through the jungle is interrupted by a variety of encounters, which Mowgli (who doesn't want to leave the jungle) is only too happy to find.

Bagheera finally walks out in disgust, and Mowgli is befriended by Baloo, a happy-go-lucky bear whose philosophy of life is to sit back and relax. Mowgli follows his example, but soon finds himself kidnapped by monkeys who take him to their leader, King Louis. Baloo goes to Bagheera for help, and the two of them manage to rescue Mowgli from the overly enthusiastic chimp.

Mowgli runs off on his own, rather than be taken away from the jungle. He meets four vultures who befriend him when they see he is all alone. Then Shere Khan appears, and Mowgli is on his own once more to face the vicious predator. Baloo jumps in and tries to interfere, but Shere Khan knocks him cold. Then the vultures offer their help, and keep the tiger occupied long enough for Mowgli to tie a burning branch to his tail. Fire is the one thing that frightens tigers to death, and Shere Khan takes off instantly for parts unknown.

Now Mowgli can remain in the jungle without any problems. Just then, however, he spies an Indian girl on the edge of the forest; his human instincts return to him, and he forsakes his jungle life to go with her. Mowgli's animal friends realize that it's all for the best.

The Jungle Book is a very easygoing film. The trouble is, it's *too* easygoing. Though it has a lot of fun to offer, and the characters are very likable, the film is singularly lacking in excitement. It ambles along in a genial fashion, but one keeps waiting for something to happen.

Visually, it is a most impressive work. The variety of jungle settings and the opportunities for effects animation (reflection in the water, glimmering moonlight, etc.) are fully realized. More importantly, the character design is excellent. Baloo, King Louie, the elephants, and other "funny" characters in the narrative are all designed amusingly, while the other characters reflect their own personality traits in the way they look: the menacing Shere Khan, the sly, hypnotic snake Kaa, the very proper panther Bagheera. This is the essence of an animated cartoon, and it is good to see the potential being utilized to the fullest extent.

On the other side of the coin there is the question of voice characterization. Seldom before had the Disney people allowed a strong voice personality to dominate a character as in *The Jungle Book*. This does not apply as

Mowgli takes the advice of Baloo the Bear and enjoys the leisurely life. © 1965 Walt Disney Productions

strongly to children as it would to adults, but when one is watching (and listening to) Baloo, one is not thinking about a bear, one is thinking about Phil Harris. Similarly, Louis Prima and George Sanders are so striking on the sound track that it's difficult to get involved with their animal characters on screen.

This is not to knock the voice work done by these people; on the contrary, it is delightful. But there is a serious question of whether one should sacrifice a three-dimensional, believable character in favor of having a voice personality (with a marquee name). The best of Disney's cartoons have outstanding voice work, but never to the extent that the audience is distracted from the character itself. (This same problem cropped up in the studio's next cartoon feature, *The Aristocats,* where again Phil Harris played a leading role.)

Mowgli arouses the ire of both Colonel Hathi and the vicious
Shere Khan. © 1965 Walt Disney. Productions

In many ways the best voice in the film is Sterling
Holloway's, used for the slithery snake, Kaa. The
Sherman brothers concocted a clever song to emphasize
Kaa's lingering "s" sound, as did most of his dialogue.
The versatile Holloway, of course, contributed voices to
more Disney cartoons than any other actor.

The songs themselves are hardly memorable, although
they suit the plot situations fairly well. The most enjoyable is "I Wanna Be Like You," which the orangutan
King Louis sings to Mowgli, the man-cub, followed
closely by Baloo's "The Bare Necessities," which explains his philosophy of life. (This song, contributed by
Terry Gilkyson, was nominated for an Academy
Award.)

The Jungle Book is not a bad film by any stretch of the
imagination. But it lacks a certain spirit, a certain
momentum at its very foundation that might have made
it memorable. As it now stands it is one of the most

forgettable of all the Disney cartoon features. The next feature the studio tackled, *The Aristocats,* topped this one in every department.

Yet *The Jungle Book* garnered some very impressive reviews. *Time* magazine, always wary in its enthusiasm for Disney projects, noted that the film had little to do with Kipling, but added that "the result is thoroughly delightful. The reasons for its success lie in Disney's own unfettered animal spirits, his ability to be childlike without being childish . . . it is the happiest possible way to remember Walt Disney." Howard Thompson in the *New York Times* called it "a perfectly dandy cartoon feature . . . grand fun for all ages." *Life*'s Richard Schickel thought it "the best thing of its kind since *Dumbo.*"

But Judith Crist said the film was "completely devoid of mood or atmosphere . . . a middle-brow cartoon of middling quality." And *Variety,* in a generally favorable review, noted that "the story development is restrained—the potential dangers are suggested and there is an overriding upbeat end in sight from the beginning—so moppet audiences may squirm at times."

They did not hesitate to give it a try, however, and *The Jungle Book* became a sensational box-office hit, earning $13 million in its domestic release alone, ranking sixth of Disney's films on *Variety*'s list of all-time box-office champs. Apparently the combination of Disney and the familiar Kipling tales was enough to pull children and their parents into theatres, especially during the holiday season.

The Jungle Book was released exactly thirty years after the debut of Disney's first animated feature, *Snow White and the Seven Dwarfs.* In the ensuing years the Disney staff had conquered the field of animation so thoroughly that there seemed nowhere else to go. Perhaps this is why the ideas for newer Disney films must be twice as good as those of the pioneer cartoons in order to equal them, for the Disney staff can no longer hope to captivate an audience simply by *being* an animated cartoon. The medium has become too familiar, and too facile, for that.

375

OTHER LIVE-ACTION FEATURE FILMS
PRODUCED BY WALT DISNEY

The Sword and the Rose—1953—directed by Ken Annakin—starring Richard Todd, Glynis Johns, James Robertson Justice, Michael Gough

Rob Roy, the Highland Rogue—1954—directed by Harold French—starring Richard Todd, Glynis Johns, James Robertson Justice, Michael Gough

The Littlest Outlaw—1955—directed by Robert Gavaldon—starring Pedro Armendariz, Joseph Calleia, Rodolfo Acosta, Andres Velasquez

The Great Locomotive Chase—1956—directed by Francis D. Lyon—starring Fess Parker, Jeffrey Hunter, Jeff York, John Lupton, Kenneth Tobey

Davy Crockett and the River Pirates—1956—directed by Norman Foster—starring Fess Parker, Buddy Ebsen, Jeff York, Kenneth Tobey, Clem Bevans

Secrets of Life—1956—directed by James Algar—True-Life Adventure

Westward Ho the Wagons—1956—directed by William Beaudine—starring Fess Parker, Kathleen Crowley, Jeff York, David Stollery, Sebastian Cabot, George Reeves

Johnny Tremain—1957—directed by Robert Stevenson—starring Hal Stalmaster, Luana Patten, Jeff York, Sebastian Cabot, Dick Beymer

The Light in the Forest—1958—directed by Herschel Daugherty—starring James MacArthur, Carol Lynley, Fess Parker, Wendell Corey, Joanne Dru

White Wilderness—1958—directed by James Algar—True-Life Adventure

Tonka—1958—directed by Lewis R. Foster—starring Sal Mineo, Philip Carey, Jerome Courtland, Rafael Campos

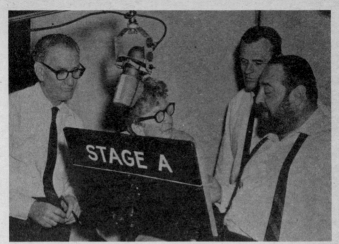

A recording session for *The Jungle Book;* storyman Larry Clemmons, veteran Disney voice man Sterling Holloway, director Wolfgang Reitherman, and Sebastian Cabot. © 1965 Walt Disney Productions

A foxy Robin Hood does his derring-do in Disney's 1973 animated *Robin Hood.* © 1970 Walt Disney Productions

Third Man on the Mountain—1959—directed by Ken Annakin—starring James MacArthur, Michael Rennie, Janet Munro, James Donald, Herbert Lom, Laurence Naismith

Toby Tyler, or Ten Weeks with a Circus—1960—directed by Charles Barton—starring Kevin Corcoran, Henry Calvin, Gene Sheldon, Bob Sweeney, Mr. Stubbs

Kidnapped—1960—directed by Robert Stevenson—starring James MacArthur, Peter Finch, Bernard Lee, Niall MacGinnis, Finlay Currie, Peter O'Toole

Jungle Cat—1960—directed by James Algar—True-Life Adventure

Ten Who Dared—1960—directed by William Beaudine—starring Brian Keith, John Beal, James Drury, R.G. Armstrong, Ben Johnson, L.Q. Jones, David Stollery

The Sign of Zorro—1960—directed by Norman Foster and Lewis R. Foster—starring Guy Williams, Henry Calvin, Gene Sheldon, Britt Lomond, George J. Lewis

The Parent Trap—1961—directed by David Swift—starring Hayley Mills, Maureen O'Hara, Brian Keith, Charlie Ruggles, Una Merkel, Leo G. Carroll, Joanna Barnes

Nikki, Wild Dog of the North—1961—directed by Jack Couffer and Don Haldane—starring Jean Coutu, Emile Genest

Greyfriars Bobby—1961—directed by Don Chaffey—starring Donald Crisp, Laurence Naismith, Alex MacKenzie, Kay Walsh, Duncan MacRae

Moon Pilot—1962—directed by James Neilson—starring Tom Tryon, Dany Saval, Brian Keith, Edmond O'Brien, Tommy Kirk, Bob Sweeney

Bernard and Bianca get set for take-off in one of the highlights of THE RESCUERS. © *Walt Disney Productions*

Bon Voyage!—1962—directed by James Neilson—starring Fred MacMurray, Jane Wyman, Michael Callan, Deborah Walley, Tommy Kirk, Kevin Corcoran

Big Red—1962—directed by Norman Tokar—starring Walter Pidgeon, Gilles Payant, Emile Genest, Janette Bertrand

Almost *Angels*—1962—directed by Steve Previn—starring Peter Weck, Hans Holt, Fritz Eckhardt, Bruni Lobel, Vincent Winter, Sean Scully

The Legend of Lobo—1962—directed by Jack Couffer—narrated by Rex Allen and the Sons of the Pioneers—animal story

In Search of the Castaways—1962—directed by Robert Stevenson—starring Hayley Mills, Maurice Chevalier, George Sanders, Wilfrid Hyde-White, Michael Anderson Jr.

Peter Ustinov and Dean Jones get ready to go out on the town in *Blackbeard's Ghost.* © 1967 Walt Disney Productions

Son of Flubber—1963—directed by Robert Stevenson—starring Fred MacMurray, Nancy Olson, Keenan Wynn, Tommy Kirk, Elliott Reid, Joanna Moore, Leon Ames, Ed Wynn, Charlie Ruggles

Miracle of the White Stallions—1963—directed by Arthur Hiller—starring Robert Taylor, Lilli Palmer, James Franciscus, Curt Jurgens, Eddie Albert, John Larch

Savage Sam—1963—directed by Norman Tokar—starring Brian Keith, Tommy Kirk, Kevin Corcoran, Dewey Martin, Jeff York, Royal Dano

Summer Magic—1963—directed by James Neilson—starring Hayley Mills, Burl Ives, Dorothy McGuire, Deborah Walley, Eddie Hodges

The Incredible Journey—1963—directed by Fletcher Markle—starring Emile Genest, John Drainie, Tommy Tweed; animal story

The Misadventures of Merlin Jones—1964—directed by Robert Stevenson—starring Tommy Kirk, Annette Funicello, Leon Ames, Stuart Erwin, Alan Hewitt

A Tiger Walks—1964—directed by Norman Tokar—starring Brian Keith, Vera Miles, Pamela Franklin, Sabu, Kevin Corcoran, Peter Brown

The Three Lives of Thomasina—1964—directed by Don Chaffey—starring Patrick McGoohan, Susan Hampshire, Karen Dotrice, Vincent Winter, Laurence Naismith, Finlay Currie

The Moon-Spinners—1964—directed by James Neilson—starring Hayley Mills, Peter McEnery, Eli Wallach, Pola Negri, Joan Greenwood, Irene Papas

Emil and the Detectives—1964—directed by Peter Tewksbury—starring Walter Slezak, Bryan Russell, Roger Mobley, Heinz Schubert

Those Calloways—1965—directed by Norman Tokar—starring Brian Keith, Vera Miles, Brandon de Wilde, Walter Brennan, Ed Wynn, Linda Evans

A momentary dilemma faces our heroes during the climactic race in *The Love Bug*. © *1968 Walt Disney Productions*

The Monkey's Uncle—1965—directed by Robert Stevenson—starring Tommy Kirk, Annette Funicello, Leon Ames, Frank Faylen, Arthur O'Connell

That Darn Cat—1965—directed by Robert Stevenson—starring Hayley Mills, Dean Jones, Dorothy Provine, Roddy McDowall, Neville Brand, Elsa Lanchester, William Demarest, Frank Gorshin

The Ugly Dachshund—1966—directed by Norman Tokar—starring Dean Jones, Suzanne Pleshette, Charlie Ruggles, Kelly Thordsen

Lt. Robin Crusoe, U.S.N.—1966—directed by Byron Paul—starring Dick Van Dyke, Nancy Kwan, Akim Tamiroff, Arthur Malet

The Fighting Prince of Donegal—1966—directed by Michael O'Herlihy—starring Peter McEnery, Susan Hampshire, Tom Adams, Gordon Jackson, Andrew Keir

Follow Me, Boys!—1966—directed by Norman Tokar—starring Fred MacMurray, Vera Miles, Lillian Gish, Charlie Ruggles, Elliott Reid, Kurt Russell, Luana Patten

Monkeys, Go Home!—1967—directed by Andrew V. McLaglen—starring Dean Jones, Maurice Chevalier, Yvette Mimieux, Bernard Woringer

The Adventures of Bullwhip Griffin—1967—directed by James Neilson—starring Roddy McDowall, Suzanne Pleshette, Karl Malden, Harry Guardino, Richard Haydn, Hermione Baddeley, Bryan Russell

The Gnome-Mobile—1967—directed by Robert Stevenson—starring Walter Brennan, Karen Dotrice, Matthew Garber, Richard Deacon, Tom Lowell, Sean McClory

The Happiest Millionaire—1967—directed by Norman Tokar—starring Fred MacMurray, Greer Garson, Tommy Steele, Geraldine Page, Lesley Ann Warren, John Davidson, Hermione Baddeley

3 · Without Walt

WHEN WALT DISNEY DIED, THERE WAS SPECULATION that the studio could not survive for long without him. But Disney left behind him a very well-oiled machine that will, in all probability, continue to grow and prosper indefinitely.

Over the years various Disney veterans had been promoted to positions of responsibility to the extent that they were able to carry on with "business as usual" after Walt's death. Seven men were left in charge of film production, doing exactly what they had been doing for the past few years.

As a result the films that have come out since Disney's death look no different from those made before his death in the 1960s. There have been gimmick comedies (the excellent *Blackbeard's Ghost, The Computer Wore Tennis Shoes*), frontier dramas (*The Wild Country, Smith!*), a true-life adventure (*King of the Grizzlies*), a musical (*The One and Only Genuine Original Family Band*), an animated feature (*The Aristocats*), a super-spectacular (*Bedknobs and Broomsticks*), and even some short subjects (*Winnie the Pooh and the Blustery Day, It's Tough to Be a Bird*).

Critical and box-office reaction has been about the same as before, even repeating the irony of ambitious or offbeat films failing financially while trivia brings in the customers.

Not even the Disney people anticipated the success of one 1969 feature, *The Love Bug*. This engaging fantasy-comedy, directed by Robert Stevenson, has what all great Disney films have always had: a good premise to start with. In this case it's a car with a mind of its own, who is instantly attracted to racing-driver Dean Jones and his mechanic Buddy Hackett, and repulsed by conniving David Tomlinson. The little Volkswagen actually has personality! The film is full of wild chases, special effects, and slapstick, plus ingratiating performances by Jones, Hackett, Tomlinson, and Michele Lee. In release for a good long time, and then repackaged on a double bill with *The Jungle Book,* the film earned a whopping $21 million in America alone, making it second only to *Mary Poppins,* and surpassing *Snow White*. An attempt to capture the same audience the following summer with *The Boatniks,* a mild comedy about a coast-guard ensign (Robert Morse) who gets involved with some bumbling thieves, led by Phil Silvers, earned a hefty amount for the studio (over $6 million domestically), but came nowhere near the success of *The Love Bug,* which was propelled, undoubtedly, by the ingenious premise of a Volkswagen with a heart and brains. A sequel went into production in early 1973.

The Aristocats came as a pleasant surprise to those who were disappointed with *The Jungle Book:* a delightful, carefree cartoon about a cat and her offspring who inherit a fortune from their late mistress and fall prey to a scheming butler who is next in line for the inheritance. They are rescued by a free-swinging alley cat named Thomas O'Malley. The film bears more than a passing resemblance to *One Hundred and One Dalmatians,* taking its most successful aspects and adapting them to this new story: making animals the main characters, with human beings in subordinate roles, and emphasizing the communication within the animal fraternity. Although, as Mike Barrier pointd out in a lengthy review of the film in *Funnyworld,* there is no plot device as ingenious as the "twilight bark" in *Dalmatians, Aristocats* does have substantial charm and humor of its own to make up for the less than inspired story line. It only seems a shame that the studio was unable to get Louis Armstrong to do the voice of Scat Cat; the character was

386

originally created with Satchmo in mind, and his infectious ad-libbing might have given the film some of its brightest moments. Still, *The Aristocats* was a big box-office hit, even more so in Europe than in America, and a healthy reaffirmation of the Disney studio's pre-eminence in the field of animation.

Robin Hood followed in 1973, a discouragingly down-to-earth rendition of the classic story, which nevertheless broke earlier box-office records. Then in 1977 came a watershed in the history of Disney animation. *The Rescuers* marked the first full-fledged collaboration between Disney's animation veterans (many of whom retired with this film) and some of the new, younger talent at the studio. Released the same year as Richard Williams' *Raggedy Ann and Andy* and Ralph Bakshi's *Wizards,* the Disney feature easily topped the competition with its strong, tightly-knit story and winning personality animation. What's more, it climbed ahead of *Robin Hood* and *The Aristocats* to become the biggest grossing animated feature in film history.

Bedknobs and Broomsticks, Disney's Christmas release for 1971, was a clear attempt to follow up the success of *Mary Poppins.* The songwriting Sherman brothers recalled, in an interview with Doug McClelland in *Record World:*

Actually, he bought the Mary Norton book before *Mary Poppins.* I remember just before everything got going on *Poppins,* we were having some trouble getting okays from P. L. Travers, the author of the stories, on the songs we had written. It was very exasperating. One day Walt came to us and said, "Don't worry, boys. I've bought another story that deals with magic. If we can't work things out with Travers, we'll be able to use your stuff in the other picture."

It was deliberately decided not to move ahead with *Bedknobs* for a while, however, because of its similarities to *Poppins.* Nevertheless, the story was

387

The Duchess is wooed by Thomas O'Malley in *The Aristocats*.

45A-21c

developed in 1964, at which time the Shermans started writing their score. After a dormant period, production resumed on a major scale in 1970. Lynn Redgrave, Leslie Caron, and Judy Carne (along with Julie Andrews) were all considered for the leading role of Eglantine, an amateur witch in wartime England, but, very wisely, Angela Lansbury was finally chosen for what is after all a rather mature role. Ron Moody was originally slated to play her vis-à-vis, but he was replaced by David Tomlinson, marking an even stronger resemblance to *Poppins,* despite the major difference in the actor's characterization.

The film did not cause the same sensation as *Poppins,* and many critics spent most of their time making comparisons, which seems unfair. *Bedknobs and Broomsticks* can stand on its own, as a thoroughly entertaining fantasy, with tuneful (if not memorable) songs and excellent special effects. The film also boasts of one sequence that ranks alongside the best of Disney: a blend of live action and animation that in many ways surpasses all previous examples of this art. Interestingly, the style of this cartoon sequence, directed by Ward Kimball, is quite different from that of the recent Disney features, which have been piloted by Wolfgang Reitherman. The drawing is funnier to begin with, and the character styling more in the classic Disney mold than in the rough-line method used in recent feature films.

The studio's next big musical feature, *Pete's Dragon* (1977), tried again to rekindle *Mary Poppins* magic, without success. Once more, the animated sequences (directed by newcomer Don Bluth), involving a giant green dragon, stole the show.

What, then, has been the impact of Disney's death? Not any in the selection and production of stories, perhaps, but a great deal in the end result. Like most great producers in the history of Hollywood, Disney was a superb editor. Others may have concocted the raw material, but Disney was the one who passed final judgment, who knew what to cut, what to change, what to redo. Even as late as *The Jungle Book*, he cut one entire sequence involving a rhinoceros because it followed the King Louie scene, and he felt that two hyperactive segments in a row would not work with an audience.

There was another vital aspect to Walt Disney as a producer. As Ward Kimball recalls: "Walt was criticized by the banks and the financial empires down through the years—'That crazy Disney, blowing all that money.' He had that way of saying, 'This is different, this is new, this is worth a try.' "

It was this spirit, a desire to do new things, whatever the cost and whatever the opposition, that made Disney great, and that made his films successful. It was a form of leadership that no organization can do without. It is the reason he will be missed.

4 · The Disney Shorts

EVERYONE KNOWS THAT IT WAS *Steamboat Willie* AND Mickey Mouse that put Walt Disney on the map. But many people tend to forget that after the studio made *Snow White* and went on to more ambitious projects, both animated and live action, Disney *continued* to turn out one-reel cartoons with Mickey, Donald, Goofy, and all the other animated stars.

Though these shorts do not offer as much as the feature films, they have many interesting aspects, and certainly deserve a closer look.

A large part of *Steamboat Willie*'s success was due to music; the novelty of the cartoon was the synchronization of cartoon action on the screen with music on the sound track. Disney knew that this delighted his audience, and from that time on music always played an important part in his short films. In fact, a good many of the Disney cartoons through the early 1930s are completely built around musical themes.

One of the best Mickey Mouse efforts of the early 1930s, *The Whoopee Party,* has Mickey and Minnie throwing a house party for their friends. The music is virtually nonstop: Minnie is playing "Sweet Rosie O'Grady" on the piano while the guests dance, Mickey doing "Maple Leaf Rag," and then the whole gang joining in on "Running Wild," in which Mickey uses mousetraps, flapping window shades, and other household utensils to provide percussion. On this number the party really starts jumping. The piano sways, and the stool hops in time. The lamps start moving in time to the

Mickey provides impromptu accompaniment for a musicale in
Steamboat Willie. © *Walt Disney Productions*

music, with chairs, bureaus, a coffeepot, a tray of sand-
wiches, a couple of hot dogs, even a bunch of matches
finding it impossible to keep still. A long shot then
shows the entire house swaying with the infectious beat
of the song. When noise brings a police patrol to calm
things down, even they join in the fun.

The whole cartoon moves to this music. Equally important, however, is what's happening on screen. *The
Whoopee Party* is typical of the Mickey Mouse cartoons
of this time. There is an incredible amount of action on
the screen; an opening shot shows a score of couples
dancing to the music. Later, when the party starts to
jump, every single inch of picture is filled with dancing
figures. What is more, nothing is out of bounds for joining the fun: a pair of shirts on the ironing board are as
likely to get up and dance as any of the animals at the
party.

394

The early Disney cartoons knew no limits when it came to such ideas; anything was fair game. As the technique grew more sophisticated, it seemed incongruous to indulge in this kind of humor, and it disappeared.

The studio was turning out about one Mickey Mouse per month in the early thirties, each one filled to overflowing with gags, gags, gags. Other studios surpassed Disney in later years with invention and characterization in the short-subject field, but no cartoons ever topped the early Mickey Mouse series for sheer volume in the gag department. *Touchdown Mickey* (1932), for instance, boasts the most frenetic football game ever conceived for a comedy film, ending with Mickey being driven underground and burrowing up to the goal line to win the game.

No effort was spared on the Mickey Mouse series, especially as it grew in popularity (in many theatres Mickey received top billing over the feature film!), producing such elaborate shorts as *The Mad Doctor* (1933), a chilling and amazingly atmospheric cartoon with all the stops pulled out to create a miniature horror film; *Mickey's Gala Premiere* (1933), in which a gaggle of Hollywood luminaries come to the debut of Mickey's latest film: John, Ethel, and Lionel Barrymore, Laurel and Hardy, Marie Dressler and Wallace Beery, Charlie Chaplin, Harold Lloyd, Buster Keaton, Harry Langdon, Douglas Fairbanks, Joe E. Brown, Wheeler and Woolsey, Joan Crawford, Mae West, George Arliss, and even Greta Garbo! (P.S. It all turns out to be a dream.)

(Offbeat ideas like *Gulliver Mickey* (1934), with giant-sized Mickey in the land of the Lilliputians, paid off nicely, as did such spoofs as *Mickey's Mellerdrammer* (1933), in which Mickey and the gang put on a production of *Uncle Tom's Cabin,* and *The Klondike Kid* (1932), an amusing takeoff of Yukon melodramas.

For Mickey's color debut in 1935, Disney returned to a musical motif, and produced one of the best cartoons ever made anywhere, *The Band Concert*. The film opens at an outdoor band concert in the park, with a responsive audience applauding the last piece. Then

Greta Garbo congratulates Mickey on his new movie in *Mickey's
Gala Premiere.* © *Walt Disney Productions; courtesy Al Kilgore*

maestro Mickey turns to the *William Tell* Overture. He literally wrings various shades of performance from his band, the effect of which is spoiled when a noisy ice-cream vendor (Donald Duck) approaches, first bursting into the music with his raucous voice, then confounding the band by playing "Turkey in the Straw" on his fife. The song is counterpoint to William Tell, and the band quickly adopts to the wrong tune, much to Mickey's chagrin. He smashes Donald's instrument in two, but the resourceful duck has an endless number of them up his sleeve.

Just as Donald gets out of the way, another crisis approaches. The "Storm" section of the piece is due, and the musicians prepare. Tympanist Horace Horsecollar removes his coat; others work into a sweat. At the same time a vicious tornado twister is nearing the park. Just as the band starts to play "The Storm," the real storm overtakes the bandstand, sending the musicians flying into the air. They don't miss a note, even though conductor Mickey is flying in and out of doors, windows, and debris (his music stand miraculously following him), and other musicians are suffering similar problems. Near the end of the piece the storm subsides and they start falling to earth, still keeping up with the music as the band members are deposited, one by one, on the branches of a barren tree. They all manage to end together, with a grand finale, and are greeted with the applause of one spectator—Donald. He takes out his fife, which prompts the band members to hurl everything in sight at him. He is swallowed up by a tuba, but manages to peer outside and play the last note as the scene fades out.

The Band Concert is a brilliant cartoon, because everything about it works so beautifully. The music itself is compelling (it obviously inspired the animators and gagmen), but the material built around it is terrific. There are nuances of expression in Mickey's character throughout this film that had seldom been explored in earlier shorts. The pacing is also entirely different from the standard Mickey Mouse comedies of the early thirties. Instead of trying to pack in a thousand gags a

Minnie prepares for her stage debut in *Mickey's Mellerdrammer*.

© Walt Disney Productions; courtesy Al Kilgore

399

minute, *The Band Concert* takes its time and builds to a crescendo, cued, naturally, by the moods of the *William Tell* Overture. Last, but not least, the color in this cartoon is superb.

In some respects this was the pinnacle of Mickey's career as a short-subject star, and a harbinger of things to come. From the very start ample footage in the MM cartoons had been devoted to Minnie, Pluto, Horace Horsecollar, Clarabelle Cow, Pegleg Pete, and Dippy Dawg, later known as Goofy. As the 1930s wore on, however, Mickey played a progressively less important role in the proceedings, some cartoons completely taken over by the character of Pluto. After the introduction of Donald Duck, it was clear Disney had another "star" to contend with, and he moved in on Mickey's territory as well. Beginning with *Mickey's Service Station*, more and more cartoons costarred Mickey, Donald, and Goofy—films like *On Ice, Moving Day, Alpine Climbers*, etc. Mickey still had his moments, in spectacular cartoons such as *Thru the Mirror* (a marvelous, surreal *Alice in Wonderland* cartoon) and *The Brave Little Tailor;* but it took special ideas and backgrounds to carry Mickey, where just a few years earlier a day in the farmyard was enough excuse for a successful Mickey Mouse endeavor.

By 1938 the handwriting was on the wall, and Disney stopped calling his shorts "Mickey Mouse Cartoons," identifying each short by its star character instead. Just a few years later Disney all but phased out his Silly Symphonies as well, leaving the field wide open for his most popular cartoon stars.

The Silly Symphonies dated back to 1929, when Carl Stalling was in charge of the music for Disney's cartoons. He suggested the idea of finding music that was evocative of some mood, and building a cartoon around the theme, with inanimate objects coming to life to suggest a season or a setting. The first such short was *The Skeleton Dance;* finding acceptance for it among movie exhibitors was difficult, but when the film caught on with audiences, the series, dubbed Silly Symphonies, was

*Maestro Mickey about to conduct the William Tell Overture in
The Band Concert.* © *Walt Disney Productions*

Donald Duck makes his screen debut in The Wise Little Hen.
© *Walt Disney Productions; courtesy Movie Star News*

launched. Still, not to take any chances, the title card for the series read, "Mickey Mouse presents a Walt Disney Silly Symphony," giving moviegoers something familiar to hold onto.

Early Silly Symphonies had such titles as *Springtime, Night, Arctic Antics*, and *Midnight in a Toy Shop*. But the sheer novelty of watching plants and objects become animated wore off fairly soon, and the series soon broadened its horizons to encompass fairy tales, with no running characters from film to film. In 1932 Disney won an Academy Award for the first Silly Symphony in color, *Flowers and Trees*. He continued to make the Symphonies in Technicolor, which gave them added interest, at a time when color was still something special.

By far the most famous Silly Symphony of all time was *The Three Little Pigs*. The cartoon is no more outstanding than any number of other entries in the series, but its theme song, "Who's Afraid of the Big Bad Wolf?", and colorful, *visual* story made it a smash hit not only in America, but around the world. A sequel made the following year, *The Big Bad Wolf*, failed to duplicate the original's success.

There are other justifiably famous Silly Symphonies, such as two seasonal items, *Santa's Workshop* (1932) and *The Night Before Christmas* (1933). Both films benefit from a rainbow collage of colors, still dazzling today; the latter also shows signs of the effects Disney's animators were trying to perfect (realistic, multicolored flames, and the warm glow around the fireplace, for instance). *Who Killed Cock Robin?* featured an amusing spoof of Mae West at the height of her popularity, whereas *Mother Goose Goes Hollywood*, made three years later, in 1938, has a brilliant array of bull's-eye caricatures of Hollywood stars, with Katharine Hepburn as Little Bo-Peep, Laurel and Hardy as Simple Simon and the Pieman, etc. Another winner that year was *Ferdinand the Bull*, a delightful visualization of Munro Leaf's story about a bull whose only aim in life is to spend his time sniffing flowers.

Disney was often quoted about the failure of one Symphony called *The Golden Touch*. It was, he said, the one time they consciously tried to inject a "message" into a cartoon; it ended with King Midas, surrounded by gold, crying for a hamburger. Though it is true that the Disney staff did steer clear of this kind of philosophizing, they did not hesitate to indulge in moralizing on a smaller scale. Such cartoons as *Elmer Elephant*, in which little Elmer is ridiculed for his ugly trunk until it enables him to become a hero, and *The Tortoise and the Hare*, with the egocentric rabbit allowing his opponent to win a race through his own overconfidence, are pretty sticky going today. (Indeed, they are even offered to the educational market for the express purpose of teaching young children these important lessons.) Other shorts, such as *Little Hiawatha*, simply become overbearingly cute. (Hiawatha's pants continually fall down as he runs after an elusive rabbit.)

The Silly Symphonies served another purpose for Disney throughout the 1930s. They provided a proving ground for experimentation, and gave the staff an opportunity to take a dry run on new and ambitious ideas. Most of the Symphonies of the mid- and late 1930s are visually superior to their companions, the Mickey Mouse series. Some of them, like 1938's *Wynken Blynken and Nod*, are visual extravaganzas.

In this filmization of the lovely Eugene Field poem, Wynken, Blynken, and Nod, three infant boys, sail through the nighttime sky in a wooden shoe, and hauntingly beautiful cloud arrangements, with luminescent stars as "fish" in the "sea" of air. They hitch onto a shooting star, which casts a dazzling light on them as it careens through the air. Then the clouds start blowing the shoe around; lightning strikes, and the three children tumble out of their shoe, sailing back to earth, where they materialize into one youngster, sleeping in his bed and dreaming this wonderful fantasy.

Wynken Blynken and Nod is as extravagant as any Disney feature; it set a standard that was probably too extravagant to maintain, with most effort being turned toward feature-film production in the late 1930s. After

A posed portrait of the Three Little Pigs. © Walt Disney Productions

W. C. Fields and Charlie McCarthy were among the many stars portrayed in *Mother Goose Goes Hollywood*. © Walt Disney Productions

1940 these unique cartoons petered out of the Disney production schedule.

Not that the character cartoons weren't done on an elaborate scale. In discussing *Window Cleaners* (1940), film historian William K. Everson commented: "Disney used height—skyscrapers, mountains, etc.—far more than other cartoon-makers, and with more concern for perspective and the convincing illusion of dizzy depths. Height gags in Warner Brothers and MGM cartoons were always just that—rapid gags that paid off quickly in a laugh, and without a buildup. Disney, on the other hand, used height much as Harold Lloyd did, to counterpoint comedy with a genuine thrill."

Around this time, however, the Disney cartoons (or at least, many of them, for there were always exceptions) started to fall into formula patterns. The Mickey-Donald-Goofy efforts usually involved some project (scaling a mountain in *Alpine Climbers,* building a ship in *Boat Builders,* etc.), which all three would begin together; then the cartoon would break down into separate segments of each character encountering his own problem, culminating in a finale where all three would come together again. The Donald Duck cartoons became increasingly predictable, and Donald's temper tantrums less funny.

Furthermore, with the 1940s, Disney began to feel his competition moving up on him. There were many rival cartoon studios operating in the 1930s, with varying degrees of success, but Disney was always in a class by himself. In the early 1940s Warner Brothers and MGM surged ahead, spurred by their new stars Bugs Bunny and Tom and Jerry. They too were making their cartoons in color, and their product became slick and handsome. Reacting to the mood of the 1940s, they adopted a loud, brash sense of humor, and sharpened the tempo of the films considerably. Though no one could touch Disney in the feature-film area, many felt that he was being eclipsed in the realm of short subjects.

The situation changed as the decade wore on. The Disney cartoons were assigned to several directors who asserted their own styles on the familiar characters, just as various men did with the Warners's characters. Charles Nichols, who had a gentle, sometimes cute approach, supervised most of the shorts with Mickey, Pluto, and Figaro the Cat. Jack Kinney started doing crazy things with Goofy, while the wildest of all were Jack Hannah's Donald Duck cartoons.

The pacing accelerated, the humor sharpened, and the technique improved (if such a thing seems possible) during this phase. Never before would there have been an inside joke such as the one in *Double Dribble,* in which the basketball players (all depicted as Goofy) are called by the names Kinney, Lounsbery, Hannah, and Sibley—all members of the Disney staff! Seldom had there been violence in Disney cartoons until now, albeit less savage than the antics of MGM's Tom and Jerry.

It is important to recall that these are generalizations, for in no series, under any director, did the studio come up with a winner every time, just as in the mild-mannered cartoons of Charles Nichols there were often some very bright, inspired creations, such as *Mickey and the Seal* (1948), in which a sea lion follows Mickey home from the zoo and joins Mickey for a bath, without the mouse's knowledge, or *Bone Bandit* (1947), a very funny Pluto cartoon with the dog battling an ambitious gopher who is using bones to support a massive underground tunnel where he stores his food.

But when one thinks of great cartoons from this period, the Kinney and Hannah endeavors usually stand out. Another interesting aspect of the cartoons at this time is that Mickey, Donald, and Goofy all became middle-class citizens; it is as if their status in life improved along with the fortunes of the country, for they began life in the Depression as barnyard characters. As the 1930s progressed (and the animation technique improved, along with the addition of color) they became slicker and less "vulgar." The 1940s cartoons often show Goofy in a business suit or as Father in a series of domestic comedies. Mickey now lives in a comfortable suburban home, and one entire Donald Duck comedy,

A publicity sketch from *Elmer Elephant* gives an indication of its general cuteness. © *Walt Disney Productions*

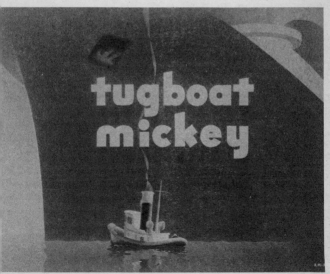

Even the title cards on Disney cartoons were impressive; here is a good example. © *Walt Disney Productions*

The New Neighbor, is devoted to the trials of living in a house next door to a pest.

The writers and directors were careful not to be hemmed in by these changes, however, and they always left room for ventures off the beaten path, as in *No Sail* (1945), in which Donald and Goofy rent a sailboat that operates on nickels. When the time is up, the sail collapses until another nickel is deposited. Unprepared for this, our friends are stranded out at sea, and their plight is shown with great melodrama; there is a beautiful image of the stark situation, a bright sun creating a yellowy sky, their boat a silhouette on the horizon. After several days Donald has whiskers and a thoroughly bedraggled look. When he goes fishing for a shark and is pulled underwater, he screams for Goofy to help, but the Goof has gotten his hands tangled up in the fishing wire, and becomes engrossed in working a cat's cradle. Eventually, the twosome returns to shore when Donald accidentally pushes his bill down the nickel slot and reactivates the boat.

In 1941 Goofy starred in a short called *How to Ride a Horse*, which was incorporated into the feature film *The Reluctant Dragon*. The incongruity of using this hapless creature to demonstrate *anything* made the spoof of a training film a big laugh-getter, and spawned a series of Goofy sports reels: *The Art of Skiing, How to Play Baseball, Olympic Champ, How to Swim, How to Play Golf, How to Play Football, Double Dribble, Goofy Gymnastics,* and *Tennis Racquet,* the latter enhanced by the comic narration of Doodles Weaver.

The late 1940s brought Donald two new adversaries to contend with: a pair of spunky chipmunks named Chip 'n' Dale. Their battles are responsible for some of the funniest and fastest Donald Duck cartoons, most notably *Up a Tree* (1955), a later effort that has one of the most frenzied strings of gags ever concocted for a Disney cartoon, as lumberjack Donald tries to cut down the chipmunks' tree, and they arrange it so the scheme backfires completely, the downed log "chasing" Donald down a sluice, through his cabin, into a mine, and into a

This title card was the signal for applause and laughter in hundreds of theatres around the world. © *Walt Disney Productions*

What a difference between the style of this cartoon and the early Mickeys; a handsome scene from *Pueblo Pluto*. © *Walt Disney Productions*

shambles.

Perhaps the best Donald Duck of all was directed by Jack King, who alternated among several characters at this time. The film is *Donald's Dilemma* (1947), a sidesplitting satire of psychological dramas with Daisy telling her story to psychiatrist Sigmund Frump. It seems that one day a flowerpot fell on Donald's head, and when he awoke he thought he was a romantic singer; what's more, he had no memory of Daisy. Overnight, he became a star, and despite all her attempts to see him, Daisy has been left out in the cold. The psychiatrist places a globe on his desk, and tells Daisy that now Donald and his voice belong to the world; she must decide if she is willing to let the world have him, or if she wants him for herself. "Which will it be?" he asks, "the world—or you?" Without hesitation, she screams "Me! Me! Me!" and smashes the globe through his desk. Daisy climbs up to the catwalk of the theatre where Donald is appearing, and drops another flowerpot on his head, restoring his original voice and his memory.

Donald's Dilemma is a great cartoon, for many reasons. Foremost is the fact that it makes the characters and their situation *real,* even while reminding you that this is a cartoon. The audience actually becomes involved with Daisy's predicament, and there are marvelous little touches to heighten the emotionalism (as when she is climbing to the catwalk near the end and almost loses her step). At the same time the cartoon is filled with hilarious visual exaggeration; when Daisy recalls that Donald gave her a cold, icy stare, a long icicle emits from his eyes, and as she waits for Donald at the stage door of the theatre, the seasons change and she is covered with snow. *Donald's Dilemma* shows how much could be done within the framework of a ten-minute cartoon, using familiar characters; it is a gem.

The 1950s saw many changes in the structure of the cartoon program at Disney. Several trends had their effect on the animation itself. First, there was the tremendous impact of UPA's initial cartoons, with Gerald McBoing and Mr. Magoo, which used "limited animation" and a stylized design that moved away from the literalism of the Disney cartoons. Critics hailed the UPA technique and downgraded Disney at the same time, but Disney answered back with a delightful short called *Toot, Whistle, Plunk, and Boom,* which not only used limited animation, but built the whole concept of the film around it, in showing the origin of musical instruments; what is more, the film was made in CinemaScope. It won the Academy Award that year as best cartoon short.

Having shown that they could do limited animation as well as anyone, the Disney staff returned to their normal routine, except that gradually the backgrounds in the cartoons became sparse and were eventually designed in an abstract form, a compromise measure adopted by such rival studios as Warner Brothers. Thus, clouds, trees, and landscapes took on a different look in the background, while Donald Duck, Goofy, and Chip 'n' Dale cavorted in full animation in the foreground. Limited animation was used as a technique where it was felt suited to the story, as in *Pigs Is Pigs* (1954).

CinemaScope was a short-lived medium for the one-reelers, as was the passing fancy of 3-D, which Disney employed for one Donald Duck cartoon, *Working for Peanuts,* as well as *Adventures in Music: Melody.*

Another trend took root at this time, however. The short subject market was dwindling, and it was becoming increasingly expensive to produce one-reel cartoons. Disney gradually phased them out altogether, replacing them with two- and three-reel "specials," digest-sized cartoons with something more to offer than the run-of-the-mill series entry.

Ben and Me (1954) had all the qualities of a feature film, though it ran less than a half hour. It *should* look like a feature; it employed virtually the entire animation staff, under the direction of Hamilton Luske. This handsome cartoon deals with Amos the Mouse, confidant of Benjamin Franklin who was really responsible for many

A scene from one of the funniest cartoons ever made, *Hold That Pose*. Notice how Goofy has evolved into a middleclass American everyman.   © *Walt Disney Productions*

An angry Donald horns in on Chip 'n' Dale in one of their many encounters.   © *Walt Disney Productions*

of Franklin's greatest ideas. This charming, if somewhat irreverent, cartoon featured Sterling Holloway as the voice of Amos.

Other "specials" included *Jack and Old Mac,* a short but interesting artistic experiment by Bill Justice in which characters are created out of words (the letters "cat" form the body of a cat, etc.); *The Truth About Mother Goose,* an elaborate featurette directed by Wolfgang Reitherman and Bill Justice illustrating the origins of three famous nursery rhymes, a London Bridge sequence being especially striking; *Paul Bunyan,* directed by Les Clark, a genial cartoon of the famous tall-tale hero with nice touches (Paul and Babe the Blue Ox built Pike's Peak in order to survey the land, and dug the Missouri River to haul logs) and a good title song; *Noah's Ark* (1959), animation of stick figures not unlike George Pal's Puppetoons, done by Bill Justice, who with several collaborators was responsible for the ingenious main titles of several Disney features; *A Symposium on Popular Songs* (1962), another Bill Justice credit with Ludwig von Drake conducting a tour of popular musical styles from ragtime to rock and roll, accompanied by some clever songs by the Sherman brothers, and equally clever animation, using paper cutouts; and *Winnie the Pooh and the Honey Tree* (1966), directed by Wolfgang Reitherman, one of the studio's loveliest works, capturing the flower of A. A. Milne's original illustrations, and taking them a few steps further, with delightful results. A sequel, *Winnie the Pooh and the Blustery Day* (1969), was equally good.

Disney filled in his short subject schedule in the 1950s by releasing the segments of his omnibus features of the 1940s as separate cartoons (*Lake Titicaca, Peter and the Wolf,* etc,), combining some for special packages (*Contrasts in Rhythm* was comprised of *Trees* and *Bumble Boogie*).

There was also an increasing number of live-action shorts at this time, which had been spurred by the initial success of *Seal Island* in 1949.

After the somewhat surprising success of the True-Life Adventures, which started racking up Academy Awards the way the Disney cartoons had done in the 1930s, a second series was established called "People and Places." When its very first entry, *The Alaskan Eskimo,* copped an Oscar, Disney knew he had another hit on his hands. These shorts were done in the same style as the True-Life films and by the same people. (*Eskimo* was photographed by Alfred Milotte, who had launched the first True-Life short, *Seal Island.*) When Disney expanded his True-Life series into the feature-length category, People and Places accelerated its output, tackling such diverse topics as *Lapland, Switzerland,* and *Seven Cities of Antarctica.* These outstanding shorts have since become staples on the school circuit.

The short subject schedule also included occasional imports from the Disney TV show, such as Ward Kimball's fascinating *Man in Space* show, a 1956 look at the future of the United States space program which time has proven to be remarkably accurate. It was prepared with the on- and off-screen participation of Dr. Werner von Braun, Dr. Heinz Haber, and Willy Ley.

Finally, there were the fictional animal sagas, always well done, always surefire fodder for the younger set: *Wetback Hound, The Horse with the Flying Tail, Yellowstone Cubs,* etc. Most of these were the work of Larry Lansburgh, who was responsible for the feature *The Littlest Outlaw,* as well as many other animal-oriented segments of the Disney TV show.

The market for short subjects has become practically nonexistent in America. Very few theatrical cartoons are being made, and those that are don't rate much attention. Therefore, when the Disney studio does decide to make a new animated short, such as *Winnie the Pooh* or the more recent *It's Tough to Be a Bird,* it is certain to stand out, just as Disney's shorts always did, even at the height of the studio system. They have always had the hallmark of quality to distinguish them from most of their competition.

Following is a list of the Disney shorts. All titles are

given in the order of their release, which may differ from the order in which they were made; such variances are clear when one compares the copyright date for a film to the release date. This list includes only the Disney shorts that received theatrical release. The categories cited after each title indicates which series the short was part of and not necessarily all the characters who appeared in it. (For instance, a Mickey Mouse short of the late 1930s might star Donald and Goofy.) The list concludes with 1967's releases.

Key to abbreviations: L = Laugh-O-Grams; A = Alice in Cartoonland; O = Oswald the Lucky Rabbit; MM = Mickey Mouse; SS = Silly Symphonies; DD = Donald Duck; G = Goofy; P = Pluto; CD = Chip 'n' Dale; TL = True-Life Adventure; PP = People and Places. Where no indication is given, the short does not fall under any series title.

1920

Newman Laugh-O-Grams — various mini-cartoons made for the Newman Theater in Kansas City, lasting less than one minute.

1922 – 1923

Bremen Town Musicians —L
Little Red Riding Hood —L
Puss in Boots —L
Jack and the Beanstalk —L
Goldie Locks and the Three Bears —L
Cinderella —L
Tommy Tucker's Tooth
Martha —a Song-o-Reel
Alice's Wonderland

1924

Alice and the Dog Catcher — A
Alice and the Three Bears —A
Alice and the Toreador —A
Alice and the Wild West Show —A
Alice Cans the Cannibals —A
Alice in Dutch at School —A
Alice Hunting in Africa —A
Alice Plays the Pipers —A
Alice the Peacemaker —A
Alice's Day at Sea —A
Alice's Fishy Story —A
Alice's Spooky Adventure —A

1925

Alice Chops the Suey —A
Alice Gets Stung —A

Alice in the Jungle—A
Alice Is Stage Struck—A
Alice Loses Out—A
Alice on the Farm—A
Alice Picks the Champ—A
Alice Plays Cupid—A
Alice Rattled by Rats—A
Alice Solves the Puzzle—A
Alice the Jail Bird—A
Alice Wins the Derby—A
Alice's Balloon Race—A
Alice's Egg Plant—A
Alice's Little Parade—A
Alice's Mysterious Mystery—A
Alice's Ornery Orphan—A
Alice's Tin Pony—A

1926

Alice at the Carnival—A
Alice at the Rodeo—A
Alice Charms the Fish—A
Alice Cuts the Ice—A
Alice Foils the Pirates—A
Alice Helps the Romance—A
Alice in the Alps—A
Alice in the Big League—A
Alice in the Klondike—A
Alice in the Woolly West—A
Alice the Beach Nut—A
Alice the Collegiate—A
Alice the Fire Fighter—A
Alice the Golf Bug—A
Alice the Lumber Jack—A
Alice the Whaler—A
Alice's Auto Race—A
Alice's Brown Derby—A

Alice's Channel Swim—A
Alice's Circus Daze—A
Alice's Knaughty Knight—A
Alice's Medicine Show—A
Alice's Monkey Business—A
Alice's Picnic—A
Alice's Spanish Guitar—A
Alice's Three Bad Eggs—A
Clara Cleans Her Teeth

1927—1928

Africa Before Dark—O
All Wet—O
The Banker's Daughter—O
Bright Lights—O
Empty Socks—O
The Fox Chase—O
Great Guns—O
Harem Scarem—O
Hot Dog—O
Hungry Hoboes—O
The Mechanical Cow—O
Neck 'n' Neck—O
The Ocean Hop—O
Oh, Teacher—O
Oh, What a Knight—O
The Ole Swimmin' Hole—O
Ozzie of the Mounted—O
Poor Papa—O
Rickety Gin—O
Ride 'Em Plowboy—O
Rival Romeos—O
Sagebrush Sadie—O
Sky Scrappers—O
Sleigh Bells—O
Tall Timber—O
Trolley Troubles—O

After being hit on the head with a flowerpot, Donald doesn't recognize his own girl friend Daisy, in the memorable short, *Donald's Dilemma*.   © *Walt Disney Productions*

If UPA could do it, so could Disney. The result: a multiaward-winning "limited animation" short, *Toot, Whistle, Plunk, and Boom*.   © *Walt Disney Productions*

1928–1929

(*Steamboat Willie* premiered November 18, 1928; after its success, two previously completed silent MM cartoons, *Plane Crazy* and *Gallopin' Gaucho* were remade with sound. Disney and Celebrity Productions released the Disney product erratically through the end of 1929, and in 1930 Columbia Pictures started national distribution of the cartoons, rereleasing on a wide basis the earlier cartoons that had already received limited release by Disney and Celebrity—hence great confusion in so-called "release dates" at this time. Following are the early titles in the order of their completion and initial distribution.)

Steamboat Willie—MM
Gallopin' Gaucho—MM
Plane Crazy—MM
Barn Dance—MM
The Opry House—MM
When the Cat's Away—MM
Skeleton Dance—SS
Barnyard Battle—MM
The Plow Boy—MM
The Karnival Kid—MM
Mickey's Follies—MM
El Terrible Toreador—MM
Mickey's Choo Choo—MM
Springtime—SS
The Jazz Fool—MM
Hell's Bells—SS
Jungle Rhythm—SS
The Merry Dwarfs—SS
Haunted House—MM
Wild Waves—MM

1930

Summer—SS
Autumn—SS
Just Mickey—MM

Cannibal Capers—SS
The Barnyard Concert—MM
Night—SS
Cactus Kid—MM
Frolicking Fish—SS
Fire Fighters—MM
Arctic Antics—SS
The Shindig—MM
Midnight in a Toy Shop—SS
The Chain Gang—MM
Monkey Melodies—SS
Gorilla Mystery—MM
The Picnic—MM
Winter—SS
Pioneer Days—MM
Playful Pan—SS

1931

Birthday Party—MM
Birds of a Feather—SS
Traffic Troubles—MM
The Castaway—MM
Mother Goose Melodies—SS
The Moose Hunt—MM
The China Plate—SS

Delivery Boy—MM
The Busy Beavers—SS
Mickey Steps Out—MM
The Cat's Out—SS
Blue Rhythm—MM
Egyptian Melodies—SS
Fishin' Around—MM
The Clock Store—SS
Barnyard Broadcast—MM
The Spider and the Fly—SS
Beach Party—MM
The Fox Hunt—SS
Mickey Cuts Up—MM
Mickey's Orphans—MM (nominated for an Academy Award)
The Ugly Duckling—SS

1932

The Bird Store—SS
Duck Hunt—MM
Grocery Boy—MM
Mad Dog—MM
Barnyard Olympics—MM
Mickey's Revue—MM
The Bears and the Bees—SS
Musical Farmer—MM
Mickey in Arabia—MM
Just Dogs—SS
Mickey's Nightmare—MM
Trader Mickey—MM
Flowers and Trees—SS (first one in color)
The Whoopee Party—MM
King Neptune—SS
Bugs in Love—SS
Touchdown Mickey—MM
The Wayward Canary—MM
The Klondike Kid—MM

Babes in the Woods—SS
Santa's Workshop—SS
Mickey's Good Deed—MM

1933

Building a Building—MM (nominated for an Academy Award)
The Mad Doctor—MM
Mickey's Pal Pluto—MM
Birds in the Spring—SS
Mickey's Mellerdrammer—MM
Ye Olden Days—MM
Father Noah's Ark—SS
The Mail Pilot—MM
Three Little Pigs—SS (Academy Award winner)
Mickey's Mechanical Man—MM
Mickey's Gala Premiere—MM
Old King Cole—SS
Lullaby Land—SS
Puppy Love—MM
Pied Piper—SS
The Steeplechase—MM
The Pet Store—MM
Giant Land—MM
The Night Before Christmas—SS

1934

Shanghaied—MM
The China Shop—SS
The Grasshopper and the Ants—SS

The Disney animators even got around to stick figures, in such 1950s efforts as *Noah's Ark*. © *1962 Walt Disney Productions*

Ernest Shepard's famous Pooh drawings come to life in Disney's *Winnie the Pooh and the Honey Tree*. © *1965 Walt Disney Productions*

Camping Out—MM
Playful Pluto—MM
Funny Little Bunnies—SS
The Big Bad Wolf—SS
Gulliver Mickey—MM
The Wise Little Hen—SS
Mickey's Steamroller—MM
The Flying Mouse—SS
Orphans' Benefit—MM
Peculiar Penguins—SS
Mickey Plays Papa—MM
Goddess of Spring—SS
The Dog-Napper—MM
Two-Gun Mickey—MM

1935

The Tortoise and the Hare—
    SS (Academy Award winner)
Mickey's Man Friday—MM
The Band Concert—MM (the first Mickey Mouse in color)
Mickey's Service Station—MM
The Golden Touch—SS
Mickey's Kangaroo—MM
The Robber Kitten—SS
Water Babies—SS
Cookie Carnival—SS
Who Killed Cock Robin?—SS (nominated for an Academy Award)
Mickey's Garden—MM
Mickey's Fire Brigade—MM
Pluto's Judgment Day—MM
On Ice—MM
Music Land—SS
Three Orphan Kittens—SS (Academy Award winner)

Cock o' the Walk—SS
Broken Toys—SS

1936

Mickey's Polo Team—MM
Orphans' Picnic—MM
Mickey's Grand Opera—MM
Elmer Elephant—SS
Three Little Wolves—SS
Thru the Mirror—MM
Moving Day—MM
Mickey's Rival—MM
Alpine Climbers—MM
Mickey's Circus—MM
Toby Tortoise Returns—SS
Donald and Pluto—MM
Three Blind Mouseketeers—SS
Mickey's Elephant—MM
The Country Cousin—SS
Mother Pluto—MM
More Kittens—SS

1937

The Worm Turns—MM
Don Donald—MM
Magician Mickey—MM
Moose Hunters—MM
Woodland Cafe—SS
Mickey's Amateurs—MM
Little Hiawatha—SS
Modern Inventions—MM
Hawaiian Holiday—MM
Clock Cleaners—MM
The Old Mill—SS (Academy Award winner)
Pluto's Quinpuplets—P
Donald's Ostrich—DD
Lonesome Ghosts—MM

421

One of the stars of *Beaver Valley*. © *Walt Disney Productions*

A colorful scene from one of the "People and Places" shorts, *Samoa*. © *Walt Disney Productions*

1938

Self Control—DD
Boat Builders—MM
Donald's Better Self—DD
The Moth and the Flame—SS
Donald's Nephews—DD
Mickey's Trailer—MM
Wynken Blynken and Nod—SS
Polar Trappers—DD
Good Scouts—DD (nominated for an Academy Award)
The Fox Hunt—DD
The Whalers—MM
Mickey's Parrot—MM
The Brave Little Tailor—MM (nominated for an Academy Award)
Farmyard Symphony—SS
Donald's Golf Game—DD
Ferdinand the Bull—Special (Academy Award winner)
Merbabies—SS
Mother Goose Goes Hollywood—SS (nominated for an Academy Award)

1939

Donald's Lucky Day—DD
Society Dog Show—MM
The Practical Pig—Special
Goofy and Wilbur—G
The Ugly Duckling—SS (Academy Award winner)
Hockey Champ—DD
Donald's Cousin Gus—DD
Beach Picnic—DD
Sea Scouts—DD
The Pointer—MM (nominated for an Academy Award)
Donald's Penguin—DD
The Autograph Hound—DD
Officer Duck—DD

1940

The Riveter—DD
Donald's Dog Laundry—DD
Tugboat Mickey—MM
Billposters—DD
Mr. Duck Steps Out—DD
Bone Trouble—P
Put-Put Troubles—DD
Donald's Vacation—DD
Pluto's Dream House—P
Window Cleaners—DD
Mr. Mouse Takes a Trip—MM
Goofy's Glider—G
Fire Chief—DD
Pantry Pirate—P

1941

Timber—DD
Pluto's Playmate—P
The Little Whirlwind—MM
Golden Eggs—DD
A Gentleman's Gentleman—P
Baggage Buster—G
A Good Time for a Dime—DD
Canine Caddy—P
Nifty Nineties—MM
Early to Bed—DD
Truant Officer Donald—DD (nominated for an Academy Award)
Orphans' Benefit—MM
Old MacDonald Duck—DD

Lend a Paw—P (Academy Award winner)
Donald's Camera—DD
The Art of Skiing—G
Chef Donald—DD
The Art of Self-Defense—G
The Village Smithy—DD
Mickey's Birthday Party—MM
Pluto Junior—P
Symphony Hour—MM
Donald's Snow Fight—DD
Donald Gets Drafted—DD
The Army Mascot—P
Donald's Garden—DD
The Sleepwalker—P
Donald's Gold Mine—DD
T-Bone for Two—P
How to Play Baseball—G
The Vanishing Private—DD
The Olympic Champ—G
How to Swim—G
Sky Trooper—DD
Pluto at the Zoo—P
How to Fish—G
Bellboy Donald—DD

1943

Der Fuehrer's Face—DD (Academy Award winner)
Education for Death—Special
Donald's Tire Trouble—DD
Pluto and the Armadillo—P
Flying Jalopy—DD
Private Pluto—P
Fall Out—Fall In—DD
Victory Vehicles—G

Reason and Emotion—Special (nominated for an Academy Award)
Figaro and Cleo—Figaro
The Old Army Game—DD
Home Defense—DD
Chicken Little—Special

1944

The Pelican and the Snipe—Special
How to Be a Sailor—G
Trombone Trouble—DD
How to Play Golf—G
Donald Duck and the Gorilla—DD
Contrary Condor—DD
Commando Duck—DD
Springtime for Pluto—P
The Plastics Inventor—DD
How to Play Football—G (nominated for an Academy Award)
First Aiders—P
Donald's Off Day—DD

1945

Tiger Trouble—G
The Clock Watcher—DD
Dog Watch—P
The Eyes Have It—DD
African Diary—G
Donald's Crime—DD (nominated for an Academy Award)
Californy er Bust—G
Canine Casanova—P
Duck Pimples—DD

The Legend of Coyote Rock—P
No Sail—G & D
Hockey Homicide—G
Cured Duck—DD
Canine Patrol—P
Old Sequoia—DD

1946

A Knight for a Day—G
Pluto's Kid Brother—P
In Dutch—P
Squatter's Rights—P (nominated for an Academy Award)
Donald's Double Trouble—DD
The Purloined Pup—P
Wet Paint—DD
Dumbbell of the Yukon—DD
Lighthouse Keeping—DD
Bath Day—Figaro
Frank Duck Brings 'em Back Alive—DD
Double Dribble—G

1947

Pluto's Housewarming—P
Rescue Dog—P
Straight Shooters—DD
Sleepytime Donald—DD
Figaro and Frankie—Figaro
Clown of the Jungle—DD
Donald's Dilemma—DD
Crazy with the Heat—D & G
Bootle Beetle—DD
Wide Open Spaces—DD
Mickey's Delayed Date—MM

Foul Hunting—G
Mail Dog—P
Chip 'n' Dale—DD (nominated for an Academy Award)
Pluto's Blue Note—P (nominated for an Academy Award)
(Disney started reissuing his old cartoons this year, beginning with *Hawaiian Holiday* and *Clock Cleaners*.)

1948

They're Off—G
The Big Wash—G
Drip Dippy Donald—DD
Mickey Down Under—MM
Daddy Duck—DD
Bone Bandit—P
Donald's Dream Voice—DD
Pluto's Purchase—P
The Trial of Donald Duck—DD
Cat Nap Pluto—P
Inferior Decorator—DD
Pluto's Fledgling—P
Soup's On—DD
Three for Breakfast—DD
Mickey and the Seal—MM (nominated for an Academy Award)
Tea for Two Hundred—DD (nominated for an Academy Award)

1949

Pueblo Pluto—P

Donald's Happy Birthday—DD
Pluto's Surprise Package—P
Sea Salts—DD
Pluto's Sweater—P
Seal Island—TL (Academy Award winner)
Winter Storage—DD
Bubble Bee—Special
Honey Harvester—DD
Tennis Racquet—G
All in a Nutshell—DD
Goofy Gymnastics—G
The Greener Yard—DD
Sheep Dog—P
Slide, Donald, Slide—DD
Toy Tinkers—DD (nominated for an Academy Award)

1950

Pluto's Heart Throb—P
Lion Around—DD
Pluto and the Gopher—P
How to Ride a Horse—G (originally part of *The Reluctant Dragon*)
The Brave Engineer—Special
Crazy Over Daisy—DD
The Wonder Dog—P
Trailer Horn—DD
Primitive Pluto—P
Puss-Cafe—P
Motor Mania—G
Beaver Valley—TL (Academy Award winner)
Pests of the West—P
Food for Feudin'—P
Hook, Lion and Sinker—DD
Camp Dog—P

Bee at the Beach—DD
Hold That Pose—G
Morris the Midget Moose—Special
Out on a Limb—DD

1951

Lion Down—G
Chicken in the Rough—CD
Cold Storage—P
Dude Duck—DD
Home Made Home—G
Corn Chips—DD
Cold War—G
Plutopia—P
Test Pilot Donald—DD
Tomorrow We Diet—G
A Lucky Number—DD
Nature's Half Acre—TL (Academy Award winner)
R'coon Dawg—MM
Get Rich Quick—G
Cold Turkey—P
Fathers Are People—G
Out of Scale—DD
No Smoking—G
Bee on Guard—DD

1952

Father's Lion—G
Donald Applecore—DD
Lambert, The Sheepish Lion—Special (nominated for an Academy Award)
Hello Aloha—G
Two Chips and a Miss—CD
Man's Best Friend—G
Let's Stick Together—DD
Two Gun Goofy—G

Disney tackles science fiction—a scene from *Eyes in Outer Space*.
© *Walt Disney Productions*

Susie, The Little Blue Coupe
—Special
Water Birds—TL (Academy
Award winner)
Teachers Are People—G
Uncle Donald's Ants—DD
The Little House—Special
Pluto's Party—P
Trick or Treat—DD
Two Weeks Vacation—G
Pluto's Christmas Tree—MM
How to Be a Detective—G

1953

Bear Country—TL (Academy
Award winner)
The Alaskan Eskimo—PP
(Academy Award winner)
Father's Day Off—G
The Simple Things—MM
For Whom the Bulls Toil—G
Melody (Adventures in
Music)—Special (Disney's
first 3-D cartoon)
Don's Fountain of Youth—
DD
Father's Weekend—G
How to Dance—G
Prowlers of the Everglades
—TL
The New Neighbor—DD
Football (Now and Then)
—Special
Rugged Bear—DD (nominat-
ed for an Academy Award)
Toot, Whistle, Plunk, and
Boom—Special (Disney's
first CinemaScope cartoon;
Academy Award winner)

Ben and Me—Special (nomi-
nated for an Academy
Award)
Working for Peanuts—DD
(made in 3-D)
How to Sleep—G
Canvas Back Duck—DD

1954

(Starting this year "specials"
will be identified as either
cartoon or live action.)
Spare the Rod—DD
Donald's Diary—DD
Stormy, The Thoroughbred
with an Inferiority Com-
plex—live action
The Lone Chipmunks—DD
Two for the Record—from
Make Mine Music
Johnny Fedora and Alice
Blue Bonnet—from Make
Mine Music
Pigs Is Pigs—cartoon (nomi-
nated for an Academy
Award)
Casey Bats Again—cartoon
The Martins and the Coys—
from Make Mine Music
Dragon Around—DD
Grin and Bear It—DD
Little Toot—from Melody
Time
Once Upon a Wintertime—
from Melody Time
Social Lion—cartoon
Willie the Operatic Whale—
from Make Mine Music

The Flying Squirrel—DD

Grand Canyonscope—DD (CinemaScope)

Siam—PP (nominated for an Academy Award)

1955

No Hunting—DD (nominated for an Academy Award)

Lake Titicaca—DD—from *Saludos Amigos*

Contrast in Rhythm—from *Melody Time*

Blame It on the Samba—DD—from *Melody Time*

Pedro—from *Saludos Amigos*

Arizona Sheepdog—live action

El Gaucho Goofy—G—from *Saludos Amigos*

Switzerland—PP (nominated for an Academy Award)

Aquarela do Brasil—from *Saludos Amigos*

The Flying Gauchito—from *The Three Caballeros*

Bearly Asleep—DD (CinemaScope)

Beezy Bear—DD (CinemaScope)

Peter and the Wolf—from *Make Mine Music*

Up a Tree—DD (CinemaScope)

Emperor Penguins—live action

Men Against the Arctic—PP (Academy Award winner)

Johnny Appleseed—from *Melody Time*

1956

Chips Ahoy—DD (CinemaScope)

Hooked Bear—cartoon (CinemaScope)

How to Have an Accident in the Home—DD

Jack and Old Mac—cartoon

Man in Space—live action (nominated for an Academy Award)

In the Bag—cartoon (CinemaScope)

Cow Dog—live action (nominated for an Academy Award)

A Cowboy Needs a Horse—cartoon

Sardinia—PP

Disneyland U.S.A.—PP

Samoa—PP (nominated for an Academy Award)

1957

Blue Men of Morocco—PP

The Wetback Hound—live action (Academy Award winner)

The Story of Anyburg U.S.A.—cartoon

Lapland—PP

The Truth About Mother Goose—cartoon (nominated for an Academy Award)

Niok—live action

Portugal—PP (nominated for an Academy Award)

Mars and Beyond—live action

Alaskan Sled Dog

1958

Wales—PP
Scotland—PP
Ama Girls—PP (Academy Award winner)
Paul Bunyan—cartoon (nominated for an Academy Award)
The Legend of Sleepy Hollow—from *Ichabod and Mr. Toad*
Seven Cities of Antarctica—PP

1959

Grand Canyon—live action (Academy Award winner)
Nature's Strangest Creatures—live action
Cruise of the Eagle—PP
Eyes in Outer Space—live action
Donald in Mathmagic Land—DD
How to Have an Accident at Work—DD
Noah's Ark—cartoon (nominated for an Academy Award)
Mysteries of the Deep—live action (nominated for an Academy Award)

1960

Gala Day at Disneyland—live action
Goliath II—cartoon (nominated for an Academy Award)

Islands of the Sea—live action (nominated for an Academy Award)
Japan—PP
The Danube—PP
The Hound That Thought He Was a Raccoon—live action
The Horse with the Flying Tail—live action (Academy Award winner)

1961

The Saga of Windwagon Smith—cartoon
Donald and the Wheel—DD
The Litterbug—DD
Aquamania—G (nominated for an Academy Award)

1962

A Symposium on Popular Songs—cartoon (nominated for an Academy Award)

1963

Yellowstone Cubs—live action
Disneyland After Dark—live action (released in 1962 in England)

1964

Golden Horseshoe Revue—live action (released in 1963 in England)
The Tattooed Police Horse—live action

What better subject for a Disney short than Disneyland? This is a ride through the Matterhorn, as seen in *Gala Day at Disneyland.* © *Walt Disney Productions*

1965

A Country Coyote Goes Hollywood—live action
Freewayphobia—cartoon
Flash the Teenage Otter—live action (released in 1964 in England)
Freewayphobia #2 (Goofy's Freeway Trouble)—cartoon

1966

Winnie the Pooh and the Honey Tree—cartoon
Run, Appaloosa, Run—live action

1967

Scrooge McDuck and Money—cartoon
The Legend of the Boy and the Eagle—live action

Additional Shorts

The above listing includes only short subjects given theatrical release in the United States. Many others were made for television, sponsors, special showings, foreign release, and 16mm distribution. Of these, it is worth noting several cartoons made for the National Film Board of Canada in 1941 and 1942: *Thrifty Pig*, featuring the Three Little Pigs, *The Seven Wise Dwarfs*, bringing Snow White's friends back to the screen, *Donald's Decision*, featuring Donald Duck, and *All Together*. The Disney characters were also used in various commercial films, from a 1939 short for Nabisco called *Mickey's Surprise Party* to a 1965 live-action documentary called *Steel and America* featuring Donald Duck in several animated sequences. Disney also made an important series of short subjects of an instructional nature for the Coordinator of Inter-American Affairs during World War II, several of which are in the permanent collection of the Museum of Modern Art.

Most of the short subjects released theatrically overseas or domestically on 16mm had their origin on the Disney TV programs, such as the popular *I'm No Fool* series with Jiminy Cricket, originally shown on the *Mickey Mouse Club* show. Finally, it is worth noting that in 1967 Disney produced two films for special exhibition in Circlevision, a 360-degree projection system used with great success at such places as Expo '67 in Montreal.

432

5 · Disney on TV

WHEN DISNEY FIRST VENTURED INTO TELEVISION, IT was on his own terms. He did a handful of Christmas specials, beginning in 1950, with no commercials interrupting the fun, just an announcement of the sponsor's name at the beginning and end of the program. He called the constant interruptions on most programs "bad showmanship."

These initial filmed hours were directed by veteran Robert Florey, who recalls: "We didn't go on location; everything was photographed at the studio, and we took all the time necessary to obtain the perfection always required by Walt Disney, without the usual pressure from a production manager."

When, in 1954, Disney finally succumbed to an offer for a weekly series, he decided to retain as much of this quality as possible. Says Florey: "He followed the march of his TV segments from the time of their conception, presiding daily at conferences with all his collaborators. He didn't have to look at a finished product, or at something in progress to sense what was right or wrong with it. He knew it at once, and if not satisfied, ordered immediate retakes or added scenes after viewing the daily rushes."

The series, broadcast Wednesday evenings on ABC-TV, was called *Disneyland,* and, in keeping with the format of the new amusement park, the show was divided into categories: Fantasyland, Adventureland, Frontierland, and Tomorrowland. The first season set the pace for the weekly series: a combination of cartoon mélanges,

433

true-life nature films, multi-episode adventures, old Disney feature films, and constant bulletins on the Disneyland park, then in progress. Walt Disney himself proved to be a most affable host. (After his first season on the air, he was nominated for an Emmy award as "Most Outstanding New Personality," but he lost to George Gobel.)

During the first season or two, there was enough material in the backlog to provide for a good many shows, with only connecting footage to be filmed, either with Disney himself or with the characters; in at least one case Hans Conried was hired to pose as the Magic Mirror from Snow White, hosting a program of excerpts from earlier feature films. A typical entry during the first season was *From Aesop to Hans Christian Andersen,* which comprised a scene from *Snow White* and the 1930s cartoons *Tortoise and the Hare, The Country Cousin, The Brave Little Tailor,* and *The Ugly Duckling.* Other hours were devoted entirely to one character, such as Goofy or Pluto.

One of the most successful shows during the first season was Ward Kimball's *Man in Space,* a fascinating survey of space travel, past, present, and future; it was considered good enough to be released theatrically, as was the major hit of the first season, *Davy Crockett.*

In addition to the spate of shows devoted to the Disneyland park, there were other programs that were, in effect, hour-long plugs for current Disney films, both current and reissued. *Operation Undersea,* the story of the filming of *20,000 Leagues Under the Sea,* won Disney an Emmy that year as Best Documentary. The following year there was *A Tribute to Joel Chandler Harris,* timed to coincide with the reissue of *Song of the South,* and *Behind the Scenes with Fess Parker,* which was telecast just in time to remind youngsters of the theatrical release of *Davy Crockett and the River Pirates.*

Some of the most fascinating shows in the series were those where Disney took his audience behind the scenes at the studio to show how cartoons are made. An entire show, *The Tricks of Our Trade,* was devoted to such footage, to the delight of Disney buffs as well as curious small fry.

The perfect host for the Disney TV show: Walt Disney, with a seeing-eye dog featured in the program *Atta Girl, Kelly*.
© 1966 Walt Disney Productions

Although *Davy Crockett* was a tremendous success, it was not until the 1957–1958 series that Disney embarked on another homegrown series, *The Saga of Andy Burnett,* starring Jerome Courtland as a young frontier hero, with Jeff York and Iron Eyes Cody in supporting roles. The series lasted for six episodes, but it was fairly routine, and it did not warrant further sequels. The 1958–1959 season was marked by two new series, however, which did much better. First, there was *The Nine Lives of Elfego Baca,* "Sheriff, Lawyer, Believer in Justice." Robert Loggia starred as the Latin lawyer with a flair for fighting and a perpetual sympathy for the underdog; James Dunn costarred as his senior law partner. Good casts (Patric Knowles, Lynn Bari, James Drury, Kenneth Tobey) marked this series, but the plotting was pretty obvious, even for children.

Better yet was *Texas John Slaughter,* starring Disney discovery Tom Tryon as a peaceful man who joins the Texas Rangers in order to rid the state of lawlessness, so he can settle down and get married. Directed by Harry Keller, a Republic Pictures Western veteran, on picturesque outdoor locations, the series benefited from tight pacing and nice scenery, but mainly Tryon's portrayal of the title character. *Slaughter* became the biggest success on the Disney show since *Davy Crockett.* Disney commented: "Every time it goes on the air, the rating goes up. So I guess we'll stick with it for a while." *Slaughter* outlasted all the other series on the show.

The 1959–1960 season saw the birth of still more miniseries: *The Swamp Fox,* starring Leslie Nielsen as the famed General Francis Marion, co-starring Dick Foran; *Moochie of the Little League,* an outgrowth of the Kevin Corcoran character from the Mickey Mouse Club; and a brief continuation of the *Elfego Baca* series, as well as four *Zorro* hours, bringing back the character from his recently completed run of half-hour shows.

The following year Disney returned to the *Davy Crockett* vein with a quarter of *Daniel Boone* sagas starring Dewey Martin, but they did not take off the way their predecessor did.

436

In the fall of 1961 Disney moved from ABC to NBC; financial considerations aside, NBC offered Disney the opportunity of broadcasting in color, as well as a sponsorship deal with RCA Victor that would emphasize the unique color qualities of the show (especially if viewed on an RCA color set). Disney had been filming the series in color all along, a wise move that has paid off many times over in recent years.

While at ABC, Disney had produced two series besides his hourly show. The more successful of the two was *The Mickey Mouse Club,* a daily children's show, which bowed on October 3, 1955; to this day there has not been another kiddie program to rival it in popularity, with the possible exception of *Sesame Street.* The daily show was a combination of live performing by the Mouseketeers, a group of personable and talented children (of whom Annette Funicello remains the most prominent) led by Jimmy Dodd; an old Mickey Mouse or Donald Duck cartoon; nature footage; and a daily serial. These serials were produced on the same scale as the weekly miniseries, and provided good, wholesome entertainment, the likes of which no other producer has been able to equal. (In fact, there have been remarkably few live-action filmed series made especially for children in the entire history of television; nowadays, the most popular kiddie programs are reruns of old nighttime situation comedies.)

The serials included *Corky and White Shadow,* an adventure tale starring Mouseketeer Darlene Gillespie and character actor Lloyd Corrigan; *Annette,* a contemporary tale of teen-age life (sort of); *The Hardy Boys,* with Tim Considine and Tommy Kirk unraveling various mysteries; and most popular of all, *Spin and Marty,* an excellent story about two boys and their life at a summer ranch, with Tim Considine and David Stollery in the title roles, and Harry Carey, Jr., Roy Barcroft, and J. Pat O'Malley among the supporting cast.

The rituals of the *Mickey Mouse Club,* including the various "days" (Talent Roundup Day, Anything Can Happen Day, Fun with Music Day, etc.), became a nationwide habit for millions of children, and the show

Texas John Slaughter (Tom Tryon) in a meditative moment.
© *Walt Disney Productions*

endured for over 300 daily episodes, enjoying a brief revival as a syndicated program in the 1960s.

Disney's other TV series for ABC was *Zorro*, starring Guy Williams as the masked avenger. Although it only lasted for two seasons (seventy-eight episodes), it became a perennial rerun on local stations around the country, making kids as conscious of the character as they had been of Davy Crockett several years back. After the show's demise in the spring of 1959, Disney employed the character on a number of hour-long episodes of his weekly show as well.

When it first appeared, the weekly hour was called *Disneyland*. For the 1959–1960 season the name was changed to *Walt Disney Presents*. And when the show moved to NBC, the name was again changed, this time with more obvious reason, to *Walt Disney's Wonderful World of Color*. Because it was a new network, and ostensibly a new show, it was decided that there would be no holdovers from the previous series, so Texas John Slaughter and his comrades bit the dust.

Not that this made Disney unhappy. He told Bill Davidson of *TV Guide:*

I gave ABC their first full-hour Western series with my Davy Crockett shows and soon the network was flooded with other Westerns. They made so much money for ABC that before long *I* found myself in a straitjacket. I no longer had the freedom of action I enjoyed in those first three years. They kept insisting that I do more and more Westerns and my show became loaded with Elfego Baca, the Swamp Fox, Texas John Slaughter, Daniel Boone. I found myself competing with *Maverick, Wyatt Earp* and every other Western myth. When I came up with a fresh idea in another field, the network executives would say no. Just to give you some notion of what they turned down, one of their rejects was "The Shaggy Dog." We made a theater movie out of it and it grossed $9,000,000.

Disney also felt that the network had strangled the *Mickey Mouse Club,* first by overloading it with commercials, then cutting it to a half hour, and then taking no interest in it at all. Associates claimed that the NBC move was like a new lease on life for the producer, who reveled in the new possibilities open to him.

The one new character to emerge from the network switch was a new cartoon creation named Ludwig von Drake, the erudite "uncle" of Donald Duck. This meant, happily, that there would be new animation for the show, although the ratio of live action to cartoon programming had increased steadily over the years, a sharp contrast to *Disneyland*'s opening season, which was a feast for admirers of Mickey, Donald, and friends.

Few running characters emerged from the new Disney show; instead, there were two- and three-part stories that generally stood alone. These became more elaborate under the NBC-color aegis than the former mini-series had been, although without their allure.

Quality was definitely up, however, and the first season of *Walt Disney's Wonderful World of Color* brought such first-rate films as *Hans Brinker, or the Silver Skates* and *The Prince and the Pauper*, starring Sean Scully and Guy Williams. Highlights of later years included *The Horse Without a Head*, made in England with a top-drawer cast (Jean-Pierre Aumont, Herbert Lom, Leo McKern, Pamela Franklin) and directed by Don Chaffey; *Johnny Shiloh*, a good Civil War yarn with Kevin Corcoran; *The Legend of Young Dick Turpin*; *The Magnificent Rebel* (the story of Tchaikovsky); *The Scarecrow of Romney Marsh* with Patrick McGoohan; *Kilroy* with newcomer Warren Berlinger and old favorites Joan Blondell and Jack Oakie; and Disney's most successful effort, *Gallegher*, based on Richard Harding Davis's stories about a young boy working for a newspaper at the turn of the century. *Gallegher*, starring Roger Mobley, was so successful in the 1964–1965 season that two sequels were filmed, *The Further Adventures of Gallegher* and *Gallegher Goes West*, one for each of the next two television seasons.

Disney consistently spent more money on his TV show than he recouped from the networks, well aware that the

Kevin Corcoran in a scene from *Moochie of the Little League*.
© *Walt Disney Productions*

difference was compensated for many times again in publicity and goodwill (as well as by foreign release of many episodes as feature films). The money has been well spent, and it is significant that in a medium where programs come and go from week to week, the Disney show has remained among the top-rated series from year to year, without fluctuation.

The only disappointment in recent years has been the increasing reliance on reruns, especially in the cartoon department. Even most of the Von Drake footage is a repeat of one of the shows originally made in the early 1960s.

Walt Disney continued to host the series all along. Ironically, the show that was broadcast the Sunday after his death in December 1966 featured Walt showing plans for his Walt Disney World in Florida. It was a most appropriate tribute to the man.

For the 1967–1968 season, the idea of a host was eliminated, and two years later the name was changed to *The Wonderful World of Disney*. It continues to win a large Sunday night audience with its by now familiar formula of animal stories, reruns of old programs, multi-episode broadcasts of Disney feature films, and newly filmed adventure tales, always done on a large scale with fine casts.

In television, just as in motion pictures, Walt Disney proved conclusively that quality *did* pay off. It's a lesson that few other television producers have heeded.

The following is an index of all one-hour programs shown in the *Disneyland, Walt Disney Presents,* and *Walt Disney's Wonderful World of Color* series. I have included theatrical feature films that were broadcast on the series, and noted where a program was subsequently released as a feature film abroad. Apparent gaps in the index are due to the large number of reruns used in the series, both from the current season and from previous years; and occasional preemptions. Disney was perhaps the first to sprinkle reruns throughout the season, a practice now commonly used, and he was certainly the first to rebroadcast shows from earlier years. This, plus the

Guy Williams as Zorro puts Sergeant Garcia (Henry Calvin) on the spot in a scene from an early *Zorro* program.   © *Walt Disney Productions*

availability of theatrical features, made it possible for Disney to film as few as eleven new hour-long shows for a full season (1965–1966). Finally, it should be noted that quite often Disney would interrupt spring reruns in May to broadcast a new show with the express purpose of promoting a film about to go into release for the summer. Most of the shows turned into feature films for Europe are available for rent on 16mm in the United States. This index concludes with the 1966–67 season.

1954—1955 season

10/27/54—*The Disneyland Story*
11/13/54—*Alice in Wonderland* (1951)
11/10/54—*Prairie—Seal Island*
11/17/54—*The Donald Duck Story*

11/24/54—*So Dear to My Heart* (1949)

12/1/54—*A Story of Dogs*

12/8/54—*Operation Undersea* (Emmy Award winner)

12/15/54—*Davy Crockett, Indian Fighter* (released as theatrical feature, along with two later episodes, in 1955; nominated for Emmy Award for best TV film editing)

12/22/54—*1954 Christmas Show*

12/29/54—*Cameras in Africa/Beaver Valley*

1/5/55—*Treasure Island* (1950) part one

1/12/55—*Treasure Island* (1950) part two

1/19/55—*Monsters of the Deep*

1/26/55—*Davy Crockett Goes to Congress*

2/2/55—*Wind in the Willows* (half of *The Adventures of Ichabod and Mr. Toad,* 1949)

2/9/55—*A Progress Report and Nature's Half Acre*

2/16/55—*Cavalcade of Songs*

2/23/55—*Davy Crockett at the Alamo* (last of trilogy)

3/2/55—*From Aesop to Hans Christian Andersen* (released theatrically in Europe)

3/9/55—*Man in Space* (later released theatrically as a short)

7/13/55—*Further Report on Disneyland*

1955—1956 season

9/14/55—*Dumbo* (1941)

9/21/55—*Behind the True-Life Cameras—Olympic Elk*

9/28/55—*Jiminy Cricket Presents Bongo*

10/5/55—*Tiburon, Sardinia, Morocco and Icebreakers*

10/12/55—*Adventures of Mickey Mouse*

10/19/55—*The Story of the Silly Symphony*

10/26/55—*The Legend of Sleepy Hollow* (half of *The Adventures of Ichabod and Mr. Toad,* 1949)

11/2/55—*The Story of Robin Hood* (1952), part one

11/9/55—*The Story of Robin Hood* (1952), part two

11/16/55—*Davy Crockett's Keelboat Race* (released theatrically, along with later episode, in 1956)

11/30/55—*The Story of the Animated Drawing*

12/7/55—*The Goofy Success Story* (written and directed by Jack Kinney, with Wolfgang Reitherman as sequence director, this compilation was released as a featurette in Europe)

12/14/55—*Davy Crockett and the River Pirates*

12/28/55—*Man and the Moon*

1/4/56—*When Knighthood Was in Flower* (originally released as *The Sword and the Rose*, 1953) part one

1/15/56—*When Knighthood Was in Flower*, part two

1/18/56—*A Tribute to Joel Chandler Harris*

2/1/56—*A Day in the Life of Donald Duck*

2/8/56—*Survival in Nature*

2/15/56—*Our Unsung Villains*

2/29/56—*A Trip Through Adventureland and Water Birds*

3/7/56—*On Vacation*

3/14/56—*Stormy the Thoroughbred* (released as a featurette in 1953)

3/21/56—*The Goofy Sports Story* (released theatrically in Europe; directed by Jack Kinney)

4/4/56—*Where Do the Stories Come From?*

5/30/56—*Behind the Scenes with Fess Parker*

1956—1957 season

9/12/56—*Antarctica, Past and Present*

9/19/56—*The Great Cat Family*

9/26/56—*Searching for Nature's Mysteries*

10/3/56—*Rob Roy* (1953), part one

10/10/56—*Rob Roy* (1953), part two

10/17/56—*Goofy's Cavalcade of Sports*

10/24/56—*Behind the Cameras in Lapland; The Alaskan Eskimo*

10/31/56—*The Plausible Impossible*

11/7/56—*Cameras in Samoa; The Holland Story*

11/14/56—*Along the Oregon Trail* (a separate story intended as a teaser for *Westward Ho the Wagons*)

11/21/56—*At Home with Donald Duck*

12/12/56—*Pluto's Day*

12/19/56—*1956 Christmas Show: A Present for Donald* (*The Three Caballeros*—1945)

Jimmy Dodd and Roy Williams lead the Mouseketeers in a rousing cheer; the most famous alumnus, Annette Funicello, can be seen third from right. © *Walt Disney Productions*

1/22/58—*The Littlest Outlaw* (1955), part one

1/29/58—*The Littlest Outlaw* (1955), part two

2/26/58—*The Saga of Andy Burnett: Land of the Enemies*

3/5/58—*The Saga of Andy Burnett: The White Man's Medicine*

3/12/58—*The Saga of Andy Burnett: The Big Council*

3/19/58—*Magic and Music*

4/9/58—*An Adventure in the Magic Kingdom*

4/16/58—*Four Tales on a Mouse*

4/30/58—*An Adventure in Art*

5/14/58—*Magic Highway U.S.A.*

1958—1959 season

(The season began with repeats of the three Davy Crockett shows.)

10/3/58—*The Nine Lives of Elfego Baca*, part one (released as a feature film abroad, using this and other segments; directed by Norman Foster, starring Robert Loggia and Lisa Montell)

10/10/58—*The Pigeon That Worked a Miracle* (released as a featurette in Europe; directed by Walter Perkins)

10/17/58—*The Nine Lives of Elfego Baca*, part two: Four Down and Five Lives to Go

10/24/58—*Rusty and the Falcon* (released theatrically abroad)

10/31/58—*Tales of Texas John Slaughter*, part one (released as a feature film abroad, using this and other segments; directed by Harry Keller, starring Tom Tryon, Robert Middleton, Norma Moore, Harry Carey, Jr.)

11/7/58—*His Majesty—The King of Beasts* (released theatrically as *The African Lion*, 1955)

11/14/58—*Tales of Texas John Slaughter*, part two: Ambush at Laredo

11/21/58—*The Boston Tea Party* (first half of *Johnny Tremain*, 1957)

11/28/58—*The Nine Lives of Elfego Baca*, part three: Lawman or Gunman

12/5/58—*The Shot That Was Heard Around the World* (part two of *Johnny Tremain*, 1957)

12/12/58—*The Nine Lives of Elfego Baca*, part four: Law and Order, Inc.

12/19/58—*From All of Us to All of You*

1/9/58— *Tales of Texas John Slaughter,* part three: Killers from Kansas

1/16/59—*Niok*

1/23/59—*Tales of Texas John Slaughter,* part four: Showdown at Sandoval (released as a feature film abroad, comprising episodes 3 and 4, directed by Harry Keller, with Tom Tryon, Norma Moore, Dan Duryea, Beverly Garland, Harry Carey, Jr. The feature title was *Gunfight at Sandoval*)

1/30/59—*The Peter Tchaikovsky Story* (released theatrically in Europe, starring Grant Williams)

2/6/59—*The Nine Lives of Elfego Baca,* part five: Attorney at Law (released as a feature called *Six Gun Law,* along with the following episode; directed by Christian Nyby, it starred Robert Loggia, James Dunn, James Drury, Lynn Bari, Kenneth Tobey, Patric Knowles)

2/13/59—*Duck Flies Coop*

2/20/59—*The Nine Lives of Elfego Baca,* part six: The Griswold Murder

2/27/59—*The Adventures of Chip 'n' Dale*

3/6/59—*Tales of Texas John Slaughter,* part five: The Man from Bitter Creek (this and the next episode comprised another European feature release, *Stampede at Bitter Creek,* directed by Harry Keller, with Tom Tryon, Stephen McNally, Grant Williams, Sidney Blackmer, Bill Williams)

3/13/59—*Highway to Trouble*

3/20/59—*Tales of Texas John Slaughter,* part six: The Slaughter Trail

3/27/59—*Toot, Whistle, Plunk, and Boom* (expanded from 1953 short)

4/24/59—*The Wetback Hound* (released theatrically in 1957)

5/29/59—*I Captured the King of the Leprechauns* (teaser for *Darby O'Gill*)

1959—1960 season

10/2/59—*A Diamond Is a Boy's Best Friend* (this and the next episode released in Europe as *Little League Moochie,* with Kevin Corcoran, James Brown, Frances Rafferty, Reginald Owen, Stuart Erwin)

10/9/59—*Wrong Way Moochie*

10/16/59—*Killers of the High Country*

450

10/23/59—*The Birth of the Swamp Fox* (first of series starring Leslie Nielsen)

10/30/59—*Brother Against Brother* (Swamp Fox)

11/6/59—*Perilous Assignment* (teaser for *Third Man on the Mountain*)

11/13/59—*Move Along, Mustangers* (Elfego Baca)

11/20/59—*Mustang Man, Mustang Maid* (Elfego Baca)

11/27/59—*A Storm Called Maria* (released theatrically in Europe; directed by Ken Nelson)

12/4/59—*The Robber Stallion* (Texas John Slaughter)

12/11/59—*Wild Horse Revenge* (Texas John Slaughter)

12/18/59—*Range War at Tombstone* (Texas John Slaughter)

1/1/60—*Tory Vengeance* (Swamp Fox)

1/8/60—*Day of Reckoning* (Swamp Fox)

1/15/60—*Redcoat Strategy* (Swamp Fox)

1/22/60—*A Case of Treason* (Swamp Fox)

1/29/60—*Wild Burro of the West*

2/5/60—*Two Happy Amigos*

2/12/60—*Desperado from Tombstone* (Texas John Slaughter)

2/19/60—*Apache Friendship* (Texas John Slaughter)

2/26/60—*Kentucky Gunslick* (Texas John Slaughter)

3/4/60—*Geronimo's Revenge* (Texas John Slaughter; this and other episodes were released as a feature abroad, *Geronimo's Revenge,* directed by James Neilson, with Tom Tryon and Darryl Hickman)

3/11/60—*This Is Your Life, Donald Duck*

3/18/60—*Friendly Enemies at Law* (Elfego Baca)

3/25/60—*Gus Tomlin Is Dead* (Elfego Baca)

4/1/60—*The Mad Hermit of Chimney Butte*

1960—1961 season

(The season opened on new day, Sunday, at 6:30, with repeats of the two later Davy Crockett shows.)

10/16/60—*Rapids Ahead and Bear Country* (first half a teaser for *Ten Who Dared*)

10/30/60—*El Bandido* (Zorro)

11/6/60—*Adios El Cuchillo* (Zorro)

11/13/60—*Donald's Silver Anniversary*

11/20/60—*Moochie of Pop Warner Football: The Pee Wees Versus City Hall*

11/27/60—*Moochie of Pop Warner Football: From Ticonderoga to Disneyland*

12/4/60—*The Warrior's Path* (Daniel Boone)

12/11/60—*And Chase the Buffalo* (Daniel Boone)

12/18/60—*Escape to Paradise* and *Water Birds* (first half a teaser for *Swiss Family Robinson*)

1/1/61—*The Postponed Wedding* (Zorro)

1/8/61—*A Woman's Courage* (Swamp Fox)

1/15/61—*Horses for Greene* (Swamp Fox)

1/22/61—*A Salute to Father*

1/29/61—*The End of the Trail* (Texas John Slaughter)

2/5/61—*A Holster Full of Law* (Texas John Slaughter, released abroad, with other episodes, as a theatrical feature)

2/19/61—*Westward Ho the Wagons* (1956), part one

2/26/61—*Westward Ho the Wagons* (1956), part two

3/5/61—*The Coyote's Lament* (released abroad theatrically)

3/12/61—*The Wilderness Road* (Daniel Boone)

3/19/61—*The Promised Land* (Daniel Boone)

3/26/61—*Man in Flight*

4/2/61— *Auld Acquaintance* (Zorro)

4/9/61—*Battle for Survival*

4/16/61—*A Trip to Tucson* (Texas John Slaughter)

4/23/61—*Frank Clell's in Town* (Texas John Slaughter)

4/30/61—*Flash, the Teenage Otter* (released theatrically both here and in Europe)

5/7/61—*Andrews Raiders* (*The Great Locomotive Chase*, 1956) part one

5/14/61—*Andrews Raiders* (*The Great Locomotive Chase*, 1956) part two

5/21/61—*Wonders of the Water World*

5/28/61—*Disneyland '61* and *Olympic Elk*

6/11/61—*Title Makers* and *Nature's Half Acre* (first half a teaser for *The Parent Trap*)

1961—1962 season

(Disney moved to NBC, got a new name, and a new time, 7:30 on Sunday.)

9/24/61—*An Adventure in Color, Mathmagic Land* (first half introducing Ludwig von Drake; second half a theatrical short of 1959)

10/1/61—*The Horsemasters*, part one (released as a feature in Europe, directed by Bill Fairchild, with Annette Funicello, Janet Munro, Tommy Kirk, Donald Pleasence, Tony Britton)

10/8/61—*The Horsemasters*, part two

10/15/61—*Chico, the Misunderstood Coyote* (released theatrically in Europe)

10/22/61—*The Hunting Instinct* (Ludwig von Drake; released theatrically in Europe; new animation directed by Hamilton Luske)

11/5/61—*Inside Donald Duck* (Ludwig von Drake)

11/12/61—*Return of True Son* (part one of *The Light in the Forest*, 1958)

11/19/61—*True Son's Revenge* (part two of *The Light in the Forest*, 1958)

11/26/61—*Holiday for Henpecked Husbands*

12/3/61—*A Fire Called Jeremiah* (released theatrically in Europe)

12/10/61—*Kids Is Kids* (Ludwig von Drake) (released theatrically in France)

12/17/61—*Backstage Party* (on the set of *Babes in Toyland*)

1/7/62—*Hans Brinker, or, The Silver Skates* (released theatrically in Europe; directed by Norman Foster, with Rony Zeander, Carin Rossby, Erik Strandwerk, all-Swedish cast), part one

1/14/62—*Hans Brinker*, part two

1/21/62—*Sancho the Homing Steer*, part one (released as a feature film in Europe: directed by Tom McGowan, with Bill Shurley, Rosita Fernandez, Arthur Custis, narrated by Rex Allen)

1/28/62—*Sancho the Homing Steer*, part two

2/4/62—*Fantasy on Skis*

2/18/62—*Comanche*, part one (released theatrically as *Tonka*, 1959)

2/25/62—*Comanche*, part two (released theatrically as *Tonka*, 1959)

3/4/62—*Carnival Time*

Donald Duck's alter ego wants him to spend his tax money foolishly in the wartime short *The New Spirit*. Acme photo

3/11/62—*The Prince and the Pauper*, part one (released theatrically in Europe, directed by Don Chaffey, with Guy Williams, Sean Scully, Laurence Naismith, Niall MacGinnis, Donald Houston)

3/18/62—*The Prince and the Pauper*, part two

3/25/62—*The Prince and the Pauper*, part three

4/1/62—*Spy in the Sky* (first half a teaser for *Moon Pilot;* second half *Eyes in Outer Space*, a 1959 short)

4/8/62—*Von Drake in Spain* (released theatrically in Europe, with animation directed by Hamilton Luske, and featuring in live action Jose Greco and Rafael de Cordova; directed by Norman Foster)

4/15/62—*Disneyland After Dark* (released theatrically in Europe, directed by William Beaudine, with Louis Armstrong, Annette Funicello, Bobby Rydell, Bobby Burgess, Kid Ory, The Osmond Brothers, and others)

5/27/62—*The Wetback Hound* (repeat of title short, plus teaser for *Big Red*)

1962—1963 season

9/23/62—*The Golden Horseshoe Revue* (released theatrically in Europe; directed by Ron Miller, with Annette Funicello, Ed Wynn, Gene Sheldon, Wally Boag)

9/30/62—*Escapade in Florence*, part one (released theatrically in Europe; directed by Steve Previn, with Tommy Kirk, Annette Funicello, Nino Castelnuovo)

10/7/62—*Escapade in Florence*, part two

10/14/62—*The Silver Fox and Sam Davenport* (released theatrically abroad)

10/21/62—*Man Is His Own Worst Enemy* (Ludwig von Drake)

10/28/62—*Sammy the Way-Out Seal*, part one (released theatrically in Europe; directed by Norman Tokar, with Robert Culp, Patricia Barry, Jack Carson, Billy Mumy)

11/4/62—*Sammy the Way-Out Seal*, part two

11/18/62—*The Magnificent Rebel*, part one (released theatrically in Europe, with Carl Boehm, Ernst Nadhering, Gabriele Porks, Ivan Desny)

11/25/62—*The Magnificent Rebel*, part two

12/2/62—*The Mooncussers*, part one (released theatrically in Europe; with Oscar Homolka, Kevin Corcoran, Joan Freeman, Ryan Garrick)

12/9/62—*The Mooncussers*, part two

12/16/62—*Hurricane Hannah*

12/23/62—*Holiday Time at Disneyland*

1/6/63—*Three Tall Tales* (Casey at the Bat, Paul Bunyan, Windwagon Smith)

1/13/63—*Little Dog Lost*

1/20/63—*Johnny Shiloh*, part one (released theatrically in Europe; with Brian Keith, Kevin Corcoran, Darryl Hickman, Skip Homeier)

1/27/63—*Johnny Shiloh*, part two

2/3/63—*Greta the Misfit Greyhound* (released theatrically abroad)

2/10/63—*Inside Outer Space* (Ludwig von Drake)

2/17/63—*Banner in the Sky*, part one (released theatrically as *Third Man on the Mountain*, 1959)

2/24/63—*Banner in the Sky*, part two (released theatrically as *Third Man on the Mountain*, 1959)

455

3/3/63—*Square Peg in a Round Hole* (Ludwig von Drake; new cartoon footage directed by Hamilton Luske in this featurette released theatrically in Europe)

3/10/63—*The Horse with the Flying Tail* (released theatrically in 1960)

3/17/63—*Kidnapped* (1960), part one

3/24/63—*Kidnapped* (1960), part two

1963—1964 season

9/29/63—*The Horse Without a Head,* part one (released theatrically in Europe; directed by Don Chaffey, with Jean-Pierre Aumont, Herbert Lom, Leo McKern, Pamela Franklin, Vincent Winter)

10/6/63—*The Horse Without a Head,* part two

10/13/63—*Fly with Von Drake* (including scenes from *Victory Through Air Power*)

10/20/63—*The Wahoo Bobcat* (released theatrically in Europe; directed by Hank Schloss)

10/27/63—*The Waltz King,* part one (released theatrically in Europe; with Kerwin Matthews, Senta Berger, Brian Aherne, directed by Steve Previn)

11/3/63—*The Waltz King,* part two

11/17/63—*The Truth About Mother Goose* (expanded from 1957 short, with Ludwig von Drake hosting)

12/1/63—*Pollyanna* (1960), part one

12/8/63—*Pollyanna* (1960), part two

12/15/63—*Pollyanna* (1960), part three

1/5/64—*The Ballad of Hector, the Stowaway Dog,* part one (released theatrically abroad as *Million Dollar Collar*)

1/12/64—*The Ballad of Hector, the Stowaway Dog,* part two

1/19/64—*Mediterranean Cruise* (Ludwig von Drake)

1/26/64—*Bristle Face,* part one

2/2/64—*Bristle Face,* part two

2/9/64—*The Scarecrow of Romney Marsh,* part one (released theatrically in Europe as *Dr. Syn, Alias the Scarecrow;* directed by James Neilson, with Patrick McGoohan, Sean Scully, Kay Walsh, Tony Britton)

2/16/64—*The Scarecrow of Romney Marsh,* part two

2/23/64—*The Scarecrow of Romney Marsh,* part three

3/1/64—*Legend of Two Gypsy Dogs*

3/8/64—*For the Love of Willadean*, part one

3/15/64—*For the Love of Willadean*, part two

3/22/64—*In Shape with Von Drake* (Ludwig von Drake)

3/29/64—*Greyfriars Bobby* (1961), part one

4/5/64—*Greyfriars Bobby* (1961), part two

4/12/64—*Jungle Cat* (1960)

5/17/64—*Disneyland Goes to the World's Fair*

1964—1965 season

9/20/64—*The Hound That Thought He Was a Raccoon* (released theatrically in 1960)

9/27/64—*Nikki, Wild Dog of the North* (1961), part one

10/4/64—*Nikki, Wild Dog of the North* (1961), part two

10/11/64—*A Rag, a Bone, a Box of Junk* (Ludwig von Drake)

10/18/64—*The Tenderfoot*, part one (released theatrically in Europe; directed by Byron Paul, with Brian Keith, Brandon de Wilde, James Whitmore, Richard Long, Donald May)

10/25/64—*The Tenderfoot*, part two

11/1/64—*The Tenderfoot*, part three

11/8/64—*One Day at Teton Marsh*

11/15/64—*Ben and Me* and *Peter and the Wolf*

11/22/64—*Toby Tyler* (1960), part one

11/29/64—*Toby Tyler* (1960), part two

12/6/64—*Big Red* (1962), part one

12/13/64—*Big Red* (1962), part two

1/3/65—*Disneyland's 10th Anniversary*

1/10/65—*Ida the Offbeat Eagle*

1/24/65—*Gallegher*, part one (released theatrically in Europe; with Roger Mobley, Edmond O'Brien, Robert Middleton, Philip Ober, Jack Warden)

1/31/65—*Gallegher*, part two

2/7/65—*Gallegher*, part three

2/28/65—Almost *Angels* (1962), part one

3/7/65—Almost *Angels* (1962), part two

3/7/65—*Almost Angels* (1962), part two

3/14/65—*Kilroy*, part one

3/21/65—*Kilroy*, part two

3/28/65—*Kilroy*, part three

4/4/65—*Kilroy*, part four

1965—1966 season

9/19/65—*Yellowstone Cubs* (released theatrically in 1963)

9/26/65—*Further Adventures of Gallegher*, part one (released theatrically in Europe, with Roger Mobley again as Gallegher, Edmond O'Brien)

10/3/65—*Further Adventures of Gallegher*, part two

10/10/65—*Further Adventures of Gallegher*, part three

10/17/65—*The Flight of the White Stallions*, part one (released theatrically as *The Miracle of the White Stallions*, 1963)

10/24/65—*The Flight of the White Stallions*, part two (released theatrically as *The Miracle of the White Stallions*, 1963)

11/7/65—*Minado the Wolverine*

11/14/65—*The Three Lives of Thomasina* (1964), part one

11/21/65—*The Three Lives of Thomasina* (1964), part two

11/28/65—*The Three Lives of Thomasina* (1964), part three

12/5/65—*Summer Magic* (1963), part one

12/12/65—*Summer Magic* (1963), part two

12/19/65—*A Country Coyote Goes Hollywood* (also released theatrically)

1/16/66—*Moon Pilot* (1962), part one

1/23/66—*Moon Pilot* (1962), part two

1/30/66—*Music for Everybody* (Ludwig von Drake)

2/13/66—*The Legend of Young Dick Turpin*, part one (released theatrically in Europe; directed by James Neilson, with David Western, Bernard Lee, George Cole, Maurice Denham)

2/20/66—*The Legend of Young Dick Turpin*, part two

2/27/66—*Ballerina*, part one (released theatrically in Europe, with Kirsten Simone, Henning Kronsane, Paul Reinghardt)

3/6/66—*Ballerina*, part two

3/13/66—*Run, Light Buck, Run*

3/20/66—*A Tiger Walks* (1964), part one

3/27/66—*A Tiger Walks* (1964), part two

4/10/66—*Concho, the Coyote Who Wasn't*

1966—1967 season

9/11/66—*Emil and the Detectives* (1964), part one

9/18/66—*Emil and the Detectives* (1964), part two

9/25/66—*The Legend of El Blanco*

10/2/66—*Savage Sam* (1963), part one

10/9/66—*Savage Sam* (1963), part two

10/16/66—*101 Problems of Hercules*

10/23/66—*Gallegher Goes West*, part one (released theatrically in Europe; with Roger Mobley, John McIntire, Beverly Garland, Darleen Carr, Jeanette Nolan, Peter Graves, Bruce Dern)

10/30/66—*Gallegher Goes West*, part two

11/13/66—*Ranger's Guide to Nature*

11/20/66—*The Moon-Spinners* (1964), part one

11/27/66—*The Moon-Spinners* (1964), part two

12/4/66—*The Moon-Spinners* (1964), part three

12/11/66—*Joker, the Amiable Ocelot*

12/18/66—*Disneyland Around the Seasons* (released theatrically abroad)

1/8/67—*Willie and the Yank*, part one

1/15/67—*Willie and the Yank*, part two

1/22/67—*Willie and the Yank*, part three (released theatrically abroad as *Mosby's Marauders*)

1/29/67—*Gallegher Goes West*, part three

2/5/67—*Gallegher Goes West*, part four

2/19/67—*The Boy Who Flew with Condors*

3/5/67—*Atta Girl, Kelly*, part one

3/12/67—*Atta Girl, Kelly*, part two

3/19/67—*Atta Girl, Kelly*, part three

3/26/67—*Man on Wheels*

4/2/67—*A Salute to Alaska* (Ludwig von Drake)

6 · Disneyana

IT IS IMPOSSIBLE TO EXAGGERATE THE SCOPE OF FILM production tackled over the years by the Disney studio.

In 1934 Disney contributed animated segments to two major studio feature films: a whimsical sequence for Fox's *Servants Entrance,* starring Janet Gaynor and Lew Ayres, and a musical number for MGM's *Hollywood Party.* There had been a previous liaison with Fox the year before when a brief clip of Mickey Mouse appeared in *My Lips Betray,* as Lillian Harvey watched a futuristic television screen in her limousine. Douglas Fairbanks Sr. introduced Mickey briefly in his 1932 feature *Around the World in Eighty Minutes.*

Hollywood Party was an odd conglomeration of plotless sketches, musical numbers, and "guest stars," tied around the theme of Jimmy Durante throwing a big party for the film colony. MGM advertised it as "Mickey Mouse's first appearance in a feature-length film," and the Mouse received costar billing with Durante, Lupe Velez, Laurel and Hardy, and the other luminaries in the film.

The sequence was shot in Technicolor, beginning with a combination live-action/animation scene of Mickey appearing at the party, and leading into an animated musical number, "Hot Chocolate Soldiers," written by Arthur Freed and Nacio Herb Brown.

References to Disney characters were common in films of the 1930s and 1940s, from Ginger Rogers selling Donald Duck toys in *Bachelor Mother* to Lawrence Tierney being shot after watching a Mickey Mouse cartoon in *Dillinger*. In Noel Coward's *Brief Encounter*, Trevor Howard commented, during a wartime film showing: "Thank Heaven for Donald Duck." And in Alfred Hitchcock's *Sabotage*, a showing of *Who Killed Cock Robin?* figures prominently in a dazzling murder scene.

Meanwhile, Disney was finding new outlets for his filmmaking expertise. In 1940 Donald Duck was pressed into service to promote the Community Chest charities in a three-minute short called *The Volunteer Worker*. The effect was so tremendous that three years later Donald starred in one of Disney's most famous noncommercial films, *The New Spirit*, commissioned by the government to inform wartime Americans of the importance of paying their taxes on time ("Spend for the Axis—or save for taxes."). The short was booked into thousands of theatres around the country, and it was said that tax returns never came in so promptly before.

Other characters were used during wartime to promote various causes; The Seven Dwarfs returned in a short made for South American audiences on the dangers of malaria, for instance.

During the war Disney produced scores of training and morale films for the army, the Office of War Information, and sundry other government agencies. This work alone is worthy of a detailed study. After the war, however, Disney began accepting other odd assignments for educational and promotional films, ranging from public-service items like *How to Have an Accident at Work* to sponsored films such as Kotex-Kleenex's *The Story of Menstruation* and *How to Catch a Cold*, or U.S. Steel's *Steel and America*. To beleaguered schoolchildren who had to suffer through dull educational films, Disney shorts have always been a breath of fresh air, no matter what the subject at hand.

Disney also joined most of the film colony in participating in various "behind the scenes" short subjects. In 1938 he allowed *Pathé Parade* to take a filmed tour of his studio, and in 1946 he appeared on screen to congratulate *Screen Snapshots* on its twenty-fifth anniversary, one of several times he appeared in that series.

In the 1950s Disney's filmmaking team was so good that they not only did receive commissions to do films but offers to work on other people's films as well. In 1956 the studio loaned its animation-effects specialist Joshua Meador to MGM to create effects for the brilliant science-fiction film *Forbidden Planet,* and seven years later Ub Iwerks was loaned to Alfred Hitchcock to work his wonders with *The Birds*.

It is safe to say that no other producer ever enjoyed greater success in more fields of filmmaking than Walt Disney; the record bears that out.

465

471

477

478

ALL TIME BESTSELLERS
FROM POPULAR LIBRARY

☐ AFTERNOON MEN—Powell	04268-0	1.95
☐ MARINA TOWER—Beardsley	04198-6	1.95
☐ SKIN DEEP—Hufford	04258-3	1.95
☐ MY HEART TURNS BACK—Patton	04241-9	2.25
☐ EARTHLY POSSESSIONS—Tyler	04214-1	1.95
☐ THE BERLIN CONNECTION—Simmel	08607-6	1.95
☐ THE BEST PEOPLE—Van Slyke	08456-1	1.95
☐ A BRIDGE TOO FAR—Ryan	08373-5	2.50
☐ THE CAESAR CODE—Simmel	08413-8	1.95
☐ DO BLACK PATENT LEATHER SHOES REALLY REFLECT UP?—Powers	08490-1	1.75
☐ THE FURY—Farris	08620-3	2.25
☐ THE HEART LISTENS—Van Slyke	08520-7	1.95
☐ TO KILL A MOCKINGBIRD—Lee	08376-X	1.75
☐ THE LAST BATTLE—Ryan	08381-6	2.25
☐ THE LAST CATHOLIC IN AMERICA—Powers	08523-2	1.50
☐ THE LONGEST DAY—Ryan	08380-8	1.95
☐ LOVE'S WILD DESIRE—Blake	08616-5	1.95
☐ THE MIXED BLESSING—Van Slyke	08491-X	1.95

Buy them at your local bookstores or use this handy coupon for ordering:

POPULAR LIBRARY
P.O. Box C730, 524 Myrtle Ave., Pratt Station, Brooklyn, N.Y. 11205

Please send me the books I have checked above. Orders for less than 5 books must include 75¢ for the first book and 25¢ for each additional book to cover mailing and handling. I enclose $_____ in check or money order.

Name_____

Address_____

City_____State/Zip_____

Please allow 4 to 5 weeks for delivery.